Executive Function in Preschool-Age Children

INTEGRATING MEASUREMENT, NEURODEVELOPMENT, AND TRANSLATIONAL RESEARCH

Edited by James A. Griffin, Peggy McCardle,
and Lisa S. Freund

American Psychological Association • Washington, DC

Published by
American Psychological Association
750 First Street, NE
Washington, DC 20002
www.apa.org

To order
APA Order Department
P.O. Box 92984
Washington, DC 20090-2984
Tel: (800) 374-2721; Direct: (202) 336-5510
Fax: (202) 336-5502; TDD/TTY: (202) 336-6123
Online: www.apa.org/pubs/books
E-mail: order@apa.org

In the U.K., Europe, Africa, and the Middle East, copies may be ordered from
American Psychological Association
3 Henrietta Street
Covent Garden, London
WC2E 8LU England

Typeset in Goudy by Circle Graphics, Inc., Columbia, MD

Printer: Sheridan Books, Ann Arbor, MI
Cover Designer: Mercury Publishing Services, Inc., Rockville, MD

The opinions and statements published are the responsibility of the authors, and such opinions and statements do not necessarily represent the policies of the American Psychological Association.

Library of Congress Cataloging-in-Publication Data

Executive function in preschool-age children : integrating measurement, neurodevelopment, and translational research / [edited by] James A. Griffin, Peggy McCardle, and Lisa S. Freund. — First edition.
    pages cm
  Includes bibliographical references and index.
    ISBN 978-1-4338-1826-4 — ISBN 1-4338-1826-4 1. Executive functions (Neuropsychology) 2. Cognition in children. 3. Control (Psychology) in children. 4. Child psychology. 5. Preschool children. I. Griffin, James Alan, 1963- II. McCardle, Peggy D. III. Freund, Lisa S.
  BF723.C5E985 2016
  155.42'3—dc23
                                    2015019980

British Library Cataloguing-in-Publication Data
A CIP record is available from the British Library.

Printed in the United States of America
First Edition

http://dx.doi.org/10.1037/14797-000

CONTENTS

CONTRIBUTORS

Danielle M. Beck, PhD, Department of Psychology, Simpson University, Redding, CA

Martha Ann Bell, PhD, Department of Psychology, Virginia Tech, Blacksburg

Karen L. Bierman, PhD, Department of Psychology, Pennsylvania State University, University Park

Clancy B. Blair, PhD, Department of Applied Psychology, New York University, New York

Stephanie M. Carlson, PhD, Institute of Child Development, University of Minnesota, Minneapolis

Margaret O'Brien Caughy, ScD, The University of Texas School of Public Health, Dallas

Nicolas Chevalier, PhD, Department of Psychology, University of Edinburgh, Edinburgh, Scotland

Caron A. C. Clark, PhD, Department of Psychology, University of Arizona, Tempe

Kimberly Cuevas, PhD, Department of Psychology, University of Connecticut, Storrs

Rebecca DelCarmen-Wiggins, PhD, National Institute of Mental Health, Rockville, MD

Jamie Hurst DeLuna, PhD, Texas Christian University Institute of Child Development, Fort Worth

Adele Diamond, PhD, Department of Psychiatry, University of British Columbia, Vancouver, British Columbia, Canada

Nancy Eisenberg, PhD, Department of Psychology, Arizona State University, Tempe

Kimberly Andrews Espy, PhD, Department of Psychology, University of Arizona, Tempe; Department of Psychology, University of Nebraska–Lincoln

Susan Faja, PhD, Autism Center, University of Washington, Seattle

Martha J. Farah, PhD, University of Pennsylvania, Philadelphia

Judith F. Feldman, PhD, Albert Einstein College of Medicine, Yeshiva University, Bronx, NY

Anna Fisher, PhD, Department of Psychology, Carnegie Mellon University, Pittsburgh, PA

Lisa S. Freund, PhD, Eunice Kennedy Shriver National Institute of Child Health and Human Development, Rockville, MD

Jennie K. Grammer, PhD, School of Education, University of California at Los Angeles

James A. Griffin, PhD, Eunice Kennedy Shriver National Institute of Child Health and Human Development, Rockville, MD

Daniel A. Hackman, PhD, University of Pennsylvania, Philadelphia

Abigail Haydon, MPH, PhD, FrameWorks Institute, Washington, DC

Scott K. Holland, PhD, Department of Pediatrics, University of Cincinnati, Cincinnati, OH

Cayce J. Hook, BA, University of Pennsylvania, Philadelphia

Tzipi Horowitz-Kraus, PhD, Department of Pediatrics, University of Cincinnati, Cincinnati, OH

Tiffany D. James, PhD, Developmental Cognitive Neuroscience Laboratory, University of Nebraska–Lincoln

Jeffery J. Jankowski, PhD, Albert Einstein College of Medicine, Yeshiva University, Bronx, NY

Heidi Kloos, PhD, University of Cincinnati, Cincinnati, OH

Gwendolyn M. Lawson, MA, University of Pennsylvania, Philadelphia

Leslie D. Leve, PhD, Oregon Social Learning Center, Eugene

Peggy McCardle, PhD, MPH, Peggy McCardle Consulting, LLC, Washington, DC

Megan M. McClelland, PhD, Oregon State University, Corvallis

Frederick J. Morrison, PhD, Department of Psychology, University of Michigan, Ann Arbor

Jennifer Mize Nelson, PhD, Department of Psychology, University of Nebraska–Lincoln

Margaret Tresch Owen, PhD, The University of Texas at Dallas

Katherine C. Pears, PhD, Oregon Social Learning Center, Eugene

Susan A. Rose, PhD, Albert Einstein College of Medicine, Yeshiva University, Bronx, NY

Marcela Torres, PhD, Department of Psychology, Pennsylvania State University, University Park

Michael T. Willoughby, PhD, RTI International, Research Triangle Park, NC

Qing Zhou, PhD, University of California, Berkeley

Executive Function in Preschool-Age Children

INTRODUCTION TO EXECUTIVE FUNCTION IN PRESCHOOL-AGE CHILDREN

JAMES A. GRIFFIN, LISA S. FREUND, PEGGY McCARDLE,
REBECCA DelCARMEN-WIGGINS, AND ABIGAIL HAYDON

If one were to gather 100 researchers, policymakers, and practitioners and ask them to rate the importance of the development of executive function (EF) skills in preschool-age children, it is likely that most, if not all, would place a high importance on such an outcome. If one were to ask the same 100 to define *executive function*, at least 100 different definitions would likely be given. Such is the state of the field—there is general agreement regarding the importance of EF in early childhood and later adolescence but little consensus on the definition and components of EF. The purpose of this volume is not to provide a consensus based on evidence from these areas. Rather, it is to reflect the current state of knowledge regarding EF measurement, neurodevelopment, and translational research. Indeed, premature consensus at this point would likely do more

The views expressed in this volume are those of the authors and do not necessarily represent those of the National Institutes of Health, the Eunice Kennedy Shriver National Institute of Child Health and Human Development, the National Institute of Mental Health, or the U.S. Department of Health and Human Services.

http://dx.doi.org/10.1037/14797-001
Executive Function in Preschool-Age Children: Integrating Measurement, Neurodevelopment, and Translational Research, J. A. Griffin, P. McCardle, and L. S. Freund (Editors)

harm than good, as it would stifle innovation and make it more difficult to study all aspects of this complex construct.

DEFINING EXECUTIVE FUNCTION

EF in young children can generally be described as comprising a number of cognitive processes that, over time, support children's ability to increasingly regulate their own behavior and, in turn, develop greater social, emotional, and cognitive competence. These cognitive processes are thought to include working memory (the ability to pay attention and remember facts while using them to complete tasks), inhibitory control (the ability to follow rules, modulate emotions, and delay gratification), and cognitive flexibility (the ability to plan, make judgments, and self-correct). The development of EF skills and abilities is fundamental to learning because they lay the foundation for adaptive, goal-directed behaviors that enable the child to override more automatic (e.g., cry, scream, run away) or impulsive (e.g., grab for or throw objects) thoughts and responses. It is crucial for young children to acquire these skills in order to be ready to learn when they begin school and to have continued academic success.

Longitudinal frameworks are critical not only to measurement but also to theories and conceptualization of EF. There have been difficulties in specifying developmental trajectories for EF, partly related to questions about whether EF is one skill or a set of skills, and partly because the age range for development is so broad. Currently, it is difficult to compare results across research findings because there is no guarantee that investigators took similar approaches to their conceptualization and measurement of EF. It is likely that developmental trajectories differ for various EF components (e.g., working memory, inhibition) and that these differences are crucial to an examination of how these components interact to support or develop more complex learning and cognitive functioning. In addition, the potential for identifying sensitive periods to guide the timing and design of interventions should emerge from studies of the trajectory of EF from early childhood to adolescence (and beyond).

OVERVIEW OF THE VOLUME

This volume was inspired by a workshop[1] and subsequent discussions of the definition, conceptualization, and measurement of EF in the preschool period. The workshop and later discussions were held with scientists from

---

[1]Executive Function in Preschool Children: Current Knowledge and Research Opportunities, Workshop, June 2010, supported by the Eunice Kennedy Shriver National Institute of Child Health and Human Development, the National Institute on Drug Abuse, and the Office of Behavioral and Social Sciences Research,

diverse fields, including developmental psychology, cognitive neuroscience, early education, and applied/clinical psychology. This volume is the result of the ideas, theories, research, and insights from these scientists and, it is hoped, may move the field toward an interdisciplinary, multilevel analytic approach to conducting EF research with preschool-age children.

For this volume, authors were charged with reviewing the current state of the research on EF competence in preschoolers, considering how best to define the construct of EF, and proposing promising areas of research ripe for advancement and translation. Recent research suggests that early EF skill development provides the critical foundation for school readiness and self-regulation. However, as has been mentioned, there has been no consistent definition or conceptualization of EF competence in the earliest years. Nor has there been agreement on how best to measure the construct or its components in the preschool period. This volume, therefore, addresses these areas and their translational implications, such as novel interventions to improve EF skills in young children from risk groups or disadvantaged backgrounds, and builds the beginnings of an agenda for future basic and translational research in EF development in the preschool period. Specifically, the volume has three overarching goals: (a) to increase the inclusion of detailed information regarding the conceptualization and measurement of EF skills in basic and translational research studies to ensure comparability; (b) to review what is known about the developmental trajectory of EF in preschoolers, including the neurobiological mechanisms and neurocircuitry underlying the development of EF and the role of EF in risk and resilience; and (c) to highlight translational implications leading to novel interventions designed to improve or enhance early EF skill development.

ORGANIZATION OF THE VOLUME

The volume contains three major parts. Part I deals with conceptualization and measurement of EF in the preschool period, tackling the thorny issues of how researchers conceptualize EF at these early stages of development, measure the skills considered components or aspects of EF, and address measurement continuity across ages—an issue especially problematic for research comparing performance of groups of children at different ages or investigating performance in the same children longitudinally. This part begins with a chapter by Diamond, who addresses the many varying definitions of EF. This

National Institutes of Health/U.S. Department of Health and Human Services (DHHS); the Administration for Children and Families, DHHS; the Institute of Education Sciences, U.S. Department of Education; and the University of Kansas Merrill Advanced Studies Center.

is followed by a chapter by Carlson, Faja, and Beck, who examine various challenges and opportunities regarding the definition and measurement of EF. Nelson, James, Chevalier, Clark, and Espy then highlight the developmental course of EF, reviewing the evidence supporting different latent construct models of EF across the lifespan. Building on these models of EF, Willoughby and Blair summarize their work developing and evaluating the psychometric properties of a battery of tasks to assess EF during early childhood. At the end of this part, Eisenberg and Zhou explore the intersection between EF and self-regulation, thus setting the stage for discussions (in subsequent parts and chapters) of the extent to which EF subserves or overlaps with other aspects of cognitive development.

Part II addresses neurodevelopment—psychobiological issues and neural pathways of EF skills from infancy into toddlerhood and beyond. First, Rose, Feldman, and Jankowski propose a developmental cascade model that links deficits in information-processing abilities among infants born prematurely to similar deficits during toddlerhood. The next chapter, by Bell and Cuevas, describes the changes in neural activity and frontal synchrony associated with development of EF skills and the ways in which two particular constructs—child temperament and parenting characteristics—contribute to individual differences in EF development. Horowitz-Kraus, Holland, and Freund then provide an overview of how advances in neuroimaging and electrophysiological techniques can be applied to the study of EF development. Fisher and Kloos conclude this part by describing extant research on the orienting and executive systems of selective sustained attention, paying particular attention to their measurement, developmental course, neural substrates, and relevance to EF.

In the final part, Part III, the chapter authors address translational research to examine risk and resilience as they pertain to EF, beginning with McClelland, Leve, and Pears, who focus on the negative effects of early risk on the development of EF, but also note that strong EF skills may buffer against the poor academic and social outcomes often associated with early environmental, genetic, or familial adversity. Lawson, Hook, Hackman, and Farah then provide an overview of the influence of socioeconomic status on EF. Next, Caughy, Owen, and DeLuna describe their experiences assessing EF among low-income, ethnic minority preschoolers and the striking disparities in EF skills within this population. Bierman and Torres provide an overview of the multiple early education and intervention programs designed to promote the development of executive function, ranging from individualized training of working memory and attentional control to school-based programs that foster social–emotional learning, sociodramatic play, and positive classroom climates. In the final chapter of the volume, Morrison and Grammer attempt to make sense of the conceptual clutter summarized in the preceding chapters, to advance several proposals to move the field forward, and to suggest areas that must be addressed in early childhood EF research. And that is our hope for this volume—that it will encourage researchers to clearly define and operationalize their conceptualization and measurement of EF and engage in rigorous, replicable basic and translational research that concomitantly increases the field's understanding of the neurobiological and behavioral mechanisms at work in EF and informs the development and testing of new interventions that can meaningfully enhance the development of EF skills in early childhood and throughout the lifespan.

I

CONCEPTUALIZATION AND MEASUREMENT OF EXECUTIVE FUNCTION

1

WHY IMPROVING AND ASSESSING EXECUTIVE FUNCTIONS EARLY IN LIFE IS CRITICAL

ADELE DIAMOND

To be successful in school or in one's career takes creativity, flexibility, self-control, and discipline. Central to all those are executive functions (EFs), including mentally playing with ideas, giving a considered response rather than an impulsive one, and being able to change course or perspectives as needed, resist temptations, and stay focused. These are core skills critical for cognitive, social, and psychological development, success in school and in life, and mental and physical health. They begin to emerge early (even during infancy) but are not fully mature until young adulthood, although EFs in early childhood are highly predictive of EF skills later in life. EFs are very sensitive to environmental factors (including negative ones such as poverty and positive ones such as sensitive parenting). Accumulating evidence indicates that several different approaches can successfully improve EFs and that improving them early in life may be absolutely critical for an individual's happiness and success throughout life and for reducing social disparities in

http://dx.doi.org/10.1037/14797-002

Executive Function in Preschool-Age Children: Integrating Measurement, Neurodevelopment, and Translational Research, J. A. Griffin, P. McCardle, and L. S. Freund (Editors)

achievement and health. Whether an approach produces sustained benefits to EFs can be determined only by assessing EFs over time using the same or comparable measures. Hence longitudinal assessment tools for the early years of life become critical to the goal of finding what works. I delve into each of these points briefly in this chapter and invite you to read the other chapters in this volume where these points are elaborated in greater depth.

EXECUTIVE FUNCTIONS DEFINED

I refer to EFs in the plural because the term refers to a family of skills, not just one skill. These skills are needed when you have to concentrate and think, when going on automatic or acting on your initial impulse might be ill-advised. In the title to this volume and in some of the other chapters within, the singular term *executive function* is used. These skills depend on a neural circuit in which prefrontal cortex plays a pivotal role (Aron, Behrens, Smith, Frank, & Poldrack, 2007; Braver, Cohen, & Barch, 2002; Eisenberg & Berman, 2010; Leh, Petrides, & Strafella, 2010; Zanto, Rubens, Thangavel, & Gazzaley, 2011).

Working Memory and Inhibitory Control

One core component of EFs is working memory (holding information in mind and working with it). Working memory is critical for making sense of anything that unfolds over time, for that always involves relating what came earlier to what came later. Understanding written or spoken language requires this because as you focus on the next phrase, the previous one is no longer present or you are no longer looking at it. Doing any math in your head requires this, as does reasoning, because it involves holding bits of information in mind and seeing how they relate. As Nelson et al. note in Chapter 3 of this volume, the ability to hold information in mind develops very early and even extremely young children can hold one or two things in mind for quite a long time. Indeed, infants of only 9 to 12 months can update the contents of their working memory, as seen on tasks such as A-not-B (Diamond, 1985; see also Chapter 7, this volume). However, being able to hold many things in mind or do any kind of mental manipulation (e.g., reordering mental representations of objects in order of size) is far slower to develop and shows a prolonged developmental progression (Bachevalier, 1990; Barrouillet, Gavens, Vergauwe, Gaillard, & Camos, 2009; Cowan, Saults, & Elliott, 2002; Luciana, Conklin, Hooper, & Yarger, 2005; Schleepen & Jonkman, 2009).

Holding a piece of information in mind for some seconds could just as correctly be described as keeping your attention focused on a piece of information for some seconds. Indeed, the distinction between these aspects of memory and attention appears to be arbitrary. They are similar in many ways including in their neural bases. The same prefrontal system that enables you to selectively remain focused on the information you want to hold in mind also helps you selectively attend to stimuli in your environment, tuning out irrelevant stimuli. Hence it is virtually impossible to try to hold something in mind that is at odds with what you are trying to keep your attention focused on in the environment (Awh & Jonides, 2001; Awh, Vogel, & Oh, 2006; Gazzaley, 2011; Gazzaley & Nobre, 2012; Zanto et al., 2011).

The other core EF skill is inhibitory control, which is more heterogeneous than working memory. It includes inhibition of attention (selective or focused attention), which is often referred to as interference control and involves inhibiting (or suppressing) attention to other things in the environment (distracters) so you can stay focused on what you want. Inhibitory control also includes inhibition of action (motor responses, including verbal ones), which includes several subtypes. Most of the subtypes are aspects of self-control: (a) inhibiting the impulse to respond or react immediately—making yourself wait or giving yourself time to give a wiser, more considered response (e.g., not sending off a blistering email, but waiting until you are calmer; giving yourself time to acquire more information before jumping to a conclusion); (b) delaying gratification—making yourself wait, forgoing an immediate pleasure for a greater reward later (often termed *delay discounting* by neuroscientists and learning theorists; Louie & Glimcher, 2010; Rachlin, Raineri, & Cross, 1991); (c) inhibiting your first inclination and substituting a more appropriate response (e.g., not butting in line but going to the end of the line, not blurting out something that could offend but saying something more considerate instead, or not giving the more natural response to a stimulus when instructed to give a different response instead); (d) holding up on making a response that had almost reached response threshold (e.g., a batter checking his or her swing); (e) resisting temptations (e.g., temptations such as eating foods that are not good for you, overindulging, trying forbidden substances, or taking something you are addicted to). The other subtypes of inhibitory control are aspects of discipline: (f) staying on task, including (f.1) finishing one's work though it might be tedious or difficult, inhibiting temptations to do something more fun, and (f.2) sustaining your attention on something for several long minutes despite distractions even if the task seems boring and pointless.

You are in good company if you think (a) and (c)—or (b), (e), and (f)—are so related as to perhaps be the same thing, or if you think the above list is so long and diverse that a single construct (inhibitory control) does not do justice to the heterogeneity or that surely the neural basis for all of these aspects of inhibitory control (e.g., inhibition at the level of attention or action, or inhibition when motivation is high [hot situations] and inhibition when motivation is minimal [cool situations]) could not possibly be the same (Dempster, 1993; Harnishfeger, 1995; Kerr & Zelazo, 2004; Nigg, 2000). Those are among the many debates concerning EFs. It is interesting that some confirmatory factor analyses find that inhibition of attention (resistance to distracter interference) and inhibition of action (inhibiting a prepotent response) are highly related and form a single factor (Friedman & Miyake, 2004). Moreover, when required to exert one type of self-control (e.g., resisting sweets) and then required immediately after to exert a second type of self-control (e.g., the Stop-Signal task), people are consistently found to be more impaired on the second task than if they did a different difficult task first that did not require self-control (e.g., math calculations; Muraven & Baumeister, 2000). One group reports that all the diverse types of self-control appear to rely on substantially similar neural bases (Cohen, Berkman, & Lieberman, 2013). However, many studies have found that interference control (inhibiting extraneous thoughts or inhibiting attention to environmental distraction) is much more strongly linked to working memory than to other forms of inhibitory control (e.g., response inhibition). In particular, selective attention and working memory appear to be very tightly linked (see above as well as Awh & Jonides, 2001; Gazzaley, 2011). Working memory and inhibition are highly interrelated. A situation might place a higher demand on one than the other, and two conditions of a task might differ more in their working memory demands or their inhibitory demands, but rarely if ever are either of these exercised in the absence of the other. How can you know what to inhibit unless you maintain your goal in working memory? How can you stay focused on the relevant information in working memory if you do not inhibit (suppress) environmental distractions and mental distractions, such as irrelevant thoughts?

Different theories of EFs postulate inhibitory control (Barkley, 2001), working memory (Cepeda & Munakata, 2007; Cohen, Dunbar, & McClelland, 1990; Morton & Munakata, 2002; Pennington, 1994), or attention (Garon, Bryson, & Smith, 2008; Rothbart & Posner, 2001) as primary. As Nelson et al. outline in Chapter 3 (this volume), early in development, working memory and inhibitory control appear to be relatively undifferentiated behaviorally, consistent with intellectual skills developing from a relatively unified, general ability in childhood to more differentiated, specific cognitive abilities with age (Garrett, 1946; Werner, 1957). There was already evidence that this characterized the development of working memory and inhibition from 4 to 14 years of age (e.g., Shing, Lindenberger, Diamond, Li, & Davidson, 2010). Willoughby and Blair (Willoughby, Blair, Wirth, & Greenberg, 2010; see also Chapter 4, this volume) and Espy and colleagues (Wiebe et al., 2011; see also Chapter 3, this volume) provided evidence that, consistent with this relative nondifferentiation early in development, working memory and inhibitory control fall along a single factor in children 3 to 5 years of age. It has also been known for some time that progressive differentiation occurs at the neural level from childhood to adolescence, with first many brain regions being recruited to exercise EFs followed by progressive fine-tuning of neural activation to prefrontal cortex and other members of the EF neural network (Durston et al., 2006). In Chapter 7 of this volume, Bell and Cuevas present new data showing that this progressive fine-tuning of neural activation also characterizes changes from infancy to the preschool period.

More Advanced Executive Functions

To shift mental sets or see something from different perspectives, you need to activate and maintain a new set or perspective in working memory and you need to inhibit the set or perspective that was just being used. Thus cognitive flexibility (also called *set shifting*) the third core EF, builds upon and requires working memory and inhibitory control (Diamond, 2010; Morasch, Raj, & Bell, 2013; see Figure 1.1). Whereas factor analyses of EFs in adults routinely come up with three factors (working memory, inhibitory control, and cognitive flexibility; Lehto, Juujärvi, Kooistra, & Pulkkinen, 2003; Miyake et al., 2000), factor analyses with children are more likely to find only two factors (working memory and inhibitory control; Hughes, Ensor, Wilson, & Graham, 2009; St Clair-Thompson & Gathercole, 2006; Wiebe et al., 2011). Not surprisingly, cognitive flexibility emerges later than working memory or inhibitory control (Cepeda, Kramer, & Gonzalez de Sather, 2001; Davidson, Amso, Anderson, & Diamond, 2006; Garon et al., 2008). Being able to flexibly switch between two rules or two ways of sorting cards on a trial-by-trial basis is utterly beyond the ability of most preschoolers, and before they are 2.5 or 3 years old there is little or no evidence that children can make a switch between blocks of trials (using one rule for all trials in one block, and a different rule for all trials in the next block; Marcovitch & Zelazo, 2009). Still more advanced EFs that build upon working memory, inhibitory control, and cognitive flexibility include reasoning, problem solving, and planning (Collins & Koechlin, 2012; Daniels, Toth, & Jacoby, 2006; Niendam et al., 2012).

DIFFERENCES AND SIMILARITIES BETWEEN EXECUTIVE FUNCTIONS AND RELATED TERMS

Self-regulation refers to processes that enable people to maintain optimal levels of emotional, motivational, and cognitive arousal (Liew, 2011). Eisenberg, Hofer, and Vaughan (2007) define emotion-related self-regulation as "processes used to manage and change if, when, and how (e.g., how intensely) one experiences emotions and emotion-related motivation and physiological states, as well as how emotions are expressed behaviorally"

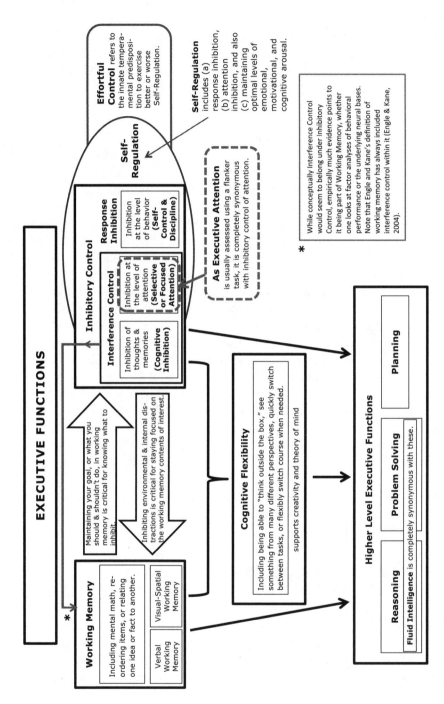

Figure 1.1. The components that together comprise executive functions (EFs) and the relation of executive functions to other related concepts. The two primary EFs are working memory and inhibitory control. Those together make cognitive flexibility possible. From those three core EFs, the higher order EFs of reasoning, problem solving, and planning are built.

(p. 288). These processes include effortfully "managing the perception of stimuli and manipulating cognitions and behavior associated with emotion, generally in the service of biological or social adaptation and/or accomplishing goals" (Eisenberg & Zhou, Chapter 5, this volume, p. 118).

Self-regulation does not include a working memory component (unlike EFs), but it overlaps substantially with the inhibitory control component of EFs (see Figure 1.1). Self-regulation refers primarily to control and regulation of one's emotions (Eisenberg, Spinrad, & Eggum, 2010; Mischel & Ayduk, 2002; Raver, 2004; Rothbart & Jones, 1998). EF researchers have historically focused more on the control of thoughts, attention, and actions; only recently have they included control of one's emotions. Whereas EF researchers have addressed emotions only as troublesome things to be inhibited, self-regulation also embraces the importance of motivation and interest as emotional responses that can be critical to the achievement of one's goals (Blair & Diamond, 2008). Historically, self-regulation has been assessed through (a) adult ratings of children's behavior, observed over the course of time in real-world settings such as home or school, and (b) observation of children's behavior when they have to delay gratification in an emotionally laden, hot situation (Mischel, Shoda, & Rodriguez, 1989) or in a frustrating situation (Kochanska, Philibert, & Barry, 2009). Historically, EFs have been assessed directly from children's performance on arbitrary laboratory-based tests far removed from the real world in fairly emotionally neutral, cool situations. Finally, EF researchers have historically focused on the brain bases for component EFs, whereas self-regulation researchers have focused more on the peripheral, autonomic nervous system, using measures such as heart rate variability or respiratory sinus arrhythmia as indices of parasympathetic nervous system activity (Porges, Doussard-Roosevelt, & Maiti, 1994). For a more thorough discussion of what self-regulation is and how it compares to EFs, see Chapter 5, this volume.

Effortful control (Rothbart & Bates, 2006) refers to an aspect of temperament, a largely innate predisposition, which involves a tendency to exercise self-regulation with ease (e.g., easily able to slow down or lower one's voice), perhaps even being too regulated (lacking in spontaneity) versus finding regulation harder or less natural. It is usually measured by parental report (Goldsmith, 1996; Rothbart, Ahadi, Hershey, & Fisher, 2001).

Executive attention (Fan, McCandliss, Sommer, Raz, & Posner, 2002; Posner & DiGirolamo, 1998; Rueda, Posner, & Rothbart, 2005) refers to the top-down regulation of attention as opposed to alerting (maintaining a state of high readiness to attend to potential stimuli) or orienting (exogenous attention—being pulled by a stimulus to attend to it). As the name and definition imply, it sounds synonymous with inhibitory control of attention. Indeed, it is usually assessed using measures of selective attention such as the flanker task (Fan et al., 2002; Rueda et al., 2005). Much confusion has been engendered by the overly broad use of the term *executive attention* to apply to such skills as working memory capacity (Engle, 2002; Erickson, 2008) and response inhibition, which is also known as the resolution of response conflict (e.g., whether to press on the left or right on a Simon-type task; Gerardi-Caulton, 2000; Jones, Rothbart, & Posner, 2003).

Fluid intelligence is the ability to reason, problem solve, and see patterns or relations among items (Cattell, 1963). It is synonymous with the reasoning and problem-solving subcomponents of EFs. No surprise then that measures of fluid intelligence (e.g., Raven's Matrices; Raven, Raven, & Court, 2004) are very highly correlated with independent measures of EFs (Boone, 1999; Conway, Kane, & Engle, 2003; Duncan, Emslie, Williams, Johnson, & Freer, 1996; Duncan et al., 2008; Engle, Tuholski, Laughlin, & Conway, 1999; Roca et al., 2010).

Working memory is often referred to as a subcomponent of EFs, although many working-memory researchers use the term *working memory* more broadly. For example, Kane and Engle define working memory as the ability to (a) maintain selected information in an active, easily retrievable state while (b) inhibiting (blocking) distracters or interference, such as from other information that might otherwise enter that active state (i.e., memory maintenance + interference control, which seems consistent with the close empirical tie between these two skills; Conway & Engle, 1994; Kane & Engle, 2000, 2002). Hasher and Zacks (1988; Zacks & Hasher, 2006) also insert interference control components into their definition of working memory: (a) gating out irrelevant information from the working-memory workspace and (b) deleting no-longer-relevant information from that limited-capacity workspace. Functions of the central executive in Baddeley's working-memory model (Baddeley, 1992; Baddeley & Hitch, 1994) include inhibitory control and cognitive flexibility: (a) multitasking, (b) shifting between tasks or retrieval strategies, and (c) the capacity to attend and inhibit in a selective manner. Working-memory researchers often use complex span tasks (also called working memory span tasks; Bailey, Dunlosky, & Kane, 2008; Barrouillet et al., 2009; Chein & Morrison, 2010; Conway et al., 2005; Pardo-Vázquez & Fernández-Rey, 2008; Unsworth, Redick, Heitz, Broadway, & Engle, 2009) to study what they call working memory but what EF researchers would call EFs (because these tasks require more subcomponents of EFs than just holding information in mind and manipulating it). It would probably cause less confusion if they were called EF tasks.

EVIDENCE OF THE IMPORTANCE OF EFs

EFs are critical for success in school. EF skills have been repeatedly found to be more important for school readiness than IQ or entry-level reading or math (e.g., Blair, 2002, 2003; Blair & Razza, 2007; Normandeau & Guay,

1998). EFs continue to be critical for school success from preschool through university, even controlling for initial achievement levels and IQ. Working memory and inhibitory control each independently predict both math and reading competence throughout the school years, and often do so much better than IQ (e.g., Alloway & Alloway, 2010; Borella, Carretti, & Pelegrina, 2010; Duckworth & Seligman, 2005; Duncan et al., 2007; Gathercole, Pickering, Knight, & Stegmann, 2004; see also Chapter 10, this volume).

EFs are also critical for job success. Poor EFs lead to poor productivity and difficulty finding and keeping a job (Bailey, 2007). EFs are important for marital harmony because people with poor EFs are more difficult to get along with, less dependable, and more likely to act on impulse (Eakin et al., 2004). Poor EFs can lead to social problems such as aggression, emotional outbursts, and crime (Broidy et al., 2003; Denson, Pedersen, Friese, Hahm, & Roberts, 2011; Moffitt et al., 2011; Saarni, 1999; Winstok, 2009). EFs are impaired in many mental health disorders (such as addictions, attention-deficit/hyperactivity disorder, obsessive–compulsive disorder, depression, conduct disorder, and schizophrenia; Baler & Volkow, 2006; Barch, 2005; Diamond, 2005; Lui & Tannock, 2007; Miller, Barnes, & Beaver, 2011; Penadés et al., 2007; Taylor Tavares et al., 2007; Verdejo-García, Bechara, Recknor, & Pérez-García, 2006). Such disorders are increasing at alarming rates (Moffitt et al., 2010; Robison, Sclar, Skaer, & Galin, 1999) and account for more lost years of life and productivity than any other illness including cancer (Prince et al., 2007). Not surprisingly, given all of these findings, poorer EFs are associated with a poorer quality of life (Davis, Marra, Najafzadeh, & Liu-Ambrose, 2010; Moffitt, 2012).

In general, these associations are particularly true for the inhibitory control component of EFs. For example, Moffitt et al. (2011) found that children, who at ages 3 through 11 had worse inhibitory control (were less persistent, more impulsive, and had poorer selective attention), as adults 30 years later had worse health (were more likely to be overweight and have substance abuse problems), earned less, committed more crimes, and were less happy than those with better inhibitory control as children, controlling for IQ, gender, social class, and their home lives and family circumstances growing up. This finding is based on a sample of 1,000 children born in the same city in the same year followed for 32 years with a 96% retention rate.

Inhibitory control is also disproportionately difficult for young children. For example, the difference in both speed and accuracy of children at all ages from 4 through 9 for always responding on the same side as a stimulus versus inhibiting that impulse and always responding on the side opposite a stimulus is greater than the difference in either their speed or accuracy for holding two associations in mind versus six (Davidson et al., 2006). This is true whether or not the same-side trials come before or after the opposite-side ones (Wright & Diamond, 2014). The opposite is true for adults: It is far harder to hold six associations in mind than two but it is no harder to always respond on the side opposite a stimulus than to always respond on the same side as a stimulus (adults' speed and accuracy for each are equivalent; Davidson et al., 2006; Lu & Proctor, 1995). Preschool and early elementary school programs that target EFs have thus wisely focused on improving inhibitory control (focused attention, self-control, and discipline; Bodrova & Leong, 2007; Kusché & Greenberg, 1994; Raver et al., 2008; Webster-Stratton & Reid, 2004). Inhibitory control is by no means fully mature by age 9; indeed, it continues to improve throughout adolescence (Bedard et al., 2002; Christakou, Brammer, & Rubia, 2011; Klein, Foerster, Hartnegg, & Fischer, 2005; Leon-Carrion, García-Orza, & Pérez-Santamaría, 2004; Luna, 2009; Olson et al., 2009; Rubia, Smith, Taylor, & Brammer, 2007; Steinberg et al., 2009).

BENEFITS OF EARLY IMPROVEMENTS OF EFs

EFs can be improved. That is true throughout life from infancy through old age (Bryck & Fisher, 2012; Diamond & Lee, 2011; Greenberg & Harris, 2012; Klingberg, 2010; Kovács & Mehler, 2009; Morrison & Chein, 2011; Muraven, 2010; Wass, Porayska-Pomsta, & Johnson, 2011). Why bother to try to improve EFs early if (a) those with poorer EFs might just be slower maturers and might catch up and (b) EFs can be improved later if the children do not catch up on their own? The early gap between those with better and worse EFs often does not disappear on its own but can grow larger over time (O'Shaughnessy, Lane, Gresham, & Beebe-Frankenberger, 2003; Riggs, Blair, & Greenberg, 2004) and EF problems (especially inhibitory control problems) in early childhood predict EF problems years later (Eigsti et al., 2006; Friedman et al., 2007; Moffitt et al., 2011; Shoda, Mischel, & Peake, 1990). Similarly, children's school readiness (which depends heavily on children's EFs) strongly predicts academic performance years later in middle school through college (Entwisle, Alexander, & Olson, 2005; McClelland, Acock, Piccinin, Rhea, & Stallings, 2013; O'Shaughnessy et al., 2003; Petit, Courtney, Maisog, Ungerleider, & Haxby, 1997; see also Chapter 12, this volume).

Prefrontal cortex is not fully mature until early adulthood (one's mid-20s; Gogtay et al., 2004; Paus et al., 1999). Some people have asked, therefore, "Isn't it nonsense to try to improve EFs in preschoolers? There isn't enough of a biological substrate to work with; wait until prefrontal cortex is more mature." In response, I think it is helpful to consider an analogy. Certainly toddlers' legs are not at their full adult extent, and they probably will not be for another 15 years or so, but with those immature legs toddlers can walk and even run. That is to say that even though the prefrontal cortex is immature, it is able to subserve EFs to some extent (not at the full adult level, but to some extent) and with training and practice, that immature prefrontal cortex can probably subserve EFs at a higher level of proficiency.

Being able to improve EFs early in a child's life may be absolutely critical because it affects the trajectory (the negative or positive feedback loop) on which a child gets launched. Children who start school with relatively poor inhibitory control tend to blurt out the answer, jump out of their seats, take things from other children, and have difficulty paying attention and completing their assignments. They are always getting scolded and get poor grades. Teachers come to expect poor performance from them and the children come to expect the same from themselves. A downward spiral of self-doubt, low expectations, and not wanting to be in school begins. Contrast that with the self-reinforcing positive feedback loop that develops when children start off with better EFs. They are able to pay attention, complete their assignments, and not misbehave. They are often praised, get good grades, and enjoy school. Teachers come to expect them to succeed and the children come to expect the same. Improving EF skills early gets children started on a trajectory for success. Conversely, letting children start school behind on EF skills is letting them get started on a negative trajectory that can be extremely difficult and expensive to reverse. It can be astonishingly difficult to change self-perceptions, self-expectations, and the expectations of others and of an institution for you once those have been formed.

The need to intervene early is probably particularly critical for children at risk because of social or economic disadvantage. They enter school with poorer EFs (Evans & Rosenbaum, 2008; Evans & Schamberg, 2009; Hackman & Farah, 2009; Lengua, Honorado, & Bush, 2007; Noble, McCandliss, & Farah, 2007; Noble, Norman, & Farah, 2005; Raizada & Kishiyama, 2010; Sektnan, McClelland, Acock, & Morrison, 2010; see also Chapter 12, this volume). Those early differences increase with time. Disadvantaged children fall progressively farther behind each school year (O'Shaughnessy et al., 2003). They also become progressively more vulnerable to mental and physical health problems (Adler & Newman, 2002; Gianaros, 2011). A small difference between at-risk and more-advantaged children in EFs early can lead to a gap in achievement and mental health that grows ever wider each passing year. Reducing or erasing that gap at the outset could nip that dynamic in the bud. Intervening early thus has enormous potential to reduce inequalities in health and its determinants.

Indeed, there is already evidence that improving EFs early improves academic achievement. The Chicago School Readiness Project (CSRP) found that children's EFs (inhibitory control of attention and action) improved significantly more in those preschool classes where Head Start teachers had been trained on CSRP than in comparison classes (Raver et al., 2011). CSRP children also improved in vocabulary, letter-naming, and math significantly more than did controls. CSRP's improvement of academic skills was mediated largely via its improvement of EFs. EFs in the spring of preschool predicted achievement 3 years later in math and reading. Thus disadvantaged children who were lucky enough to have been randomly assigned to a CSRP class tended to continue to perform better in school 3 years later, and that was primarily mediated through their improved EFs (Li-Grining, Raver, & Pess, 2011).

MECHANISMS BY WHICH SOCIAL AND ECONOMIC DISADVANTAGE CAN IMPAIR EF DEVELOPMENT

The flip side of the neural plasticity that makes possible improvements in EFs due to environmental influences such as school curricula is that EFs are also particularly vulnerable to impairment by disadvantageous environmental influences. Growing up in poverty, in a community characterized by violence, moving often, having divorced parents, being removed from one's parents, or being a member of a minority that is discriminated against each increases one's stress (e.g., Blair et al., 2011; Bradley & Corwyn, 2002; Evans, 2004; Goodman, McEwen, Dolan, Schafer-Kalkhoff, & Adler, 2005). A plethora of evidence shows that stress impairs EFs and that EFs are exceptionally vulnerable to stress. When a person is stressed, prefrontal cortex gets flooded with too much dopamine (Arnsten, 2000; Cerqueira, Mailliet, Almeida, Jay, & Sousa, 2007; Roth, Tam, Ida, Yang, & Deutch, 1988) and the activity of the neural circuit that includes prefrontal cortex becomes less synchronized (Liston, McEwen, & Casey, 2009). One cannot think clearly and the ability to exercise self-control is weakened (Arnsten, 1998; Liston et al., 2009; Mueller et al., 2010; Oaten & Cheng, 2005; Steinhauser, Maier, & Hübner, 2007). Stressful life circumstances not only directly affect a child growing up in such circumstances, but also affect his or her parents and their ability to think clearly and be caring role models. Not only is their stress detrimental to their ability to be good parents but their child will pick up on their stress, which will increase the stress the child feels.

Another way that social or economic disadvantage can get inside the brain and affect prefrontal cortex and EFs is via parenting. For example, parents who are too fearful and overly protective or too controlling, coercive, or harsh tend to have children with worse EFs than do parents who are more supportive of their child's developing autonomy (Bernier, Carlson, & Whipple, 2010; Eddy, Leve, & Fagot, 2001; Karreman, van Tuijl, van Aken, & Dekovic, 2006; Matte-Gagné & Bernier, 2011). Homes with a richer oral language environment (especially where utterances are more elaborated and conceptually rich, where parents ask open-ended questions and model how to problem solve out loud while their child is working on a problem, and where children are encouraged to think out loud and ask questions) tend to produce children with better EFs (Hackman & Farah, 2009; Hart & Risley, 1992; Matte-Gagné & Bernier, 2011; Vallotton & Ayoub, 2011). Parents can also aid their child's development of EFs by scaffolding or supporting their child's attempts at problem solving or exercising self-control so their child can succeed when, without their help, their child would not (Bernier et al., 2010; Bibok, Carpendale, & Müller, 2009; Hughes & Ensor, 2009; Landry, Smith, Swank, Assel, & Vellet, 2001). This assistance can take the form of guiding questions; helping their child stay on task; helping their child wait rather than giving the immediate, impulsive response; making critical features more salient for their child; helping their child handle frustration and keep going; reducing the number of possible options for problem solution; and so on, thus bootstrapping a process by which children can gradually come to solve problems and exercise self-control on their own (Bibok et al., 2009). One way that scaffolding and a rich verbal environment might aid EF development is through improving the child's verbal ability, which in turn then supports EF development (Landry et al., 2001; Matte-Gagné & Bernier, 2011; Vygotsky, 1978).

Sensitive and responsive parenting and secure attachment can buffer children against the negative effects of environmental risk on EFs (Bernier, Carlson, Deschênes, & Matte-Gagné, 2012; Bernier et al., 2010; Kochanska, Murray, & Harlan, 2000; Landry et al., 2001; Matte-Gagné & Bernier, 2011; Rhoades, Greenberg, Lanza, & Blair, 2011; Robinson, Burns, & Davis, in press; see also Chapter 11, this volume). Such fostering of better EF development translates directly into better grades in school (Sektnan et al., 2010) and better resiliency in general (Obradović, 2010). For a more extended discussion of the mechanisms by which socioeconomic disadvantage can impair EFs, and how this can be minimized, see the chapters in Part III of this volume, especially Chapters 10 and 11.

MEASUREMENT TOOLS FOR ASSESSING EF DEVELOPMENT

To investigate the factors mediating and moderating the effects of environmental risk on EFs and to investigate the causal relations between EFs and academic performance, tools for measuring EFs that can be used over a broad age range and that are valid not only for middle-class, European American children but also for children at social or economic disadvantage are needed. Zelazo has been working with others on the National Institutes of Health Toolbox to develop brief EF measures for use with people ages 3 through 85 (Weintraub et al., 2010). Diamond and colleagues have EF measures that can be used with people ages 4 through 85, but each takes about 10 to 12 minutes to administer (Davidson et al., 2006; Diamond, Barnett, Thomas, & Munro, 2007).

There are many EF tasks appropriate for the 3- to 5-year-old age range, including the Dimensional Change Card Sort (DCCS), Day-Night (Gerstadt, Hong, & Diamond, 1994), Tapping (Diamond & Taylor, 1996; also called the Hands task [Hughes, 1996]), Appearance-Reality (Flavell, 1986, 1993), Ambiguous Figures (Gopnik & Rosati, 2001), False Belief (Perner, Leekam, & Wimmer, 1987), Matrix Classification (Inhelder & Piaget, 1959/1964), and Go/No-Go (Livesey & Morgan, 1991). It has been hard to find EF tasks on which children of only 2.5 or 3 years can succeed, however. Carlson and colleagues (e.g., see Chapter 2, this volume) have been at the forefront of efforts to devise measures that can be used for children 2 through 5 years of age. The combined work of several people in the field seems to have produced one progression of performance on very similar tasks from 2 to 5 years of age (see Table 1.1): By roughly 2.5 years of age, children can do intradimensional switching (reversal tasks: e.g., first putting trucks with trucks, and stars with stars, and then switching to put trucks with stars, and stars with trucks; Brooks, Hanauer, Padowska, & Rosman, 2003; Perner & Lang, 2002). By roughly 3.5 years of age, children can do extradimensional switching (switch between dimensions) from one block of trials to another but only if the dimensions are physically separated on the stimulus cards (e.g., color is a property of background rather than of the stimuli themselves, thus instead of white cards with a red truck or blue star, the front of the cards are

TABLE 1.1
Developmental Progression in the Age at Which Children
Can First Switch Rules When Sorting Cards

Tasks that require switching rules	Age in years at which most children can first succeed
Intradimensional switch: Reversal Tasks[a]	2½
Extradimensional switches (sort by 1 dimension and then by another):	
DCCS With Separated Dimensions[b]	3½
DCCS (Standard)—Integrated Dimensions[c]	4½
DCCS–Mixed Block (switching dimensions randomly across trials)[d]	7½

Note. DCCS = Dimensional Change Card Sorting task.
[a]On Reversal Tasks, first stimuli of Type 1 (say, cars) go in the left bin (stimuli of Type 2 [say, animals] go in the right bin); then when the rules reverse, stimuli of Type 1 go in the right bin and Type 2 stimuli go in the left bin. [b]For DCCS with Separated Dimensions, the stimulus on the card is always black or white with a black outline, and color appears elsewhere on the card (either as the background or as a color patch on the other side of the card). [c]For DCCS (standard), the stimuli themselves are colored and the rest of the card is white. First, the participant sorts by one dimension for some trials and then there is a single switch to sorting by the other dimension for a block of trials. In other words, there are two single-task blocks. [d]For DCCS–Mixed Block, there are several switches of sorting by one dimension and then the other. These occur randomly over trials often after only 1, 2, or 3 trials. This is called a mixed-task block. Note how much longer it takes most children to master this.

red or blue and the trucks and stars are drawn entirely in black; Diamond, Carlson, & Beck, 2005; Kloo & Perner, 2005). By roughly 4.5 years of age, children can switch between dimensions from one block of trials to another, even when both dimensions are properties of the same objects (DCCS; Zelazo, Reznick, & Piñon, 1995). It is not until about 7.5 years of age, however, that children can flexibly switch between dimensions on a trial-by-trial basis (Cohen, Bixenman, Meiran, & Diamond, 2001), and not until about 10.5 years of age that they can begin to perform well on the Wisconsin Card Sorting Task (Chelune & Baer, 1986; Welsh, Pennington, & Groisser, 1991).

There is a dearth of research on the early development of EFs among low-income children, children living in sparsely populated rural areas, children who are not of European American descent, and especially among children who are both poor and members of ethnic minorities (the children at greatest risk for school failure and for mental and physical health problems). Work such as that by Caughy et al. (see Chapter 12, this volume) and Willoughby and Blair (see Chapter 4, this volume) is starting to fill that gap but much more work is needed. The timetable of EF development among monolingual North American children of European descent cannot be assumed to be true of all children. There is already evidence that, at least during early childhood, EFs develop faster in East Asian children (Lewis et al., 2009; Oh & Lewis, 2008; Sabbagh, Xu, Carlson, Moses, & Lee, 2006) and in children who are bilingual (Bialystok & Martin, 2004; Kovács & Mehler, 2009).

To test rural children, especially those of low income, the commonly used computerized tests of EFs are not always practical. Willoughby and colleagues (Willoughby & Blair, 2011; Willoughby et al., 2010; see also Chapter 4, this volume) have developed a flip-book version of EF measures, free of technological or electrical requirements. The flip-book version has its own drawbacks, however. One must forgo the collection of reaction-time data, which is often more sensitive than percentage of correct responses (e.g., Durston, Thomas, Worden, Yang, & Casey, 2002; Simpson & Riggs, 2005). Even with training and clear instructions, there is considerable room for between-tester differences in tone of voice, pacing, and other aspects of task administration. For example, although testers are instructed to flip pages at the rate of one page every 2 seconds, there is almost surely more between-tester variability in rate than if a computer controls the timing. A computer takes away much of the opportunity for intertester variations in task administration and reduces opportunities for human error. A final drawback is that the flip-book battery is labor and time intensive; it requires the presence of two staff persons per test administration (increasing labor costs) and it takes 2 hours. The pros and cons of each EF measure and method of administration need to be carefully considered as was indicated above when asking adults for their subjective assessments of children's behavior in real-world settings (as is often done by self-regulation researchers) was contrasted with obtaining objective assessments of children's actual behavior on decontextualized, arbitrary laboratory tasks.

Researchers often assume that a measure labeled an EF measure is (a) really assessing EFs and (b) dependent on frontal cortex and interconnected brain regions thought to subserve EFs. Often those assumptions go untested. Any task requires multiple abilities, and children may have difficulty with a task not because of the ability the researcher was targeting but because of some other requirement of the task. Prefrontal cortex is late maturing; it is not impossible that earlier maturing brain regions subserve EF abilities in very young children. In Chapter 7 (this volume), Bell and Cuevas present initial electroencephalogram evidence of frontal activation during EF performance in preschoolers. Preschoolers exhibited task-related increases in medial frontal power and medial frontal-posterior coherence. (Medial frontal cortex is just behind prefrontal cortex.)

SUMMARY

One of the most critical societal needs is to develop effective, scalable, sustainable, and affordable strategies for supporting children from the youngest age possible, their parents, and their early child-care providers to get children started with good EFs when they first enter school, thereby launching them on a promising, positive trajectory, improving their life prospects and preventing problems, rather than trying to treat problems after they have been allowed to develop. To be able to determine whether a strategy is successful or not, sensitive and valid measures of EFs that can be administered longitudinally are absolutely essential.

REFERENCES

Adler, N. E., & Newman, K. (2002). Socioeconomic disparities in health: Pathways and policies. *Health Affairs, 21*, 60–76. http://dx.doi.org/10.1377/hlthaff.21.2.60

Alloway, T. P., & Alloway, R. G. (2010). Investigating the predictive roles of working memory and IQ in academic attainment. *Journal of Experimental Child Psychology, 106*, 20–29. http://dx.doi.org/10.1016/j.jecp.2009.11.003

Arnsten, A. F. T. (1998). The biology of being frazzled. *Science, 280*, 1711–1712. http://dx.doi.org/10.1126/science.280.5370.1711

Arnsten, A. F. T. (2000). Stress impairs prefrontal cortical function in rats and monkeys: Role of dopamine D1 and norepinephrine alpha-1 receptor mechanisms. *Progress in Brain Research, 126*, 183–192. http://dx.doi.org/10.1016/S0079-6123(00)26014-7

Aron, A. R., Behrens, T. E., Smith, S., Frank, M. J., & Poldrack, R. A. (2007). Triangulating a cognitive control network using diffusion-weighted magnetic resonance imaging (MRI) and functional MRI. *Journal of Neuroscience, 27,* 3743–3752. http://dx.doi.org/10.1523/JNEUROSCI.0519-07.2007

Awh, E., & Jonides, J. (2001). Overlapping mechanisms of attention and spatial working memory. *Trends in Cognitive Sciences, 5,* 119–126. http://dx.doi.org/10.1016/S1364-6613(00)01593-X

Awh, E., Vogel, E. K., & Oh, S. H. (2006). Interactions between attention and working memory. *Neuroscience, 139,* 201–208. http://dx.doi.org/10.1016/j.neuroscience.2005.08.023

Bachevalier, J. (1990). Ontogenetic development of habit and memory formation in primates. *Annals of the New York Academy of Sciences, 608,* 457–484. http://dx.doi.org/10.1111/j.1749-6632.1990.tb48906.x

Baddeley, A. (1992). Working memory. *Science, 255,* 556–559. http://dx.doi.org/10.1126/science.1736359

Baddeley, A. D., & Hitch, G. J. (1994). Developments in the concept of working memory. *Neuropsychology, 8,* 485–493. http://dx.doi.org/10.1037/0894-4105.8.4.485

Bailey, C. E. (2007). Cognitive accuracy and intelligent executive function in the brain and in business. *Annals of the New York Academy of Sciences, 1118,* 122–141. http://dx.doi.org/10.1196/annals.1412.011

Bailey, H., Dunlosky, J., & Kane, M. J. (2008). Why does working memory span predict complex cognition? Testing the strategy affordance hypothesis. *Memory & Cognition, 36,* 1383–1390. http://dx.doi.org/10.3758/MC.36.8.1383

Baler, R. D., & Volkow, N. D. (2006). Drug addiction: The neurobiology of disrupted self-control. *Trends in Molecular Medicine, 12,* 559–566. http://dx.doi.org/10.1016/j.molmed.2006.10.005

Barch, D. M. (2005). The cognitive neuroscience of schizophrenia. *Annual Review of Clinical Psychology, 1,* 321–353. http://dx.doi.org/10.1146/annurev.clinpsy.1.102803.143959

Barkley, R. A. (2001). The inattentive type of ADHD as a distinct disorder: What remains to be done. *Clinical Psychology: Science and Practice, 8,* 489–493. http://dx.doi.org/10.1093/clipsy.8.4.489

Barrouillet, P., Gavens, N., Vergauwe, E., Gaillard, V., & Camos, V. (2009). Working memory span development: A time-based resource-sharing model account. *Developmental Psychology, 45,* 477–490. http://dx.doi.org/10.1037/a0014615

Bedard, A.-C., Nichols, S., Barbosa, J. A., Schachar, R., Logan, G. D., & Tannock, R. (2002). The development of selective inhibitory control across the life span. *Developmental Neuropsychology, 21,* 93–111. http://dx.doi.org/10.1207/S15326942DN2101_5

Bernier, A., Carlson, S. M., Deschênes, M., & Matte-Gagné, C. (2012). Social factors in the development of early executive functioning: A closer look at the care-giving environment. *Developmental Science, 15,* 12–24. http://dx.doi.org/10.1111/j.1467-7687.2011.01093.x

Bernier, A., Carlson, S. M., & Whipple, N. (2010). From external regulation to self-regulation: Early parenting precursors of young children's executive functioning. *Child Development, 81,* 326–339. http://dx.doi.org/10.1111/j.1467-8624.2009.01397.x

Bialystok, E., & Martin, M. M. (2004). Attention and inhibition in bilingual children: Evidence from the dimensional change card sort task. *Developmental Science, 7,* 325–339. http://dx.doi.org/10.1111/j.1467-7687.2004.00351.x

Bibok, M. B., Carpendale, J. I. M., & Müller, U. (2009). Parental scaffolding and the development of executive function. *New Directions for Child and Adolescent Development, 2009,* 17–34. http://dx.doi.org/10.1002/cd.233

Blair, C. (2002). School readiness. Integrating cognition and emotion in a neurobiological conceptualization of children's functioning at school entry. *American Psychologist, 57,* 111–127. http://dx.doi.org/10.1037/0003-066X.57.2.111

Blair, C. (2003). *Self-regulation and school readiness.* Champaign, IL: ERIC Clearinghouse on Elementary and Early Childhood Education.

Blair, C., & Diamond, A. (2008). Biological processes in prevention and intervention: The promotion of self-regulation as a means of preventing school failure. *Development and Psychopathology, 20,* 899–911. http://dx.doi.org/10.1017/S0954579408000436

Blair, C., Granger, D. A., Willoughby, M., Mills-Koonce, R., Cox, M., Greenberg, M. T., . . . the FLP Investigators. (2011). Salivary cortisol mediates effects of poverty and parenting on executive functions in early childhood. *Child Development, 82,* 1970–1984. http://dx.doi.org/10.1111/j.1467-8624.2011.01643.x

Blair, C., & Razza, R. P. (2007). Relating effortful control, executive function, and false belief understanding to emerging math and literacy ability in kindergarten. *Child Development, 78,* 647–663. http://dx.doi.org/10.1111/j.1467-8624.2007.01019.x

Bodrova, E., & Leong, D. J. (2007). *Tools of the mind: The Vygotskian approach to early childhood education* (2nd ed.). New York, NY: Merrill/Prentice Hall.

Boone, K. B. (1999). Neuropsychological assessment of executive functions: Impact of age, education, gender, intellectual level, and vascular status on executive test scores. In B. R. Miller & J. L. Cummings (Eds.), *The human frontal lobes: Functions and disorders* (pp. 247–260). New York, NY: Guilford Press.

Borella, E., Carretti, B., & Pelegrina, S. (2010). The specific role of inhibition in reading comprehension in good and poor comprehenders. *Journal of Learning Disabilities, 43,* 541–552. http://dx.doi.org/10.1177/0022219410371676

Bradley, R. H., & Corwyn, R. F. (2002). Socioeconomic status and child development. *Annual Review of Psychology, 53,* 371–399. http://dx.doi.org/10.1146/annurev.psych.53.100901.135233

Braver, T. S., Cohen, J. D., & Barch, D. M. (2002). The role of the prefrontal cortex in normal and disordered cognitive control: A cognitive neuroscience perspective. In D. T. Stuss & R. T. Knight (Eds.), *Principles of frontal lobe function* (pp. 428–447). Oxford, England: Oxford University Press. http://dx.doi.org/10.1093/acprof:oso/9780195134971.003.0027

Broidy, L. M., Nagin, D. S., Tremblay, R. E., Bates, J. E., Brame, B., Dodge, K. A., . . . Vitaro, F. (2003). Developmental trajectories of childhood disruptive behaviors and adolescent delinquency: A six-site, cross-national study. *Developmental Psychology, 39*, 222–245.

Brooks, P. J., Hanauer, J. B., Padowska, B., & Rosman, H. (2003). The role of selective attention in preschoolers' rule use in a novel dimensional card sort. *Cognitive Development, 18*, 195–215. http://dx.doi.org/10.1016/S0885-2014(03)00020-0

Bryck, R. L., & Fisher, P. A. (2012). Training the brain: Practical applications of neural plasticity from the intersection of cognitive neuroscience, developmental psychology, and prevention science. *American Psychologist, 67*, 87–100. http://dx.doi.org/10.1037/a0024657

Cattell, R. B. (1963). Theory of fluid and crystallized intelligence: A critical experiment. *Journal of Educational Psychology, 54*(1), 1–22. http://dx.doi.org/10.1037/h0046743

Cepeda, N. J., Kramer, A. F., & Gonzalez de Sather, J. C. (2001). Changes in executive control across the life span: Examination of task-switching performance. *Developmental Psychology, 37*, 715–730. http://dx.doi.org/10.1037/0012-1649.37.5.715

Cepeda, N. J., & Munakata, Y. (2007). Why do children perseverate when they seem to know better: Graded working memory, or directed inhibition? *Psychonomic Bulletin & Review, 14*, 1058–1065. http://dx.doi.org/10.3758/BF03193091

Cerqueira, J. J., Mailliet, F., Almeida, O. F. X., Jay, T. M., & Sousa, N. (2007). The prefrontal cortex as a key target of the maladaptive response to stress. *The Journal of Neuroscience, 27*, 2781–2787. http://dx.doi.org/10.1523/JNEUROSCI.4372-06.2007

Chein, J. M., & Morrison, A. B. (2010). Expanding the mind's workspace: Training and transfer effects with a complex working memory span task. *Psychonomic Bulletin & Review, 17*, 193–199. http://dx.doi.org/10.3758/PBR.17.2.193

Chelune, G. J., & Baer, R. A. (1986). Developmental norms for the Wisconsin Card Sorting test. *Journal of Clinical and Experimental Neuropsychology, 8*, 219–228. http://dx.doi.org/10.1080/01688638608401314

Christakou, A., Brammer, M., & Rubia, K. (2011). Maturation of limbic corticostriatal activation and connectivity associated with developmental changes in temporal discounting. *NeuroImage, 54*, 1344–1354. http://dx.doi.org/10.1016/j.neuroimage.2010.08.067

Cohen, J. D., Dunbar, K., & McClelland, J. L. (1990). On the control of automatic processes: A parallel distributed processing account of the Stroop effect. *Psychological Review, 97*, 332–361. http://dx.doi.org/10.1037/0033-295X.97.3.332

Cohen, J. R., Berkman, E. T., & Lieberman, M. D. (2013). Intentional and incidental self-control in ventrolateral PFC. In D. T. Stuss & R. T. Knight (Eds.), *Principles of frontal lobe function* (2nd ed., pp. 417–440). New York, NY: Oxford University Press.

Cohen, S., Bixenman, M., Meiran, N., & Diamond, A. (2001, May). *Task switching in children*. Paper presented at the South Carolina Bicentennial Symposium on Attention, University of South Carolina, Columbia, SC.

Collins, A., & Koechlin, E. (2012). Reasoning, learning, and creativity: Frontal lobe function and human decision-making. *PLoS Biology, 10*(3), e1001293. http://dx.doi.org/10.1371/journal.pbio.1001293

Conway, A. R. A., & Engle, R. W. (1994). Working memory and retrieval: A resource-dependent inhibition model. *Journal of Experimental Psychology: General, 123*, 354–373. http://dx.doi.org/10.1037/0096-3445.123.4.354

Conway, A. R. A., Kane, M. J., Bunting, M. F., Hambrick, D. Z., Wilhelm, O., & Engle, R. W. (2005). Working memory span tasks: A methodological review and user's guide. *Psychonomic Bulletin & Review, 12*, 769–786. http://dx.doi.org/10.3758/BF03196772

Conway, A. R. A., Kane, M. J., & Engle, R. W. (2003). Working memory capacity and its relation to general intelligence. *Trends in Cognitive Sciences, 7*, 547–552. http://dx.doi.org/10.1016/j.tics.2003.10.005

Cowan, N., Saults, J. S., & Elliott, E. M. (2002). The search for what is fundamental in the development of working memory. *Advances in Child Development and Behavior, 29*, 1–49. http://dx.doi.org/10.1016/S0065-2407(02)80050-7

Daniels, K. A., Toth, J. P., & Jacoby, L. L. (2006). The aging of executive functions. In F. I. M. Craik & E. Bialystok (Eds.), *Lifespan cognition: Mechanisms of change* (pp. 9–11). London, England: Oxford University Press.

Davidson, M. C., Amso, D., Anderson, L. C., & Diamond, A. (2006). Development of cognitive control and executive functions from 4 to 13 years: Evidence from manipulations of memory, inhibition, and task switching. *Neuropsychologia, 44*, 2037–2078. http://dx.doi.org/10.1016/j.neuropsychologia.2006.02.006

Davis, J. C., Marra, C. A., Najafzadeh, M., & Liu-Ambrose, T. (2010). The independent contribution of executive functions to health related quality of life in older women. *BMC Geriatrics, 10*(1), 16–23. http://dx.doi.org/10.1186/1471-2318-10-16

Dempster, F. N. (1993). Resistance to interference: Developmental changes in a basic processing mechanism. In M. L. Howe & R. Rasnak (Eds.), *Emerging themes in cognitive development: Vol. 1. Foundations* (pp. 3–27). New York, NY: Springer-Verlag.

Denson, T. F., Pedersen, W. C., Friese, M., Hahm, A., & Roberts, L. (2011). Understanding impulsive aggression: Angry rumination and reduced self-control capacity are mechanisms underlying the provocation–aggression relationship. *Personality and Social Psychology Bulletin, 37*, 850–862. http://dx.doi.org/10.1177/0146167211401420

Diamond, A. (1985). Development of the ability to use recall to guide action, as indicated by infants' performance on AB. *Child Development, 56*, 868–883. http://dx.doi.org/10.2307/1130099

Diamond, A. (2005). Attention-deficit disorder (attention-deficit/hyperactivity disorder without hyperactivity): A neurobiologically and behaviorally distinct disorder from attention-deficit/hyperactivity disorder (with hyperactivity). *Development and Psychopathology, 17*, 807–825. http://dx.doi.org/10.1017/S0954579405050388

Diamond, A. (2010). The evidence base for improving school outcomes by addressing the whole child and by addressing skills and attitudes, not just content. *Early Education and Development, 21,* 780–793. http://dx.doi.org/10.1080/10409289.2010.514522

Diamond, A., Barnett, W. S., Thomas, J., & Munro, S. (2007). Preschool program improves cognitive control. *Science, 318,* 1387–1388. http://dx.doi.org/10.1126/science.1151148

Diamond, A., Carlson, S. M., & Beck, D. M. (2005). Preschool children's performance in task switching on the dimensional change card sort task: Separating the dimensions aids the ability to switch. *Developmental Neuropsychology, 28,* 689–729. http://dx.doi.org/10.1207/s15326942dn2802_7

Diamond, A., & Lee, K. (2011). Interventions shown to aid executive function development in children 4 to 12 years old. [Research Support, N.I.H., Extramural Review]. *Science, 333,* 959–964. http://dx.doi.org/10.1126/science.1204529

Diamond, A., & Taylor, C. (1996). Development of an aspect of executive control: Development of the abilities to remember what I said and to "do as I say, not as I do." *Developmental Psychobiology, 29,* 315–334. http://dx.doi.org/10.1002/(SICI)1098-2302(199605)29:4<315::AID-DEV2>3.0.CO;2-T

Duckworth, A. L., & Seligman, M. E. P. (2005). Self-discipline outdoes IQ in predicting academic performance of adolescents. *Psychological Science, 16,* 939–944. http://dx.doi.org/10.1111/j.1467-9280.2005.01641.x

Duncan, G. J., Dowsett, C. J., Claessens, A., Magnuson, K., Huston, A. C., Klebanov, P., . . . Japel, C. (2007). School readiness and later achievement. *Developmental Psychology, 43,* 1428–1446. http://dx.doi.org/10.1037/0012-1649.43.6.1428

Duncan, J., Emslie, H., Williams, P., Johnson, R., & Freer, C. (1996). Intelligence and the frontal lobe: The organization of goal-directed behavior. *Cognitive Psychology, 30,* 257–303. http://dx.doi.org/10.1006/cogp.1996.0008

Duncan, J., Parr, A., Woolgar, A., Thompson, R., Bright, P., Cox, S., . . . Nimmo-Smith, I. (2008). Goal neglect and Spearman's *g:* Competing parts of a complex task. *Journal of Experimental Psychology: General, 137,* 131–148. http://dx.doi.org/10.1037/0096-3445.137.1.131

Durston, S., Davidson, M. C., Tottenham, N., Galvan, A., Spicer, J., Fossella, J. A., & Casey, B. J. (2006). A shift from diffuse to focal cortical activity with development. *Developmental Science, 9,* 1–8. http://dx.doi.org/10.1111/j.1467-7687.2005.00454.x

Durston, S., Thomas, K. M., Worden, M. S., Yang, Y., & Casey, B. J. (2002). The effect of preceding context on inhibition: An event-related fMRI study. *NeuroImage, 16,* 449–453. http://dx.doi.org/10.1006/nimg.2002.1074

Eakin, L., Minde, K., Hechtman, L., Ochs, E., Krane, E., Bouffard, R., . . . Looper, K. (2004). The marital and family functioning of adults with ADHD and their spouses. *Journal of Attention Disorders, 8,* 1–10. http://dx.doi.org/10.1177/108705470400800101

Eddy, J. M., Leve, L. D., & Fagot, B. I. (2001). Coercive family processes: A replication and extension of Patterson's coercion model. *Aggressive Behavior, 27,* 14–25. http://dx.doi.org/10.1002/1098-2337(20010101/31)27:1<14::AID-AB2>3.0.CO;2-2

Eigsti, I. M., Zayas, V., Mischel, W., Shoda, Y., Ayduk, O., Dadlani, M. B., . . . Casey, B. J. (2006). Predicting cognitive control from preschool to late adolescence and young adulthood. *Psychological Science, 17*, 478–484. http://dx.doi.org/10.1111/j.1467-9280.2006.01732.x

Eisenberg, D. P., & Berman, K. F. (2010). Executive function, neural circuitry, and genetic mechanisms in schizophrenia. *Neuropsychopharmacology, 35*, 258–277. http://dx.doi.org/10.1038/npp.2009.11

Eisenberg, N., Hofer, J., & Vaughan, C. (2007). Effortful control and its socioemotional consequences, *Handbook of emotion regulation* (pp. 287–306). New York, NY: Guilford Press.

Eisenberg, N., Spinrad, T. L., & Eggum, N. D. (2010). Emotion-related self-regulation and its relation to children's maladjustment. *Annual Review of Clinical Psychology, 6*, 495–525. http://dx.doi.org/10.1146/annurev.clinpsy.121208.131208

Engle, R. W. (2002). Working memory capacity as executive attention. *Current Directions in Psychological Science, 11*, 19–23. http://dx.doi.org/10.1111/1467-8721.00160

Engle, R. W., Tuholski, S. W., Laughlin, J. E., & Conway, A. R. (1999). Working memory, short-term memory, and general fluid intelligence: A latent-variable approach. *Journal of Experimental Psychology: General, 128*, 309–331. http://dx.doi.org/10.1037/0096-3445.128.3.309

Entwisle, D. R., Alexander, K. L., & Olson, L. S. (2005). First grade and educational attainment by age 22: A new story. *American Journal of Sociology, 110*, 1458–1502. http://dx.doi.org/10.1086/428444

Erickson, M. A. (2008). Executive attention and task switching in category learning: Evidence for stimulus-dependent representation. *Memory & Cognition, 36*, 749–761. http://dx.doi.org/10.3758/MC.36.4.749

Evans, G. W. (2004). The environment of childhood poverty. *American Psychologist, 59*, 77–92. http://dx.doi.org/10.1037/0003-066X.59.2.77

Evans, G. W., & Rosenbaum, J. (2008). Self-regulation and the income achievement gap. *Early Childhood Research Quarterly, 23*, 504–514. http://dx.doi.org/10.1016/j.ecresq.2008.07.002

Evans, G. W., & Schamberg, M. A. (2009). Childhood poverty, chronic stress, and adult working memory. *Proceedings of the National Academy of Sciences of the United States of America, 106*, 6545–6549. http://dx.doi.org/10.1073/pnas.0811910106

Fan, J., McCandliss, B. D., Sommer, T., Raz, A., & Posner, M. I. (2002). Testing the efficiency and independence of attentional networks. *Journal of Cognitive Neuroscience, 14*, 340–347. http://dx.doi.org/10.1162/089892902317361886

Flavell, J. H. (1986). The development of children's knowledge about the appearance-reality distinction. *American Psychologist, 41*, 418–425. http://dx.doi.org/10.1037/0003-066X.41.4.418

Flavell, J. H. (1993). The development of children's understanding of false belief and the appearance-reality distinction. *International Journal of Psychology, 28*, 595–604. http://dx.doi.org/10.1080/00207599308246944

Friedman, N. P., Haberstick, B. C., Willcutt, E. G., Miyake, A., Young, S. E., Corley, R. P., & Hewitt, J. K. (2007). Greater attention problems during childhood predict poorer executive functioning in late adolescence. *Psychological Science, 18,* 893–900. http://dx.doi.org/10.1111/j.1467-9280.2007.01997.x

Friedman, N. P., & Miyake, A. (2004). The relations among inhibition and interference control functions: A latent-variable analysis. *Journal of Experimental Psychology: General, 133,* 101–135. http://dx.doi.org/10.1037/0096-3445.133.1.101

Garon, N., Bryson, S. E., & Smith, I. M. (2008). Executive function in preschoolers: A review using an integrative framework. *Psychological Bulletin, 134,* 31–60. http://dx.doi.org/10.1037/0033-2909.134.1.31

Garrett, H. E. (1946). A developmental theory of intelligence. *American Psychologist, 1,* 372–378. http://dx.doi.org/10.1037/h0056380

Gathercole, S. E., Pickering, S. J., Knight, C., & Stegmann, Z. (2004). Working memory skills and educational attainment: Evidence from National Curriculum assessments at 7 and 14 years of age. *Applied Cognitive Psychology, 18,* 1–16. http://dx.doi.org/10.1002/acp.934

Gazzaley, A. (2011). Influence of early attentional modulation on working memory. *Neuropsychologia, 49,* 1410–1424. http://dx.doi.org/10.1016/j.neuropsychologia.2010.12.022

Gazzaley, A., & Nobre, A. C. (2012). Top-down modulation: Bridging selective attention and working memory. *Trends in Cognitive Sciences, 16,* 129–135. http://dx.doi.org/10.1016/j.tics.2011.11.014

Gerardi-Caulton, G. (2000). Sensitivity to spatial conflict and the development of self-regulation in children 24–36 months of age. *Developmental Science, 3,* 397–404. http://dx.doi.org/10.1111/1467-7687.00134

Gerstadt, C. L., Hong, Y. J., & Diamond, A. (1994). The relationship between cognition and action: Performance of children 3½–7 years old on a Stroop-like day–night test. *Cognition, 53,* 129–153. http://dx.doi.org/10.1016/0010-0277(94)90068-X

Gianaros, P. J. (2011, January). Socioeconomic health disparities: A health neuroscience and lifecourse perspective. *Psychological Science Agenda, 25*(1). Retrieved from http://www.apa.org/science/about/psa/2011/01/health-disparities.aspx

Gogtay, N., Giedd, J. N., Lusk, L., Hayashi, K. M., Greenstein, D., Vaituzis, A. C., . . . Thompson, P. M. (2004). Dynamic mapping of human cortical development during childhood through early adulthood. *Proceedings of the National Academy of Sciences of the United States of America, 101,* 8174–8179. http://dx.doi.org/10.1073/pnas.0402680101

Goldsmith, H. H. (1996). Studying temperament via construction of the Toddler Behavior Assessment Questionnaire. *Child Development, 67,* 218–235. http://dx.doi.org/10.2307/1131697

Goodman, E., McEwen, B. S., Dolan, L. M., Schafer-Kalkhoff, T., & Adler, N. E. (2005). Social disadvantage and adolescent stress. *Journal of Adolescent Health, 37,* 484–492. http://dx.doi.org/10.1016/j.jadohealth.2004.11.126

Gopnik, A., & Rosati, A. (2001). Duck or rabbit? Reversing ambiguous figures and understanding ambiguous representations. *Developmental Science, 4,* 175–183. http://dx.doi.org/10.1111/1467-7687.00163

Greenberg, M. T., & Harris, A. R. (2012). Nurturing mindfulness in children and youth: Current state of research. *Child Development Perspectives, 6,* 161–166. http://dx.doi.org/10.1111/j.1750-8606.2011.00215.x

Hackman, D. A., & Farah, M. J. (2009). Socioeconomic status and the developing brain. *Trends in Cognitive Sciences, 13,* 65–73. http://dx.doi.org/10.1016/j.tics.2008.11.003

Harnishfeger, K. K. (1995). The development of cognitive inhibition: Theories, definitions, and research evidence. In F. N. Dempster & C. J. Brainerd (Eds.), *New perspective on interference and inhibition in cognition* (pp. 175–204). San Diego, CA: Academic Press. http://dx.doi.org/10.1016/B978-012208930-5/50007-6

Hart, B., & Risley, T. R. (1992). American parenting of language-learning children: Persisting differences in family-child interactions observed in natural home environments. *Developmental Psychology, 28,* 1096–1105. http://dx.doi.org/10.1037/0012-1649.28.6.1096

Hasher, L., & Zacks, R. T. (1988). Working memory, comprehension, and aging: A review and a new view. In G. H. Bower (Ed.), *The psychology of learning and motivation: Advances in research and theory* (Vol. 22, pp. 193–225). San Diego, CA: Academic Press.

Hughes, C. (1996). Control of action and thought: Normal development and dysfunction in autism: A research note. *Journal of Child Psychology and Psychiatry, 37,* 229–236. http://dx.doi.org/10.1111/j.1469-7610.1996.tb01396.x

Hughes, C. H., & Ensor, R. A. (2009). How do families help or hinder the emergence of early executive function? *New Directions for Child and Adolescent Development, 2009,* 35–50. http://dx.doi.org/10.1002/cd.234

Hughes, C. H., Ensor, R. A., Wilson, A., & Graham, A. (2009). Tracking executive function across the transition to school: A latent variable approach. *Developmental Neuropsychology, 35,* 20–36. http://dx.doi.org/10.1080/87565640903325691

Inhelder, B., & Piaget, J. (1964). *The early growth of logic in the child: Classification and seriation* (E. A. Lunzer & D. Papert, Trans.). New York, NY: Harper & Row. (Original work published 1959)

Jones, L. B., Rothbart, M. K., & Posner, M. I. (2003). Development of executive attention in preschool children. *Developmental Science, 6,* 498–504. http://dx.doi.org/10.1111/1467-7687.00307

Kane, M. J., & Engle, R. W. (2000). Working-memory capacity, proactive interference, and divided attention: Limits on long-term memory retrieval. *Journal of Experimental Psychology: Learning, Memory, and Cognition, 26,* 336–358. http://dx.doi.org/10.1037/0278-7393.26.2.336

Kane, M. J., & Engle, R. W. (2002). The role of prefrontal cortex in working-memory capacity, executive attention, and general fluid intelligence: An individual-differences perspective. *Psychonomic Bulletin & Review, 9,* 637–671. http://dx.doi.org/10.3758/BF03196323

Karreman, A., van Tuijl, C., van Aken, M. A. G., & Dekovic, M. (2006). Parenting and self-regulation in preschoolers: A meta-analysis. *Infant and Child Development, 15,* 561–579. http://dx.doi.org/10.1002/icd.478

Kerr, A., & Zelazo, P. D. (2004). Development of "hot" executive function: The children's gambling task. *Brain and Cognition, 55,* 148–157. http://dx.doi.org/10.1016/S0278-2626(03)00275-6

Klein, C., Foerster, F., Hartnegg, K., & Fischer, B. (2005). Lifespan development of pro- and anti-saccades: Multiple regression models for point estimates. *Developmental Brain Research, 160,* 113–123. http://dx.doi.org/10.1016/j.devbrainres.2005.06.011

Klingberg, T. (2010). Training and plasticity of working memory. *Trends in Cognitive Sciences, 14,* 317–324. http://dx.doi.org/10.1016/j.tics.2010.05.002

Kloo, D., & Perner, J. (2005). Disentangling dimensions in the Dimensional Change Card Sorting task. *Developmental Science, 8,* 44–56.

Kochanska, G., Murray, K. T., & Harlan, E. T. (2000). Effortful control in early childhood: Continuity and change, antecedents, and implications for social development. *Developmental Psychology, 36,* 220–232.

Kochanska, G., Philibert, R. A., & Barry, R. A. (2009). Interplay of genes and early mother–child relationship in the development of self-regulation from toddler to preschool age. *Journal of Child Psychology and Psychiatry, 50,* 1331–1338. http://dx.doi.org/10.1111/j.1469-7610.2008.02050.x

Kovács, A. M., & Mehler, J. (2009). Flexible learning of multiple speech structures in bilingual infants. *Science, 325,* 611–612. http://dx.doi.org/10.1126/science.1173947

Kusché, C. A., & Greenberg, M. T. (1994). *The PATHS Curriculum.* Seattle, WA: Developmental Research and Programs.

Landry, S. H., Smith, K. E., Swank, P. R., Assel, M. A., & Vellet, S. (2001). Does early responsive parenting have a special importance for children's development or is consistency across early childhood necessary? *Developmental Psychology, 37,* 387–403. http://dx.doi.org/10.1037/0012-1649.37.3.387

Leh, S. E., Petrides, M., & Strafella, A. P. (2010). The neural circuitry of executive functions in healthy subjects and Parkinson's Disease. *Neuropsychopharmacology, 35,* 70–85. http://dx.doi.org/10.1038/npp.2009.88

Lehto, J. E., Juujärvi, P., Kooistra, L., & Pulkkinen, L. (2003). Dimensions of executive functioning: Evidence from children. *British Journal of Developmental Psychology, 21,* 59–80. http://dx.doi.org/10.1348/026151003321164627

Lengua, L. J., Honorado, E., & Bush, N. R. (2007). Contextual risk and parenting as predictors of effortful control and social competence in preschool children. *Journal of Applied Developmental Psychology, 28*(1), 40–55. http://dx.doi.org/10.1016/j.appdev.2006.10.001

Leon-Carrion, J., García-Orza, J., & Pérez-Santamaría, F. J. (2004). Development of the inhibitory component of the executive functions in children and adolescents. *International Journal of Neuroscience, 114,* 1291–1311. http://dx.doi.org/10.1080/00207450490476066

Lewis, C., Koyasu, M., Oh, S., Ogawa, A., Short, B., & Huang, Z. (2009). Culture, executive function, and social understanding. *New Directions for Child and Adolescent Development, 2009*(123), 69–85. http://dx.doi.org/10.1002/cd.236

Liew, J. (2011). Effortful control, executive functions, and education: Bringing self-regulatory and social–emotional competencies to the table. *Child Development Perspectives, 6*, 105–111. http://dx.doi.org/10.1111/j.1750-8606.2011.00196.x

Li-Grining, C. P., Raver, C. C., & Pess, R. A. (2011, April). *Academic impacts of the Chicago School Readiness Project: Testing for evidence in elementary school.* Paper presented at the Society for Research in Child Development Biennial Meeting, Montreal, Quebec, Canada.

Liston, C., McEwen, B. S., & Casey, B. J. (2009). Psychosocial stress reversibly disrupts prefrontal processing and attentional control. *Proceedings of the National Academy of Sciences of the United States of America, 106*, 912–917. http://dx.doi.org/10.1073/pnas.0807041106

Livesey, D. J., & Morgan, G. A. (1991). The development of response inhibition in 4- and 5-year-old children. *Australian Journal of Psychology, 43*, 133–137. http://dx.doi.org/10.1080/00049539108260137

Louie, K., & Glimcher, P. W. (2010). Separating value from choice: Delay discounting activity in the lateral intraparietal area. *The Journal of Neuroscience, 30*, 5498–5507. http://dx.doi.org/10.1523/JNEUROSCI.5742-09.2010

Lu, C. H., & Proctor, R. W. (1995). The influence of irrelevant location information on performance: A review of the Simon and spatial Stroop effects. *Psychonomic Bulletin & Review, 2*, 174–207. http://dx.doi.org/10.3758/BF03210959

Luciana, M., Conklin, H. M., Hooper, C. J., & Yarger, R. S. (2005). The development of nonverbal working memory and executive control processes in adolescents. *Child Development, 76*, 697–712. http://dx.doi.org/10.1111/j.1467-8624.2005.00872.x

Lui, M., & Tannock, R. (2007). Working memory and inattentive behavior in a community sample of children. *Behavioral and Brain Functions, 3*, 12. http://dx.doi.org/10.1186/1744-9081-3-12

Luna, B. (2009). Developmental changes in cognitive control through adolescence. *Advances in Child Development and Behavior, 37*, 233–278. http://dx.doi.org/10.1016/S0065-2407(09)03706-9

Marcovitch, S., & Zelazo, P. D. (2009). A hierarchical competing systems model of the emergence and early development of executive function. *Developmental Science, 12*, 1–18. http://dx.doi.org/10.1111/j.1467-7687.2008.00754.x

Matte-Gagné, C., & Bernier, A. (2011). Prospective relations between maternal autonomy support and child executive functioning: Investigating the mediating role of child language ability. *Journal of Experimental Child Psychology, 110*, 611–625. http://dx.doi.org/10.1016/j.jecp.2011.06.006

McClelland, M. M., Acock, A. C., Piccinin, A., Rhea, S. A., & Stallings, M. C. (2013). Relations between preschool attention span-persistence and age 25 educational outcomes. *Early Childhood Research Quarterly, 28*, 314–324.

Miller, H. V., Barnes, J. C., & Beaver, K. M. (2011). Self-control and health outcomes in a nationally representative sample. *American Journal of Health Behavior, 35*, 15–27. http://dx.doi.org/10.5993/AJHB.35.1.2

Mischel, W., & Ayduk, O. (2002). Self-regulation in a cognitive–affective personality system: Attentional control in the service of the self. *Self and Identity, 1*, 113–120. http://dx.doi.org/10.1080/152988602317319285

Mischel, W., Shoda, Y., & Rodriguez, M. I. (1989). Delay of gratification in children. *Science, 244*, 933–938. http://dx.doi.org/10.1126/science.2658056

Miyake, A., Friedman, N. P., Emerson, M. J., Witzki, A. H., Howerter, A., & Wager, T. D. (2000). The unity and diversity of executive functions and their contributions to complex "frontal lobe" tasks: A latent variable analysis. *Cognitive Psychology, 41*, 49–100. http://dx.doi.org/10.1006/cogp.1999.0734

Moffitt, T. E. (2012, January). Childhood self-control predicts adult health, wealth, and crime. *Multi-disciplinary symposium improving the well-being of children and youth*. Copenhagen, Denmark.

Moffitt, T. E., Arseneault, L., Belsky, D., Dickson, N., Hancox, R. J., Harrington, H., . . . Caspi, A. (2011). A gradient of childhood self-control predicts health, wealth, and public safety. *Proceedings of the National Academy of Sciences of the United States of America, 108*, 2693–2698. http://dx.doi.org/10.1073/pnas.1010076108

Moffitt, T. E., Caspi, A., Taylor, A., Kokaua, J., Milne, B. J., Polanczyk, G., & Poulton, R. (2010). How common are common mental disorders? Evidence that lifetime prevalence rates are doubled by prospective versus retrospective ascertainment. *Psychological Medicine, 40*, 899–909. http://dx.doi.org/10.1017/S0033291709991036

Morasch, K. C., Raj, V. R., & Bell, M. A. (2013). The development of cognitive control from infancy through childhood. In D. Resiberg (Ed.), *Oxford handbook of cognitive psychology* (pp. 989–999). New York, NY: Oxford University Press. http://dx.doi.org/10.1093/oxfordhb/9780195376746.013.0062

Morrison, A. B., & Chein, J. M. (2011). Does working memory training work? The promise and challenges of enhancing cognition by training working memory. *Psychonomic Bulletin & Review, 18*, 46–60. http://dx.doi.org/10.3758/s13423-010-0034-0

Morton, J. B., & Munakata, Y. (2002). Active versus latent representations: A neural network model of perseveration, dissociation, and decalage. *Developmental Psychobiology, 40*, 255–265. http://dx.doi.org/10.1002/dev.10033

Mueller, S. C., Maheu, F. S., Dozier, M., Peloso, E., Mandell, D., Leibenluft, E., . . . Ernst, M. (2010). Early-life stress is associated with impairment in cognitive control in adolescence: An fMRI study. *Neuropsychologia, 48*, 3037–3044. http://dx.doi.org/10.1016/j.neuropsychologia.2010.06.013

Muraven, M. (2010). Building self-control strength: Practicing self-control leads to improved self-control performance. *Journal of Experimental Social Psychology, 46*, 465–468. http://dx.doi.org/10.1016/j.jesp.2009.12.011

Muraven, M., & Baumeister, R. F. (2000). Self-regulation and depletion of limited resources: Does self-control resemble a muscle? *Psychological Bulletin, 126*, 247–259. http://dx.doi.org/10.1037/0033-2909.126.2.247

Niendam, T. A., Laird, A. R., Ray, K. L., Dean, Y. M., Glahn, D. C., & Carter, C. S. (2012). Meta-analytic evidence for a superordinate cognitive control network subserving diverse executive functions. *Cognitive, Affective & Behavioral Neuroscience, 12*, 241–268. http://dx.doi.org/10.3758/s13415-011-0083-5

Nigg, J. T. (2000). On inhibition/disinhibition in developmental psychopathology: Views from cognitive and personality psychology and a working inhibition taxonomy. *Psychological Bulletin, 126*, 220–246. http://dx.doi.org/10.1037/0033-2909.126.2.220

Noble, K. G., McCandliss, B. D., & Farah, M. J. (2007). Socioeconomic gradients predict individual differences in neurocognitive abilities. *Developmental Science, 10*, 464–480. http://dx.doi.org/10.1111/j.1467-7687.2007.00600.x

Noble, K. G., Norman, M. F., & Farah, M. J. (2005). Neurocognitive correlates of socioeconomic status in kindergarten children. *Developmental Science, 8*, 74–87. http://dx.doi.org/10.1111/j.1467-7687.2005.00394.x

Normandeau, S., & Guay, F. (1998). Preschool behavior and first-grade school achievement: The mediational role of cognitive self-control. *Journal of Educational Psychology, 90*, 111–121. http://dx.doi.org/10.1037/0022-0663.90.1.111

Oaten, M., & Cheng, K. (2005). Academic examination stress impairs self-control. *Journal of Social and Clinical Psychology, 24*, 254–279. http://dx.doi.org/10.1521/jscp.24.2.254.62276

Obradović, J. (2010). Effortful control and adaptive functioning of homeless children: Variable-focused and person-focused analyses. *Journal of Applied Developmental Psychology, 31*, 109–117. http://dx.doi.org/10.1016/j.appdev.2009.09.004

Oh, S., & Lewis, C. (2008). Korean preschoolers' advanced inhibitory control and its relation to other executive skills and mental state understanding. *Child Development, 79*, 80–99. http://dx.doi.org/10.1111/j.1467-8624.2007.01112.x

Olson, E. A., Collins, P. F., Hooper, C. J., Muetzel, R., Lim, K. O., & Luciana, M. (2009). White matter integrity predicts delay discounting behavior in 9- to 23-year-olds: A diffusion tensor imaging study. *Journal of Cognitive Neuroscience, 21*, 1406–1421. http://dx.doi.org/10.1162/jocn.2009.21107

O'Shaughnessy, T., Lane, K. L., Gresham, F. M., & Beebe-Frankenberger, M. (2003). Children placed at risk for learning and behavioral difficulties: Implementing a school-wide system of early identification and prevention. *Remedial and Special Education, 24*, 27–35. http://dx.doi.org/10.1177/074193250302400103

Pardo-Vázquez, J. L., & Fernández-Rey, J. (2008). External validation of the computerized, group administrable adaptation of the "operation span task." *Behavior Research Methods, 40*, 46–54. http://dx.doi.org/10.3758/BRM.40.1.46

Paus, T., Zijdenbos, A., Worsley, K., Collins, D. L., Blumenthal, J., Giedd, J. N., . . . Evans, A. C. (1999). Structural maturation of neural pathways in children and adolescents: In vivo study. *Science, 283*, 1908–1911. http://dx.doi.org/10.1126/science.283.5409.1908

Penadés, R., Catalán, R., Rubia, K., Andrés, S., Salamero, M., & Gastó, C. (2007). Impaired response inhibition in obsessive compulsive disorder. *European Psychiatry, 22*, 404–410. http://dx.doi.org/10.1016/j.eurpsy.2006.05.001

Pennington, B. F. (1994). The working memory function of the prefrontal cortices: Implications for developmental and individual differences in cognition. In M. M. Haith, J. Benson, R. Roberts, & B. F. Pennington (Eds.), *The development of future oriented processes* (pp. 243–289). Chicago, IL: University of Chicago Press.

Perner, J., & Lang, B. (2002). What causes 3-year-olds' difficulty on the dimensional change card sorting task? *Infant and Child Development, 11*, 93–105. http://dx.doi.org/10.1002/icd.299

Perner, J., Leekam, S. R., & Wimmer, H. (1987). Three-year-olds' difficulty with false belief: The case for a conceptual deficit. *British Journal of Developmental Psychology, 5*, 125–137. http://dx.doi.org/10.1111/j.2044-835X.1987.tb01048.x

Petit, L., Courtney, S. M., Maisog, J. M., Ungerleider, L. G., & Haxby, J. V. (1997). Frontal spatial working memory areas anterior to the frontal and supplementary eye fields studied with fMRI in humans. *Society for Neuroscience Abstracts, 23*, 1679.

Porges, S. W., Doussard-Roosevelt, J. A., & Maiti, A. K. (1994). Vagal tone and the physiological regulation of emotion. *Monographs of the Society for Research in Child Development, 59*(2–3), 167–186. http://dx.doi.org/10.1111/j.1540-5834.1994.tb01283.x

Posner, M. I., & DiGirolamo, G. J. (1998). Executive attention: Conflict, target detection, and cognitive control. In R. Parasuraman (Ed.), *The attentive brain* (pp. 401–423). Cambridge, MA: MIT Press.

Prince, M., Patel, V., Saxena, S., Mmaj, M., Maselko, J., Phillips, M., & Rahman, A. (2007). No health without mental health. *The Lancet, 370*, 859–877.

Rachlin, H., Raineri, A., & Cross, D. (1991). Subjective probability and delay. *Journal of the Experimental Analysis of Behavior, 55*, 233–244. http://dx.doi.org/10.1901/jeab.1991.55-233

Raizada, R. D., & Kishiyama, M. M. (2010). Effects of socioeconomic status on brain development, and how cognitive neuroscience may contribute to levelling the playing field. *Frontiers in Human Neuroscience, 4*, 1–11.

Raven, J., Raven, J. C., & Court, J. H. (2004). *Manual for Raven's Progressive Matrices and Vocabulary Scales.* San Antonio, TX: Pearson Assessment.

Raver, C. C. (2004). Placing emotional self-regulation in sociocultural and socioeconomic contexts. *Child Development, 75*, 346–353. http://dx.doi.org/10.1111/j.1467-8624.2004.00676.x

Raver, C. C., Jones, S. M., Li-Grining, C. P., Metzger, M., Smallwood, K., & Sardin, L. (2008). Improving preschool classroom processes: Preliminary findings from a randomized trial implemented in Head Start settings. *Early Childhood Research Quarterly, 63*, 253–255.

Raver, C. C., Jones, S. M., Li-Grining, C., Zhai, F., Bub, K., & Pressler, E. (2011). CSRP's impact on low-income preschoolers' preacademic skills: Self-regulation as a mediating mechanism. *Child Development, 82*, 362–378.

Rhoades, B. L., Greenberg, M. T., Lanza, S. T., & Blair, C. (2011). Demographic and familial predictors of early executive function development: Contribution of a person-centered perspective. *Journal of Experimental Child Psychology, 108*, 638–662. http://dx.doi.org/10.1016/j.jecp.2010.08.004

Riggs, N. R., Blair, C. B., & Greenberg, M. T. (2004). Concurrent and 2-year longitudinal relations between executive function and the behavior of 1st and 2nd grade children. *Child Neuropsychology, 9*, 267–276. http://dx.doi.org/10.1076/chin.9.4.267.23513

Robinson, J. B., Burns, B. M., & Davis, D. W. (in press). Maternal scaffolding and attention regulation in children living in poverty. *Journal of Applied Developmental Psychology.*

Robison, L. M., Sclar, D. A., Skaer, T. L., & Galin, R. S. (1999). National trends in the prevalence of attention-deficit/hyperactivity disorder and the prescribing of methylphenidate among school-age children: 1990–1995. *Clinical Pediatrics, 38*, 209–217. http://dx.doi.org/10.1177/000992289903800402

Roca, M., Parr, A., Thompson, R., Woolgar, A., Torralva, T., Antoun, N., . . . Duncan, J. (2010). Executive function and fluid intelligence after frontal lobe lesions. *Brain: A Journal of Neurology, 133*, 234–247. http://dx.doi.org/10.1093/brain/awp269

Roth, R. H., Tam, S. Y., Ida, Y., Yang, J. X., & Deutch, A. Y. (1988). Stress and the mesocorticolimbic dopamine systems. *Annals of the New York Academy of Sciences, 537*, 138–147. http://dx.doi.org/10.1111/j.1749-6632.1988.tb42102.x

Rothbart, M. K., Ahadi, S. A., Hershey, K. L., & Fisher, P. (2001). Investigations of temperament at three to seven years: The Children's Behavior Questionnaire. *Child Development, 72*, 1394–1408. http://dx.doi.org/10.1111/1467-8624.00355

Rothbart, M. K., & Bates, J. E. (2006). Temperament. In W. Damon & N. Eisenberg (Eds.), *Handbook of child psychology: Vol. 3. Social, emotional, and personality development* (pp. 105–176). New York, NY: Wiley.

Rothbart, M. K., & Jones, L. B. (1998). Temperament, self-regulation, and education. *School Psychology Review, 27*, 479–491.

Rothbart, M. K., & Posner, M. I. (2001). Mechanism and variation in the development of attentional networks. In C. A. Nelson & M. Luciana (Eds.), *Handbook of developmental cognitive neuroscience* (pp. 353–363). Cambridge, MA: MIT Press.

Rubia, K., Smith, A. B., Taylor, E., & Brammer, M. (2007). Linear age-correlated functional development of right inferior fronto-striato-cerebellar networks during response inhibition and anterior cingulate during error-related processes. *Human Brain Mapping, 28*, 1163–1177. http://dx.doi.org/10.1002/hbm.20347

Rueda, M. R., Posner, M. I., & Rothbart, M. K. (2005). The development of executive attention: Contributions to the emergence of self-regulation. *Developmental Neuropsychology, 28*, 573–594. http://dx.doi.org/10.1207/s15326942dn2802_2

Saarni, C. (1999). *The development of emotional competence.* New York, NY: Guilford Press.

Sabbagh, M. A., Xu, F., Carlson, S. M., Moses, L. J., & Lee, K. (2006). The development of executive functioning and theory of mind. A comparison of Chinese and U.S. preschoolers. *Psychological Science, 17*, 74–81. http://dx.doi.org/10.1111/j.1467-9280.2005.01667.x

Schleepen, T. M., & Jonkman, L. M. (2009). The development of non-spatial working memory capacity during childhood and adolescence and the role of interference control: An N-back task study. *Developmental Neuropsychology, 35*, 37–56. http://dx.doi.org/10.1080/87565640903325733

Sektnan, M., McClelland, M. M., Acock, A., & Morrison, F. J. (2010). Relations between early family risk, children's behavioral regulation, and academic achievement. *Early Childhood Research Quarterly, 25*, 464–479. http://dx.doi.org/10.1016/j.ecresq.2010.02.005

Shing, Y. L., Lindenberger, U., Diamond, A., Li, S. C., & Davidson, M. C. (2010). Memory maintenance and inhibitory control differentiate from early childhood to adolescence. *Developmental Neuropsychology, 35*, 679–697. http://dx.doi.org/10.1080/87565641.2010.508546

Shoda, Y., Mischel, W., & Peake, P. K. (1990). Predicting adolescent cognitive and self-regulatory competencies from preschool delay of gratification: Identifying diagnostic conditions. *Developmental Psychology, 26*, 978–986. http://dx.doi.org/10.1037/0012-1649.26.6.978

Simpson, A., & Riggs, K. J. (2005). Inhibitory and working memory demands of the day–night task in children. *British Journal of Developmental Psychology, 10*, 1–17.

St Clair-Thompson, H. L., & Gathercole, S. E. (2006). Executive functions and achievements in school: Shifting, updating, inhibition, and working memory. *The Quarterly Journal of Experimental Psychology, 59*, 745–759. http://dx.doi.org/10.1080/17470210500162854

Steinberg, L., Graham, S., O'Brien, L., Woolard, J., Cauffman, E., & Banich, M. (2009). Age differences in future orientation and delay discounting. *Child Development, 80*, 28–44. http://dx.doi.org/10.1111/j.1467-8624.2008.01244.x

Steinhauser, M., Maier, M., & Hübner, R. (2007). Cognitive control under stress: How stress affects strategies of task-set reconfiguration. *Psychological Science, 18*, 540–545. http://dx.doi.org/10.1111/j.1467-9280.2007.01935.x

Taylor Tavares, J. V., Clark, L., Cannon, D. M., Erickson, K., Drevets, W. C., & Sahakian, B. J. (2007). Distinct profiles of neurocognitive function in unmedicated unipolar depression and bipolar II depression. *Biological Psychiatry, 62*, 917–924. http://dx.doi.org/10.1016/j.biopsych.2007.05.034

Unsworth, N., Redick, T. S., Heitz, R. P., Broadway, J. M., & Engle, R. W. (2009). Complex working memory span tasks and higher-order cognition: A latent-variable analysis of the relationship between processing and storage. *Memory, 17*, 635–654. http://dx.doi.org/10.1080/09658210902998047

Vallotton, C., & Ayoub, C. (2011). Use your words: The role of language in the development of toddlers' self-regulation. *Early Childhood Research Quarterly, 26*, 169–181. http://dx.doi.org/10.1016/j.ecresq.2010.09.002

Verdejo-García, A., Bechara, A., Recknor, E. C., & Pérez-García, M. (2006). Executive dysfunction in substance dependent individuals during drug use and abstinence: An examination of the behavioral, cognitive, and emotional correlates of addiction. *Journal of the International Neuropsychological Society*, *12*, 405–415. http://dx.doi.org/10.1017/S1355617706060486

Vygotsky, L. S. (1978). *Mind in society: The development of higher psychological processes*. Cambridge, MA: Harvard University Press.

Wass, S., Porayska-Pomsta, K., & Johnson, M. H. (2011). Training attentional control in infancy. *Current Biology*, *21*, 1543–1547. http://dx.doi.org/10.1016/j.cub.2011.08.004

Webster-Stratton, C., & Reid, M. J. (2004). Strengthening social and emotional competence in young children: The foundation for early school readiness and success. *Infants and Young Children*, *17*, 96–113. http://dx.doi.org/10.1097/00001163-200404000-00002

Weintraub, S., Tulksy, D., Dikmen, S., Heaton, R., Havlik, R., Fox, N., & Borosh, B. (2010). *The NIH Toolbox for assessment of neurological and behavioral function: The cognition team experience*. Evanston, IL: Center on Education Research and Outcomes, Evanston Northwestern Healthcare.

Welsh, M. C., Pennington, B. F., & Groisser, D. B. (1991). A normative–developmental study of executive function: A window on prefrontal function in children. *Developmental Neuropsychology*, *7*, 131–149. http://dx.doi.org/10.1080/87565649109540483

Werner, H. (1957). The concept of development from a comparative and organismic point of view. In D. B. Harris (Ed.), *The concept of development: An issue in the study of human behaviour* (pp. 125–148). Minneapolis, MN: Jones Press.

Wiebe, S. A., Sheffield, T., Nelson, J. M., Clark, C. A., Chevalier, N., & Espy, K. A. (2011). The structure of executive function in 3-year-olds. *Journal of Experimental Child Psychology*, *108*, 436–452. http://dx.doi.org/10.1016/j.jecp.2010.08.008

Willoughby, M. T., & Blair, C. B. (2011). Test–retest reliability of a new executive function battery for use in early childhood. *Child Neuropsychology*, *17*, 564–579. http://dx.doi.org/10.1080/09297049.2011.554390

Willoughby, M. T., Blair, C. B., Wirth, R. J., & Greenberg, M. (2010). The measurement of executive function at age 3 years: Psychometric properties and criterion validity of a new battery of tasks. *Psychological Assessment*, *22*, 306–317. http://dx.doi.org/10.1037/a0018708

Winstok, Z. (2009). From self-control capabilities and the need to control others to proactive and reactive aggression among adolescents. *Journal of Adolescence*, *32*, 455–466. http://dx.doi.org/10.1016/j.adolescence.2008.08.006

Wright, A., & Diamond, A. (2014). An effect of inhibitory load in children while keeping working memory load constant. [Special issue on Development of Executive Function during Childhood]. *Frontiers in Psychology*, *5*, 213. http://dx.doi.org/10.3389/fpsyg.2014.00213

Zacks, R. T., & Hasher, L. (2006). Aging and long-term memory: Deficits are not inevitable. In E. Bialystock & F. I. M. Craik (Eds.), *Lifespan cognition: Mechanisms of change* (pp. 162–177). New York, NY: Oxford University Press. http://dx.doi.org/10.1093/acprof:oso/9780195169539.003.0011

Zanto, T. P., Rubens, M. T., Thangavel, A., & Gazzaley, A. (2011). Causal role of the prefrontal cortex in top-down modulation of visual processing and working memory. *Nature Neuroscience, 14,* 656–661. http://dx.doi.org/10.1038/nn.2773

Zelazo, P. D., Reznick, J. S., & Piñon, D. E. (1995). Response control and the execution of verbal rules. *Developmental Psychology, 31,* 508–517. http://dx.doi.org/10.1037/0012-1649.31.3.508

2

INCORPORATING EARLY DEVELOPMENT INTO THE MEASUREMENT OF EXECUTIVE FUNCTION: THE NEED FOR A CONTINUUM OF MEASURES ACROSS DEVELOPMENT

STEPHANIE M. CARLSON, SUSAN FAJA, AND DANIELLE M. BECK

Executive function (EF) refers to higher order, self-regulatory cognitive processes that aid in the monitoring and control of thought and action (for a review, see Carlson, Zelazo, & Faja, 2013). Components of EF that have been identified include working memory, attentional flexibility, and inhibitory control processes such as resistance to temptation. EF is primarily associated with the prefrontal cortex (PFC) and most knowledge about EF stems from neuroimaging data and clinical observations of children and adults with brain lesions or medical conditions known to affect prefrontal functioning. Several studies using various measures of self-control in children have suggested that EF may play an important role in cognitive and social development, such as theory of mind, pretend play, emotion regulation, moral conduct, and school readiness (e.g., Blair & Razza, 2007; Carlson, Mandell, & Williams, 2004;

Preparation of this chapter was supported in part by R01HD051495 to Stephanie M. Carlson.

http://dx.doi.org/10.1037/14797-003
Executive Function in Preschool-Age Children: Integrating Measurement, Neurodevelopment, and Translational Research, J. A. Griffin, P. McCardle, and L. S. Freund (Editors)

Carlson & Wang, 2007; Carlson & White, 2013; Shoda, Mischel, & Peake, 1990). Conversely, disruptions in EF are implicated in a number of childhood disorders and are associated with poor social and academic adjustment (e.g., Casey, Tottenham, & Fossella, 2002; Hughes & Ensor, 2011; Rodriguez, Mischel, & Shoda, 1989), persisting even decades later (Casey et al., 2011; Moffitt et al., 2011; see Carlson & Zelazo, 2011, for commentary).

Despite its clear importance, tracing early EF development, identifying its major components, and determining its role in child outcomes have been hampered by a lack of appropriate behavioral measures of EF. Researchers in recent years have used a mix of tabletop behavioral and computerized tasks, including tasks tapping multiple (but often unspecified) aspects of EF, tasks that are not developmentally sensitive in the age group of interest (i.e., they produce floor or ceiling effects), or tasks that are not child-friendly (which have a high refusal rate). Furthermore, researchers often use the same measures over time to investigate development; however, very few of these tasks have been systematically evaluated for reliability. Each of these factors introduces measurement error in the construct of EF.

A primary challenge to measurement of EF is that despite considerable empirical, clinical, and theoretical attention, consensus on its definition has remained elusive. Some definitions have emphasized associated brain structures whereas others have attempted to delineate the organization of diverse but interrelated cognitive processes. For example, one approach draws a distinction between automatic versus controlled processes, with the executive domain being tapped during actions requiring controlled effort (Atkinson & Shiffrin, 1968; Shiffrin & Schneider, 1977), as summarized by Hughes and Graham (2002). Thus, EF is necessarily involved in situations that require planning, decision making, error correction or troubleshooting, initiation of novel action sequences, overcoming a habitual response, or pursuing goals (Anderson, 2002; Norman & Shallice, 1986; Shallice & Burgess, 1991). Another definition emphasizes the function of executive cognitive processes in supporting self-regulation and development of social cognitive competence (Blair, Zelazo, & Greenberg, 2005; Sokol, Müller, Carpendale, Young, & Iarocci, 2010). We first review approaches to refining the definition of EF and implications for methodology.

FUNCTIONAL DEFINITIONS OF EXECUTIVE FUNCTION

Most discussions of EF specify it as a unitary construct or a metaconstruct that encompasses multiple subcomponents, or some combination of the two. For example, EFs can be understood as overarching self-regulatory abilities that coordinate more basic or domain-specific cognitive processes in the service of goal-oriented behaviors (Neisser, 1967). Others posit a definition that is even more broadly encompassing, where EF is defined as "the control, supervisory, or self-regulatory functions that organize and direct all cognitive activity, emotional response, and overt behavior" (Isquith, Crawford, Espy, & Gioia, 2005, p. 209).

In contrast, others have attempted to parse EF into distinct functions. Definitions that emphasize problem solving or goal achievement include the subfunctions of attention to external stimuli (i.e., noticing the problem), formation of goals and strategies, planning, controlling attention, verification that plans and actions have been implemented appropriately, and trouble-shooting (e.g., Burgess, 1997; Luria, 1973; Shallice, 1988). Other cognitive divisions include maintenance of information in working memory, inhibition of prepotent responding, planning, rule use, error correction, detection of and resistance to interference, mental flexibility, and shifting and sustaining of attention in the service of a goal (Blair et al., 2005; Dempster, 1992; Welsh, Pennington, & Groisser, 1991; Zelazo, Carter, Reznick, & Frye, 1997). Finally, some have divided EF into cognitive regulation (e.g., working memory, attention maintenance or shifting), behavioral regulation (e.g., initiation of movements, sustaining motor performance over time, motor inhibition), and emotional regulation (e.g., modulating mood, self-soothing strategies; Nigg, 2000; Powell & Voeller, 2004), or into simple (e.g., delay, low working memory) versus complex (e.g., conflict, high working memory) task demands (e.g., Carlson, 2005; Garon, Bryson, & Smith, 2008).

These various ways of parsing EF have raised current controversy as to whether EF is a unitary construct or consists of interrelated, but distinct, components—referred to as the "unity versus diversity" issue (e.g., Barkley, Edwards, Laneri, Fletcher, & Metevia, 2001; Brocki & Bohlin, 2004; Isquith, Gioia, & Espy, 2004; Miyake et al., 2000). One methodological approach to this problem relies on a factorial analysis of performance on a number of EF tests that purportedly tap distinct EF components (e.g., short-term memory span, simple inhibition tasks) and compares them to performance on complex problem-solving activities thought to require multiple EFs (e.g., Wisconsin Card Sorting Test [WCST], Tower of Hanoi). Then, confirmatory factor analysis is used to test the empirical results of the a priori theoretical model (e.g., a single latent variable) against alternative models (e.g., several latent variables). In their seminal study with young adults, Miyake et al. (2000) followed this approach and extracted three correlated latent variables from several commonly used EF tasks, believed to represent inhibition, working memory, and shifting, which contributed differentially to performance on complex EF tasks. In developmental studies of this kind, the tripartite EF model identified by Miyake et al. (2000) appears to be in place by middle childhood (Lehto, Juujärvi, Kooistra, & Pulkkinen, 2003; McAuley & White, 2011).

Huizinga, Dolan, and van der Molen (2006) employed confirmatory factor analysis with individuals ages 7, 11, 15, and 21 years and found partial support for the Miyake model, as only the working memory and shifting measures (and not the inhibition measures) loaded onto latent variables. Miyake's group subsequently also found evidence for this more parsimonious two-factor model consisting of working memory and shifting, with the inhibition measures being distributed across them (Miyake & Friedman, 2012).

In contrast, most research of this kind with preschoolers finds a one-factor solution to be most parsimonious (Wiebe, Espy, & Charak, 2008; Wiebe et al., 2011; but see Hughes, 1998; Miller, Giesbrecht, Müller, McInerney, & Kerns, 2012). Wiebe et al. (2008) used a battery of preschool EF measures including three tasks considered a priori to demand working memory and seven tasks requiring inhibitory processes. Seven models were tested; for reasons of goodness of fit and parsimony, the unitary executive control model was preferred. Together, the evidence for a unitary EF factor in preschool and at least two distinct components (working memory and shifting) in later childhood appears to be consistent with increased specialization of cortical brain activity with age (e.g., Durston et al., 2006). A degree of circular reasoning in the factorial approach, however, merits caution. In the end, the factors are determined by the researcher's initial choice of tasks, as well as any shared method variance among tasks loading on a factor, and so the approach begs the question of which is being confirmed: the structure of EF or the investigator's model of its structure (e.g., see Miller et al., 2012). Nonetheless, the factorial approach represents an empirical starting point in generating hypotheses about EF processes that can be experimentally tested in order to clarify the definition of EF for future research. Rather than attempt to resolve ongoing definitional controversies, we refer to the term *EF* as denoting both a class of cognitive processes (working memory, inhibition, shifting, etc.) and an overarching coordination of these processes in achieving a certain goal (i.e., to a functional characterization of EF).

DIMENSIONS OF EXECUTIVE FUNCTION

In our own work, we have identified two major dimensions of EF using task analyses in studies of preschool children. The first dimension involves conflict versus delay. Conflict tasks require children to initiate a goal-directed behavior in the face of conflicting stimulus properties, such as in a Stroop-like task. In the Day-Night task, for example, children are instructed to say "day" when shown a drawing of the moon and stars and to say "night" when shown a yellow sun (Gerstadt, Hong, & Diamond, 1994). Delay tasks, on the other hand, require children to postpone a dominant response or resist temptation in the short term for a larger delayed reward, such as in a delay-of-gratification task (e.g., waiting until the examiner says "go" before playing a game or eating a snack). Kochanska, Murray, and Harlan (2000) and Carlson and Moses (2001) reported that these aspects of self-regulation in preschoolers emerged as separate factors in a principal components analysis, and this was replicated in confirmatory factor analysis by Carlson, White, and Davis-Unger (2014), although the two factors are correlated. Performance across both conflict EF and delay EF shows dramatic improvement during the preschool period (Carlson, 2005), yet they have shown different patterns of relations to other constructs. For example, conflict EF, but not delay EF, has been shown to be predicted by early parenting (Bernier, Carlson, & Whipple, 2010) and to be significantly related to children's theory of mind and representational understanding of pretense (Carlson & Moses, 2001; Carlson et al., 2014; Davis-Unger & Carlson, 2008). In addition, bilingual children performed significantly better on conflict EF than did monolingual children; however, there was no bilingual advantage on delay tasks (Carlson & Choi, 2009; Carlson & Meltzoff, 2008; Poulin-Dubois, Blaye, Coutya, & Bialystok, 2011). Conversely, delay, but not conflict, task performance was significantly predicted by sleep regulation in infancy (Bernier, Carlson, Bordeleau, & Carrier, 2010) and related to more mature pretend actions (Carlson et al., 2014). The different task demands of conflict versus delay may tap separate neurological structures, suggesting they may also be useful in understanding brain development. Delay tasks, for instance, have been shown to provide assessment of orbitofrontal cortex (OFC) function, whereas conflict tasks activate both the OFC and PFC (Berlin, Rolls, & Kischka, 2004; Monterosso, Ehrman, Napier, O'Brien, & Childress, 2001; Zelazo & Cunningham, 2007).

The second dimension concerns the affective–motivational context of the task, with some being relatively cool (emotionally neutral) and others being relatively hot (emotionally motivating, usually in the presence of rewards). Traditionally, most research has focused on the cool components of EF. Cool aspects of EF are associated with the dorsolateral PFC and are likely elicited by certain logic problems or tasks such as the WCST (Grant & Berg, 1948) or Dimensional Change Card Sort (DCCS; Frye, Zelazo, & Palfai, 1995; Zelazo, 2006) where cards must be sorted by various characteristics (e.g., shape and color). Hot EF, on the other hand, is believed to depend on the OFC, which has close connections with the limbic system (e.g., Iowa Gambling Task; Bechara, Damasio, Damasio, & Anderson, 1994). Thus, situations that are emotionally charged or social in nature tend to call on hot EF and OFC activation (for an overview see Zelazo & Carlson, 2012).

Despite general improvements in EF across the preschool period, research has shown differential patterns of development for cool and hot EF as well as meaningful individual differences in task performance within a particular age range. However, relatively little is known about how motivational or affectively charged stimuli influence young children's EF. Under some circumstances, children seem to perform better on hot versions of EF tasks (Qu & Zelazo, 2007; Zelazo, Qu, & Kesek, 2010), although other reports suggest children do better on cool versions (Carlson, Davis, & Leach, 2005; Prencipe & Zelazo, 2005; Talwar, Carlson, & Lee, 2011). Similar to the distinction between conflict and delay tasks, individual differences on tasks of hot and cool EF have been shown to be important in distinguishing concurrent and later functioning. For example, preschoolers who perform better on cool measures of EF have been shown to have higher verbal ability and academic achievement in kindergarten. No such relations to hot EF were found (Brock, Rimm-Kaufman, Nathanson, & Grimm, 2009; Hongwanishkul, Happaney, Lee, & Zelazo, 2005). It should be noted that these dimensions are usually confounded in the EF literature, with conflict tasks being cool and delay tasks being hot. Relatively hot versions of conflict tasks are used successfully including the hot DCCS (Beck, Schaefer, Pang, & Carlson, 2011; Qu & Zelazo, 2007; Talwar et al., 2011) and the Less Is More task (Carlson et al., 2005). Nevertheless, it has been challenging to make a delay task carry the same meaning when cooling it down by asking the child to wait or resist temptation on behalf of someone else (Beck et al., 2011; Prencipe & Zelazo, 2005).

MEASUREMENT CHALLENGES AND RECOMMENDATIONS

Methodological advances in recent years make investigation of development of EF and measurement of disruptions to this system among young children increasingly feasible. First, a variety of tasks have been created that are sensitive to development and account for the linguistic, motor, and sustained attention skills of young children, including the DCCS (Zelazo, 2006), the Day-Night task (Gerstadt et al., 1994), Less Is More (Carlson et al., 2005) and Shape School (Espy, 1997). Second, Carlson (2005) made a significant contribution to the understanding of which EF tasks are sensitive to age-related changes by measuring the performance of 600 children ages 2 to 6 years across 24 tasks. An age effect was found for 65% of the tasks administered and Carlson predicted that effects would have been detected with task modifications to reduce floor and ceiling effects for the remaining 35%. This broad investigation of EF during the preschool period provides useful information for researchers regarding the difficulty of many common EF tasks. Examination of performance on these tasks might also aid in selecting measures for correlational analyses that are likely to yield the most within-group variability. Third, the National Institutes of Health (NIH) Toolbox Cognition Battery was developed for life span (age 3–85) assessment of cognitive and language skills including EF (Bauer & Zelazo, 2014). In a pediatric validation study, two computerized measures of EF (DCCS and Flanker) were tested in approximately 85 children ages 3 to 6 and were found to be reliable and valid (Zelazo et al., 2013). Finally, such methodological advances have clinical relevance, by enabling researchers to develop norms for typically developing children against which to measure potentially serious deviations or delays.

Regarding clinical populations, theories that seek to reduce EF to a single construct (e.g., inhibition) may be limited in distinguishing between disorders, whereas an approach that integrates multiple subfunctions is likely to be more appropriate (Zelazo et al., 1997). Jacobs and Anderson (2002) provided recommendations and examples for developing scoring systems based on problem-solving strategy or qualitative errors, rather than mastery or overall performance. For instance, these authors found that the latency to make a second move in a Tower of London task distinguished children and adolescents with frontal lobe pathology from children with damage to other regions (Anderson, Anderson, & Lajoie, 1996; Shallice, 1982). Such deficits in planning efficiency may be masked in investigations that consider only the initial latency between seeing the problem and making the first move. This approach goes beyond documenting the existence of executive dysfunction, which is observed in many childhood disorders, to establishing why the disorder produces observed dysexecutive behaviors. In addition, microanalytic coding may offer more sensitive approaches to distinguishing among relatively basic functions such as visuospatial skills or memory and metacognitive components of performance including planning or flexibility. These approaches may also be useful in linking mental processes with underlying brain structures. Another consideration raised by Hughes and Graham (2002) is to examine associations rather than dissociations between domains within EF and correlates of EF (e.g., social function, theory of mind), especially when exploring relations between observed impairments and preserved functions in various developmental disorders (e.g., attention-deficit/ hyperactivity disorder, conduct disorder, and autism spectrum disorder). Last, the mode of administration may be especially important in interpreting the findings with patient populations. An example of this is the discrepant findings produced by administering EF tasks to individuals with autism spectrum disorders via computer versus an experimenter. In computer-delivered versions of card sorting and tower tasks, the social and motivational aspects of the task are reduced, and individuals with autism generally perform better under these circumstances than in the traditional versions delivered face to face (see Kenworthy et al., 2008, for a review of this topic, but see also Williams & Jarrold, 2013). Computer-administered tasks also have a higher beginning age boundary among typically developing preschoolers, who have difficulty mapping their responses to a screen or keypad and staying on-task with a computer before age 4–5 years, especially without an adult examiner present. This concern is lessening now with touch-tablet games, with which even 2-year-olds are able to symbolically map and execute their responses (Carlson & Zelazo, 2015).

Despite recent interest in the development of EF and increasingly sophisticated methods, examining EF in children continues to present challenges. For instance, the same tasks may tap different skills at different time points during development. For example, Perner and Lang (2002) varied the nature of task demands in an attention-shifting task administered to preschoolers. Three-year-olds, but not 4-year-olds, were affected by the complexity of the task. Executive tasks for very young children must take into consideration limitations in other domains including language comprehension, literacy, and fluency, which emerge later in development. The NIH Toolbox measures of EF, for example, have not worked well for children under age 4 in our lab, or for children under age 5 in our fieldwork with children of low socioeconomic status, because the starting level is too difficult to comprehend, a finding confirmed by Akshoomoff et al. (2014). Conversely, tasks that are known to be difficult for older children and adults may be trivially easy for young children. For example, the Stroop task assumes word reading of color names to be fluent and automatic. For prereaders, the task is simple. The Grass-Snow variant, in which children need to point to a white card for "grass" and to a green card for "snow," is a more appropriate test for young children, although most reach a ceiling on it by 4.5 years of age (Carlson, 2005; Hughes & Graham, 2002). There might also be individual variability across participants in the magnitude of task complexity or the novelty of the tasks presented; thus, the executive demands may differ among same-aged children. For example, temperamentally inhibited children might find it easier to withhold a response during inhibitory control tasks such as Go/No-Go than more exuberant children would (Lamm et al., 2014). This variability presents a particular challenge to those who seek to develop standard or comparable methods for studying children with rapidly developing abilities or for making comparisons between typical and atypical development at various ages.

Another methodological concern is that tasks with high internal validity may miss important aspects of real-world EF (i.e., ecological validity). One approach to this issue is to design tasks that seek to replicate aspects of real-world EF in the laboratory (e.g., the Clean-Up task; Kochanska & Aksan, 1995). Another approach is to collect information about EF and self-regulation in various settings through parent or teacher surveys, such as the Children's Behavior Questionnaire (CBQ; Rothbart, Ahadi, Hershey, & Fisher, 2001), the Child Behavior Rating Scale (CBRS; Bronson, Goodson, Layzer, & Love, 1990), and the Behavior Rating Inventory of Executive Function—Preschool version (BRIEF-P; Gioia, Isquith, Guy, & Kenworthy,

2000). Gioia and Isquith (2004) recommended a model of assessment that includes both carefully defined measures of specific process components and ecologically valid assessments of real-world function. However, correlations between adult-report and laboratory measures of EF tend to be modest at best (BRIEF-P, see Anderson, Anderson, Northam, Jacobs, & Mikiewicz, 2002, and Liebermann, Giesbrecht, & Müller, 2007; CBQ, see Hongwanishkul et al., 2005; CBRS, see Schmitt, Pratt, & McClelland, 2014).

A cornerstone of longitudinal and pre-/post-intervention studies is having measures that are reliable within an individual over time. Research investigating test–retest reliability of EF measures in children has been limited and results have varied. Some studies have reported same-day test–retest reliability on the Tower of Hanoi to be adequate; however, mean scores on the second administration of the task were more than one standard deviation higher than on the first administration (Aman, Roberts, & Pennington, 1998; Gnys & Willis, 1991), suggesting this task might be prone to practice effects, and the reliability estimate does not hold up in every study (Bishop, Aamodt-Leeper, Creswell, McGurk, & Skuse, 2001). Test–retest reliability on a variety of other EF measures has been reported to be within an acceptable range. An extensive study using several tasks of EF with 7- to 12-year-olds, including Self-Ordered Pointing, developmental Stroop tasks, and Go/No-Go, reported good reliability on all tasks with an average retest interval of 4 months, despite a small N (Archibald & Kerns, 1999). In a study of the psychometric properties of 11 impulsivity measures (including Stroop and delay tasks) in typical and behaviorally disordered children ages 6 to 16, 73% of the tasks had at least one dependent variable with adequate temporal stability (Kindlon, Mezzacappa, & Earls, 1995).

Nonetheless, very few measures appropriate for preschoolers have been subjected to test–retest reliability analyses. In one exception, Beck et al. (2011) tested children ages 2.5 to 4.5 years and found acceptable same-day reliability on both hot and cool versions of Carlson's (2010) EF scale as well as a delay-of-gratification choice task. The intraclass correlation for level 4 on the scale (analogous to the standard DCCS task by Zelazo, 2006) was .94, and there were no significant practice or fatigue effects. Similarly, both the NIH Toolbox DCCS and Flanker tasks had excellent retest reliability, although the latter also showed significant practice effects (Zelazo et al., 2013). These findings suggest that certain EF measures can be given repeatedly in intervention studies or longitudinal designs.

Some investigators have attempted to extract developmental sequences from EF task batteries. In Carlson's (2005) analysis of multiple EF measures in a large sample of preschoolers, although the ordering of specific tasks varied from age to age, inhibition tasks routinely were passed earlier than working memory tasks and the very hardest tasks consistently involved both inhibition and working memory demands (e.g., Reverse Categorization at age 2; standard DCCS at age 3; Backward Digit Span at ages 3 and 4; advanced DCCS at ages 5 and 6). Similarly, P. Anderson (2002) inferred the following developmental sequence of EF components from an integrative review: attentional control (i.e., inhibition), information processing (i.e., processing speed), cognitive flexibility (i.e., switching), and goal setting. Romine and Reynolds (2005) inferred sequences from the age at which performance leveled off, based on a meta-analysis of ages 5 through 22 and average effect sizes of age-related change in performance. They found the following sequence: inhibition of perseveration, set maintenance, nonverbal fluency, planning, and verbal fluency.

One design for detecting sequences, rarely used in this research area, is to give children slightly different versions of the same task that assess different components of EF or levels of difficulty (see Wellman & Liu, 2004, for the successful use of this design for assessing the developmental sequence for theory-of-mind tasks). By examining the mean performance on each version or the percentage of children who pass each version at each age, one can infer the order in which aspects of EF are acquired. Also, a scalogram analysis could examine how many children pass all of the hypothesized easier versions of the task before a hypothesized more difficult task. That is, if the ordering of component tasks from easiest to hardest is A, B, C, D, then the outcome of interest is how many children passed A, B, and C but not D; A and B but not C and D; and A but not B, C, and D.

The Minnesota Executive Function Scale (MEFS) applies this method to the DCCS by involving a series of rules that gradually increase in difficulty, thus making it developmentally sensitive for children ages 2 to 7 (Carlson & Zelazo, 2014). The scale (presented on a touchscreen tablet) is age-adaptive, brief (4 minutes on average), and suitable for a wide range of EF ability. The original tabletop version of the EF scale was assessed with more than 2,500 children in multiple labs and found to be reliable, with good internal validity (conforms to an ordinal scale), convergent validity (correlates with other EF tasks such as the NIH Toolbox and Head-Toes-Knees-Shoulders), and divergent validity (low correlation with IQ; Carlson & Harrod, 2013). This measure has been used to assess EF in clinical populations (Doom et al., 2014; Fuglestad et al., 2014; Hostinar, Stellern, Schaefer, Carlson, & Gunnar, 2012) and preschoolers at risk (Chu, vanMarle, & Geary, 2013; vanMarle, Chu, Li, & Geary, 2014). It is related to emotional competence in preschoolers (Martins, Osório, Veríssimo, & Martins, 2014) and predicts kindergarten readiness and first-grade math achievement over and above IQ (Carlson & Harrod, 2013; Hassinger-Das, Jordan, Glutting, Irwin, & Dyson, 2014). The tablet version is highly concordant with the original tabletop version (intraclass correlation = .95; Carlson & Zelazo, 2015) yet is much easier to administer, and scores can be retrieved automatically. The MEFS is built around a core set of identified EF skills (e.g., working memory, inhibitory control, and set shifting), is appropriate across a wide age range by incorporating graduated levels, and will be extremely valuable for providing age norms and tracking intra- and interindividual changes in EF that occur as a result of development, training, or planned interventions. However, it remains to be seen how well this measure predicts long-term outcomes of interest.

Longitudinal studies are most ideal to detect sequences, but few exist. Several longitudinal studies have examined the Tower of Hanoi or Tower of London task, with a focus on developmental sequences in strategy use (McNamara, DeLucca, & Berg, 2007) and family, cognitive, school achievement, and social adjustment correlates (Friedman et al., 2007; Jacobson & Pianta, 2007). On inhibitory tasks, one striking sequence identified is that performance on a delay-of-gratification task at age 4 predicts, and thus may be a developmental precursor for, performance on inhibitory tasks such as the Go/No-Go task in adolescence (Eigsti et al., 2006) and after age 40 (Casey et al., 2011). Longitudinal studies of children from 2 to 4 years (Carlson et al., 2004; Hughes & Ensor, 2005, 2007), and even from infancy to 4 years (Morasch & Bell, 2011), showed stable individual differences in EF (aggregates of inhibition, working memory, and shifting tasks), indicating the predictive validity of early EF for later EF, as well as for related skills such as theory of mind and, ultimately, academic achievement and educational attainment (McClelland, Acock, Piccinin, Rhea, & Stallings, 2013).

Psychometric research on EF in early childhood is just beginning. It will benefit from further development of age-appropriate tasks that tap into the core aspects of EF and can be administered in a variety of settings across the preschool period. These efforts will provide age norms and ultimately reveal more about the early organization and differentiation of EF at both the behavioral and brain levels of analysis.

REFERENCES

Akshoomoff, N., Newman, E., Thompson, W. K., McCabe, C., Bloss, C. S., Chang, L., . . . Jernigan, T. L. (2014). The NIH Toolbox Cognition Battery: Results from a large normative developmental sample (PING). *Neuropsychology, 28,* 1–10.

Aman, C. J., Roberts, R. J., Jr., & Pennington, B. F. (1998). A neuropsychological examination of the underlying deficit in attention-deficit/hyperactivity disorder: Frontal lobe versus right parietal lobe theories. *Developmental Psychology, 34,* 956–969. http://dx.doi.org/10.1037/0012-1649.34.5.956

Anderson, P. (2002). Assessment and development of executive function (EF) during childhood. *Child Neuropsychology, 8,* 71–82. http://dx.doi.org/10.1076/chin.8.2.71.8724

Anderson, P., Anderson, V. A., & Lajoie, G. (1996). The Tower of London Test: Validation and standardization for pediatric populations. *The Clinical Neuropsychologist, 10*, 54–65. http://dx.doi.org/10.1080/13854049608406663

Anderson, V. A., Anderson, P., Northam, E., Jacobs, R., & Mikiewicz, O. (2002). Relationships between cognitive and behavioral measures of executive function in children with brain disease. *Child Neuropsychology, 8*, 231–240. http://dx.doi.org/10.1076/chin.8.4.231.13509

Archibald, S., & Kerns, K. (1999). Identification and description of new tests of executive functioning in children. *Child Neuropsychology, 5*, 115–129. http://dx.doi.org/10.1076/chin.5.2.115.3167

Atkinson, R. C., & Shiffrin, R. M. (1968). Human memory: A proposed system and its control processes. In W. K. Spence & J. T. Spence (Eds.), *The psychology of learning and motivation: Advances in research and theory* (Vol. 2, pp. 89–195). Oxford, England: Academic Press.

Barkley, R. A., Edwards, G., Laneri, M., Fletcher, K., & Metevia, L. (2001). Executive functioning, temporal discounting, and sense of time in adolescents with attention-deficit/hyperactivity disorder (ADHD) and oppositional defiant disorder (ODD). *Journal of Abnormal Child Psychology, 29*, 541–556. http://dx.doi.org/10.1023/A:1012233310098

Bauer, P. J., & Zelazo, P. D. (2014). The National Institutes of Health Toolbox for the assessment of neurological and behavioral function: A tool for developmental science. *Child Development Perspectives, 8*, 119–124. http://dx.doi.org/10.1111/cdep.12080

Bechara, A., Damasio, A. R., Damasio, H., & Anderson, S. W. (1994). Insensitivity to future consequences following damage to human prefrontal cortex. *Cognition, 50*, 7–15. http://dx.doi.org/10.1016/0010-0277(94)90018-3

Beck, D. M., Schaefer, C., Pang, K., & Carlson, S. M. (2011). Executive function in preschool children: Test–retest reliability. *Journal of Cognition and Development, 12*, 169–193. http://dx.doi.org/10.1080/15248372.2011.563485

Berlin, H. A., Rolls, E. T., & Kischka, U. (2004). Impulsivity, time perception, emotion and reinforcement sensitivity in patients with orbitofrontal cortex lesions. *Brain: A Journal of Neurology, 127*, 1108–1126. http://dx.doi.org/10.1093/brain/awh135

Bernier, A., Carlson, S. M., Bordeleau, S., & Carrier, J. (2010). Relations between physiological and cognitive regulatory systems: Infant sleep regulation and subsequent executive functioning. *Child Development, 81*, 1739–1752. http://dx.doi.org/10.1111/j.1467-8624.2010.01507.x

Bernier, A., Carlson, S. M., & Whipple, N. (2010). From external regulation to self-regulation: Early parenting precursors of young children's executive functioning. *Child Development, 81*, 326–339. http://dx.doi.org/10.1111/j.1467-8624.2009.01397.x

Bishop, D. V. M., Aamodt-Leeper, G., Creswell, C., McGurk, R., & Skuse, D. H. (2001). Individual differences in cognitive planning on the Tower of Hanoi task: Neuropsychological maturity or measurement error? *Journal of Child Psychology and Psychiatry, 42,* 551–556. http://dx.doi.org/10.1111/1469-7610.00749

Blair, C., & Razza, R. P. (2007). Relating effortful control, executive function, and false belief understanding to emerging math and literacy ability in kindergarten. *Child Development, 78,* 647–663. http://dx.doi.org/10.1111/j.1467-8624.2007.01019.x

Blair, C., Zelazo, P. D., & Greenberg, M. T. (2005). The measurement of executive function in early childhood. *Developmental Neuropsychology, 28,* 561–571. http://dx.doi.org/10.1207/s15326942dn2802_1

Brock, L. L., Rimm-Kaufman, S. E., Nathanson, L., & Grimm, K. J. (2009). The contributions of "hot" and "cool" executive function to children's academic achievement, learning-related behaviors, and engagement in kindergarten. *Early Childhood Research Quarterly, 24,* 337–349. http://dx.doi.org/10.1016/j.ecresq.2009.06.001

Brocki, K. C., & Bohlin, G. (2004). Executive functions in children aged 6 to 13: A dimensional and developmental study. *Developmental Neuropsychology, 26,* 571–593. http://dx.doi.org/10.1207/s15326942dn2602_3

Bronson, M. B., Goodson, B. D., Layzer, J. I., & Love, J. M. (1990). *Child Behavior Rating Scale.* Cambridge, MA: Abt Associates.

Burgess, P. W. (1997). Theory and methodology in executive function and research. In P. Rabbitt (Ed.), *Methodology of frontal and executive function* (pp. 81–116). Hove, England: Psychology Press.

Carlson, S. M. (2005). Developmentally sensitive measures of executive function in preschool children. *Developmental Neuropsychology, 28,* 595–616. http://dx.doi.org/10.1207/s15326942dn2802_3

Carlson, S. M. (2010, June). *Measurement: Developmentally sensitive approaches to measuring executive functions in preschoolers.* Invited presentation in the NICHD workshop on Executive Function in Preschool Children: Current Knowledge and Research Opportunities, Bethesda, MD.

Carlson, S. M., & Choi, H. P. (2009, April). Bilingual and bicultural: Executive function in Korean and American children. In K. G. Millett (Chair), *Cognitive effects of bilingualism: A look at executive function and theory of mind.* Symposium conducted at the biennial meeting of the Society for Research in Child Development, Denver, CO.

Carlson, S. M., Davis, A. C., & Leach, J. G. (2005). Less is more: Executive function and symbolic representation in preschool children. *Psychological Science, 16,* 609–616. http://dx.doi.org/10.1111/j.1467-9280.2005.01583.x

Carlson, S. M., & Harrod, J. (2013, April). Validation of the Executive Function Scale for Early Childhood. In J. Griffin (Chair), *Developing the next generation of preschool outcome measures: The Interagency School Readiness Measurement Consortium.* Poster session presented at the biennial meeting of the Society for Research in Child Development, Seattle, WA.

Carlson, S. M., Mandell, D. J., & Williams, L. (2004). Executive function and theory of mind: Stability and prediction from ages 2 to 3. *Developmental Psychology, 40*, 1105–1122. http://dx.doi.org/10.1037/0012-1649.40.6.1105

Carlson, S. M., & Meltzoff, A. N. (2008). Bilingual experience and executive functioning in young children. *Developmental Science, 11*, 282–298. http://dx.doi.org/10.1111/j.1467-7687.2008.00675.x

Carlson, S. M., & Moses, L. J. (2001). Individual differences in inhibitory control and children's theory of mind. *Child Development, 72*, 1032–1053. http://dx.doi.org/10.1111/1467-8624.00333

Carlson, S. M., & Wang, T. (2007). Inhibitory control and emotion regulation in preschool children. *Cognitive Development, 22*, 489–510. http://dx.doi.org/10.1016/j.cogdev.2007.08.002

Carlson, S. M., & White, R. E. (2013). Executive function, pretend play, and imagination. In M. Taylor (Ed.), *The Oxford handbook of the development of imagination* (pp. 161–174). New York, NY: Oxford University Press.

Carlson, S. M., White, R. E., & Davis-Unger, A. (2014). Evidence for a relation between executive function and pretense representation in preschool children. *Cognitive Development, 29*, 1–16. http://dx.doi.org/10.1016/j.cogdev.2013.09.001

Carlson, S. M., & Zelazo, P. D. (2011). The value of control and the influence of values. *Proceedings of the National Academy of Sciences of the United States of America, 108*, 16861–16862. http://dx.doi.org/10.1073/pnas.1113235108

Carlson, S. M., & Zelazo, P. D. (2014). *Minnesota Executive Function Scale—Early Childhood Version: Test manual*. St. Paul, MN: Reflection Sciences.

Carlson, S. M., & Zelazo, P. D. (2015). *Minnesota Executive Function Scale—Early Childhood Version: Technical report*. St. Paul, MN: Reflection Sciences.

Carlson, S. M., Zelazo, P. D., & Faja, S. (2013). Executive function. In P. D. Zelazo (Ed.), *The Oxford handbook of developmental psychology: Vol. 1. Body and mind* (pp. 706–743). New York, NY: Oxford University Press.

Casey, B. J., Somerville, L. H., Gotlib, I. H., Ayduk, O., Franklin, N. T., Askren, M. K., . . . Shoda, Y. (2011). Behavioral and neural correlates of delay of gratification 40 years later. *Proceedings of the National Academy of Sciences of the United States of America, 108*, 14998–15003. http://dx.doi.org/10.1073/pnas.1108561108

Casey, B. J., Tottenham, N., & Fossella, J. (2002). Clinical, imaging, lesion, and genetic approaches toward a model of cognitive control. *Developmental Psychobiology, 40*, 237–254. http://dx.doi.org/10.1002/dev.10030

Chu, F. W., vanMarle, K., & Geary, D. C. (2013). Quantitative deficits of preschool children at risk for mathematical learning disability. *Frontiers in Psychology, 4*, 195. http://dx.doi.org/10.3389/fpsyg.2013.00195

Davis-Unger, A. C., & Carlson, S. M. (2008). Children's teaching: Relations to theory of mind and executive function. *Mind, Brain, and Education, 2*, 128–135. http://dx.doi.org/10.1111/j.1751-228X.2008.00043.x

Dempster, F. (1992). The rise and fall of the inhibitory mechanism: Toward a unified theory of cognitive development and aging. *Developmental Review, 12,* 45–75. http://dx.doi.org/10.1016/0273-2297(92)90003-K

Doom, J. R., Gunnar, M. R., Georgieff, M. K., Kroupina, M. G., Frenn, K., Fuglestad, A. J., & Carlson, S. M. (2014). Beyond stimulus deprivation: Iron deficiency and cognitive deficits in postinstitutionalized children. *Child Development, 85,* 1805–1812.

Durston, S., Davidson, M. C., Tottenham, N., Galvan, A., Spicer, J., Fossella, J. A., & Casey, B. J. (2006). A shift from diffuse to focal cortical activity with development. *Developmental Science, 9,* 1–8. http://dx.doi.org/10.1111/j.1467-7687.2005.00454.x

Eigsti, I., Zayas, V., Mischel, W., Shoda, Y., Ayduk, O., Dadlani, M. B., . . . Casey, B. J. (2006). Predicting cognitive control from preschool to late adolescence and young adulthood. *Psychological Science, 17,* 478–484.

Espy, K. (1997). The shape school: Assessing executive function in preschool children. *Developmental Neuropsychology, 13,* 495–499. http://dx.doi.org/10.1080/87565649709540690

Friedman, N. P., Haberstick, B. C., Willcutt, E. G., Miyake, A., Young, S. E., Corley, R. P., & Hewitt, J. K. (2007). Greater attention problems during childhood predict poorer executive functioning in late adolescence. *Psychological Science, 18,* 893–900. http://dx.doi.org/10.1111/j.1467-9280.2007.01997.x

Frye, D., Zelazo, P. D., & Palfai, T. (1995). Theory of mind and rule-based reasoning. *Cognitive Development, 10,* 483–527. http://dx.doi.org/10.1016/0885-2014(95)90024-1

Fuglestad, A. J., Whitley, M. L., Carlson, S. M., Boys, C. J., Eckerle, J. K., Fink, B. A., & Wozniak, J. R. (2014). Executive functioning deficits in preschool children with Fetal Alcohol Spectrum Disorders. *Child Neuropsychology,* 1–16. Advance online publication. http://dx.doi.org/10.1080/09297049.2014.933792

Garon, N., Bryson, S. E., & Smith, I. M. (2008). Executive function in preschoolers: A review using an integrative framework. *Psychological Bulletin, 134,* 31–60. http://dx.doi.org/10.1037/0033-2909.134.1.31

Gerstadt, C. L., Hong, Y. J., & Diamond, A. (1994). The relationship between cognition and action: Performance of children 3½–7 years old on a Stroop-like day–night test. *Cognition, 53,* 129–153. http://dx.doi.org/10.1016/0010-0277(94)90068-X

Gioia, G. A., & Isquith, P. K. (2004). Ecological assessment of executive function in traumatic brain injury. *Developmental Neuropsychology, 25,* 135–158. http://dx.doi.org/10.1080/87565641.2004.9651925

Gioia, G. A., Isquith, P. K., Guy, S. C., & Kenworthy, L. (2000). Behavior rating inventory of executive function. *Child Neuropsychology, 6,* 235–238. http://dx.doi.org/10.1076/chin.6.3.235.3152

Gnys, J. A., & Willis, W. G. (1991). Validation of executive function tasks with young children. *Developmental Neuropsychology, 7,* 487–501. http://dx.doi.org/10.1080/87565649109540507

Grant, D. A., & Berg, E. A. (1948). A behavioral analysis of degree of reinforcement and ease of shifting to new responses in a Weigl-type card-sorting problem. *Journal of Experimental Psychology, 38*, 404–411. http://dx.doi.org/10.1037/h0059831

Hassinger-Das, B., Jordan, N. C., Glutting, J., Irwin, C., & Dyson, N. (2014). Domain-general mediators of the relation between kindergarten number sense and first-grade mathematics achievement. *Journal of Experimental Child Psychology, 118*, 78–92. http://dx.doi.org/10.1016/j.jecp.2013.09.008

Hongwanishkul, D., Happaney, K. R., Lee, W. S., & Zelazo, P. D. (2005). Assessment of hot and cool executive function in young children: Age-related changes and individual differences. *Developmental Neuropsychology, 28*, 617–644. http://dx.doi.org/10.1207/s15326942dn2802_4

Hostinar, C. E., Stellern, S. A., Schaefer, C., Carlson, S. M., & Gunnar, M. R. (2012). Associations between early life adversity and executive function in children adopted internationally from orphanages. *Proceedings of the National Academy of Sciences of the United States of America, 109*(Suppl. 2), 17208–17212. http://dx.doi.org/10.1073/pnas.1121246109

Hughes, C. (1998). Executive function in preschoolers: Links with theory of mind and verbal ability. *British Journal of Developmental Psychology, 16*, 233–253. http://dx.doi.org/10.1111/j.2044-835X.1998.tb00921.x

Hughes, C., & Ensor, R. (2005). Executive function and theory of mind in 2-year-olds: A family affair? *Developmental Neuropsychology, 28*, 645–668. http://dx.doi.org/10.1207/s15326942dn2802_5

Hughes, C., & Ensor, R. (2007). Executive function and theory of mind: Predictive relations from ages 2 to 4. *Developmental Psychology, 43*, 1447–1459. http://dx.doi.org/10.1037/0012-1649.43.6.1447

Hughes, C., & Ensor, R. (2011). Individual differences in growth in executive function across the transition to school predict externalizing and internalizing behaviors and self-perceived academic success at 6 years of age. *Journal of Experimental Child Psychology, 108*, 663–676. http://dx.doi.org/10.1016/j.jecp.2010.06.005

Hughes, C., & Graham, A. (2002). Measuring executive functions in childhood: Problems and solutions? *Child and Adolescent Mental Health, 7*, 131–142. http://dx.doi.org/10.1111/1475-3588.00024

Huizinga, M., Dolan, C. V., & van der Molen, M. W. (2006). Age-related change in executive function: Developmental trends and a latent variable analysis. *Neuropsychologia, 44*, 2017–2036. http://dx.doi.org/10.1016/j.neuropsychologia.2006.01.010

Isquith, P. K., Crawford, J. S., Espy, K. A., & Gioia, G. A. (2005). Assessment of executive function in preschool-aged children. *Mental Retardation and Developmental Disabilities Research Reviews, 11*, 209–215. http://dx.doi.org/10.1002/mrdd.20075

Isquith, P. K., Gioia, G. A., & Espy, K. A. (2004). Executive function in preschool children: Examination through everyday behavior. *Developmental Neuropsychology, 26*, 403–422. http://dx.doi.org/10.1207/s15326942dn2601_3

Jacobs, R., & Anderson, V. (2002). Planning and problem solving skills following focal frontal brain lesions in childhood: Analysis using the Tower of London. *Child Neuropsychology, 8,* 93–106. http://dx.doi.org/10.1076/chin.8.2.93.8726

Jacobson, L. A., & Pianta, R. C. (2007, April). *Executive function skills and children's academic and social adjustment to sixth grade.* Poster session presented at the biennial meeting of the Society for Research in Child Development, Boston, MA.

Kenworthy, L., Yerys, B. E., Anthony, L. G., & Wallace, G. L. (2008). Understanding executive control in autism spectrum disorders in the lab and in the real world. *Neuropsychology Review, 18,* 320–338. http://dx.doi.org/10.1007/s11065-008-9077-7

Kindlon, D., Mezzacappa, E., & Earls, F. (1995). Psychometric properties of impulsivity measures: Temporal stability, validity and factor structure. *Journal of Child Psychology and Psychiatry, 36,* 645–661. http://dx.doi.org/10.1111/j.1469-7610.1995.tb02319.x

Kochanska, G., & Aksan, N. (1995). Mother–child mutually positive affect, the quality of child compliance to requests and prohibitions, and maternal control as correlates of early internalization. *Child Development, 66,* 236–254. http://dx.doi.org/10.2307/1131203

Kochanska, G., Murray, K. T., & Harlan, E. T. (2000). Effortful control in early childhood: Continuity and change, antecedents, and implications for social development. *Developmental Psychology, 36,* 220–232. http://dx.doi.org/10.1037/0012-1649.36.2.220

Lamm, C., Walker, O. L., Degnan, K. A., Henderson, H. A., Pine, D. S., McDermott, J. M., & Fox, N. A. (2014). Cognitive control moderates early childhood temperament in predicting social behavior in 7-year-old children: An ERP study. *Developmental Science, 17,* 667–681. http://dx.doi.org/10.1111/desc.12158

Lehto, J. E., Juujärvi, P., Kooistra, L., & Pulkkinen, L. (2003). Dimensions of executive functioning: Evidence from children. *British Journal of Developmental Psychology, 21,* 59–80. http://dx.doi.org/10.1348/026151003321164627

Liebermann, D., Giesbrecht, G. F., & Müller, U. (2007). Cognitive and emotional aspects of self-regulation in preschoolers. *Cognitive Development, 22,* 511–529. http://dx.doi.org/10.1016/j.cogdev.2007.08.005

Luria, A. R. (1973). *The working brain: An introduction to neuropsychology* (B. Haigh, Trans.). New York, NY: Basic Books.

Martins, E. C., Osório, A., Veríssimo, M., & Martins, C. (2014). Emotion understanding in preschool children: The role of executive functions. *International Journal of Behavioral Development.* Advance online publication. http://dx.doi.org/10.1177/0165025414556096

McAuley, T., & White, D. A. (2011). A latent variables examination of processing speed, response inhibition, and working memory during typical development. *Journal of Experimental Child Psychology, 108,* 453–468. http://dx.doi.org/10.1016/j.jecp.2010.08.009

McClelland, M. M., Acock, A. C., Piccinin, A., Rhea, S. A., & Stallings, M. C. (2013). Relations between preschool attention span-persistence and age 25 educational outcomes. *Early Childhood Research Quarterly, 28*, 314–324. http://dx.doi.org/10.1016/j.ecresq.2012.07.008

McNamara, J. P. H., DeLucca, T. L., & Berg, W. K. (2007, March). *Children's executive functioning: A longitudinal and microgenetic study.* Poster presented at the biennial meeting of the Society for Research in Child Development, Boston, MA.

Miller, M. R., Giesbrecht, G. F., Müller, U., McInerney, R. J., & Kerns, K. A. (2012). A latent variable approach to determining the structure of executive function in preschool children. *Journal of Cognition and Development, 13*, 395–423. http://dx.doi.org/10.1080/15248372.2011.585478

Miyake, A., & Friedman, N. P. (2012). The nature and organization of individual differences in executive functions: Four general conclusions. *Current Directions in Psychological Science, 21*, 8–14. http://dx.doi.org/10.1177/0963721411429458

Miyake, A., Friedman, N. P., Emerson, M. J., Witzki, A. H., Howerter, A., & Wager, T. D. (2000). The unity and diversity of executive functions and their contributions to complex "Frontal Lobe" tasks: A latent variable analysis. *Cognitive Psychology, 41*, 49–100. http://dx.doi.org/10.1006/cogp.1999.0734

Moffitt, T. E., Arseneault, L., Belsky, D., Dickson, N., Hancox, R. J., Harrington, H., . . . Caspi, A. (2011). A gradient of childhood self-control predicts health, wealth, and public safety. *Proceedings of the National Academy of Sciences of the United States of America, 108*, 2693–2698. http://dx.doi.org/10.1073/pnas.1010076108

Monterosso, J., Ehrman, R., Napier, K. L., O'Brien, C. P., & Childress, A. R. (2001). Three decision-making tasks in cocaine-dependent patients: Do they measure the same construct? *Addiction, 96*, 1825–1837. http://dx.doi.org/10.1046/j.1360-0443.2001.9612182512.x

Morasch, K. C., & Bell, M. A. (2011). The role of inhibitory control in behavioral and physiological expressions of toddler executive function. *Journal of Experimental Child Psychology, 108*, 593–606. http://dx.doi.org/10.1016/j.jecp.2010.07.003

Neisser, U. (1967). *Cognitive psychology.* Englewood Cliffs, NJ: Prentice-Hall.

Nigg, J. T. (2000). On inhibition/disinhibition in developmental psychopathology: Views from cognitive and personality psychology and a working inhibition taxonomy. *Psychological Bulletin, 126*, 220–246. http://dx.doi.org/10.1037/0033-2909.126.2.220

Norman, D., & Shallice, T. (1986). Attention to action: Willed and automatic control of behaviour. In R. Davidson, G. Schwartz, & D. Shapiro (Eds.), *Consciousness and self-regulation* (Vol. 4, pp. 1–18). New York, NY: Plenum Press.

Perner, J., & Lang, B. (2002). What causes 3-year-olds' difficulty on the dimensional change card sorting task? *Infant and Child Development, 11*, 93–105. http://dx.doi.org/10.1002/icd.299

Poulin-Dubois, D., Blaye, A., Coutya, J., & Bialystok, E. (2011). The effects of bilingualism on toddlers' executive functioning. *Journal of Experimental Child Psychology, 108*, 567–579. http://dx.doi.org/10.1016/j.jecp.2010.10.009

Powell, K. B., & Voeller, K. K. (2004). Prefrontal executive function syndromes in children. *Journal of Child Neurology, 19*, 785–797.

Prencipe, A., & Zelazo, P. D. (2005). Development of affective decision making for self and other: Evidence for the integration of first- and third-person perspectives. *Psychological Science, 16*, 501–505. http://dx.doi.org/10.1111/j.0956-7976.2005.01564.x

Qu, L., & Zelazo, P. D. (2007). The facilitative effect of positive stimuli on 3-year-olds' flexible rule use. *Cognitive Development, 22*, 456–473. http://dx.doi.org/10.1016/j.cogdev.2007.08.010

Rodriguez, M. L., Mischel, W., & Shoda, Y. (1989). Cognitive person variables in the delay of gratification of older children at risk. *Journal of Personality and Social Psychology, 57*, 358–367. http://dx.doi.org/10.1037/0022-3514.57.2.358

Romine, C. B., & Reynolds, C. R. (2005). A model of the development of frontal lobe functioning: Findings from a meta-analysis. *Applied Neuropsychology, 12*, 190–201. http://dx.doi.org/10.1207/s15324826an1204_2

Rothbart, M. K., Ahadi, S. A., Hershey, K. L., & Fisher, P. (2001). Investigations of temperament at three to seven years: The Children's Behavior Questionnaire. *Child Development, 72*, 1394–1408. http://dx.doi.org/10.1111/1467-8624.00355

Schmitt, S. A., Pratt, M. E., & McClelland, M. M. (2014). Examining the validity of behavioral self-regulation tools in predicting preschoolers' academic achievement. *Early Education and Development, 25*, 641–660. Advance online publication. http://dx.doi.org/10.1080/10409289.2014.850397

Shallice, T. (1982). Specific impairments of planning. *Philosophical Transactions of the Royal Society of London. Series B, Biological Sciences, 298*, 199–209. http://dx.doi.org/10.1098/rstb.1982.0082

Shallice, T. (1988). *From neuropsychology to mental structure*. Cambridge, England: Cambridge University Press.

Shallice, T., & Burgess, P. W. (1991). Deficits in strategy application following frontal lobe damage in man. *Brain: A Journal of Neurology, 114*, 727–741. http://dx.doi.org/10.1093/brain/114.2.727

Shiffrin, R. M., & Schneider, W. (1977). Controlled and automatic human information processing: II. Perceptual learning, automatic attending and a general theory. *Psychological Review, 84*, 127–190. http://dx.doi.org/10.1037/0033-295X.84.2.127

Shoda, Y., Mischel, W., & Peake, P. K. (1990). Predicting adolescent cognitive and self-regulatory competencies from preschool delay of gratification. *Developmental Psychology, 26*, 978–986. http://dx.doi.org/10.1037/0012-1649.26.6.978

Sokol, B. W., Müller, U., Carpendale, J. I. M., Young, A. R., & Iarocci, G. (Eds.). (2010). *Self- and social-regulation: Social interaction and the development of social understanding and executive functions*. New York, NY: Oxford University Press.

Talwar, V., Carlson, S. M., & Lee, K. (2011). Effects of a punitive environment on children's executive functioning: A natural experiment. *Social Development, 20*, 805–824. http://dx.doi.org/10.1111/j.1467-9507.2011.00617.x

vanMarle, K., Chu, F. W., Li, Y., & Geary, D. C. (2014). Acuity of the approximate number system and preschoolers' quantitative development. *Developmental Science*. Advance online publication.

Wellman, H. M., & Liu, D. (2004). Scaling of theory-of-mind tasks. *Child Development, 75*, 523–541. http://dx.doi.org/10.1111/j.1467-8624.2004.00691.x

Welsh, M. C., Pennington, B. F., & Groisser, D. B. (1991). A normative–developmental study of executive function: A window on prefrontal function in children. *Developmental Neuropsychology, 7*, 131–149. http://dx.doi.org/10.1080/87565649109540483

Wiebe, S. A., Espy, K. A., & Charak, D. (2008). Using confirmatory factor analysis to understand executive control in preschool children: I. Latent structure. *Developmental Psychology, 44*, 575–587. http://dx.doi.org/10.1037/0012-1649.44.2.575

Wiebe, S. A., Sheffield, T., Nelson, J. M., Clark, C. A. C., Chevalier, N., & Espy, K. A. (2011). The structure of executive function in 3-year-olds. *Journal of Experimental Child Psychology, 108*, 436–452. http://dx.doi.org/10.1016/j.jecp.2010.08.008

Williams, D., & Jarrold, C. (2013). Assessing planning and set-shifting abilities in autism: Are experimenter-administered and computerized versions of tasks equivalent? *Autism Research, 6*, 461–467. http://dx.doi.org/10.1002/aur.1311

Zelazo, P. D. (2006). The Dimensional Change Card Sort (DCCS): A method of assessing executive function in children. *Nature Protocols, 1*, 297–301. http://dx.doi.org/10.1038/nprot.2006.46

Zelazo, P. D., Anderson, J. E., Richler, J., Wallner-Allen, K., Beaumont, J. L., & Weintraub, S. (2013). II. NIH Toolbox Cognition Battery (CB): Measuring executive function and attention. *Monographs of the Society for Research in Child Development, 78*(4), 16–33. http://dx.doi.org/10.1111/mono.12032

Zelazo, P. D., & Carlson, S. M. (2012). Hot and cool executive function in childhood and adolescence: Development and plasticity. *Child Development Perspectives*. Advance online publication. http://dx.doi.org/10.1111/j.1750-8606.2012.00246.x

Zelazo, P. D., Carter, A., Reznick, J. S., & Frye, D. (1997). Early development of executive function: A problem-solving framework. *Review of General Psychology, 1*, 198–226. http://dx.doi.org/10.1037/1089-2680.1.2.198

Zelazo, P. D., & Cunningham, W. A. (2007). Executive function: Mechanisms underlying emotion regulation. In J. J. Gross (Ed.), *Handbook of emotion regulation* (pp. 135–158). New York, NY: Guilford Press.

Zelazo, P. D., Qu, L., & Kesek, A. C. (2010). Hot executive function: Emotion and the development of cognitive control. In S. D. Calkins & M. A. Bell (Eds.), *Child development at the intersection of emotion and cognition* (pp. 97–111). Washington, DC: American Psychological Association.

3

STRUCTURE, MEASUREMENT, AND DEVELOPMENT OF PRESCHOOL EXECUTIVE FUNCTION

JENNIFER MIZE NELSON, TIFFANY D. JAMES, NICOLAS CHEVALIER, CARON A. C. CLARK, AND KIMBERLY ANDREWS ESPY

Human behavior is partly determined by instincts, reflexes, and impulses, but it is also largely driven by the goals that one wishes to reach. Goal attainment may conflict with instincts and automatic responses, and as such, requires intentional regulation of thoughts and actions, which is commonly referred to as *executive function* (EF). EF allows individuals to respond flexibly and adaptively to an ever-changing environment and thus is effortful, is a complex tertiary process, and matures in a protracted manner throughout childhood and adolescence. Age-related changes in EF have tremendous consequences for children's social development (e.g., Carlson & Moses, 2001), school achievement (e.g., Blair & Razza, 2007; Bull, Espy, Wiebe, Sheffield, & Nelson, 2011; Clark, Pritchard, & Woodward, 2010), and problem behavior (Espy,

This work was supported by National Institutes of Health grants MH065668 and DA023653. We thank the participating families and acknowledge the invaluable assistance with data collection and coding by research technicians and graduate and undergraduate students of the Developmental Cognitive Neuroscience Laboratory, University of Nebraska–Lincoln.

http://dx.doi.org/10.1037/14797-004
Executive Function in Preschool-Age Children: Integrating Measurement, Neurodevelopment, and Translational Research, J. A. Griffin, P. McCardle, and L. S. Freund (Editors)

Sheffield, Wiebe, Clark, & Moehr, 2011). Although EF development spans the entirety of childhood, dramatic changes occur over the preschool period (e.g., Carlson, 2005; Espy, 1997; Wiebe, Sheffield, & Espy, 2012). Those changes are often interpreted as reflecting quantitative changes in efficiency of the underlying cognitive processes. However, they could also partly result from qualitative changes, particularly in the structure of EF.

The structure of EF, or more precisely the extent to which EF corresponds to a unitary construct or encompasses separable components, has long been debated in both children and adults. In Baddeley and Hitch's (1974) model of working memory, information manipulation and control was thought to be achieved by a unitary central executive component. Similarly, Norman and Shallice (1986) proposed a unitary view of the supervisory attentional system in charge of conflict resolution. In contrast to these early cognitive models, the neuropsychological investigation of adult patients with brain lesions, especially of the prefrontal cortex, has revealed a variety of executive difficulty profiles (Damasio & Anderson, 2003), which hints at the multiplicity of executive components. More recently, using confirmatory factor analysis (CFA), the seminal study by Miyake et al. (2000) showed that measures of EF load onto three correlated latent factors in adults (see also Friedman et al., 2008). These findings suggest that EF is not unitary in adults, yet it is composed of three major components that, although separable, also share significant variance: (a) inhibition of spontaneous or irrelevant responses, (b) information updating in working memory, and (c) set shifting, that is, the ability to switch between multiple tasks. As separable as these components may be, they are thought to share common processes, potentially related to inhibition at the representational level or goal maintenance (Miyake et al., 2000).

The view of EF as partially separable in adults largely prevails nowadays (but see McCabe, Roediger, McDaniel, Balota, & Hambrick, 2010). As a result, a similarly separable structure of EF has been expected among young children despite less thorough research to date (Garon, Bryson, & Smith, 2008). Therefore, recent empirical support for a possible unitary EF structure in the preschool years (see below) has been met with some resistance. At the cerebral level, EF is supported by a distributed frontal-parietal neural network whose activation largely, if not completely, overlaps executive components (McNab et al., 2008), suggesting that executive components mostly share the same neural substrates (although activation in specific regions for each executive component also is observed; Collette et al., 2005).

The structure of EF has been probed in children. As in adults, EF has been found to fall into three main components in school-age children (Huizinga, Dolan, & van der Molen, 2006; Lehto, Juujärvi, Kooistra, & Pulkkinen, 2003), although the separability of all components is not always observed (St Clair-Thompson & Gathercole, 2006; van der Sluis, de Jong, & van der

Leij, 2007). This partial separation in school age is consistent with the distinct developmental trajectories for the main executive components derived from children's observed performance on specific tasks. Working memory task performance develops steadily throughout childhood (e.g., Gathercole, Pickering, Ambridge, & Wearing, 2004), whereas set shifting undergoes a slower rate of growth in school age (e.g., Cepeda, Kramer, & Gonzalez de Sather, 2001) and inhibition develops at a rapid rate through age 8 (e.g., Best, Miller, & Jones, 2009). Therefore, EF seemingly undergoes little structural change from school age on. In blatant contrast, recent evidence suggests that the structure of EF earlier in childhood, during the preschool period, may be more unitary (Fuhs & Day, 2011; Hughes, Ensor, Wilson, & Graham, 2009; Wiebe, Espy, & Charak, 2008; Wiebe et al., 2011).

The unitary structure of EF at preschool age and the partial separability observed later in development could be reconciled by hypothesizing that inhibition, set shifting, and working memory (maintenance or updating) progressively differentiate from each other with age. Such a hypothesis matches the claim that cognitive processes are initially applied to any type of information and progressively specialize in the processing of more delineated types of information with age and experience (Karmiloff-Smith, 1998, 2009). Indeed, it has been proposed that executive components develop sequentially, with working memory emerging first, followed by response inhibition, and finally set shifting (Garon et al., 2008). Although empirical support is missing to date, such a sequence may suggest that each new executive component emerges by differentiating itself from extant components. Indeed, it is largely believed that set shifting relies on the other executive components at preschool age (Diamond, 2006; Garon et al., 2008). A differentiation of executive components with age may result from increasing brain connectivity that reflects neural network reorganization and specialization in some executive components (Crone & Ridderinkhof, 2011; Johnson, 2011). Indeed, it is highly plausible that the frontal, striatal, and parietal brain regions associated with EF undergo substantial changes in brain size, cortical thickness, and connectivity during childhood (e.g., Giedd & Rapoport, 2010; Sowell et al., 2004) and that EF is associated with increasingly selective and focal activation of such regions with age (e.g., Casey, Thomas, Davidson, Kunz, & Franzen, 2002; Durston et al., 2006). However, these studies addressing age-related changes in brain activation were conducted at school age exclusively and may not necessarily imply structure changes.

In brief, the extant studies suggest that EF may be a unitary structure in preschoolers and that the executive components may progressively separate with age, although it is still unclear whether such a separation may occur over the preschool period or later in development. To address this issue, the structure of EF needs to be assessed with the same battery of tasks at multiple time points with the same sample throughout the preschool period. Although this period spans only a few years, it is the stage of tremendous improvement in EF and qualitative changes in neural development, which poses a number of methodological challenges. In this chapter we describe a longitudinal study in which preschool children were administered the same battery of EF tasks beginning at age 3 years in 9-month intervals until the age of 5 years, 3 months. In the course of the chapter we outline several steps taken to date toward examining the structure of EF and whether and how structural changes occur across these age points.

MEASUREMENT AND ANALYTIC CONSIDERATIONS

Confirmatory Factor Analysis (CFA) is uniquely suited for evaluating the structure of EF and thus has been recognized and implemented as a statistical approach in the EF literature in recent years for samples of adults (e.g., Miyake et al., 2000), older children (e.g., Huizinga et al., 2006; Lehto et al., 2003; van der Sluis et al., 2007), and, most recently, those of preschool age (e.g., Hughes et al., 2009; Wiebe et al., 2008, 2011). Indeed, a central component of the program of research described in the present chapter is the use of CFA to characterize the latent structure of EF that underlies preschool children's observed performance on EF tasks. Factor analysis in general has a history of use for identifying the latent structure of EF, particularly exploratory factor analysis (EFA) and principal component analysis (PCA; see Wiebe et al., 2008, for a review of studies using these analytic approaches). Any factor analysis approach has the benefit of using the distributions of children's manifest performance scores on a variety of tasks to determine whether performance across those tasks can be best summarized by one or several latent common factors. The pattern of convergence and divergence empirically reveals how individual tasks load on the determined number of latent factors. The scientist then interprets and labels each factor based on underlying cognitive abilities likely shared among the tasks that load on each factor but that differ between the factors. In addition to these benefits, CFA in particular is by name a confirmatory analysis, meaning that unlike exploratory approaches such as EFA and PCA, it allows for theory- and hypothesis-driven testing of different specified latent structures of EF. CFA demands the investigator specify an a priori hypothesized structure in which each individual task in a battery loads on one of a prespecified number of latent factors. The analysis then generates fit statistics for a given model that allows both for determining whether the model adequately fits or represents the data and for comparing the model fit statistics with those from other competing models (also specified a priori) to identify a best-fitting model.

In addition to its capability of empirically comparing competing models to arrive at a best-fitting latent representation of a construct of interest (EF in our case), CFA, and structural equation modeling (SEM) more broadly, has the added ability to identify purer representations of latent constructs. For example, children's performance on most individual EF tasks requires executive skills in addition to other skills (e.g., language or knowledge of colors). Some EF tasks within a battery may even share some of these nonexecutive demands. This uncertainty about how much variance in a given task is due to the executive demands of the task has been termed the impurity problem (Friedman et al., 2008). CFA, in part, offers a remedy to the impurity problem. A latent construct statistically represents all of the shared variance among a set of individual observed variables, while leaving behind any nonoverlapping variance. Therefore, identification of a latent EF construct that fits well in representing the overlapping variance across a battery of observed tasks with varied nonexecutive demands results in a purer measure of EF than any individual task alone. One important caveat is that care must be taken by the researcher in determining what common substantive construct (e.g., EF in our case) is represented by the overlapping latent variance. The benefit of increased confidence in the purity of latent constructs is most relevant when examining relationships between multiple latent constructs, such as when examining the correlation between two latent constructs or when examining the longitudinal growth of a given construct or its role as a predictor or outcome of other key constructs (see Bull et al., 2011, or Espy et al., 2011, for examples of relating latent EF to academic outcomes and child behavior). We can be assured in these contexts that we are dealing with constructs that are less contaminated by measurement error than are observed data on the test measures themselves.

On a final note, both developmental and methodological considerations call for careful selection of an EF task battery in the quest to model the latent structure of EF longitudinally across the preschool period. With respect to development, the rapid changes in EF as children mature during the preschool years can pose a challenge for task selection. Ideal tasks need to remain developmentally sensitive across all of the age points included in a longitudinal study to allow for modeling of growth in the underlying construct with age; this means that tasks should be possible for the youngest children to complete (to avoid floor effects) but remain challenging for the oldest children (to avoid ceiling effects). This longitudinal variability is best captured by tasks with accuracy measures on a continuous metric as opposed to pass/fail. In addition, preschool children can vary dramatically from one another in their development of the nonexecutive skills required to complete most EF tasks (e.g., general background knowledge, attention span, language competence). Therefore, tasks that minimize demands on nonexecutive skills and capitalize on knowledge likely mastered by the majority of preschool children are preferred. With respect to methodology, the identification of statistical techniques (e.g., CFA, longitudinal latent growth modeling) to best answer a research question, such as whether and how the structure of EF changes in preschool, can and should guide the selection of tasks. Specifically, for a comparison of different models with tasks grouped by executive and nonexecutive demands, tasks within a battery should be balanced so that multiple tasks tap each of the latent constructs to be modeled (e.g., working memory demands and inhibition demands, but also separately, tasks that incorporate language demands and those that do not). This balancing of nonexecutive demands across the executive demands then allows for a higher likelihood of achieving purity of the best-fitting latent constructs, as they will be represented by multiple tasks that allow for pooling shared variance across the tasks specific to the latent construct.

In sum, the goal of the remainder of this chapter is to illustrate EF task battery selection in the context of a longitudinal study spanning the preschool years and to demonstrate the application of CFA and longitudinal latent growth modeling in an attempt to uncover the longitudinal latent structure of EF in preschool. We set out to include in this study a battery made up of multiple tasks, each with putative demands on the three components of EF documented among older children and adults (i.e., working memory, inhibition, and set shifting). First, we describe this battery in detail and present descriptive statistics and distributional properties of the task accuracy measures at each of the four age points. In this process, we discuss the developmental and methodological challenges we had to consider in moving from the individual tasks into the latent modeling. Second, we used CFA to compare at each age point a unitary EF structure with a multiple latent factor model based on the components of EF. These analyses allowed us to draw conclusions about the preferred structure and the relations between the multiple latent components of EF at each age. Finally, on the basis of the findings from our cross-sectional CFAs, we describe our attempt to model the longitudinal latent growth of EF across the preschool period and conclude with a discussion of the challenges of applying traditional latent growth modeling to such a dynamic and rapidly changing construct as EF at preschool age.

DATA ILLUSTRATION

Participants and Procedures

The full sample in our longitudinal study comprised 388 preschool children (195 girls and 193 boys) recruited from and representative of two Midwestern study sites (286 non-Hispanic White, 31 Hispanic, 20 African

American, 1 Asian American, and 50 multiracial). The majority of the children were enrolled at age 3 years ($n = 228$) and participated in four data collection sessions (at ages 3 years; 3 years, 9 months; 4 years, 6 months; and 5 years, 3 months). Further, a cohort sequential design was used such that a smaller number of additional children were enrolled at each of the subsequent age points beyond 3 years, with each child then participating in the remaining sessions (total n at 3 years 9 months = 276; total n at 4 years 6 months = 319; total n at 5 years 3 months = 364). The purpose of the cohort sequential design was to allow for analysis of possible confounding practice effects, which preliminary analyses suggested were minimal. Extensive screening was conducted prior to enrollment to ensure the sample was typically developing and stratified by social risk (40.2% qualified for public medical assistance; see Wiebe et al., 2011, for more details about the sample and study recruitment and enrollment procedures).

At each data collection session, children were individually administered the battery of EF tasks in a fixed order by a trained research technician in a child-friendly laboratory setting. The child's parent (most often mother) was present in the room completing study paperwork. To allow for testing of the latent structure of EF in preschool, the EF task battery was composed of multiple tasks, each with putative demands on the three components of EF documented among older children and adults (i.e., working memory, inhibition, and set shifting). Each task was either scored or coded offline by trained undergraduate research assistants. Brief descriptions of the tasks and the dependent variables selected to represent task performance in study analyses are provided in Table 3.1 (more details available in Wiebe et al., 2011). In addition, Table 3.2 includes task-level descriptive information for each of the four study age points.

Analytic Observations

Following from the descriptive analysis of the EF tasks, several observations from descriptive analysis of the EF tasks pointed to important considerations relevant to the developmental period of preschool and critical for identifying an analytic strategy to further address our goals. First, because of large amounts of missing data (Shape School Switch and Trails-P) that were age related, the two tasks with more set-shifting demands were not included in the structure and longitudinal analyses, consistent with the literature highlighting the later development of set-shifting skills among preschoolers (Garon et al., 2008). Second, we were aware as we initiated our longitudinal analyses that early floor effects, later ceiling effects, and differences in the patterns by which children's scores on the tasks changed with age could affect our attempts to establish longitudinal invariance prior to testing longitudinal

TABLE 3.1
Executive Function Tasks

Task	Description	Dependent variable and possible range
Working Memory[a]		
Nine Boxes (9B)	Cartoon character figurines are hidden in each of nine colored boxes. Child opens one box per trial, boxes are scrambled between trials, and child must remember boxes searched on previous trials to find all figurines in fewest trials possible.	No. of maximum consecutive correct trials, possible range = 1 to 9
Delayed Alternation (DA)	Child is trained that a small reward alternates between two wells in a testing board, each covered with an identical cup neutral in color. Maximal reward is obtained if the child correctly alternates searches based on the last rewarded location.	No. of maximum consecutive correct trials – number of maximum consecutive incorrect trials, possible range = –16 to 16
Nebraska Barnyard (NB)	Child is trained to associate nine pictures of farm animals with the color and location of squares on which the animals appear in a grid on a computer screen. Animal pictures are then removed, and child reproduces animal sequences by pressing corresponding squares on a touch screen. Sequence length increases as task continues.	No. of correct trials (assigning .33 points to each correct 1-sequence trial in transition from training to test trials, and 1 point for each correct trial with sequence of 2 or more), possible range = 0 to 21
Inhibition[a]		
Big-Little Stroop (BL)	Each stimulus is a line drawing of an everyday object with smaller objects embedded within it. The smaller objects vary between matching and conflicting with the larger object. Child views stimuli on a computer screen and names the smaller objects.	No. of correct conflict trials/no. of total conflict trials, possible range = 0 to 1

Task	Description	Scoring
Go/No-Go (GNG)	Child presses a button on a button box when target stimuli appear on a computer screen (to catch fish) but suppresses pressing the button when nontarget stimuli appear (to let sharks swim away).	d prime $(d') = (z$-score value of false alarm rate right-tail $p)$ $- (z$-score value of hit rate right-tail $p)$, where false alarm is % incorrect on nontarget trials and hit rate is % correct on target trials
Shape School Inhibit (SSB)	Cartoon stimuli appear one at a time on a computer screen. Child names the color of stimuli that have happy faces and suppresses naming and remains silent for stimuli that have sad faces.	No. of correct inhibit trials/no. of total inhibit trials, possible range = 0 to 1
Snack Delay (SD)	Child stands and is told to suppress talking and moving (stay frozen) in the face of distraction and tempting reward (handful of M&Ms under a glass in front of them) until a bell is rung signaling the child to eat the candies.	Sum of hand movement across 5-second epochs before child ate candies or task ended at 4 minutes (0 = lots of movement, .5 = slight movement, 1 = no movement each epoch), possible range = 0 to 48
Set-Shifting[a]		
Shape School Switch (SSD)	Cartoon stimuli appear one at a time on a computer screen. Child switches between naming the color (red or blue) of stimuli who are not wearing hats and naming the shape (circle or square) of stimuli who are wearing hats.	No. of correct switch trials/no. of total switch trials, where switch trials = trials with a different cue (hat or hatless) than the preceding trial, possible range = 0 to 1
Trails-P (TR)	Child is instructed to use an ink stamper to switch between marking members of a family of dogs and their corresponding bone treats in ascending order from smallest (e.g., baby doggie, tiny bones) to largest (e.g., daddy doggie, largest bones).	No. of correct stamps/no. of total stamps

Note. The following are citations for the executive function (EF) tasks: 9B (Diamond, Prevor, Callender, & Druin, 1997), DA (Espy, Kaufmann, McDiarmid, & Glisky, 1999; Goldman, Rosvold, Vest, & Galkin, 1971), NB (Hughes, Dunn, & White, 1998), BL (Kochanska, Murray, & Harlan, 2000), GNG (Simpson & Riggs, 2006), SSB (Espy, 1997), SD (Kochanska, Murray, Jacques, Koenig, & Vandegeest, 1996; Korkman, Kirk, & Kemp, 1998), SSD (Espy, 1997), and TR (Espy & Cwik, 2004).
[a]The EF tasks are grouped here according to the component of EF on which each task was expected to place the greatest demand.

TABLE 3.2
Descriptive Statistics for the Executive Function Tasks at Each Age

	Task, age	n	M	SD	Observed range	% at floor	% at ceiling
				Working memory			
9B	3y, 0m	228	4.32	1.60	2–9	0.00	1.75
	3y, 9m	276	4.92	1.71	2–9	0.00	2.17
	4y, 6m	319	5.23	1.79	2–9	0.00	5.96
	5y, 3m	364	5.74	1.88	2–9	0.00	10.16
DA	3y, 0m	227	−0.37	3.96	−16–16	0.88	0.88
	3y, 9m	275	2.61	4.86	−10–16	0.00	6.18
	4y, 6m	319	6.20	5.55	−5–16	0.00	14.11
	5y, 3m	364	7.54	5.81	−6–16	0.00	21.70
NB	3y, 0m	222	2.88	1.57	0–9	4.05	0.00
	3y, 9m	276	4.90	2.07	.33–10	0.00	0.00
	4y, 6m	319	6.98	2.60	0–13	0.31	0.00
	5y, 3m	364	8.91	2.41	2.33–15.67	0.00	0.00
				Inhibition			
BL	3y, 0m	222	0.29	0.29	0–1	21.17	3.15
	3y, 9m	272	0.64	0.34	0–1	7.72	14.34
	4y, 6m	314	0.85	0.23	0–1	2.55	37.26
	5y, 3m	355	0.94	0.11	.08–1	0.00	60.85
GNG	3y, 0m	221	0.25	0.75	−1.37–2.39	0.00	0.00
	3y, 9m	274	1.38	1.02	−1.27–3.12	0.00	4.74
	4y, 6m	319	2.31	0.82	−.58–3.12	0.00	23.20
	5y, 3m	363	2.74	0.53	−.17–3.12	0.00	49.86
SSB	3y, 0m	191	0.38	0.42	0–1	42.41	23.56
	3y, 9m	263	0.75	0.37	0–1	12.17	59.32
	4y, 6m	317	0.92	0.21	0–1	2.84	77.29
	5y, 3m	364	0.95	0.15	0–1	1.10	83.52
SD	3y, 0m	214	12.21	11.42	0–48	14.95	0.47
	3y, 9m	268	17.96	10.93	0–44.5	7.84	0.00
	4y, 6m	318	21.85	9.40	0–44	2.83	0.00
	5y, 3m	363	25.54	9.84	0–48	0.83	0.28
				Set shifting			
SSD	3y, 0m	152	0.26	0.26	0–1	40.79	0.66
	3y, 9m	242	0.57	0.29	0–1	8.68	8.26
	4y, 6m	314	0.73	0.24	0–1	1.91	21.66
	5y, 3m	364	0.84	0.19	0–1	0.82	32.69
TR	3y, 0m	179	0.70	0.19	.07–1	0.00	8.94
	3y, 9m	262	0.82	0.13	.38–1	0.00	13.74
	4y, 6m	315	0.86	0.12	.18–1	0.00	23.49
	5y, 3m	355	0.90	0.11	.52–1	0.00	39.15

Note. M = mean; SD = standard deviation. 9B = Nine Boxes; DA = Delayed Alternation; NB = Nebraska Barnyard; BL = Big-Little Stroop; GNG = Go/No-Go; SSB = Shape School Inhibit; SD = Snack Delay; SSD = Shape School Switch; TR = Trails-P.

growth in the EF construct. Thus, nonideal distributions had to be trimmed at the relevant age points (see below for details). Third, as is common in longitudinal studies (particularly those conducted with a behaviorally challenging population such as preschool children), some data were missing across the tasks and age points (see Table 3.2). The option to use the expectation maximization (EM) algorithm in Mplus (Muthén & Muthén, 2006) when conducting CFA and SEM was an added benefit of selecting these models to answer our research questions about EF structure and growth. The EM algorithm capitalizes on the collected data points so that children are not listwise deleted from analyses due to missing data for a subset of the manifest EF tasks.

Results

Preschool EF Structure

To explore the structure of EF in preschool children and as a comparison with the previous structure literature in older children and adults, unitary and two-factor EF models were compared at each of the four age points. A nested-model comparison was evaluated at each age based on a chi-square difference test using the log likelihood values and scaling correction factors with the MLR estimator. If these models were not statistically different at the .05 level, then the simpler unitary model was retained as best-fitting based on parsimony (Bollen, 1989). The unitary model was constructed of all seven EF tasks representing working memory and inhibition constructs. In light of previous findings in older children and adults, the two-factor EF model was split into a Working Memory (WM) latent factor and an Inhibition latent factor. Additional alternative structure models have been considered in our 3-year-old sample, and no other nonexecutive structures fit significantly better (Wiebe et al., 2011). Model fit was evaluated using the root mean square error of approximation (RMSEA; Browne & Cudeck, 1993) and the comparative fit index (CFI). Models with an RMSEA value less than .06 and a CFI value greater than .95 (Hu & Bentler, 1999; Yu, 2002) were considered good in fit.

Some of the tasks had poor distributional qualities, as measured by skewness and kurtosis, and were trimmed to three standard deviations from the mean prior to analysis. The measures with a skewness or kurtosis value above 3 or below −3 were Delayed Alternation at age 3 years; Big-Little Stroop at ages 4 years, 6 months and 5 years, 3 months; Go/No-Go at age 5 years, 3 months; and Shape School Inhibit condition at ages 4 years, 6 months and 5 years, 3 months. After these variables were trimmed to 3 standard deviations from the mean, only Big-Little Stroop at ages 4 years, 6 months (skewness = −2.13; kurtosis = 3.99) and 5 years, 3 months (skewness = −1.94; kurtosis = 3.76) and

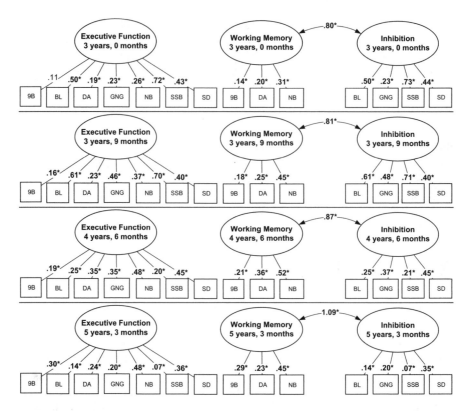

Figure 3.1. The unitary executive function and two-factor executive function models at each age. The two-factor executive function model at age 5 years, 3 months had a non-positive definite residual covariance matrix due to a correlation between the Working Memory latent and Inhibition latent greater than 1. 9B = 9 Boxes; BL = Big-Little Stroop; DA = Delayed Alternation; GNG = Go/No-Go; NB = Nebraska Barnyard; SSB = Shape School Inhibit; SD = Snack Delay.
*p < .05.

Shape School Inhibit condition at ages 4 years, 6 months (skewness = –2.65; kurtosis = 6.33) and 5 years, 3 months (skewness = –3.01; kurtosis = 9.35) had a less-than-ideal skewness or kurtosis value.

The unitary EF model and the two-factor EF model for each age are presented in Figure 3.1. Model fit statistics for each unitary EF and two-factor EF model were all within acceptable to excellent fit range (see Table 3.3). At each age, the unitary EF model was preferred for parsimony, as the two-factor EF model did not fit significantly better according to the chi-square difference test (see Table 3.3). In the two-factor EF models, the WM and Inhibition latent factors were highly correlated, all above .8. This correlation increased with age, and the two-factor EF model at age 5 years, 3 months had a nonpositive definite matrix due to a correlation above 1 between the WM

TABLE 3.3
Goodness-of-Fit Indexes and Tests of Model Comparison
for the Unitary and Two-Factor Executive Function Models at Each Age

Model	Model fit statistics				Model comparisons		
	LL	Free parameters	RMSEA	CFI	$\Delta\chi^{2\,a}$	Δ df	p_{diff}
3y, 0m							
Unitary	−1705.35	21	.00	1.00			
Two-factor	−1704.52	22	.00	1.00	1.95	1	.16
3y, 9m							
Unitary	−2372.17	21	.04	.96			
Two-factor	−2371.02	22	.04	.97	2.28	1	.13
4y, 6m							
Unitary	−2434.41	21	.05	.93			
Two-factor	−2433.72	22	.05	.93	1.31	1	.25
5y, 3m							
Unitary	−2093.60	21	.03	.97			
Two-factor	−2093.36	22	.04	.96	.42	1	.52

Note. LL = lower limit; RMSEA = root mean square error of approximation; CFI = comparative fit index.
[a]χ^2 difference = −2 × log likelihood difference/difference test scaling correction.

and Inhibit latents. The high correlation between the WM latent and the Inhibit latent suggests that these two factors have little distinction from each other, and the increased correlation with age suggests the factors are not differentiating within this period as one would expect on the basis of research on older children and adults. Also not surprising, because of the high correlation between the WM latent and the Inhibit latent factors, is that the factor loadings for the tasks changed very little, if at all, from the unitary EF model to the two-factor EF model.

Measurement Invariance of the Preferred Preschool EF Structure

Measurement invariance across the four age points was evaluated for the preferred EF structure, the unitary factor. Growth in the latent factor mean can be compared when the measurement model is invariant, which is tested in a series of nested models constraining the measurement parameters (item loadings and intercepts) to be equal across the four age points (Meredith, 1993; Meredith & Horn, 2001). Model fit statistics and nested model comparisons based on the chi-square difference test were conducted in the same manner as for the EF structure models.

The unitary EF model at each age was incorporated into one model, where the unitary EF factors were allowed to correlate, to test measurement invariance prior to estimating a latent growth model. The first step is a baseline model where all parameters are freely estimated. This baseline model

TABLE 3.4
Longitudinal Measurement Invariance Tests
for the Unitary Executive Function Model

Model	Model fit statistics				Model comparisons		
	LL	Free parameters	RMSEA	CFI	$\Delta\chi^2$ [a]	Δ df	p_{diff}
Baseline[b]	−8190.24	132	.02	.96	—	—	—
Full metric[c]	−8302.48	111	.05	.82	211.07	21	<.0001 +
Partial metric[d]							
9B	−8192.56	129	.02	.96	4.46	3	0.216 +
BL	−8233.43	129	.04	.90	71.22	3	<.0001 +
DA	−8192.76	129	.02	.96	4.85	3	0.184 +
GNG	−8204.63	129	.03	.94	21.45	3	<.0001 +
NB	−8200.01	129	.03	.95	20.47	3	<.0001 +
SSB	−8239.77	129	.04	.89	81.66	3	<.0001 +
SD	−8190.95	129	.02	.96	1.49	3	0.685 +
Partial metric[e]	−8195.86	123	.02	.96	11.19	9	0.263 +
Final partial metric[f]	−8197.32	119	.02	.96	2.33	4	0.675 *
Scalar[g]	−8502.34	110	.07	.55	897.41	9	<.0001 #

Note. LL = lower limit; RMSEA = root mean square error of approximation; CFI = comparative fit index.
9B = Nine Boxes; BL = Big-Little Stroop; DA = Delayed Alternation; GNG = Go/No-Go; NB = Nebraska Barnyard; SSB = Shape School Inhibit; SD = Snack Delay.
[a]χ^2difference = −2 × log likelihood difference/difference test scaling correction; [b]baseline = no invariance constraints; [c]full metric = metric invariance constraints across the four age points for each task with all tasks constrained simultaneously; [d]partial metric = metric invariance constraints across the four age points for each task in isolation; [e]partial metric = metric invariance constraints across the four age points only for metric invariant tasks (9B, DA, and SD); [f]final partial metric = metric invariance constraints across the four age points for 9B, DA, and SD, plus pairwise metric invariant constraints for BL, GNG, NB, and SSB; [g]scalar = scalar invariance constraints for all metric invariant parameters.
+Model compared to baseline model. *Model compared to partial metric[b] model. #Model compared to final partial metric model.

had good fit (RMSEA = .02; CFI = .96; see Table 3.4). All tasks significantly loaded onto the single-factor EF latent, except for 9 Boxes at age 3 years, which was marginal ($p = .07$); 9 Boxes significantly loaded at the other age points. We suspect that this loading pattern could be due to a location perseveration strategy at earlier ages. The loadings for Big-Little Stroop and Shape School Inhibit were dramatically lower at the later ages. We suspect that this pattern could be due to the ceiling effects described earlier in the discussion of task-specific distributional properties. All of the unitary EF factors were highly correlated (.75–.96), with higher correlations among adjacent age factors, as expected. Correlated residual errors were allowed among the same tasks across the four age points.

Next, metric invariance was tested across all tasks simultaneously by constraining all factor loadings to be equal across each age within each task. Metric invariance across all tasks failed, so partial metric invariance was tested by testing the metric invariance of each task (see Table 3.4). Metric invariance held for 9 Boxes, Delayed Alternation, and Snack Delay across all four time points. For the remaining tasks, metric invariance was tested for each pairwise age comparison within each task. Of these tasks, metric invariance held for Big-Little Stroop at 3 years and 4 years, 6 months; for Go/No-Go at 3 years and 5 years, 3 months; for Noisy Book at 4 years, 6 months and 5 years, 3 months; and for Shape School Inhibit condition at 3 years and 3 years, 9 months. The remaining parameter constraints resulted in significantly worse model fit and were therefore allowed to freely estimate. For the parameters where metric invariance was met, scalar invariance (item intercepts) was tested as the final step to satisfy measurement invariance or partial measurement invariance to allow for latent growth modeling. None of the metric invariant parameters were scalar invariant. These models reveal that we do not have sufficient partial measurement invariance to model latent growth, suggesting that the factors are not equivalent in their measurement across the four age points. The final partial metric invariant model had good fit (RMSEA = .02; CFI = .96; see Table 3.4), and the unitary EF factors remained highly correlated (.75–.96; see Figure 3.2).

DISCUSSION

EF often is most conspicuous in its absence, and yet child development is littered with examples of skills which, upon closer inspection, are not absent in young children but simply different in nature. Although developmental psychology has sometimes been guilty of downward extension of measures and models of psychological constructs from adults to children, recent years have seen a wealth of executive tasks developed specifically for use with preschoolers—tasks that are simple in terms of their language and motor requirements and that are engaging for this young population (e.g., Carlson, 2005; Espy, 1997; Espy & Cwik, 2004). The development of these measures not only raises questions regarding psychometrics and utility but also allows for closer examination of the ways in which EF in young children may be distinct from EF in adults. By using multiple age-appropriate measures in a longitudinal design, we gain a very powerful approach for answering questions regarding both quantitative and qualitative change in EF as a latent psychological construct. However, this chapter has also highlighted numerous challenges and difficulties associated with the longitudinal study of a higher order ability that undergoes dramatic change across the preschool period.

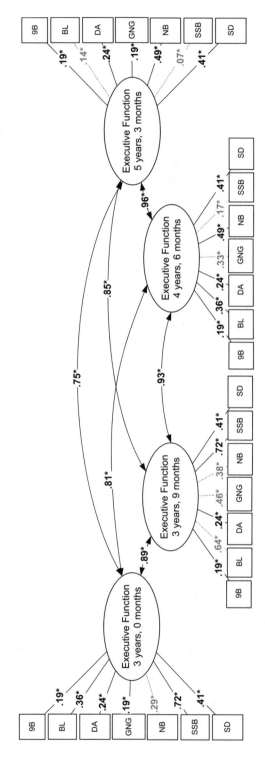

Figure 3.2. Final longitudinal executive function partial metric invariance model. 9B = Nine Boxes; BL = Big-Little Stroop; DA = Delayed Alternation; GNG = Go/No-Go; NB = Nebraska Barnyard; SSB = Shape School Inhibit; SD = Snack Delay.
* *p* < .05.

At every study point from early preschool to kindergarten age, our data indicated that the most parsimonious model of EF as a latent construct is a single-factor model, a model that differs qualitatively from that found in many studies of adults and school-age children (Friedman et al., 2008; Huizinga et al., 2006; Lehto et al., 2003; Miyake et al., 2000; St Clair-Thompson & Gathercole, 2006). This apparent lack of fractionation in EF across the preschool period supports the notion that putative components of EF identified in the adult literature (i.e., updating, inhibition, set shifting) share a common substrate that links performance across tasks (Miyake et al., 2000). Garon and colleagues (2008) argued that basic elements of attention, which emerge early in development (Ruff & Rothbart, 1996), may be foundational for EF development. This hypothesis accords with models of attention as a hierarchically integrated system organized roughly in accordance with neural architecture (Berger & Posner, 2000; Rueda, Posner, & Rothbart, 2005). Basic arousal and attention orienting, mediated by the hindbrain and midbrain respectively, may gradually come under voluntary control with the maturation of the prefrontal cortex and associated subcortical–cortical connections.

Another candidate for the core component underlying EF is goal representation, with children increasingly being able to maintain representations of intended goals or task rules in the face of interference or conflict. Indeed, this developmental shift seems to have guided differential measure selection among adults and school-age children compared with preschoolers. Studies in adults and school-age children emphasize working memory updating (assessed by N-back tasks) as one of the main executive components (Friedman et al., 2008; Miyake et al., 2000; St Clair-Thompson & Gathercole, 2006), whereas work in preschoolers mainly uses measures assessing working memory maintenance (assessed by span tasks) because very young children perform at floor on measures that require manipulating information (Wiebe et al., 2008). If goal maintenance in working memory accounts for the commonality across executive components (Chevalier et al., 2012; Friedman et al., 2008; Miyake et al., 2000), then it is not surprising that working memory maintenance and inhibition share substantial variance in preschoolers, but working memory updating and inhibition are more separable by middle childhood. However, even as working memory task selection shifts from a focus on goal maintenance to updating among older children and adults, it is clear from the middle-childhood and adult CFA literature that in these later ages identified EF factors are more differentiated yet remain highly correlated (r range of .30–.75), further supporting the notion of an underlying unity to all EF processes (Friedman, Corley, Hewitt, & Wright, 2009; Friedman et al., 2007; Huizinga et al., 2006; Lehto et al., 2003; Miyake et al., 2000; van der Sluis et al., 2007).

Contrary to our expectations, we showed no evidence for differentiation in EF across the preschool period. In fact, the correlation between WM and Inhibition factors increased with age. If we are to reconcile these findings with theoretical and empirical literature suggesting that cognitive development proceeds from relatively diffuse and generalized organization to more specialized, differentiated organization (Bell & Fox, 1992; Durston & Casey, 2006; Karmiloff-Smith, 1998, 2009; Undheim, 1978), we need to assume that differentiation occurs later in childhood. Certainly, the few studies that have employed CFA to examine age-related change in the structure of EF in older children have reported a differentiated structure only during middle childhood (Lee, Ho, & Bull, 2011; Shing, Lindenberger, Diamond, Li, & Davidson, 2010). In a similar way, studies focused on intellectual ability have shown that correlations between different IQ scales and subscales decrease through childhood, suggesting gradual differentiation in these cognitive skills as well (Hülür, Wilhelm, & Robitzsch, 2011; Li et al., 2004; although see Tucker-Drob, 2009, for an exception). A plausible explanation for the increasing correlations between WM and Inhibition latent factors in the current study is perhaps that intraindividual stability in performance across the various EF tasks may become more stable, owing to fewer fluctuations in arousal and attention during assessment sessions or even to the ceiling effects observed by kindergarten age. This explanation, however, is out of keeping with the fact that correlations between tasks appeared fairly stable over time and, if anything, factor loadings for the inhibition measures had decreased by age 5 years, 3 months. It is clear from these issues that continued follow-up of this cohort will be necessary to fully test the differentiation hypothesis.

Although the configuration of latent EF was similar across all study time points, in that EF consistently was most parsimoniously represented by a single latent variable, tests for measurement invariance revealed that the relation between latent EF and children's performance on manifest measures was not equivalent over time. Failure to achieve metric invariance (i.e., invariance of factor loadings, λs) for all EF measures indicates that the weighting of latent EF relative to error variance in contributing to manifest task performance varied over time (Kline, 2010; Steinmetz, Schmidt, Tina-Booh, Wieczorek, & Schwartz, 2009). In a similar way, failure to achieve scalar invariance (invariance of intercepts, τs) indicates that a zero score for mean latent EF did not consistently result in the same mean score for a given EF task (Brown, 2006). In essence, for any given value on the latent EF factor, the relation to the manifest tasks was not stable over time.

Unfortunately, these noninvariant associations mean that it is not clear whether quantitative change over time is at the level of the EF construct itself or at the level of the task properties as defined by the models considered (Ferrer, Balluerka, & Widaman, 2008). Therefore, our study suggests that modeling growth in latent EF in this customary way may not be tenable. Perhaps one could argue that the traditional approach of first determining longitudinal invariance in a latent construct over time prior to modeling its latent growth may not be most appropriate. After all, this approach was adopted from the well-accepted procedure of determining invariance in a construct across multiple groups (e.g., boys and girls) prior to, for example, examining latent mean differences in the construct across the groups. The multiple-group comparison approach assumes independence between the groups, yet in the longitudinal context, repeated observations and repeated latent constructs are not independent. Future efforts may be more fruitful if a more novel approach to growth modeling were employed, such as bypassing the need for longitudinal invariance and instead integrating the modeling of latent growth for each task individually with modeling of second-order growth in a latent EF construct.

Although failure to achieve measurement invariance is disappointing in some respects, it is not altogether unexpected if one returns to the whole reason we did the study. EF as a latent construct is assumed to be developmentally dynamic; on the basis of neural organization data (Thatcher, 1992), we might expect qualitative changes in EF organization during the period that will be reflected in manifest indicators to latent loadings. Noninvariance raises the interesting possibility that there may be qualitative differences in how EF manifests itself in task performance across the preschool age range. One possibility is that task performance at very young ages is more dependent on or grows from other abilities (e.g., language or motor skills) and that shared variance between tasks may in part be indicative of interindividual differences in these other skills. For instance, it is likely that a child with higher language abilities at age 3 years will also have better mental representations of verbal to object mappings. Utilization of this crystallized language knowledge would likely have a positive impact on performance on all EF tasks. In future studies, it may be that these other abilities need to be more carefully modeled to isolate variance attributable to them from variance in EF.

Some comments should also be made regarding tasks at the manifest level, as manifest task properties no doubt have a profound influence on the structure that one is able to model. Notably, floor and ceiling effects presented a major challenge across this lengthy follow-up period. For instance, it was not feasible to include measures of cognitive flexibility for all ages, given that so few children were able to complete or understand the demands of the tasks selected to assess this domain. In some respects, this problem may actually support a fractionated model of EF, where a relatively complex skill such as cognitive flexibility gradually emerges as a function of development in other skills. Similarly, mean performance on the inhibition tasks rapidly increased between age 3 years and 3 years, 9 months and often reached ceiling levels by age 5 years, 3 months. This pattern clearly affected the sensitivity of these tasks, as illustrated by the fact that factor loadings for Big-Little Stroop were dramatically lower by age 5 years, 3 months. Therefore, tasks that may have excellent sensitivity at young ages may quickly lose sensitivity over time, which impairs invariance in task to latent loadings. For many of these tasks, we have collected reaction-time data that may offer greater sensitivity to developmental change at some ages as well as allow us to measure speed–accuracy trade-offs that may occur with EF maturation.

The issues raised above serve only to caution against inferences regarding development of a latent construct based on children's manifest performance alone. Movement toward a greater understanding of how EF as a higher order, latent construct develops over this critical preschool period is largely dependent on state-of-the-art methods that can isolate unique executive processes from the lower order skills that they regulate. Second-order growth-curve modeling is one method that appears promising in this respect. However, the design issues and measurement challenges associated with this method mean that it is, at present, a difficult undertaking. In many respects, the rapid development that we aim to capture is also the most challenging aspect of this research endeavor. Nonetheless, consistently high correlations between latent EF measured at 3 years all the way through kindergarten age indicate that, regardless of whether EF at early preschool age differs in its fundamental nature, individual differences are stable, meaningful, and highly predictive of children's abilities at the important time of transition to formal education. This fact, in itself, serves as sufficient justification for the continued study of this elusive development construct.

REFERENCES

Baddeley, A. D., & Hitch, G. J. (1974). Working memory. In G. H. Bower (Ed.), *The psychology of learning and motivation* (Vol. 8, pp. 47–89). New York, NY: Academic Press.

Bell, M. A., & Fox, N. A. (1992). The relations between frontal brain electrical activity and cognitive development during infancy. *Child Development, 63,* 1142–1163. http://dx.doi.org/10.2307/1131523

Berger, A., & Posner, M. I. (2000). Pathologies of brain attentional networks. *Neuroscience and Biobehavioral Reviews, 24,* 3–5.

Best, J. R., Miller, P. H., & Jones, L. L. (2009). Executive functions after age 5: Changes and correlates. *Developmental Review, 29,* 180–200. http://dx.doi.org/10.1016/j.dr.2009.05.002

Blair, C., & Razza, R. P. (2007). Relating effortful control, executive function, and false belief understanding to emerging math and literacy ability in kindergarten. *Child Development, 78,* 647–663. http://dx.doi.org/10.1111/j.1467-8624.2007.01019.x

Bollen, K. A. (1989). *Structural equations with latent variables*. New York, NY: Wiley.

Brown, T. (2006). *Confirmatory factor analysis for applied research*. New York, NY: Guilford Press.

Browne, M. W., & Cudeck, R. (1993). Alternative ways of assessing model fit. In K. Bollen & J. S. Long (Eds.), *Testing structural equation models* (pp. 136–162). Newbury Park, CA: Sage.

Bull, R., Espy, K. A., Wiebe, S. A., Sheffield, T. D., & Nelson, J. M. (2011). Using confirmatory factor analysis to understand executive control in preschool children: Sources of variation in emergent mathematic achievement. *Developmental Science, 14,* 679–692. http://dx.doi.org/10.1111/j.1467-7687.2010.01012.x

Carlson, S. M. (2005). Developmentally sensitive measures of executive function in preschool children. *Developmental Neuropsychology, 28,* 595–616. http://dx.doi.org/10.1207/s15326942dn2802_3

Carlson, S. M., & Moses, L. J. (2001). Individual differences in inhibitory control and children's theory of mind. *Child Development, 72,* 1032–1053. http://dx.doi.org/10.1111/1467-8624.00333

Casey, B. J., Thomas, K. M., Davidson, M. C., Kunz, K., & Franzen, P. L. (2002). Dissociating striatal and hippocampal function developmentally with a stimulus-response compatibility task. *The Journal of Neuroscience, 22,* 8647–8652.

Cepeda, N. J., Kramer, A. F., & Gonzalez de Sather, J. C. (2001). Changes in executive control across the life span: Examination of task-switching performance. *Developmental Psychology, 37,* 715–730. http://dx.doi.org/10.1037/0012-1649.37.5.715

Chevalier, N., Sheffield, T. D., Nelson, J. M., Clark, C. A. C., Wiebe, S. A., & Espy, K. A. (2012). Underpinnings of the costs of flexibility in preschool children: The roles of inhibition and working memory. *Developmental Neuropsychology, 37,* 99–118. http://dx.doi.org/10.1080/87565641.2011.632458

Clark, C. A. C., Pritchard, V. E., & Woodward, L. J. (2010). Preschool executive functioning abilities predict early mathematics achievement. *Developmental Psychology, 46,* 1176–1191. http://dx.doi.org/10.1037/a0019672

Collette, F., Van der Linden, M., Laureys, S., Delfiore, G., Degueldre, C., Luxen, A., & Salmon, E. (2005). Exploring the unity and diversity of the neural substrates of executive functioning. *Human Brain Mapping, 25,* 409–423. http://dx.doi.org/10.1002/hbm.20118

Crone, E. A., & Ridderinkhof, K. R. (2011). The developing brain: From theory to neuroimaging and back. *Developmental Cognitive Neuroscience, 1,* 101–109. http://dx.doi.org/10.1016/j.dcn.2010.12.001

Damasio, A. R., & Anderson, S. W. (2003). The frontal lobes. In K. M. Heilman & E. Valenstein (Eds.), *Clinical neuropsychology* (4th ed., pp. 404–446). New York, NY: Oxford University Press.

Diamond, A. (2006). The early development of executive functions. In E. Bialystok & F. I. M. Craik (Eds.), *Lifespan cognition mechanisms of change* (pp. 70–95). Oxford, England: Oxford University Press. http://dx.doi.org/10.1093/acprof:oso/9780195169539.003.0006

Diamond, A., Prevor, M. B., Callender, G., & Druin, D. P. (1997). Prefrontal cortex cognitive deficits in children treated early and continuously for PKU. *Monographs of the Society for Research in Child Development, 62*, i–v, 1–208. http://dx.doi.org/10.2307/1166208

Durston, S., & Casey, B. J. (2006). What have we learned about cognitive development from neuroimaging? *Neuropsychologia, 44*, 2149–2157. http://dx.doi.org/10.1016/j.neuropsychologia.2005.10.010

Durston, S., Davidson, M. C., Tottenham, N., Galvan, A., Spicer, J., Fossella, J. A., & Casey, B. J. (2006). A shift from diffuse to focal cortical activity with development. *Developmental Science, 9*, 1–8. http://dx.doi.org/10.1111/j.1467-7687.2005.00454.x

Espy, K. A. (1997). The Shape School: Assessing executive function in preschool children. *Developmental Neuropsychology, 13*, 495–499. http://dx.doi.org/10.1080/87565649709540690

Espy, K. A., & Cwik, M. F. (2004). The development of a trial making test in young children: The TRAILS-P. *The Clinical Neuropsychologist, 18*, 411–422. http://dx.doi.org/10.1080/138540409052416

Espy, K. A., Kaufmann, P. M., McDiarmid, M. D., & Glisky, M. L. (1999). Executive functioning in preschool children: Performance on A-not-B and other delayed response format tasks. *Brain and Cognition, 41*, 178–199. http://dx.doi.org/10.1006/brcg.1999.1117

Espy, K. A., Sheffield, T. D., Wiebe, S. A., Clark, C. A., & Moehr, M. J. (2011). Executive control and dimensions of problem behaviors in preschool children. *Journal of Child Psychology and Psychiatry, 52*, 33–46. http://dx.doi.org/10.1111/j.1469-7610.2010.02265.x

Ferrer, E., Balluerka, N., & Widaman, K. F. (2008). Factorial invariance and the specification of second-order latent growth models. *Methodology, 4*, 22–36. http://dx.doi.org/10.1027/1614-2241.4.1.22

Friedman, N. P., Corley, R. P., Hewitt, J. K., & Wright, K. P., Jr. (2009). Individual differences in childhood sleep problems predict later cognitive executive control. *Sleep, 32*, 323–333.

Friedman, N. P., Haberstick, B. C., Willcutt, E. G., Miyake, A., Young, S. E., Corley, R. P., & Hewitt, J. K. (2007). Greater attention problems during childhood predict poorer executive functioning in late adolescence. *Psychological Science, 18*, 893–900. http://dx.doi.org/10.1111/j.1467-9280.2007.01997.x

Friedman, N. P., Miyake, A., Young, S. E., Defries, J. C., Corley, R. P., & Hewitt, J. K. (2008). Individual differences in executive functions are almost entirely genetic in origin. *Journal of Experimental Psychology: General, 137*, 201–225. http://dx.doi.org/10.1037/0096-3445.137.2.201

Fuhs, M. W., & Day, J. D. (2011). Verbal ability and executive functioning development in preschoolers at Head Start. *Developmental Psychology, 47*, 404–416. http://dx.doi.org/10.1037/a0021065

Garon, N., Bryson, S. E., & Smith, I. M. (2008). Executive function in preschoolers: A review using an integrative framework. *Psychological Bulletin, 134*, 31–60. http://dx.doi.org/10.1037/0033-2909.134.1.31

Gathercole, S. E., Pickering, S. J., Ambridge, B., & Wearing, H. (2004). The structure of working memory from 4 to 15 years of age. *Developmental Psychology, 40*, 177–190. http://dx.doi.org/10.1037/0012-1649.40.2.177

Giedd, J. N., & Rapoport, J. L. (2010). Structural MRI of pediatric brain development: What have we learned and where are we going? *Neuron, 67*, 728–734. http://dx.doi.org/10.1016/j.neuron.2010.08.040

Goldman, P. S., Rosvold, H. E., Vest, B., & Galkin, T. W. (1971). Analysis of the delayed-alternation deficit produced by dorsolateral prefrontal lesions in the rhesus monkey. *Journal of Comparative and Physiological Psychology, 77*, 212–220. http://dx.doi.org/10.1037/h0031649

Hu, L., & Bentler, P. M. (1999). Cutoff criteria for fit indexes in covariance structure analysis: Conventional criteria versus new alternatives. *Structural Equation Modeling, 6*, 1–55. http://dx.doi.org/10.1080/10705519909540118

Hughes, C., Dunn, J., & White, A. (1998). Trick or treat? Uneven understanding of mind and emotion and executive dysfunction in "hard-to-manage" preschoolers. *Journal of Child Psychology and Psychiatry, 39*, 981–994. http://dx.doi.org/10.1111/1469-7610.00401

Hughes, C., Ensor, R., Wilson, A., & Graham, A. (2009). Tracking executive function across the transition to school: A latent variable approach. *Developmental Neuropsychology, 35*, 20–36. http://dx.doi.org/10.1080/87565640903325691

Huizinga, M., Dolan, C. V., & van der Molen, M. W. (2006). Age-related change in executive function: Developmental trends and a latent variable analysis. *Neuropsychologia, 44*, 2017–2036. http://dx.doi.org/10.1016/j.neuropsychologia.2006.01.010

Hülür, G., Wilhelm, O., & Robitzsch, A. (2011). Intelligence differentiation in early childhood. *Journal of Individual Differences, 32*, 170–179. http://dx.doi.org/10.1027/1614-0001/a000049

Johnson, M. H. (2011). Interactive specialization: A domain-general framework for human functional brain development? *Developmental Cognitive Neuroscience, 1*, 7–21. http://dx.doi.org/10.1016/j.dcn.2010.07.003

Karmiloff-Smith, A. (1998). Development itself is the key to understanding developmental disorders. *Trends in Cognitive Sciences, 2*, 389–398. http://dx.doi.org/10.1016/S1364-6613(98)01230-3

Karmiloff-Smith, A. (2009). Nativism versus neuroconstructivism: Rethinking the study of developmental disorders. *Developmental Psychology, 45*, 56–63. http://dx.doi.org/10.1037/a0014506

Kline, R. B. (2010). *Principles and practice of structural equation modeling*. New York, NY: Guilford Press.

Kochanska, G., Murray, K. T., & Harlan, E. T. (2000). Effortful control in early childhood: Continuity and change, antecedents, and implications for social development. *Developmental Psychology, 36*, 220–232. http://dx.doi.org/10.1037/0012-1649.36.2.220

Kochanska, G., Murray, K., Jacques, T. Y., Koenig, A. L., & Vandegeest, K. A. (1996). Inhibitory control in young children and its role in emerging internalization. *Child Development, 67*, 490–507. http://dx.doi.org/10.2307/1131828

Korkman, M., Kirk, U., & Kemp, S. (1998). *NEPSY: A developmental neuropsychological assessment.* San Antonio, TX: Psychological Corporation.

Lee, K., Ho, R., & Bull, R. (2011, August). *Studying developmental differences in executive functions: Task design and methods of analysis.* Paper presented at the 5th International Conference on Memory, York, England.

Lehto, J. E., Juujärvi, P., Kooistra, L., & Pulkkinen, L. (2003). Dimensions of executive functioning: Evidence from children. *British Journal of Developmental Psychology, 21*, 59–80. http://dx.doi.org/10.1348/026151003321164627

Li, S.-C., Lindenberger, U., Hommel, B., Aschersleben, G., Prinz, W., & Baltes, P. B. (2004). Transformations in the couplings among intellectual abilities and constituent cognitive processes across the life span. *Psychological Science, 15*, 155–163. http://dx.doi.org/10.1111/j.0956-7976.2004.01503003.x

McCabe, D. P., Roediger, H. L., III, McDaniel, M. A., Balota, D. A., & Hambrick, D. Z. (2010). The relationship between working memory capacity and executive functioning: Evidence for a common executive attention construct. *Neuropsychology, 24*, 222–243. http://dx.doi.org/10.1037/a0017619

McNab, F., Leroux, G., Strand, F., Thorell, L., Bergman, S., & Klingberg, T. (2008). Common and unique components of inhibition and working memory: An fMRI, within-subjects investigation. *Neuropsychologia, 46*, 2668–2682. http://dx.doi.org/10.1016/j.neuropsychologia.2008.04.023

Meredith, W. (1993). Measurement invariance, factor analysis, and factorial invariance. *Psychometrika, 58*, 525–543. http://dx.doi.org/10.1007/BF02294825

Meredith, W., & Horn, J. (2001). The role of factorial invariance in modeling growth and change. In L. M. Collins & A. G. Sayer (Eds.), *New methods for the analysis of change* (pp. 203–240). Washington, DC: American Psychological Association.

Miyake, A., Friedman, N. P., Emerson, M. J., Witzki, A. H., Howerter, A., & Wager, T. D. (2000). The unity and diversity of executive functions and their contributions to complex "frontal lobe" tasks: A latent variable analysis. *Cognitive Psychology, 41*, 49–100. http://dx.doi.org/10.1006/cogp.1999.0734

Muthén, L. K., & Muthén, B. O. (2006). *Mplus user's guide* (4th ed.). Los Angeles, CA: Authors.

Norman, D. A., & Shallice, T. (1986). Attention to action: Willed and automatic control of behavior. In R. J. Davidson, G. E. Schwartz, & D. Shapiro (Eds.), *Consciousness and self-regulation* (Vol. 4, pp. 1–18). New York, NY: Plenum Press.

Rueda, M. R., Posner, M. I., & Rothbart, M. K. (2005). The development of executive attention: Contributions to the emergence of self-regulation. *Developmental Neuropsychology, 28*, 573–594. http://dx.doi.org/10.1207/s15326942dn2802_2

Ruff, H. A., & Rothbart, M. K. (1996). *Attention in early development: Themes and variations.* New York, NY: Oxford University Press.

Shing, Y. L., Lindenberger, U., Diamond, A., Li, S. C., & Davidson, M. C. (2010). Memory maintenance and inhibitory control differentiate from early childhood to adolescence. *Developmental Neuropsychology, 35*, 679–697. http://dx.doi.org/10.1080/87565641.2010.508546

Simpson, A., & Riggs, K. J. (2006). Conditions under which children experience inhibitory difficulty with a "button-press" go/no-go task. *Journal of Experimental Child Psychology, 94*, 18–26. http://dx.doi.org/10.1016/j.jecp.2005.10.003

Sowell, E. R., Thompson, P. M., Leonard, C. M., Welcome, S. E., Kan, E., & Toga, A. W. (2004). Longitudinal mapping of cortical thickness and brain growth in normal children. *The Journal of Neuroscience, 24*, 8223–8231. http://dx.doi.org/10.1523/JNEUROSCI.1798-04.2004

St Clair-Thompson, H. L., & Gathercole, S. E. (2006). Executive functions and achievements in school: Shifting, updating, inhibition, and working memory. *The Quarterly Journal of Experimental Psychology, 59*, 745–759. http://dx.doi.org/10.1080/17470210500162854

Steinmetz, H., Schmidt, P., Tina-Booh, A., Wieczorek, S., & Schwartz, S. H. (2009). Testing measurement invariance using multigroup CFA: Differences between educational groups in human values measurement. *Quality & Quantity: International Journal of Methodology, 43*, 599–616. http://dx.doi.org/10.1007/s11135-007-9143-x

Thatcher, R. W. (1992). Cyclic cortical reorganization during early childhood. *Brain and Cognition, 20*, 24–50. http://dx.doi.org/10.1016/0278-2626(92)90060-Y

Tucker-Drob, E. M. (2009). Differentiation of cognitive abilities across the life span. *Developmental Psychology, 45*, 1097–1118. http://dx.doi.org/10.1037/a0015864

Undheim, J. O. (1978). Broad ability factors in 12- to 13-year-old children, the theory of fluid and crystallized intelligence and the differentiation hypothesis. *Journal of Educational Psychology, 70*, 433–443. http://dx.doi.org/10.1037/0022-0663.70.3.433

van der Sluis, S., de Jong, P. F., & van der Leij, A. (2007). Executive functioning in children and its relation with reasoning, reading, and arithmetic. *Intelligence, 35*, 427–449. http://dx.doi.org/10.1016/j.intell.2006.09.001

Wiebe, S. A., Espy, K. A., & Charak, D. (2008). Using confirmatory factor analysis to understand executive control in preschool children: I. Latent structure. *Developmental Psychology, 44*, 575–587. http://dx.doi.org/10.1037/0012-1649.44.2.575

Wiebe, S. A., Sheffield, T. D., & Espy, K. A. (2012). Separating the fish from the sharks: A longitudinal study of preschool response inhibition. *Child Development, 83*, 1245–1261. http://dx.doi.org/10.1111/j.1467-8624.2012.01765.x

Wiebe, S. A., Sheffield, T., Nelson, J. M., Clark, C. A. C., Chevalier, N., & Espy, K. A. (2011). The structure of executive function in 3-year-olds. *Journal of Experimental Child Psychology, 108*, 436–452. http://dx.doi.org/10.1016/j.jecp.2010.08.008

Yu, C.-Y. (2002). *Evaluating cutoff criteria of model fit indices for latent variable models with binary and continuous outcomes* (Doctoral dissertation). University of California, Los Angeles.

4

LONGITUDINAL MEASUREMENT OF EXECUTIVE FUNCTION IN PRESCHOOLERS

MICHAEL T. WILLOUGHBY AND CLANCY B. BLAIR

We find no sense in talking about something unless we specify how we measure it; a definition by the method of measuring a quantity is the one sure way of avoiding talking nonsense. (Bondi, 1964, p. 65)

Although Sir Hermann Bondi was a mathematician and cosmologist, his quotation about the importance of using measurement to define a phenomenon seems especially apropos for those interested in studying executive functions in early childhood. *Executive function* (EF) is an umbrella term that refers to a range of cognitive abilities involved in the control and coordination of information in the service of goal-directed actions (Fuster, 1997; Miller & Cohen, 2001). As such, EF can be defined as a supervisory system that is important for planning, reasoning ability, and integration of thought and action (Shallice, Burgess, & Robertson, 1996). At a more fine-grained level,

Support for this research was provided by the Eunice Kennedy Shriver National Institute of Child Health and Human Development (NICHD) grants R01 HD51502 and P01 HD39667, with cofunding from the National Institute on Drug Abuse, and Institute of Education Sciences (IES) grant R324A120033. The views expressed in this manuscript are those of the authors and do not necessarily represent the opinions and positions of the IES or the NICHD.

http://dx.doi.org/10.1037/14797-005
Executive Function in Preschool-Age Children: Integrating Measurement, Neurodevelopment, and Translational Research, J. A. Griffin, P. McCardle, and L. S. Freund (Editors)

however, EF, as studied in the cognitive development literature, has come to refer to specific interrelated information-processing abilities that enable the resolution of conflicting information: working memory, defined as the holding in mind and updating of information while performing some operation on it; inhibitory control, defined as the inhibition of prepotent or automatized responding when engaged in task completion; and mental flexibility, defined as the ability to shift attentional focus or what is referred to as cognitive set among distinct but related dimensions or aspects of a given task (Garon, Bryson, & Smith, 2008; Zelazo & Müller, 2002).

In this chapter, we summarize our ongoing efforts to develop and rigorously evaluate a battery of EF tasks for use across the early childhood period (i.e., 3–5 years of age). When we began working in this area approximately 10 years ago, relatively few task batteries represented the tripartite organization of EF (inhibitory control [IC], working memory [WM], and attention shifting [AS]) that had undergone rigorous psychometric evaluations—including use with children from disadvantaged settings that yielded scalable scores to facilitate estimates of within-person changes in ability and that were amenable for use by lay interviewers (without expertise in EF) in large-scale, field-based settings. In the sections that follow, we summarize our ongoing efforts to develop such a task battery.

Although space constraints prohibit our clarifying many of the ways in which our work links to that of others, we begin by briefly acknowledging the work of three research groups who laid important foundations for the study of EF in early childhood. Espy and colleagues provided seminal work in the development of psychometrically sound and developmentally appropriate tasks designed to measure EF in preschoolers (their work is summarized in Chapter 3 of this volume). Zelazo and colleagues have provided important conceptual and theoretical framing of ideas about the emergence of EF in early childhood (Marcovitch & Zelazo, 2009; Zelazo, Carter, Reznick, & Frye, 1997; Zelazo et al., 2003) and developed the Dimensional Change Card Sort (DCCS) task (Zelazo, 2006), which is demonstrably the most widely used EF task in early childhood (ongoing efforts to revise the DCCS are summarized in Chapter 2, this volume). Finally, Diamond and colleagues made fundamental contributions to the study of EF in early childhood. Their work initially included demonstrations that nascent EF abilities were first evident in infancy (Diamond, 1990a, 1990b; Diamond & Baddeley, 1996). Their work subsequently involved the use of a sample of children with phenylketonuria to test fundamental questions about the role of dopamine in early EF (Diamond & Baddeley, 1996; Diamond, Prevor, Callendar, & Druin, 1997) as well as creative task manipulations to more precisely delineate the specific cognitive processes required for successful performance of EF tasks (Diamond, Carlson, & Beck, 2005; Diamond, Kirkham, & Amso, 2002; Gerstadt, Hong,

& Diamond, 1994). In the time since we began our work, a number of other research groups have begun to develop and evaluate omnibus tasks or task batteries that are designed to measure EF and self-regulatory functioning more generally (Cameron Ponitz et al., 2008; Garon, Smith, & Bryson, 2014; Murray & Kochanska, 2002; Smith-Donald, Raver, Hayes, & Richardson, 2007). These ongoing efforts supplement existing norm-referenced task batteries that measure EF across a wide age range, though they are not necessarily optimized for use in early childhood—especially with 3-year-olds (e.g., Korkman, Kirk, & Kemp, 1998; Luciana & Nelson, 2002). The proliferation of task development efforts is a testament to the keen multidisciplinary interest in EF in early childhood.

Carlson (2005) provided a synopsis and empirical comparison of 24 tasks that have frequently been used to measure EF in early childhood. A review of those tasks helped to identify limitations common to many that should be addressed in any new measure development efforts. First, numerous tasks exhibited binary distributions and were characterized as primarily informing pass/fail distinctions in ability. Although pass/fail distinctions are appropriate for some questions, they mask individual differences in EF ability, which are frequently of interest. Binary and bimodal distributions may result from a task having too few items or items that do not sufficiently vary in difficulty, or rapidly changing ability levels among young children. Second, tasks differed in terms of their difficulty level. Hence, interest in between- and within-group (longitudinal change) comparisons may be conditional on the specific tasks that were chosen. Third, many tasks were developed for use in laboratory settings. As such, they have often been administered by highly trained staff (e.g., graduate students) and may involve uncommon test materials that are not easily reproducible, which may limit their wide-scale use by lay interviewers in the context of large-scale studies. Fourth, many existing tasks were putatively designed to be integrative—combining WM, IC, and AS in a single measure. These omnibus measures did not allow for testing whether EF is uni- versus multidimensional in early childhood. Fifth, a perennial problem in assessment of preschool-age children is identifying tasks that are sufficiently easy for younger or disadvantaged children, who are characterized by nascent EF abilities, yet sufficiently difficult for older or precocious children with relatively advanced abilities. It is imperative that tasks (batteries) avoid floor and ceiling effects.

Under the auspices of National Institute of Child Health and Human Development (NICHD) funding (R01 HD51502), we initially sought to develop a test battery that addressed these limitations. We were specifically interested in developing tasks that represented a broad range of ability levels and that yielded individual differences in EF ability levels between 3 and 5 years of age. Moreover, we wanted tasks that were highly portable, that presented tasks in a uniform format, and that included highly scripted instructions, making them amenable for use by lay data collectors who had limited experience in standardized testing and no content knowledge of EF. In addition, we constructed tasks such that one person administered the tasks while a second person recorded child responses, to reduce the cognitive demand for data collectors and improve data quality. Finally, we were interested in tasks that were both appropriate for young children and ostensibly designed to measure the distinct components of EF (understanding that there are no completely pure measures of WM, IC, or AS) that have been critical for testing fundamental questions about the organization of EF in early childhood.

Our work proceeded in three stages. The first stage involved an iterative process of task development and pilot testing and concluded by administering the first complete task battery in a cross-sectional sample of children between the ages of 3 and 5 years. The second stage involved introducing the task battery into a population-based longitudinal sample of 1,292 children and families followed from birth (i.e., the Family Life Project [FLP]; P01 HD39667). The third stage of our work is ongoing (currently funded by Institute of Education Sciences grant R324A120033) and has involved a new round of task revisions and the migration of the battery from a flip-book to a computer-based administration format. The accomplishments and major insights that arose in each stage of work are summarized below.

STAGE 1: INITIAL TASK DEVELOPMENT

We initially set out to identify extant tasks that had been used with preschool-age children that putatively measured three aspects of EF—IC, WM, and AS—and that could be adapted for use with very young children who resided in low-income households. The focus on young and disadvantaged children was to facilitate our intended Stage 2 work, which involved direct assessments of EF in 3- to 5-year-old children who were part of the FLP, an NICHD-funded population-based cohort that oversampled low-income and, in North Carolina, African American families.

The initial set of tasks was developed as a series of card games that were intended to provide a uniform testing format. Nine potential tasks were trimmed to six following our experiences with pilot testing (some tasks were difficult for the youngest children to understand). Pilot testing also revealed that a card game format was not ideal, as cards required sorting after each administration and the likelihood of sorting-related errors was high. We subsequently created bound flip-book versions of each task, which eliminated sorting problems and facilitated the scripting of instructions for administrators (the opened flip-book sat between the experimenter and the child; one page presented a stimulus to the child and the other page provided scripted instructions that were read to the child by the experimenter or that otherwise prompted the experimenter as to what to do). We worked with a commercial artist to develop professional-looking stimuli, a graphic designer and printer to construct bound flip-books, and a computer programmer who developed software to record child responses into laptops.

Using the flip-book format, we engaged in an extended period of iterative pilot testing and task modification with a total of 120 children. During this period, no formal data were collected. Rather, two data collector teams independently tested children to gain impressions of how tasks worked and what modifications might be useful. Conference calls involving data collectors and investigators led to recommended changes, implemented by a graphic designer and subsequently pilot tested again. Major emphases were developing language that described task objectives in ways that were understandable to young children and structuring tasks in ways that minimized language demands on children in order to respond. A synopsis of the final set of tasks retained from this initial task development period follows.

Task Descriptions

Two tasks were developed that putatively measured working memory. The Working Memory Span task was based on principles described by Engle, Kane, and collaborators (e.g., Kane & Engle, 2003), with the object of holding multiple representations in mind simultaneously and selectively responding to only one. In this task, children are presented with a line drawing of an animal with a colored dot above it, both located within the outline of a house. The examiner asks the child to name the animal and then to name the color of the dot. The examiner then turns to a page that shows only the outline of the house from the previous page and asks the child which animal was or lived in the house. The task requires children to perform the operation of naming and holding in mind two pieces of information simultaneously and to activate the animal name while overcoming interference occurring from having named the color. The number of houses on each page scales difficulty level. The Pick the Picture (PtP) task is a self-ordered pointing task (Cragg & Nation, 2007; Petrides & Milner, 1982). Children are presented with a set of identical pictures that appear on a series of consecutive pages. On each page, they are instructed to pick a new picture that had not been previously selected so that all of the pictures "get a turn." The arrangement of pictures within each set is randomly changed across trials so that spatial location is not informative. The number of pictures contained in each set scales difficulty level.

Three tasks were developed that putatively measured inhibitory control. The Silly Sounds Stroop (SSS) task was derived from the Day-Night task developed by Gerstadt and colleagues (1994). While showing the children pictures of a cat and dog, the experimenter introduces the idea that, in the Silly Sounds game, dogs make the sounds of cats and vice versa. Children are then presented with pictures of dogs and cats and asked what sound a particular animal makes in the Silly Sounds game (i.e., children are to "bark" for each cat picture and "meow" for each dog picture). The second task that putatively measured inhibitory control is the Animal Go/No-Go (GNG) task. This is a standard go/no-go task (e.g., Durston et al., 2002) presented in a flip-book format. Children are presented with a large button that makes a clicking noise when depressed. Children are instructed to click their button every time they see an animal on the flip-book page unless that animal is a pig. Each page depicts one of seven possible animals. The task presented varying numbers of go trials prior to each no-go trial. The third task that putatively measured inhibitory control is the Spatial Conflict (SC) task. The SC is a Simon task of a type that is commonly used in research on EF in children (e.g., Davidson, Amso, Anderson, & Diamond, 2006; Gerardi-Caulton, 2000). Children receive a response card with a picture of a car on the left side and picture of a boat on the right side. The flip-book pages depict either a car or boats. The child is instructed to touch the car on his or her response card when the flip-book page shows a car and to touch the boat on the response card when the page shows a boat. Cars and boats are initially depicted in the center of the flip-book page (to teach the task). Across a series of trials, cars and boats are depicted laterally, with cars (boats) always appearing on the left (right) side of the flip-book page (above the car [boat] on the response card). Eventually test items begin to appear in which cars and boats are depicted contralaterally (spatial location is no longer informative). In subsequent work, it was determined that the SC task was too easy for 4- and 5-year-olds. Hence, a variation of the task, called the Spatial Conflict Arrows task, was developed. It was identical in structure to SC except that the stimuli were arrows and the response card showed two "buttons" (black circles). Children were to touch the left (right) button when the arrow on the flip-book page pointed to the left (right) side of the page. Similar to the SC task, initially all left (right) pointing arrows appeared above the left (right) button; however, during test trials, left (right) pointing arrows appeared above the right (left) button.

One task was developed that putatively measured attention shifting. The Something's the Same (StS) task was a simplified version of Jacques and Zelazo's (2001) Flexible Item Selection task. In our variation, children are shown a page containing two pictures that are similar along one dimension (content, color, or size). The experimenter explicitly states the dimension of similarity. The next page presents the same two pictures, plus a new third picture. The third picture is similar to one of the first two pictures along a dimension that is different from that of the similarity of the first two pictures (e.g., if the first two pictures were similar in shape, the third card would be similar to one of the first two along the dimension of color or size). Children are asked to choose one of the two original pictures that is the same as the new picture.

Key Results

Following the period of iterative pilot testing ($N = 120$ participants), data were collected from a convenience sample ($N = 229$ children) in North Carolina and Pennsylvania. Children ranged from 3.0 to 5.8 years of age and were recruited to ensure adequate cross-age variation. The primary analytic objectives of Stage 1 work on the battery were to use confirmatory factor analysis (CFA) to test its dimensionality, to test whether it exhibited equivalent measurement properties for distinct subsets of youth, to examine the criterion validity, and to evaluate whether performance exhibited the expected improvements as a function of chronological age. Given space constraints, we present an abbreviated explanation of three key results.

First, our EF tasks were best represented by a single latent factor, $\chi^2_{(9)} = 4.0$, $p = .91$, comparative fit index (CFI) = 1.0, root mean square error of approximation (RMSEA) = 0.00. With one exception, the EF latent variable explained approximately one third of the variance of each task (Spatial Conflict: $R^2 = .07$; Go/No-Go: $R^2 = .29$; Working Memory Span: $R^2 = .34$; Silly Sounds Stroop: $R^2 = .40$; Flexible Item Selection: $R^2 = .41$; Self-Ordered Pointing: $R^2 = .47$). Nearly two thirds of the observed variation in each task was a combination of measurement error and systematic variation unique to that task. As we elaborate below, the modest amount of shared variation among EF tasks eventually led us to reconsider the use of CFA methods for purposes of combining task scores. At the time, however, our findings aligned nicely with other CFA examinations of EF batteries (Miyake et al., 2000; Wiebe, Espy, & Charak, 2008). Moreover, the excellent fit of the one-factor model, also similar to other analyses involving preschool-age children (Hughes, Ensor, Wilson, & Graham, 2009; Wiebe et al., 2008), argued against the relevance of the tripartite organization of EF in early childhood.

Second, a series of multiple-groups CFA models were estimated to test the measurement invariance of the one-factor model separately by child sex (male vs. female) and age group (3–3.99 vs. 4–5 years), parental education (less than vs. 4+ year degree), and household income (median split of $50,000/household). In other words, we tested whether tasks were equally good indicators of the construct of EF across subgroups of children. At least partial measurement invariance was established for all comparisons (i.e., at least a subset of the tasks could take on equivalent measurement properties across all subgroups of children). This invariance provided evidence that the task battery worked, in a psychometric sense, equivalently for a wide range of children. Measurement invariance facilitated our ability to make meaningful cross-group comparisons. Comparisons of latent means indicated that girls outperformed boys (Cohen's $d = .75$), older children outperformed younger children (Cohen's $d = 1.3$), children whose parents had a bachelor's degree or higher outperformed children whose parents did not (Cohen's $d = .54$), and children from higher income households outperformed children from lower income households (Cohen's $d = 0.44$) on the EF battery (all $ps < .01$).

Third, in the total sample, the EF latent variable was negatively correlated with a latent variable of parent-reported attention–deficit/hyperactivity disorder (ADHD) symptomatology ($\varphi = -.45$, $p < .0001$) and positively correlated with a direct screening assessment (i.e., Wechsler Preschool and Primary Scale of Intelligence [WPPSI] subtests) of children's IQ ($\varphi = .77$, $p < .0001$). These results were in the expected direction and provided initial evidence supporting the criterion validity of the battery. Fourth, EF factor scores were positively correlated with chronological age ($r = .55$, $p < .0001$) and exhibited linear change from age 3 years to 6 years. An inspection of box-and-whisker plots of EF factor scores plotted by age group demonstrated that although children's performance on the EF battery showed the expected linear changes with increasing age, there were substantial individual differences in ability level within any given age (see Figure 4.1). The ability of the EF task battery to preserve individual differences within age group makes it an ideal measure for measuring longitudinal change.

In sum, at the conclusion of the first stage of our measurement development work, we had developed a set of tasks that had undergone extensive pilot testing and revision, that were presented in a uniform and easily portable format, and that could be easily administered by data collectors with no expertise in EF. Analyses indicated that children's performance on six tasks was optimally represented by a single latent factor and that EF tasks worked in an equivalent way for children of different sexes, ages, and family backgrounds. Group differences in latent EF ability were evident for females versus males, older versus younger children, and children from more (parental education, household income) versus less advantaged homes. Criterion validity was established by demonstrating that children's performance on the battery correlated with parent-reported ADHD behaviors and their performance on two screening indicators of IQ. Finally, although there was evidence of developmental improvements in performance on the battery, individual differences in ability were evident for children of the same age.

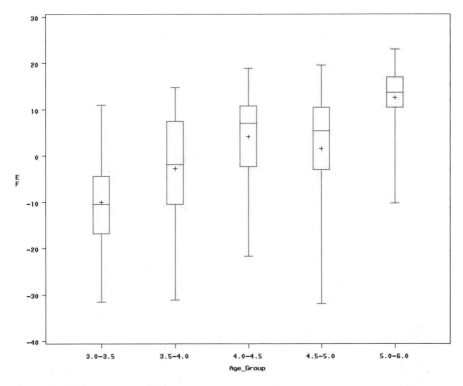

Figure 4.1. Developmental change in executive function (EF) task battery (factor scores) from age 3 to 6 years.

STAGE 2: LARGE-SCALE EVALUATION OF THE EXECUTIVE FUNCTION BATTERY IN THE FAMILY LIFE PROJECT

With the successful completion of measure development activities in Stage 1, the EF task battery was administered at the age 3-, 4-, and 5-year assessments of the FLP. The FLP is an NICHD-funded program project that was designed to study young children and their families who lived in two of the four major geographical areas of the United States with high poverty rates. Three counties in Eastern North Carolina and three counties in Central Pennsylvania were selected to be indicative of the Black South and Appalachia, respectively. The FLP adopted a developmental epidemiological design in which sampling procedures were employed to recruit a representative sample of 1,292 children whose families resided in one of the six counties at the time of the child's birth. Low-income families in both states and African American families in North Carolina were oversampled (African American families were not oversampled in Pennsylvania because the target communities were at least 95% non–African American). Interested readers are referred to a monograph-length description of study recruitment strategies and detailed descriptions of participating families and their communities (Vernon-Feagans, Cox, & Family Life Project Key Investigators, 2013). In this section, we summarize the knowledge that was gained, specifically as it related to our EF task development efforts, from embedding the EF battery in the FLP study.

The inclusion of the EF task battery at the age 3-year assessment of the FLP sample provided the first sufficiently large sample to begin evaluating the psychometric properties of each task individually, as well as their contribution to the overall battery. Three key results emerged from this study (see Willoughby, Blair, Wirth, & Greenberg, 2010). First, 91% of children who participated in the age 3-year home visit successfully completed one or more EF tasks (median = 4 of 5 tasks; note that the PtP task was not administered at the age 3-year assessment). Compared with children who completed one or more EF tasks, children who were unable to complete any tasks were more likely to be male (77% vs. 47%, $p < .0001$), to have a primary caregiver who was unmarried (57% vs. 42%, $p = .005$), and to differ on their estimated full-scale IQ score using two subtests from the WPPSI ($M = 75.9$ vs. $M = 95.1$, $p < .0001$). The WPPSI scores, in particular, indicated that children who were unable to complete any EF tasks were developmentally delayed. Second, a CFA indicated that a one-factor model fit the task scores well ($\chi^2_{(5)} = 3.5$, $p = .62$, CFI = 1.0, RMSEA = 0.00). Although a two-factor model also fit the task scores well ($\chi^2_{(4)} = 2.4$, $p = .66$, CFI = 1.0, RMSEA = 0.00), the two-factor model did not provide a statistically significant improvement in model fit relative to the two-factor model ($\chi^2_{(1)} = 1.1$, $p = .30$). Hence, consistent with other relevant studies and the results from data collected in Stage 1, EF abilities were again best conceptualized as unidimensional (undifferentiated) in preschoolers. Third, a final set of CFA models was estimated to establish the criterion validity of the EF task battery. One latent variable represented children's performance on the EF task battery (each task was an indicator of underlying EF ability). The other two latent variables represented criterion measures: multiple informant (parent, day-care provider, research assistant) ratings of ADHD behaviors and estimated intellectual functioning (based on performance on Block Design and Receptive Vocabulary subtests of the WPPSI). This three-factor model fit the observed data well ($\chi^2_{(32)} = 36.0$, $p = .29$, CFI = 1.0, RMSEA = 0.01). The EF latent variable was strongly negatively correlated with ADHD ($\varphi = -.71$, $p < .001$) and strongly positively correlated with IQ ($\varphi = .94$, $p < .001$). These results replicated those obtained in Stage 1. Although the large correlation between EF and IQ was not inconsistent with results that were observed in the adult literature (Kane, Hambrick, & Conway, 2005), the modest magnitude of the correlations between individual EF tasks and IQ was discrepant with the large correlation between the latent variable representation of EF tasks and IQ. This finding raised additional concerns about whether CFA methods were the most appropriate way to represent individual differences in task performance.

In addition to replicating tests regarding the dimensionality and criterion validity of the EF battery, the large sample size of the FLP provided the first opportunity to evaluate the psychometric properties of individual tasks. We relied extensively on item response theory (IRT) methods for psychometric evaluation of individual EF tasks. IRT methods had three advantages that were directly relevant to our work. First, IRT methods provide a principled approach for testing differential item functioning (DIF). DIF is a formal approach for evaluating whether individual items on each EF task work equally well for subgroups of participants. Ruling out DIF ensured that any observed group differences in ability were not an artifact of differential measurement operations. Second, IRT methods provided an explicit strategy for generating task scores that took into account the fact that test items varied with respect to their difficulty level and discrimination properties. Failing to take into account differences in how each item behaves results in under- or overweighting particular items. Incorrectly weighting items can lead to scale scores that are biased and therefore less accurate when comparing individuals (or groups) within or across time (Edwards & Wirth, 2009; Wirth & Edwards, 2007). A third advantage of IRT methods was the ability to compute test information curves, which characterize variations in the precision of measurement of each task as a function of a child's true ability level. Test information curves consistently indicated that all of the tasks in our battery did a relatively better job of measuring lower than higher levels of true EF ability. These results informed subsequent efforts at task revisions (see Stage 3, below). We used data from the age 4-year assessment to provide an extended introduction to the merits of IRT methods for purposes of task evaluation (Willoughby, Wirth, & Blair, 2011).

A test–retest study was embedded in the FLP age 4-year assessment (Willoughby & Blair, 2011). Over a 6-week period, every family who completed a home visit ($n = 145$) was invited to complete a follow-up (retest) visit 2 to 4 weeks later. The follow-up visit consisted of the re-administration of EF tasks by the same research assistant who administered them at the first visit. Of the 145 families who were invited to participate, 141 accepted (97%). The mean (median) number of days that passed between the initial and retest visits was 18 (16) days, with a range of 12 to 42 days. One child whose family agreed to participate in the retest visit was unable to complete any tasks, so there were only 140 retest observations. Whereas retest correlations of individual task scores were of moderate magnitude (mean $r = .60$; range = .52–.66), CFA demonstrated exceptionally high retest reliability ($\varphi = .95$) of the latent construct that represented overall EF ability. At the time, we, like others before us (Ettenhofer, Hambrick, & Abeles, 2006), interpreted this pattern of results as evidence to support the administration of multiple tasks and the use of CFA methods to represent individual differences in underlying ability that was common across tasks. However, in retrospect, this discrepancy in results could also be used as an indictment against the use of CFA methods with EF data. We return to this idea at the conclusion of this chapter.

The inclusion of the EF task battery at the FLP age 5-year assessment yielded three major findings (Willoughby, Blair, Wirth, & Greenberg, 2012). First, 99% ($N = 1,036$) of the children who participated in this visit were able to complete one or more of the tasks (median = 6 of 6), representing an 8% increase in the completion rate from the age 3-year assessment. As before, those children unable to complete any tasks tended to exhibit a variety of physical and developmental delays that prohibited their participation in any direct child testing. Because of the inclusive nature of the FLP sampling scheme (oversample low-income families, no exclusionary criteria except intention to move and speaking English as a primary language), the 99% completion rate provided direct support for the use of this battery with children from diverse backgrounds. Second, also consistent with results from the age 3-year assessment, children's performance on EF tasks continued to be optimally characterized by a single factor, $\chi^2_{(9)} = 6.3$, $p = .71$, CFI = 1.0, RMSEA = 0.00. This finding indicated that the differentiation of EF ability into more fine-grained dimensions likely occurs after the start of formal schooling (see Shing, Lindenberger, Diamond, Li, & Davidson, 2010, for supporting evidence). Third, a series of CFA models, based on $N = 1,058$ children who participated in either the age 5-year or prekindergarten (i.e., a visit that occurred prior to the start of kindergarten) visits, or both, were used to test whether children's performance on the EF battery was significantly related to performance on achievement tests. A two-factor model (one each for EF and academic achievement) fit the data well, $\chi^2_{(43)} = 135.1$, $p < .0001$, CFI =.96, RMSEA = 0.05. The latent variables representing EF and academic achievement were strongly and positively correlated ($\varphi = .70$, $p < .001$). Moreover, follow-up analyses indicated that the EF latent variable was moderately to strongly correlated with individual achievement scores as well (φ ECLS-K Math = .62, φ WJ Applied Problems = .63, φ WJ Quantitative Concepts = .62, φ WJ Letter–Word = .39, and φ TOPEL Phonological = .56, all ps < .001). Although these results validated the EF battery as an indicator of academic school readiness, the latent variable representation of EF may have inflated the magnitude of these effects.

By embedding the EF battery in the FLP, we were able to test the longitudinal measurement properties of the EF battery as well as characterize the degree of developmental change in children's performance from 3 to 5 years of age. To be clear, whereas previous results tested the measurement equivalence of items (tasks) across defined subgroups of youth (e.g., gender, family poverty level), here we tested whether the measurement parameters for items on a task and tasks on the battery were invariant across time (i.e., for children from 3 to 5 years of age). Establishing longitudinal invariance of items (tasks) was a necessary precursor to modeling developmental changes in performance across time (failure to establish longitudinal invariance can result in scores that are not on the same metric). Three results emerged from this work. First, all six individual EF tasks exhibited strong measurement invariance across time (Willoughby, Wirth, & Blair, 2012). That is, item thresholds and factor loadings could take on identical values at 3-, 4-, and 5-year assessments without degrading model fit. Moreover, the EF battery, defined by a latent variable with the six individual tasks as indicators, exhibited partial strong invariance over time. Whereas some tasks were differentially strong indicators of EF ability at different ages, two (StS, PtP) had invariant properties that facilitated the creation of a scalable battery score (note that the magnitude of differences in noninvariant tasks was modest; these differences were detected as a result of excessive statistical power associated with our large sample size).

Second, given our previous emphasis on the importance of aggregating children's performance across tasks in order to obtain a reliable indicator of true EF ability, we estimated changes in children's performance on a battery score (i.e., a latent variable estimate of ability at each age) using second-order latent growth curve models (Willoughby, Wirth, & Blair, 2012). Results indicated substantial age-related improvements in latent EF ability across time (approximately a one tenth of a standard deviation improvement in ability with each passing month). Moreover, the rate of growth was faster between 3 and 4 years than it was between 4 and 5 years (60% of total change between the age 3-year and 5-year assessments occurred between the age 3-year assessment and the age 4-year assessment). However, the 2-year stability of latent EF ability (i.e., the correlation between age 3 and age 5 latent variables) was $\varphi = .86$, which was nearly as large as the 2-week stability of latent EF ability in the test–retest study ($\varphi = .95$). Moreover, despite evidence for developmental improvements in latent EF ability, individual differences were evident in level but not rate of change (i.e., for intercepts but not slopes) in latent EF across time. These results contributed to our increasing concerns about whether CFA methods were appropriate for representing individual differences EF ability.

Third, the battery was explicitly developed in a modular format, with each task taking approximately 5 minutes to complete, to accommodate limited attention spans of young children. Although the modular format also allowed for the possibility of creating shortened versions of the battery, we were unable to provide empirically informed recommendations regarding which specific subsets of tasks were optimal for representing EF in situations where the administration of the full battery of tasks was not possible. We subsequently addressed this question by examining the maximal reliability for latent EF for all possible three-task combinations for children between 3 and 5 years of age (Willoughby, Pek, & Blair, 2013). The major result of this work was that although every possible combination of three tasks resulted in worse maximal reliability than did the administration of the full set of tasks, some three-task combinations were better than others and may have been justifiable given time savings and reductions in participant burden.

In summary, at the conclusion of Stage 2, we replicated and extended the empirical results from Stage 1 by demonstrating that children's performance on EF tasks was represented by a single latent factor at ages 3, 4, and 5 years and that individual differences in EF ability were correlated with multi-informant ratings of ADHD symptomatology as well as direct assessments of children's intelligence and academic achievement. Mixed evidence resulted from the retest reliability study. Whereas the retest reliability of individual tasks was moderate, the retest reliability of the latent variable approached unity. In terms of developmental questions, the items on all six EF tasks exhibited strong longitudinal invariance across time, whereas two of the six tasks exhibited partial strong longitudinal invariance across time (the remaining four tasks were differentially strong indicators of true EF ability at different ages). Extending the results from Stage 1, which were based on between-group comparisons of children of differing ages, Stage 2 demonstrated substantial improvements in children's performance on EF tasks across time. Finally, we used a principled approach for the creation of short forms of the battery.

STAGE 3: COMPUTERIZED ASSESSMENT

Since its inception, our measurement development work has been primarily focused on the creation of a highly portable, easily administered, and uniformly presented battery that assesses the full domain of EF abilities, that is appropriate for serial use (including longitudinal data collection and progress monitoring), and that has been demonstrated to work with preschool-age children from a wide range of socioeconomic backgrounds. Despite some initial success at these efforts, at the end of Stage 2 work, we identified three structural and one empirical limitation of the current battery that precluded its wider scale use. First, the flip-book version of the EF battery required two data collectors for administration and scoring. The requirement of two data collectors was both costly and impractical in many potential settings. Second, the flip-book version of the battery required commercial software for recording child responses into laptops, for executing programs that translate the observed child responses into item-level scores, and, when desired, for converting item-level responses into IRT scores. Many potential end users would not have the interest or the technical sophistication required to use and adapt existing software programs to meet their specific needs, nor would they want to incur the associated annual software licensing costs. Third, although highly structured in content, the flip-book version of the tasks did not afford quality control for subtle aspects of task administration that may have major impacts on the quality of data collected (e.g., the rate of presentation of items, an appreciation for how many attempts should be made to teach the task to the child before it is abandoned). Fourth, the tasks did a poorer job of measuring high (advanced) than measuring low (immature) levels of EF ability. An inherent tension in task development is the creation of tasks that are accessible for children with low ability levels but that also become sufficiently challenging for children with high ability levels.

Using competitively awarded funds from a 2-year American Recovery and Reinvestment Act supplement to our aforementioned NICHD R01 study and new (current) funds from the National Center for Special Education Research at the IES (Grant R324A120033), we are in the process of fully computerizing the battery and attending to each of these limitations as well as improving the battery in important ways. Stage 3 research is organized around six improvements. First, the computerized battery eliminated the need for two-person administration. Child responses to EF tasks are captured by the touch screen (the inclusion of a touch screen eliminates the data collector, whose sole purpose was recording child responses). Second, by creating a stand-alone piece of software that delivers test stimuli, records child responses, and provides item and task-level scoring, we eliminated the costs and technical complications associated with reliance on third-party software solutions. Third, the use of touch-screen technology allowed the possibility of including reaction time as a supplement to accuracy information for children's responses to tasks, which may facilitate improved precision of measurement for children at higher ability levels. Fourth, moving to a computerized interface has expedited task development, modification, and piloting efforts (graphic design and printing costs and time are eliminated). Fifth, we are in the process of collecting normative data that will facilitate making cross-sample inferences about children's ability with respect to age, gender, race or ethnicity, and household poverty level. Sixth, the computerized platform is well suited for translating the battery into other languages. The ability to translate will enable researchers to attend to demographic changes that are occurring at the national level (e.g., increasing Hispanic population), facilitate research that is focused on the role of bilingualism as a support of EF development (e.g., Carlson & Meltzoff, 2008), and facilitate cross-cultural research on EF (e.g., Lan, Legare, Ponitz, Li, & Morrison, 2011).

Our initial computerization efforts have resulted in a number of important insights that may be useful to other task developers. For example, although we initially hoped to use touch-screen tablet computers in order to mimic the layout of our flip-book tasks, this goal was abandoned after we determined that test stimuli appeared distorted to children when images were viewed from an angle (e.g., when children slouched in their seat during testing). Hence, in our current prototype, we use a stand-alone, upright monitor that sits directly in front of the child and is connected to a laptop that is used by the interviewer. Through pilot testing, we have determined that capacitive touch-screen technology is superior to resistive touch-screen technology. Only the former registers even the lightest of touches, which are common among young children. Capacitive technology also allows children to use their fingers to touch screens, which is more natural than asking them to use a stylus. Finally, through computerization, we are able to standardize multiple aspects of task delivery (e.g., the interstimulus time intervals; linking child performance on training items to determination of whether the task should be administered).

FUTURE DIRECTIONS

On the basis of our work to date, we see three important areas for future research related to the measurement of EF. First, researchers are continually developing new measures of EF. However, many of these new tasks have not undergone rigorous formal psychometric evaluations. Moreover, differences in task difficulty and discrimination levels, as well as idiosyncratic scoring approaches, make it difficult to compare the results across studies that used different EF measures. However, this is not a problem unique to the study of EF in early childhood. Fortunately, there exists a long tradition in psychometrics of linking and equating scores across tasks (Kolen & Brennan, 2004). It may be advantageous to the field if a concerted effort were made to link or equate scores on the most commonly used tasks in an effort to facilitate cross-study comparisons of tasks that shared a common metric. This linkage would enhance the creation of a more cumulative and interpretable body of research.

Second, as we alluded to in the summary of Stage 2 work, we are increasingly concerned about the routine use of CFA methods as a means for representing individual differences in EF ability across a battery of EF tasks. An essential problem is that children's performance on individual EF tasks tend to be weakly correlated; hence, there is little shared variation across the tasks. The routine use of CFA methods results in latent variables that account for very little variation in individual tasks (i.e., the majority of observed variation in any EF task is relegated to the residual term) but that nonetheless provide an excellent fit to the observed data (i.e., CFA models do an excellent job of reproducing weak correlations among individual tasks). On the basis of a recent targeted review of the literature, the relatively poor intertask correlations appear to be true of all direct assessments of EF—not just our tasks—and for participants of varying ages—not just preschool-age children (see Willoughby, Holochwost, Blanton, & Blair, 2014). An important direction for future research involves resolving the best way to characterize individual differences in performance-based indicators of EF. This effort will require consideration of theoretical and statistical criteria and may well result in formulations of the latent construct of EF that are inconsistent with conventional measurement wisdom.

Finally, an ongoing issue by no means unique to EF concerns the need to clearly and unambiguously differentiate the construct from related constructs, including effortful control and the ability to delay gratification, as well as general intelligence. One way in which to consider the relation of EF to these related aspects of self-regulation is to consider the extent to which demand for EF occurs in an emotionally valenced context. Strong incentives, as in delay of gratification, placed an added demand on EF and speak to processes of self-regulation more generally (Blair, 2010, 2014). Similarly, without question, general intelligence is important for and related to EF ability; however, the direction of the relation and amount of overlap between the two constructs remain unclear. Here it is important for the field to consider that general intelligence, as its name implies, is the more general construct, whereas EF is the more specific. A key distinction in intelligence research is that between crystallized and fluid abilities (Horn & Cattell, 1966). Crystallized abilities are those that reflect highly learned and acquired knowledge, such as vocabulary, language ability, and general information. In contrast, fluid abilities are those that require reasoning and on-the-spot problem solving. Indicators of fluid abilities include puzzle completion and pattern completion types of tasks that present novel information requiring to-be-learned solutions. Executive functions, particularly working memory, are domain-general skills that underlie, perhaps to a substantial extent, performance on fluid intelligence tasks (Blair, 2006; Carpenter, Just, & Shell, 1990; Kane et al., 2005). An important direction for future research on EF is to consider the extent to which the development of EF may underlie the development of fluid intelligence and the extent to which development in fluid intelligence may be an important contributor to the development of crystallized abilities. Although such an investment hypothesis has been around for some time (Cattell, 1971), only a few studies have directly examined it and provide limited support for it (Ferrer & McArdle, 2004). A key construct relevant to EF as well as to fluid and crystallized intelligence is processing speed. Performance on simple reaction-time tasks is a reliable albeit moderate correlate of general intelligence and also of EF. The role of processing speed in EF ability, and perhaps in the relation between EF and intelligence, remains to be addressed. Work with adult samples suggests that age-related decline in processing speed rather than in fluid intelligence or EF accounts for age-related decline in general intelligence (Salthouse, 1996). As such, it may be that increases in processing speed play a facilitating role in development in early childhood.

EF specifically and self-regulation more generally are currently hot topics in the developmental literature. Although hot topics in science invariably fade, many enduring aspects of research on EF have helped to advance the field's understanding of child development. An important direction for ongoing research on the construct, however, concerns the need for increased precision in its definition and measurement. We expect that increasing efforts to utilize psychometric theory to design and evaluate EF tasks will help the field reach a consensus on how best to operationalize the construct and that this consensus will in turn lead to advances in theory and research. We also expect that efforts to use what is known about the neurobiology of EF will help direct understanding of how to best operationalize the construct. Executive functions are associated with the prefrontal cortex (PFC) and can be powerfully affected by stress and other statelike influences. Evidence from neuroimaging studies with adults indicates that similar levels of measured ability can be associated with distinct profiles of neural activity (e.g., Callicott et al., 2003). In combination with findings of experimental studies indicating that EF ability can be depleted, the neurobiology of the PFC and EF suggests that information about brain activity in response to EF test batteries can provide valuable information about individual differences in ability. Indeed, efforts to improve the measurement of EF will have direct consequences for substantive research that is focused on the neurobiological foundations of EF, as well as the translational research opportunities related to EF as it relates to prevention efforts, which are the foci of the second and third parts of this volume.

REFERENCES

Blair, C. (2006). How similar are fluid cognition and general intelligence? A developmental neuroscience perspective on fluid cognition as an aspect of human cognitive ability. *Behavioral and Brain Sciences, 29*, 109–125.

Blair, C. (2010). Stress and the development of self-regulation in context. *Child Development Perspectives, 4*, 181–188. http://dx.doi.org/10.1111/j.1750-8606.2010.00145.x

Blair, C. B. (2014). Stress and the development of executive functions: Experiential canalization of brain and behavior. In P. Zelazo & M. Sera (Eds.), *Minnesota symposia on child psychology: Developing cognitive control processes: Mechanisms, implications, and interventions* (Vol. 37, pp. 145–180). Hoboken, NJ: Wiley.

Bondi, H. (1964). *Relativity and common sense*. London, England: Heinemann Educational Books.

Callicott, J. H., Mattay, V. S., Verchinski, B. A., Marenco, S., Egan, M. F., & Weinberger, D. R. (2003). Complexity of prefrontal cortical dysfunction in schizophrenia: More than up or down. *The American Journal of Psychiatry, 160*, 2209–2215. http://dx.doi.org/10.1176/appi.ajp.160.12.2209

Cameron Ponitz, C. E., McClelland, M. M., Jewkes, A. M., Connor, C. M., Farris, C. L., & Morrison, F. J. (2008). Touch your toes! Developing a direct measure of behavioral regulation in early childhood. *Early Childhood Research Quarterly, 23*, 141–158. http://dx.doi.org/10.1016/j.ecresq.2007.01.004

Carlson, S. M. (2005). Developmentally sensitive measures of executive function in preschool children. *Developmental Neuropsychology, 28*, 595–616. http://dx.doi.org/10.1207/s15326942dn2802_3

Carlson, S. M., & Meltzoff, A. N. (2008). Bilingual experience and executive functioning in young children. *Developmental Science, 11*, 282–298. http://dx.doi.org/10.1111/j.1467-7687.2008.00675.x

Carpenter, P. A., Just, M. A., & Shell, P. (1990). What one intelligence test measures: A theoretical account of the processing in the Raven Progressive Matrices Test. *Psychological Review, 97*, 404–431.

Cattell, R. B. (1971). *Abilities: Their structure, growth, and action*. Boston, MA: Houghton Mifflin.

Cragg, L., & Nation, K. (2007). Self-ordered pointing as a test of working memory in typically developing children. *Memory, 15*, 526–535. http://dx.doi.org/10.1080/09658210701390750

Davidson, M. C., Amso, D., Anderson, L. C., & Diamond, A. (2006). Development of cognitive control and executive functions from 4 to 13 years: Evidence from manipulations of memory, inhibition, and task switching. *Neuropsychologia, 44*, 2037–2078. http://dx.doi.org/10.1016/j.neuropsychologia.2006.02.006

Diamond, A. (1990a). The development and neural bases of memory functions as indexed by the AB and delayed response tasks in human infants and infant monkeys. *Annals of the New York Academy of Sciences, 608*, 267–317. http://dx.doi.org/10.1111/j.1749-6632.1990.tb48900.x

Diamond, A. (1990b). Developmental time course in human infants and infant monkeys, and the neural bases of, inhibitory control in reaching. *Annals of the New York Academy of Sciences, 608*, 637–676. http://dx.doi.org/10.1111/j.1749-6632.1990.tb48913.x

Diamond, A., & Baddeley, A. (1996). Evidence for the importance of dopamine for prefrontal cortex functions early in life. *Philosophical Transactions of the Royal Society of London. Series B, Biological Sciences, 351*, 1483–1494. http://dx.doi.org/10.1098/rstb.1996.0134

Diamond, A., Carlson, S. M., & Beck, D. M. (2005). Preschool children's performance in task switching on the dimensional change card sort task: Separating the dimensions aids the ability to switch. *Developmental Neuropsychology, 28*, 689–729. http://dx.doi.org/10.1207/s15326942dn2802_7

Diamond, A., Kirkham, N., & Amso, D. (2002). Conditions under which young children can hold two rules in mind and inhibit a prepotent response. *Developmental Psychology, 38*, 352–362. http://dx.doi.org/10.1037/0012-1649.38.3.352

Diamond, A., Prevor, M. B., Callendar, G., & Druin, D. P. (1997). Prefrontal cognitive deficits in children treated early and continuously for PKU. *Monographs of the Society for Research in Child Development, 62*(4), i–v, 1–208.

Durston, S., Thomas, K. M., Yang, Y. H., Ulug, A. M., Zimmerman, R. D., & Casey, B. J. (2002). A neural basis for the development of inhibitory control. *Developmental Science, 5*, F9–F16. http://dx.doi.org/10.1111/1467-7687.00235

Edwards, M. C., & Wirth, R. J. (2009). Measurement and the study of change. *Research in Human Development, 6*(2–3), 74–96. http://dx.doi.org/10.1080/15427600902911163

Ettenhofer, M. L., Hambrick, D. Z., & Abeles, N. (2006). Reliability and stability of executive functioning in older adults. *Neuropsychology, 20*, 607–613. http://dx.doi.org/10.1037/0894-4105.20.5.607

Ferrer, E., & McArdle, J. J. (2004). An experimental analysis of dynamic hypotheses about cognitive abilities and achievement from childhood to early adulthood. *Developmental Psychology, 40*, 935–952. http://dx.doi.org/10.1037/0012-1649.40.6.935

Fuster, J. M. (1997). *The prefrontal cortex: Anatomy, physiology, and neuropsychology of the frontal lobe.* New York, NY: Lippincott-Raven Press.

Garon, N., Bryson, S. E., & Smith, I. M. (2008). Executive function in preschoolers: A review using an integrative framework. *Psychological Bulletin, 134*, 31–60. http://dx.doi.org/10.1037/0033-2909.134.1.31

Garon, N., Smith, I. M., & Bryson, S. E. (2014). A novel executive function battery for preschoolers: Sensitivity to age differences. *Child Neuropsychology, 20*, 713–736. http://dx.doi.org/10.1080/09297049.2013.857650

Gerardi-Caulton, G. (2000). Sensitivity to spatial conflict and the development of self-regulation in children 24–36 months of age. *Developmental Science, 3*, 397–404. http://dx.doi.org/10.1111/1467-7687.00134

Gerstadt, C. L., Hong, Y. J., & Diamond, A. (1994). The relationship between cognition and action: Performance of children 3½–7 years old on a Stroop-like day–night test. *Cognition, 53*, 129–153. http://dx.doi.org/10.1016/0010-0277(94)90068-X

Horn, J. L., & Cattell, R. B. (1966). Refinement and test of the theory of fluid and crystallized general intelligences. *Journal of Education Psychology, 57*, 253–270.

Hughes, C., Ensor, R., Wilson, A., & Graham, A. (2009). Tracking executive function across the transition to school: A latent variable approach. *Developmental Neuropsychology, 35*, 20–36. http://dx.doi.org/10.1080/87565640903325691

Jacques, S., & Zelazo, P. D. (2001). The Flexible Item Selection Task (FIST): A measure of executive function in preschoolers. *Developmental Neuropsychology, 20*, 573–591. http://dx.doi.org/10.1207/S15326942DN2003_2

Kane, M. J., & Engle, R. W. (2003). Working-memory capacity and the control of attention: The contributions of goal neglect, response competition, and task set to Stroop interference. *Journal of Experimental Psychology: General, 132*, 47–70. http://dx.doi.org/10.1037/0096-3445.132.1.47

Kane, M. J., Hambrick, D. Z., & Conway, A. R. A. (2005). Working memory capacity and fluid intelligence are strongly related constructs: Comment on Ackerman, Beier, and Boyle (2005). *Psychological Bulletin, 131*, 66–71. http://dx.doi.org/10.1037/0033-2909.131.1.66

Kolen, M. J., & Brennan, R. L. (2004). *Test equating, scaling, and linking: Methods and practices* (2nd ed.). New York, NY: Springer-Verlag.

Korkman, M., Kirk, U., & Kemp, S. (1998). *NEPSY: A developmental neuropsychological assessment manual.* San Antonio, TX: Psychological Corporation.

Lan, X., Legare, C. H., Ponitz, C. C., Li, S., & Morrison, F. J. (2011). Investigating the links between the subcomponents of executive function and academic achievement: A cross-cultural analysis of Chinese and American preschoolers. *Journal of Experimental Child Psychology, 108*, 677–692. http://dx.doi.org/10.1016/j.jecp.2010.11.001

Luciana, M., & Nelson, C. A. (2002). Assessment of neuropsychological function through use of the Cambridge Neuropsychological Testing Automated Battery: Performance in 4- to 12-year-old children. *Developmental Neuropsychology, 22*, 595–624. http://dx.doi.org/10.1207/S15326942DN2203_3

Marcovitch, S., & Zelazo, P. D. (2009). A hierarchical competing systems model of the emergence and early development of executive function. *Developmental Science, 12*, 118. http://dx.doi.org/10.1111/j.1467-7687.2008.00754.x

Miller, E. K., & Cohen, J. D. (2001). An integrative theory of prefrontal cortex function. *Annual Review of Neuroscience, 24*, 167–202. http://dx.doi.org/10.1146/annurev.neuro.24.1.167

Miyake, A., Friedman, N. P., Emerson, M. J., Witzki, A. H., Howerter, A., & Wager, T. D. (2000). The unity and diversity of executive functions and their contributions to complex "frontal lobe" tasks: A latent variable analysis. *Cognitive Psychology, 41*, 49–100. http://dx.doi.org/10.1006/cogp.1999.0734

Murray, K. T., & Kochanska, G. (2002). Effortful control: Factor structure and relation to externalizing and internalizing behaviors. *Journal of Abnormal Child Psychology, 30*, 503–514. http://dx.doi.org/10.1023/A:1019821031523

Petrides, M., & Milner, B. (1982). Deficits on subject-ordered tasks after frontal- and temporal-lobe lesions in man. *Neuropsychologia, 20*, 249–262. http://dx.doi.org/10.1016/0028-3932(82)90100-2

Salthouse, T. A. (1996). The processing-speed theory of adult age differences in cognition. *Psychological Review, 103*, 403–428.

Shallice, T., Burgess, P., & Robertson, I. (1996). The domain of supervisory processes and temporal organization of behavior. *Philosophical Transactions of the Royal Society of London. Series B, Biological Sciences, 351*, 1405–1412. http://dx.doi.org/10.1098/rstb.1996.0124

Shing, Y. L., Lindenberger, U., Diamond, A., Li, S. C., & Davidson, M. C. (2010). Memory maintenance and inhibitory control differentiate from early childhood to adolescence. *Developmental Neuropsychology, 35*, 679–697.

Smith-Donald, R., Raver, C. C., Hayes, T., & Richardson, B. (2007). Preliminary construct and concurrent validity of the Preschool Self-Regulation Assessment (PSRA) for field-based research. *Early Childhood Research Quarterly, 22*, 173–187. http://dx.doi.org/10.1016/j.ecresq.2007.01.002

Vernon-Feagans, L., Cox, M., & Family Life Project Key Investigators. (2013). The Family Life Project: An epidemiological and developmental study of young children living in poor rural communities. *Monographs of the Society for Research in Child Development, 78*(5), 1–150.

Wiebe, S. A., Espy, K. A., & Charak, D. (2008). Using confirmatory factor analysis to understand executive control in preschool children: I. Latent structure. *Developmental Psychology, 44*, 575–587. http://dx.doi.org/10.1037/0012-1649.44.2.575

Willoughby, M., & Blair, C. (2011). Test–retest reliability of a new executive function battery for use in early childhood. *Child Neuropsychology, 17*, 564–579. http://dx.doi.org/10.1080/09297049.2011.554390

Willoughby, M. T., Blair, C. B., Wirth, R. J., & Greenberg, M. (2010). The measurement of executive function at age 3 years: Psychometric properties and criterion validity of a new battery of tasks. *Psychological Assessment, 22*, 306–317. http://dx.doi.org/10.1037/a0018708

Willoughby, M. T., Blair, C. B., Wirth, R. J., & Greenberg, M. (2012). The measurement of executive function at age 5: Psychometric properties and relationship to academic achievement. *Psychological Assessment, 24*, 226–239. http://dx.doi.org/10.1037/a0025361

Willoughby, M. T., Holochwost, S. J., Blanton, Z. E., & Blair, C. B. (2014). Executive functions: Formative versus reflective measurement. *Measurement: Interdisciplinary Research and Perspectives, 12*, 69–95. http://dx.doi.org/10.1080/15366367.2014.929453

Willoughby, M. T., Pek, J., & Blair, C. B. (2013). Measuring executive function in early childhood: A focus on maximal reliability and the derivation of short forms. *Psychological Assessment, 25*, 664–670. http://dx.doi.org/10.1037/a0031747

Willoughby, M. T., Wirth, R. J., & Blair, C. B. (2011). Contributions of modern measurement theory to measuring executive function in early childhood: An empirical demonstration. *Journal of Experimental Child Psychology, 108*, 414–435. http://dx.doi.org/10.1016/j.jecp.2010.04.007

Willoughby, M. T., Wirth, R. J., & Blair, C. B. (2012). Executive function in early childhood: Longitudinal measurement invariance and developmental change. *Psychological Assessment, 24*, 418–431. http://dx.doi.org/10.1037/a0025779

Wirth, R. J., & Edwards, M. C. (2007). Item factor analysis: Current approaches and future directions. *Psychological Methods, 12,* 58–79. http://dx.doi.org/10.1037/1082-989X.12.1.58

Zelazo, P. D. (2006). The Dimensional Change Card Sort (DCCS): A method of assessing executive function in children. *Nature Protocols, 1,* 297–301. http://dx.doi.org/10.1038/nprot.2006.46

Zelazo, P. D., Carter, A., Reznick, J. S., & Frye, D. (1997). Early development of executive function: A problem-solving framework. *Review of General Psychology, 1,* 198–226. http://dx.doi.org/10.1037/1089-2680.1.2.198

Zelazo, P. D., & Müller, U. (2002). Executive function in typical and atypical development. In U. Goswami (Ed.), *Blackwell handbook of childhood cognitive development* (pp. 445–469). Oxford, England: Blackwell.

Zelazo, P. D., Müller, U., Frye, D., Marcovitch, S., Argitis, G., & Boseovski, J., . . . Sutherland, A. (2003). The development of executive function in early childhood. *Monographs of the Society for Research in Child Development, 68*(3), vii–137.

5

CONCEPTIONS OF EXECUTIVE FUNCTION AND REGULATION: WHEN AND TO WHAT DEGREE DO THEY OVERLAP?

NANCY EISENBERG AND QING ZHOU

Until recently, work on executive function (EF) and on emotion-related self-regulation proceeded on separate tracks with relatively little overlap. EF, especially that of children, was the domain of neuroscientists, clinicians, and educational psychologists interested in academic or cognitive functioning (e.g., Barkley, 1996; Fuster, 2002; Hill, 2004) and, somewhat later, developmental scientists studying cognitive functioning (e.g., Espy et al., 2004; Frye, Zelazo, & Burack, 1998). Emotion regulation was studied mostly by developmental and clinical scientists concerned with children's socioemotional functioning, including maladjustment (e.g., Eisenberg & Fabes, 1992) and temperament (see Rothbart & Bates, 2006), with much of this work being conducted since 2000 (Adrian, Zeman, & Veits, 2011).

The writing of this chapter was supported by grants to Nancy Eisenberg from the National Institute of Mental Health and the Eunice Kennedy Shriver National Institute of Child Health and Human Development.

http://dx.doi.org/10.1037/14797-006

Executive Function in Preschool-Age Children: Integrating Measurement, Neurodevelopment, and Translational Research, J. A. Griffin, P. McCardle, and L. S. Freund (Editors)

Although investigators examining these topics with children have recently started to use similar measures and become more aware of findings across the bodies of research, the bodies of work remain somewhat isolated from the others mainly because of a lack of clarity of the connection between EF and self-regulation. In this chapter, we consider conceptions of the two constructs and their similarities and differences.

WHAT IS EXECUTIVE FUNCTION?

Most investigators agree that EF includes working memory, inhibition of responses, and set shifting. Moreover, the construct often explicitly includes flexibility, planning, evaluating errors and correcting them, fluency, anticipation, goal establishment, judgment, and decision making (see Diamond, 2006; Hammond, Bibok, & Carpendale, 2010; Zelazo, Carlson, & Kesek, 2008; see also Chapter 1, this volume). There has been just as much disagreement among investigators as to the terminology and definitions of the components of EF. For example, Zelazo et al. (2008) wrote of problem representation, planning, execution (intending and/or rule use), and evaluation (error detection and/or correction), whereas Blair, Zelazo, and Greenberg (2005) emphasized working memory and inhibition of prepotent responding. Miyake et al. (2000) discussed updating and monitoring of working memory representations and shifting between tasks or mental sets. In addition, EF generally is characterized as top-down or higher order (Carlson, 2005; Nelson, de Haan, & Thomas, 2006), goal-directed (Fuster, 2002), and involving problem solving (Zelazo et al., 2008) and control or regulation of automatic or prepotent processes (see Garon, Bryson, & Smith, 2008).

WHAT IS SELF-REGULATION?

The term *self-regulation* has been used in even more diverse ways and varied subdisciplines of the psychological sciences than has EF. A comprehensive definition of regulation is a process by which the individual modulates his or her thought, affect, behavior, or attention in either deliberate or automated use of specific skills toward guiding and maintaining goal-directed activities over time and as context changes (Karoly, 1993).

As already noted, most investigators studying children have been interested in the construct labeled *emotion regulation*, although some also discuss the construct of *self-regulation*. Some developmental scientists define emotion regulation without an emphasis on self-controlled regulatory processes. For example, according to Kopp and Neufeld (2003), emotion regulation during the early years is a developmental process that represents the deployment of intrinsic and extrinsic processes—at whatever maturity level the young child is at—to manage arousal states for: (a) affective biological and social adaptations, and (b) to achieve individual goals. (p. 360)

Thus, extrinsic processes, including adults' regulation of the child's emotion through processes such as soothing, are defined as part of emotion regulation. In a similar way, Thompson (1994) defined emotion regulation as "extrinsic and intrinsic processes responsible for monitoring, evaluating, and modifying emotional reactions, especially their intensive and temporal features, to achieve one's goals" (pp. 27–28), and Cicchetti, Ganiban, and Barnett (1991) defined it as "the intra- and extraorganismic factors by which emotional arousal is redirected, controlled, modulated, and modified to enable an individual to function adaptively in emotionally arousing situations" (p. 15).

Cole, Martin, and Dennis (2004) suggested an even broader definition: changes associated with activated emotions, including changes in the emotion itself and other psychological processes. In other words, they included in the rubric of emotion regulation two types of regulatory aspects: emotions as regulatory (changes that appear to result from the activated emotion, including in the external environment) and emotion as regulated. As a consequence, if the child's behavior had an unintentional or unknown effect on another person, this is considered emotion regulation because it regulates aspects of the external environment.

One issue, therefore, is whether a given conceptualization of emotion regulation includes regulation of emotion that is due to external forces. Of course, forces outside of children (e.g., parents) often contribute to their regulation, especially with young children, but these forces are also at play at times with older children and adults (e.g., through social or physical support or the receipt of help in dealing with a stressor). A second issue is whether one includes the regulatory effects of emotion on the behavior of others in the definition of emotion regulation. One person's emotion clearly can modulate the emotion and behavior of others. However, these types of control or regulatory processes seem somewhat different from attempts by an individual to manage one's own emotions, especially those effortfully initiated and executed by the self at a cognitive, motivational, or behavioral level. Eisenberg and Spinrad (2004) suggested that investigators differentiate conceptually and semantically between these broader definitions of emotion regulation and the narrower domain of regulation in which the individual is attempting to modulate his or her own emotion; they suggested that the latter be labeled *emotion-related self-regulation*, defined as

the process of initiating, avoiding, inhibiting, maintaining, or modulating the occurrence, form, intensity, or duration of internal feeling states, emotion-related physiological responses, attentional processes, motivational states, and/or the behavioral concomitants of emotion in the service of accomplishing affect-related biological or social adaptation or achieving individual goals. (p. 338)

Other semantic labels could be used; the point is that it is useful to differentiate in some manner among various ways in which emotion is modulated and itself modulates the environment and behavior. Consistent with Eisenberg and Spinrad's (2004) definition, Blair and Diamond (2008) argued that self-regulation refers to

the primarily *volitional* [italics added] cognitive and behavioral processes through which an individual maintains levels of emotional, motivational, and cognitive arousal that are conducive to positive adjustment and adaptation, as reflected in positive social relationships, productivity, achievement, and a positive sense of self. (p. 900)

Two related distinctions discussed in the field are between those regulatory processes that are effortfully managed versus automatic and between regulatory processes that are conscious versus unconscious. For example, Gross and Thompson (2007) defined emotion regulation as a "heterogeneous set of processes by which emotions are themselves regulated. . . . [They] may be automatic or controlled, conscious or unconscious processes. . ." (pp. 7–8). It is clear that some processes involved in emotional (and behavioral) control are unconscious and difficult to control, whereas others are more willfully controlled. However, many willfully controlled processes may not be very conscious at most times (albeit not unconscious in the sense of not being accessible at all) and, with practice, might become automatic in many situations.

Eisenberg and Spinrad (2004) used the term *emotion-related self-regulation* to not only differentiate between internal and external sources of regulation but also to try to differentiate control processes that are more effortful from those that are more involuntary. Their aforementioned definition includes effortfully (but not very consciously at times) managing the perception of stimuli and manipulating cognitions and behavior associated with emotion, generally in the service of biological or social adaptation and/or accomplishing goals.

Voluntary control of emotion or behavior is believed to be substantially based on what Rothbart has labeled *effortful control* (EC). EC is one of the major dimensions of temperament and is defined as "the efficiency of executive attention—including the ability to inhibit a dominant response and/or to activate a subdominant response, to plan, and to detect errors" (Rothbart & Bates, 2006, p. 129). In addition to planning and detecting errors, EC involves the following: (a) effortful attention focusing (the tendency to maintain attentional focus on task-related channels); (b) attention shifting (the capacity to intentionally shift the attentional focus to desired channels, thereby avoiding unintentional focusing on particular channels; Derryberry

& Rothbart, 1988); (c) inhibitory control (i.e., the capacity to suppress positively toned impulses and thereby resist the execution of inappropriate approach tendencies; Derryberry & Rothbart, 1988; Evans & Rothbart, 2007) and (d) activation control (i.e., the capacity to perform an action when there is a strong tendency to avoid; Evans & Rothbart, 2007; or, stated differently, the capacity to suppress negatively toned impulses and thereby resist the execution of inappropriate avoidance tendencies; Derryberry & Rothbart, 1988). In addition, many tasks used to assess EC involve successfully resolving conflict tasks that require the ability to make decisions in the presence of discrepant or conflicting stimuli (e.g., Flanker and Stroop tasks; Rothbart & Bates, 2006).

The aforementioned processes are willful or effortful in that they can be used by the individual to achieve goals and can be turned on and off as needed. The capacities involved in EC can be viewed as tools for the regulation of emotion, cognition, motivation, and behavior, although some aspects of EC probably are more involved than others in various specific regulatory tasks (e.g., attentional control is probably more involved in modulation of felt sadness than is inhibitory control). It is highly unlikely that attempts at EC are always or typically consciously enacted (in that the person is actively aware of engaging in them), and we would argue that these processes are often automatically used. Nonetheless, EC is conceptualized as top-down control rather than bottom-up control, with its core being executive attention (Rothbart & Bates, 2006).

Eisenberg and Spinrad (2004) further differentiated between the constructs of control (defined as inhibition or constraint) and regulation (actually, self-regulation, as defined above). Self-regulation is viewed as including optimal levels of control as well as other abilities (e.g., activation control, or the ability to willfully initiate subdominant behaviors, even when one does not really wish to do so; Evans & Rothbart, 2007). Consistent with the ideas of Block and Block (1980) and Cole, Michel, and Teti (1994), they argued that well-regulated individuals are not overly controlled or undercontrolled; rather, optimal regulation often involves moderate and flexible levels of control. Thus, the well-regulated individual can be constrained when necessary but can be spontaneous when there is no need for constraint.

Similar to others who have noted a range of control- or regulation-related processes (e.g., Derryberry & Rothbart, 1997; Gross & Thompson, 2007), Eisenberg and Spinrad (2004) suggested that, in contrast to EC, some control-related processes are less flexible, relatively involuntary, and so automatic that they are difficult to bring under voluntary control. We have used the term *reactive control* to refer to the relatively involuntary aspects of control. Reactive control includes temperamentally based reactive behaviors such as impulsivity and behavioral inhibition (Kagan, 1998) that are associated with motivational tendencies (e.g., approach and avoidance tendencies, respectively). Similar distinctions have been made by other researchers (e.g., Carver, 2005). Of course, both effortful and reaction control, as well as emotion, likely contribute to the ways in which individuals attempt to modulate emotion, cognition, and behavior and their success in doing so (also see Blair & Ursche, 2011; Compas, Connor-Smith, Saltzman, Thomsen, & Wadsworth, 2001; Zelazo & Cunningham, 2007).

Effortful and reactive control can be differentiated statistically as well as conceptually. In three studies with either preschool-age or school-age children, we have found separate latent constructs for effortful and reactive control constructs (Eisenberg et al., 2004, 2013; Spinrad et al., 2006; Valiente et al., 2003). Moreover, we have found some unique or differential prediction of outcomes by effortful and reactive control (e.g., Eisenberg et al., 2000, 2004; Spinrad et al., 2006; Valiente et al., 2003).

TASKS USED TO ASSESS EXECUTIVE FUNCTION AND EXECUTIVE CONTROL AND THEIR ASSOCIATION

The tasks people use to measure EF, self-regulation, or EC often depend on the investigator's definition of the constructs and on the positioning of the research historically and in terms of discipline or subdiscipline. However, one can make some generalizations about tasks traditionally or typically used to assess these constructs.

Executive Function Tasks

Tasks used to tap EF tend to involve abstract, higher order cognitive processing and frequently assess working memory, inhibitory control, and/or attentional control (e.g., shifting attention). Because working memory tasks are not similar to those used to measure self-regulation and usually are not considered part of that construct, we do not discuss them here (see Garon et al., 2008, for examples).

Garon et al. (2008) discussed several typical EF tasks that clearly involve primarily higher order cognitive processes. One type involves a child holding a given rule in mind, responding in a manner consistent with this rule, and inhibiting an opposing prepotent response. For example, on one common task, children are asked to tap twice with a wooden dowel when the experimenter taps once, and once when the experimenter taps twice (Diamond & Taylor, 1996; knocking versus tapping with the hand is a common variation for young children).

Another set of tasks discussed by Garon et al. (2008) involves forming an arbitrary stimulus–response (S-R) set in the first phase and shifting to a new S-R set in the second phase. In one such spatial response shifting task, a reward is placed under one of two identical cups when concealed behind a screen. Once the reward has been successfully retrieved by the child for a certain number of consecutive trials, the side where it is hidden is reversed. In another, slightly different type of task, the procedure is similar to that just described but the first mental set involves attention to one aspect of the stimuli (e.g., color of an object to be sorted) and the shifting phase involves shifting attention to a new aspect of the stimuli (e.g., sorting by shape, as in the Dimensional Change Card Sort [DCCS]; see Jacques & Zelazo, 2001; Zelazo & Frye, 1998).

The aforementioned tasks are most commonly used to assess EF and are less frequently used to measure self-regulation and EC. In addition to those sorts of tasks, some investigators have considered delay-of-gratification tasks as well as some of the tasks involving behavioral inhibitory control (including some of Kochanska, Murray, & Harlan's [2000] tasks discussed in the next section) to be measures of EF (e.g., Carlson, 2005; Garon et al., 2008; Gerardi-Caulton, 2000). Thus, some investigators have operationalized EF in a much broader manner than have others, including tasks that involve motivational pulls and motor restraint as well as higher order cognitive skills.

Self-Regulation/Effortful Control Tasks

In contrast to EF, emotion regulation and EC often have been assessed with parent- or teacher-report questionnaires about children's regulation, including their attentional control, inhibitory control, persistence (e.g., grit), and emotion regulation (e.g., Capaldi & Rothbart, 1992; Duckworth & Quinn, 2009; Gartstein & Rothbart, 2003; Putnam, Gartstein, & Rothbart, 2006; Rothbart, Ahadi, Hershey, & Fisher, 2001; Shields & Cicchetti, 1997; see also Eisenberg, Morris, & Spinrad, 2005). Some questionnaire measures of regulation contain few items measuring components of EF (e.g., Shields & Cicchetti, 1997). Although most questionnaire measures of regulation refer to situations involving the regulation of emotions, some items on EC questionnaires tap situations involving higher order cognitive skills in relatively nonemotional contexts (e.g., "Prepares for trips and outings by planning things s/he will need"), as well as the use of attention and inhibitory skills in situations involving rewards and punishments and hence, emotionally driven motivation ("Is usually able to resist temptation when told s/he is not supposed to do something"; Rothbart et al., 2001).

In addition, a range of observational measures have been used to measure EC. For example, Kochanska and colleagues (Kochanska, Murray, & Coy, 1997; Kochanska et al., 2000; Kochanska, Murray, Jacques, Koenig, & Vandegeest, 1996) constructed batteries of observational tasks to assess the EC, especially inhibitory control, of toddlers, preschoolers, and young schoolchildren. These batteries typically assess toddlers' or children's ability to (a) delay gratification, (b) slow down motor behavior, (c) suppress or initiate activity to a signal, or (d) effortfully manage attention. Other researchers have used somewhat similar tasks to assess effortful inhibitory control in school-age children and adolescents (e.g., Eisenberg et al., 2001; Olson, Schilling, & Bates, 1999; White et al., 1994).

In typical delay-of-gratification tasks, a child is asked to wait to touch or play with an attractive toy, wait to open a gift, or delay eating a tasty snack (Grolnick, Bridges, & Connell, 1996; Kochanska et al., 1997, 2000; Kochanska, Tjebkes, & Forman, 1998). These tasks involve inhibiting behavior upon command; in contrast, other delay tasks used with young children assess the ability or tendency to voluntarily make the choice to delay a reward (e.g., eating pretzels) for a period of time to obtain a larger reward (Mischel, Ebbesen, & Raskoff Zeiss, 1972; Prencipe & Zelazo, 2005). Performance on tasks in which children are told to delay or can choose to delay to obtain a larger reward may reflect not only attentional and behavioral control but also impulsivity (i.e., reactive undercontrol), especially for those children who cannot delay by means of exerting EC.

Tasks that require inhibition of motor activities include those in which children are asked to draw a line as slowly as possible (e.g., Kochanska et al., 2000) or to make a toy turtle and rabbit negotiate a path slowly and quickly, respectively (researchers then look at the difference in timing from a baseline and care taken in staying on the path; Kochanska et al., 2000). A typical task designed to measure the abilities to both suppress and initiate motor activity is a version of Simon Says. Such tasks measure the child's ability to follow instructions given by, for example, one toy animal (initiate activity) and to ignore instructions given by a different toy animal (suppress activity; Kochanska et al., 1996; Reed, Pien, & Rothbart, 1984).

An attention control task in Kochanska et al.'s (2000) battery is a Stroop-like task in which a child has to name the smaller fruit rather than the larger fruit in pictures where the image of the smaller fruit is embedded in that of the larger one. Other computer-based tasks assessing attentional control are similar to EF tasks. For example, children are asked to respond on a computer key to certain target stimuli and to restrain from responding to other stimuli (e.g., National Institute of Child Health and Human Development Early Child Care Research Network, 2003; Sulik et al., 2010). In addition to the aforementioned behavioral measures, tasks that assess persistence on a frustrating task have been used to assess EC (e.g., Eisenberg et al., 2000).

A frequently used behavioral measure of emotion regulation is Saarni's (1984) task that assesses children's control of facial or behavioral indicators of disappointment when receiving a disappointing gift. It is assumed that even preschoolers know that it is socially appropriate to appear grateful rather than upset when receiving a gift. The measure probably taps modulation of emotion and/or effortful inhibitory control of the expression of emotion (Cole, Zahn-Waxler, & Smith, 1994; Eisenberg et al., 2001). Anger control was recently examined in a different way—in response to losing a game to a peer who cheated. In this creative study, Smith, Hubbard, and Laurenceau (2011) measured facial, self-reported, and physiological responses to this upsetting experience and documented several different profiles of response. These sorts of measures, although they may tap individual differences in emotion as well as regulation, likely are more direct indices of emotion regulation than are pure measures of EF or EC.

RELATIONS BETWEEN EXECUTIVE
FUNCTION AND REGULATION

As already discussed, some definitions of EF include self-regulation or equate the two constructs (e.g., Carlson, 2005; Hrabok & Kerns, 2010). For example, Blair et al. (2005) defined EF as including "a number of cognitive processes that are integral to the emerging self-regulation of behavior and developing social and cognitive competence in young children" (p. 561).

Zelazo and Cunningham (2007) suggested that when the problem to be solved is modulating emotion, EF and emotion regulation are the same, but when modulation of emotion occurs in the service of solving another problem, then EF involves emotion regulation. Blair and Ursche (2011) argued that EF not only facilitates self-regulation but is sometimes a consequence of regulation of lower order, more automatic emotion, attention, and stress response systems. If individuals are not optimally regulated (e.g., are highly stressed), they will be unlikely to flexibly control attention, which will undercut EF. Blair and Ursche (2011) further suggested that executive attention (which Rothbart views as the core of EC) is "a relatively fast psychophysical phenomenon" whereas EF is "somewhat slower and more consciously effortful or deliberate" (p. 307); thus, executive attention is viewed by these authors as the attentional component of EF that is necessary for directing cognitive resources in situations that require more sophisticated EF (e.g., resolving conflict by holding information in working memory, inhibiting automatic responses, shifting cognitive set).

How similar conceptions of EF and self- or emotion regulation are depends on whether or not one defines regulation as involving the effortful or volitional aspects of self-regulation. There are quite obvious differences between EF and regulation if one includes external regulators (e.g., parents calming their child to provide regulation) or the effects of a child's own emotion on the social environment in the construct of regulation. Moreover, reactive control processes do not overlap as well as effortful processes overlap with EF processes (although reactive processes may be modulated by EF and/or EC and affect the degree to which the latter processes are evoked).

The overlap between the constructs of EF and effortful self-regulation is very obvious when the definition of the latter includes only the more effortful, internally based capacities used for the control/regulation of cognition, motivation, behavior, and/or physiological responding. In the remainder of this chapter, we focus primarily on contrasting EF with conceptions of self-regulation that involve volitional control.

Even when one considers typical definitions and measures of EF and EC or self-regulation, one can identify a number of similarities and differences between the constructs (Eisenberg, 2010; Zhou, Chen, & Main, 2012). In terms of similarities, both EF and EC focus on being able to manage attention as needed to adapt or reach a goal; indeed, executive attention is considered the core of EC (Rothbart & Bates, 2006). Furthermore, planning and error detection are part of both EF and EC. Both emphasize involvement of frontal lobes and executive attention (Hrabok & Kerns, 2010; Rothbart & Bates, 2006). Both constructs also include inhibitory processes, although EF is discussed more in relation to the managing of internal cognitive and attentional processes (e.g., on Stroop-type measures) whereas EC is most often discussed as involving inhibition of motivationally, emotionally driven behaviors (although attention focusing could be viewed as often based on inhibition of nonfocal cognitive and attentional distracters). Nonetheless, similar measures of inhibition (go/no-go tasks, peg-tapping tasks, Stroop tasks) are increasingly used to assess both constructs.

Activational control is a core type of EC (Derryberry & Rothbart, 1988). Similarly, sometimes EF has been described as involving the willful activation of behavior as needed for goal completion (e.g., Zelazo, Carter, Reznick, & Frye, 1997), although goal-directed action would not be the same as activation control unless the goal to be completed is subordinate to another desired behavior or goal (i.e., the individual has to force him- or herself to engage in goal-directed behavior because he or she would rather do something else).

Coping behaviors have been viewed as the regulation of emotion in stressful contexts (Compas et al., 2001; Eisenberg, Fabes, & Guthrie, 1997) and have been positively related to children's use of active coping (Lengua & Long, 2002). Sometimes coping efforts (e.g., active coping, distraction) map fairly well onto executive control skills (if the focus is on goal-directed behavior) and sometimes they do not (e.g., avoidant coping, venting).

There are also a number of differences in conceptualizations of EF and EC. First, modulation of emotion is more often viewed as fundamental to EC than it is to EF. Indeed, in Rothbart's model (see Rothbart & Bates, 2006), temperamental EC regulates temperamental reactivity, including emotional reactivity. Conversely, as already noted, working memory is a core component of EF but not of EC, although working memory can be a tool for implementing regulation (see Hofmann, Friese, Schmeichel, & Baddeley, 2011), and individual differences in working memory have been related to individual differences in regulation (Bernier, Carlson, & Whipple, 2010; Schmeichel, Volokhov, & Demaree, 2008). In addition, parasympathetic nervous system processes (e.g., heart rate variability, vagal tone, or respiratory sinus arrhythmia) are discussed as physiological regulation but generally are ignored in discussions of EF (see Appelhans & Luecken, 2006).

There is also a relative difference in the focus on hot versus cool EF-type cognition. Mischel and colleagues (e.g., Metcalfe & Mischel, 1999) distinguished between a hot emotion system (quick emotional processing and reflexive approach-avoidance reactions to emotionally evocative stimuli) and a cool, cognitive system of self-regulation (specializing in complex, reflective cognitive processing and planful reactions to emotionally neutral stimuli). We would argue that the hot system reflects reactive temperamentally based processes (i.e., reactive overcontrol or undercontrol and emotion) whereas the cooler system is more clearly involved in EF and EC. However, EF and EC tasks can vary in terms of the degree to which hot, reactive processes are in conflict with cooler processes. Zelazo and Cunningham (2007) proposed a neural model of EF that positions hot and cool EF on a continuum of reflective processing and emphasizes the way in which relatively hot and relatively cool components interact when one is solving a problem. They argue that hot EF is often elicited by problems involving the regulation of emotion and motivation (e.g., rewards or losses), whereas cool EF tends to be elicited by abstract, decontextualized problems (e.g., sorting tasks). An alternative view is that EF does not change in quality but sometimes is used in hot contexts involving emotion and motivation.

Building on this idea, in general, researchers studying emotion regulation have been particularly interested in contexts involving emotion (e.g., delay, frustration) or hot EF task abilities, although they sometimes use measures of cool functioning. Hot responding has been of concern because of its relevance for behaviors such as externalizing problems and the expression of emotion. In contrast, many EF researchers have been less interested in such hot contexts and tend to focus on the decontextualized, cool tasks, although, as already noted, some view the hot tasks (e.g., delay tasks, tasks involving rewards and losses) as tapping EF (e.g., Garon et al., 2008).

RELATIONS BETWEEN MEASURES OF EXECUTIVE FUNCTION AND EFFORTFUL CONTROL

A number of investigators have used batteries of tasks that include procedures typically used to assess EC and EF. Often tasks traditionally used to measure EF and EC have been significantly intercorrelated. For example,

Gerardi-Caulton (2000) found that a typical cold EF task (resolving conflict between identity and location for 24- to 36-month-olds) related to adult-reported EC and behavioral measures of EC (also see Blair & Razza, 2007). Similarly, Hongwanishkul, Happaney, Lee, and Zelazo (2005) found small to moderate correlations between cool EF (working memory and flexible rule use) and parent-reported EC, although they did not find correlations between hot EF (measured by gambling and delay tasks) and parent-reported EC among 3- to 5-year-olds. Ellis, Rothbart, and Posner (2004) found a significant relation between mother-reported (but not self-reported) EC and adolescents' performance on a computerized measure of executive attention (a Flanker task). Li-Grining (2007) found moderate correlations between measures of delayed gratification and executive control. Muris, van der Pennen, Sigmond, and Mayer (2008) reported a correlation between a measure of attentional EC (but not another, less verified measure that included inhibitory and attentional EC) and some behavioral measures of 8- to 12-year-olds' EF. Using similar measures and samples, Verstraeten, Vasey, Claes, and Bijttebier (2010) found a similar but much weaker pattern of correlations, and primarily for one of two samples of children. In a longitudinal study, the abilities to resist temptation and focus on a delay-of-gratification task during the preschool years predict better performance on an inhibitory (i.e., a go/ no-go) task at 14 years (Eigsti et al., 2006). Thus, in general, some small to moderate patterns of relations have been found between typical measures of EC and EF.

In addition, researchers sometimes have found that some tasks typically used to measure EF (sometimes labeled *low cognitive impulsivity*) loaded on the same factor with tasks typically used to assess regulation (including delay tasks; e.g., Allan & Lonigan, 2011; Olson, Bates, & Bayles, 1990; White et al., 1994; see also Kindlon et al., 1995). For example, Prencipe et al. (2011) found that four tasks of EF and/or regulation, including two cold tasks (a color word Stroop and backward digit span) typically used to assess EF and two hot tasks (a gambling task and delay discounting) often seen as tasks of self-regulation (albeit viewed by Prencipe et al., 2011, as indices of EF) loaded on one factor. Similarly, with children age 36 to 71 months, Allan and Lonigan (2011) tested single and multiple factors for measures of hot (e.g., tasks involving delay, executing a task quickly for points for a reward) and cool EC tasks and found that the measures were best characterized by a single factor. This pattern of findings is consistent with the fact that neuroscientists have found that the same parts of the brain—for example, the right ventrolateral prefrontal cortex (Cohen & Lieberman, 2010)—are involved in a variety of self-regulation tasks, including motor response inhibition, delay of gratification, regulating emotion, thought inhibition, and memory inhibition.

In other studies, however, measures of impulse control and measures of more cognitive aspects of EF have tended to load on separate factors, although the factors were not always entirely pure in this regard (e.g., Carlson & Moses, 2001; Olson et al., 1990). Moreover, although Bernier et al. (2010) obtained two factors, the measures of impulse control were all from the same task and highly similar, which might have caused them to load on a factor separate from the other measures of EF. Similarly, Willoughby, Kupersmidt, Voegler-Lee, and Bryant (2011) found that two hot and two cool measures of regulation loaded on separate factors; however, their two hot measures were very similar (both delay tasks involving food).

Sulik et al. (2010) administered a battery of tasks to measure self-regulation to a sample of high-risk Hispanic, European American, and African American children. The battery included tasks that typically measure EC (Don't Peek, Bird/Dragon, Gift Wrap, Waiting for Bow, Rabbit/Turtle, Yarn Tangle) and some that are used to assess EF (Knock/Tap, a computer-based continuous performance task in which a child has to hit a key when he or she sees a certain picture but not others), as well as teacher-reported EC.

In a series of confirmatory factor analyses, they obtained evidence for a one-factor model that demonstrated factorial, metric, and partial scalar equivalence across the three racial/ethnic groups (Sulik et al., 2010). When they conducted two-factor exploratory factor analyses, the three delay or persistence tasks (Gift Wrap, Waiting for Bow, and Yarn Tangle) primarily loaded on one factor, whereas the other behavioral tasks tapping both EC and EF loaded on a second factor, providing some support for the distinction of delay or persistence tasks from other EC and/or EF tasks, despite the small eigenvalue on the second factor. In the confirmatory factor analyses, the Bayesian information criterion statistic did not clearly favor a one- versus two-factor multigroup model; however, the correlations between the factors in the two-factor model were .75 or above in each racial/ethnic group, suggesting that the two factors were highly related. When two factors were tested separately in each ethnic group, the model would not converge for the Hispanic group, so the one-factor model was clearly preferable for that subgroup. Thus, it is not entirely clear if typical EF and EC tasks load on one or two intercorrelated factors; differences in results likely depend in large part on the tasks used in the given study.

CONCLUSION

The degree of overlap between both conceptual definitions and measures for EF and regulation/EC depends on the role of involuntary and/or unconscious behavior in EC and the degree to which EF is assessed with tasks involving hot motivation. EF skills have traditionally been seen as tools that more (e.g., inhibition) or less (working memory) involve regulation but all may contribute to modulation of cognition, emotion, and behavior. When theory and research on EF and on conceptions of self-regulation emphasizing volitional or effortful processes is considered, the major difference is in regard to the tasks chosen and the focus on relatively hot versus cool decontextualized processes (or contexts). The role of working memory, a major component of EF but not of constructs of self-regulation (including emotion regulation or coping), depends partly on the complexity of tasks used to assess these constructs and is more central to complex EF tasks. It is clear that the ideas and findings in research on EF and self-regulation/EC are increasingly overlapping and are of great relevance to one another. Future research should also further investigate the specific roles and processes of various EF skills (e.g., inhibition, set shifting) in individuals' regulation of cognition, emotion, and behaviors in various contexts or situations (e.g., coping with stressors, regulating facial expression of emotions, responding to reward or punishment). It would be useful to further clarify, however, the complex role of motivation—for example, the desires to obtain rewards and avoid losing rewards or facing aversive outcomes—and, more generally, subcortical functioning in EF and self-regulation.

REFERENCES

Adrian, M., Zeman, J., & Veits, G. (2011). Methodological implications of the affect revolution: A 35-year review of emotion regulation assessment in children. *Journal of Experimental Child Psychology, 110*, 171–197. http://dx.doi.org/10.1016/j.jecp.2011.03.009

Allan, N. P., & Lonigan, C. J. (2011). Examining the dimensionality of effortful control in preschool children and its relation to academic and socioemotional indicators. *Developmental Psychology, 47*, 905–915. http://dx.doi.org/10.1037/a0023748

Appelhans, B. M., & Luecken, L. J. (2006). Heart rate variability as an index of regulated emotional responding. *Review of General Psychology, 10*, 229–240. http://dx.doi.org/10.1037/1089-2680.10.3.229

Barkley, R. A. (1996). Linkages between attention and executive functions. In G. R. Lyon & N. A. Krasnegor (Eds.), *Attention, memory, and executive function* (pp. 307–325). Baltimore, MD: Paul H. Brookes.

Bernier, A., Carlson, S. M., & Whipple, N. (2010). From external regulation to self-regulation: Early parenting precursors of young children's executive functioning. *Child Development, 81*, 326–339. http://dx.doi.org/10.1111/j.1467-8624.2009.01397.x

Blair, C., & Diamond, A. (2008). Biological processes in prevention and intervention: The promotion of self-regulation as a means of preventing school failure. *Development and Psychopathology, 20,* 899–911. http://dx.doi.org/10.1017/S0954579408000436

Blair, C., & Razza, R. P. (2007). Relating effortful control, executive function, and false belief understanding to emerging math and literacy ability in kindergarten. *Child Development, 78,* 647–663. http://dx.doi.org/10.1111/j.1467-8624.2007.01019.x

Blair, C., & Ursche, A. (2011). A bi-directional model of executive functions and self-regulation. In K. D. Vohs & R. F. Baumeister (Eds.), *Handbook of self-regulation: Research, theory, and applications* (pp. 300–320). New York, NY: Guilford Press.

Blair, C., Zelazo, P. D., & Greenberg, M. T. (2005). The measurement of executive function in early childhood. *Developmental Neuropsychology, 28,* 561–571. http://dx.doi.org/10.1207/s15326942dn2802_1

Block, J. H., & Block, J. (1980). The role of ego-control and ego-resiliency in the organization of behavior. In W. A. Collins (Ed.), *The Minnesota Symposia on Child Psychology: Vol. 13. Development of cognition, affect, and social relations* (pp. 39–101). Hillsdale, NJ: Erlbaum.

Capaldi, D. M., & Rothbart, M. K. (1992). Development and validation of an early adolescent temperament measure. *The Journal of Early Adolescence, 12,* 153–173. http://dx.doi.org/10.1177/0272431692012002002

Carlson, S. M. (2005). Developmentally sensitive measures of executive function in preschool children. *Developmental Neuropsychology, 28,* 595–616. http://dx.doi.org/10.1207/s15326942dn2802_3

Carlson, S. M., & Moses, L. J. (2001). Individual differences in inhibitory control and children's theory of mind. *Child Development, 72,* 1032–1053. http://dx.doi.org/10.1111/1467-8624.00333

Carver, C. S. (2005). Impulse and constraint: Perspectives from personality psychology, convergence with theory in other areas, and potential for integration. *Personality and Social Psychology Review, 9,* 312–333. http://dx.doi.org/10.1207/s15327957pspr0904_2

Cicchetti, D., Ganiban, J., & Barnett, D. (1991). The development of emotion regulation. In K. Dodge & J. Garber (Eds.), *Contributions from the study of high-risk populations to understanding the development of emotion regulation* (pp. 15–48). New York, NY: Cambridge University Press.

Cohen, J. R., & Lieberman, M. D. (2010). The common neural basis of exerting neural self-control in multiple domains. In R. R. Hassin, K. N. Oscher, & Y. Trope (Eds.), *Self control in society, mind, and brain* (pp. 141–160). New York, NY: Oxford University Press.

Cole, P. M., Martin, S. E., & Dennis, T. A. (2004). Emotion regulation as a scientific construct: Methodological challenges and directions for child development research. *Child Development, 75,* 317–333. http://dx.doi.org/10.1111/j.1467-8624.2004.00673.x

Cole, P. M., Michel, M. K., & Teti, L. O. (1994). The development of emotion regulation and dysregulation: A clinical perspective. *Monographs of the*

Society for Research in Child Development, 59(2–3), 73–100. http://dx.doi. org/10.2307/1166139

Cole, P. M., Zahn-Waxler, C., & Smith, K. D. (1994). Expressive control during a disappointment: Variations related to preschoolers' behavior problems. *Developmental Psychology, 30,* 835–846. http://dx.doi.org/10.1037/0012-1649. 30.6.835

Compas, B. E., Connor-Smith, J. K., Saltzman, H., Thomsen, A. H., & Wadsworth, M. E. (2001). Coping with stress during childhood and adolescence: Problems, progress, and potential in theory and research. *Psychological Bulletin, 127,* 87–127. http://dx.doi.org/10.1037/0033-2909.127.1.87

Derryberry, D., & Rothbart, M. K. (1988). Arousal, affect, and attention as components of temperament. *Journal of Personality and Social Psychology, 55,* 958–966. http://dx.doi.org/10.1037/0022-3514.55.6.958

Derryberry, D., & Rothbart, M. K. (1997). Reactive and effortful processes in the organization of temperament. *Development and Psychopathology, 9,* 633–652. http://dx.doi.org/10.1017/S0954579497001375

Diamond, A. (2006). The early development of executive functions. In E. Bialystock & F. I. M. Craik (Eds.), *Lifespan cognition: Mechanisms of change* (pp. 70–95). Oxford, England: Oxford University Press. http://dx.doi.org/10.1093/acprof: oso/9780195169539.003.0006

Diamond, A., & Taylor, C. (1996). Development of an aspect of executive control: Development of the abilities to remember what I said and to "do as I say, not as I do." *Developmental Psychobiology, 29,* 315–334. http://dx.doi.org/10.1002/ (SICI)1098-2302(199605)29:4<315::AID-DEV2>3.0.CO;2-T

Duckworth, A. L., & Quinn, P. D. (2009). Development and validation of the short grit scale (Grit-S). *Journal of Personality Assessment, 91,* 166–174. http://dx.doi. org/10.1080/00223890802634290

Eigsti, I.-M., Zayas, V., Mischel, W., Shoda, Y., Ayduk, O., Dadlani, M. B., . . . Casey, B. J. (2006). Predicting cognitive control from preschool to late adolescence and young adulthood. *Psychological Science, 17,* 478–484. http://dx.doi. org/10.1111/j.1467-9280.2006.01732.x

Eisenberg, N. (2010, June). *Executive functioning and children's regulation: Conceptual issues.* Paper presented at the National Institute of Child Health and Human Development Workshop on Executive Function in Preschool Children: Current Knowledge and Research Opportunities, Bethesda, MD.

Eisenberg, N., Cumberland, A., Spinrad, T. L., Fabes, R. A., Shepard, S. A., Reiser, M., . . . Guthrie, I. K. (2001). The relations of regulation and emotionality to children's externalizing and internalizing problem behavior. *Child Development, 72,* 1112–1134. http://dx.doi.org/10.1111/1467-8624.00337

Eisenberg, N., Edwards, A., Spinrad, T. L., Sallquist, J., Eggum, N. D., & Reiser, M. (2013). Are effortful and reactive control unique constructs in young children? *Developmental Psychology, 49,* 2082–2094. http://dx.doi.org/10.1037/ a0031745

Eisenberg, N., & Fabes, R. A. (1992). Emotion, regulation, and the development of social competence. In M. S. Clark (Ed.), *Review of personality and social psychology: Vol. 14. Emotion and social behavior* (pp. 119–150). Newbury Park, CA: Sage.

Eisenberg, N., Fabes, R. A., & Guthrie, I. K. (1997). Coping with stress. The roles of regulation and development. In S. A. Wolchik & I. N. Sandler (Eds.), *Handbook of children's coping: Linking theory and intervention* (pp. 41–70). New York, NY: Plenum Press.

Eisenberg, N., Guthrie, I. K., Fabes, R. A., Shepard, S., Losoya, S., Murphy, B. C., . . . Reiser, M. (2000). Prediction of elementary school children's externalizing problem behaviors from attentional and behavioral regulation and negative emotionality. *Child Development, 71,* 1367–1382. http://dx.doi.org/10.1111/1467-8624.00233

Eisenberg, N., Morris, A. S., & Spinrad, T. L. (2005). Emotion-related regulation: The construct and its measurement. In D. M. Teti (Ed.), *Handbook of research methods in developmental psychology* (pp. 423–442). Oxford, England: Blackwell.

Eisenberg, N., & Spinrad, T. L. (2004). Emotion-related regulation: Sharpening the definition. *Child Development, 75,* 334–339. http://dx.doi.org/10.1111/j.1467-8624.2004.00674.x

Eisenberg, N., Spinrad, T. L., Fabes, R. A., Reiser, M., Cumberland, A., Shepard, S. A., . . . Thompson, M. (2004). The relations of effortful control and impulsivity to children's resiliency and adjustment. *Child Development, 75,* 25–46. http://dx.doi.org/10.1111/j.1467-8624.2004.00652.x

Ellis, L. K., Rothbart, M. K., & Posner, M. I. (2004). Individual differences in executive attention predict self-regulation and adolescent psychosocial behaviors. In R. E. Dahl & L. P. Spear (Eds.), *Adolescent brain development: Vulnerabilities and opportunities* (pp. 337–340). New York, NY: New York Academy of Sciences.

Espy, K. A., McDiarmid, M. M., Cwik, M. F., Stalets, M. M., Hamby, A., & Senn, T. E. (2004). The contribution of executive functions to emergent mathematic skills in preschool children. *Developmental Neuropsychology, 26,* 465–486. http://dx.doi.org/10.1207/s15326942dn2601_6

Evans, D. E., & Rothbart, M. K. (2007). Developing a model for adult temperament. *Journal of Research in Personality, 41,* 868–888. http://dx.doi.org/10.1016/j.jrp.2006.11.002

Frye, D., Zelazo, P. D., & Burack, J. A. (1998). Cognitive complexity and control: I. Theory of mind in typical and atypical development. *Current Directions in Psychological Science, 7,* 116–121. http://dx.doi.org/10.1111/1467-8721.ep10774754

Fuster, J. M. (2002). Physiology of executive functions: The perception–action cycle. In D. T. Stuss & R. T. Knight (Eds.), *Principles of frontal lobe function* (pp. 96–108). New York, NY: Oxford University Press.

Garon, N., Bryson, S. E., & Smith, I. M. (2008). Executive function in preschoolers: A review using an integrative framework. *Psychological Bulletin, 134*, 31–60. http://dx.doi.org/10.1037/0033-2909.134.1.31

Gartstein, M. A., & Rothbart, M. K. (2003). Studying infant temperament via the Revised Infant Behavior Questionnaire. *Infant Behavior and Development, 26*, 64–86. http://dx.doi.org/10.1016/S0163-6383(02)00169-8

Gerardi-Caulton, G. (2000). Sensitivity to spatial conflict and the development of self-regulation in children 24–36 months of age. *Developmental Science, 3*, 397–404. http://dx.doi.org/10.1111/1467-7687.00134

Grolnick, W. S., Bridges, L. J., & Connell, J. P. (1996). Emotion regulation in 2-year-olds: Strategies and emotional expression in four contexts. *Child Development, 67*, 928–941. http://dx.doi.org/10.2307/1131871

Gross, J. J., & Thompson, R. A. (2007). Emotion regulation: Conceptual foundations. In J. J. Gross (Ed.), *Handbook of emotion regulation* (pp. 3–24). New York, NY: Guilford Press.

Hammond, S. I., Bibok, M. B., & Carpendale, J. I. M. (2010). Theoretical perspectives on self and social regulation. In B. W. Sokol, U. Muller, J. I. M. Carpendale, A. R. Young, & G. Iarocci (Eds.), *Self and social regulation: Social interaction and the development of social understanding and executive functions* (pp. 1–34). Oxford, England: Oxford University Press.

Hill, E. L. (2004). Evaluating the theory of executive dysfunction in autism. *Developmental Review, 24*, 189–233. http://dx.doi.org/10.1016/j.dr.2004.01.001

Hofmann, W., Friese, M., Schmeichel, B. J., & Baddeley, A. D. (2011). Working memory and self-regulation. In K. D. Vohs & R. F. Baumeister (Eds.), *Handbook of self-regulation. Research, theory, and applications* (pp. 204–225). New York, NY: Guilford Press.

Hongwanishkul, D., Happaney, K. R., Lee, W. S. C., & Zelazo, P. D. (2005). Assessment of hot and cool executive function in young children: Age-related changes and individual differences. *Developmental Neuropsychology, 28*, 617–644. http://dx.doi.org/10.1207/s15326942dn2802_4

Hrabok, M., & Kerns, K. A. (2010). The development of self-regulation: A neuropsychological perspective. In B. W. Sokol, U. Muller, J. I. M. Carpendale, A. R. Young, & G. Iarocci (Eds.), *Self and social regulation: Social interaction and the development of social understanding and executive functions* (pp. 129–154). Oxford, England: Oxford University Press.

Jacques, S., & Zelazo, P. D. (2001). The Flexible Item Selection Task (FIST): A measure of executive function in preschoolers. *Developmental Neuropsychology, 20*, 573–591. http://dx.doi.org/10.1207/S15326942DN2003_2

Kagan, J. (1998). Biology and the child. In W. Damon (Series Ed.) & N. Eisenberg (Vol. Ed.), *Handbook of child psychology: Vol. 3. Social, emotional, and personality development* (pp. 177–235). New York, NY: Wiley.

Karoly, P. (1993). Mechanisms of self-regulation: A systems view. *Annual Review of Psychology, 44*, 23–52. http://dx.doi.org/10.1146/annurev.ps.44.020193.000323

Kindlon, D., Mezzacappa, E., & Earls, F. (1995). Psychometric properties of impulsivity measures: Temporal stability, validity, and factor structure. *The Journal of Child Psychology and Psychiatry, 36*, 645–661. http://dx.doi.org/10.1111/j.1469-7610.1995.tb02319.x

Kochanska, G., Murray, K., & Coy, K. C. (1997). Inhibitory control as a contributor to conscience in childhood: From toddler to early school age. *Child Development, 68*, 263–277. http://dx.doi.org/10.2307/1131849

Kochanska, G., Murray, K. T., & Harlan, E. T. (2000). Effortful control in early childhood: Continuity and change, antecedents, and implications for social development. *Developmental Psychology, 36*, 220–232. http://dx.doi.org/10.1037/0012-1649.36.2.220

Kochanska, G., Murray, K., Jacques, T. Y., Koenig, A. L., & Vandegeest, K. A. (1996). Inhibitory control in young children and its role in emerging internalization. *Child Development, 67*, 490–507. http://dx.doi.org/10.2307/1131828

Kochanska, G., Tjebkes, T. L., & Forman, D. R. (1998). Children's emerging regulation of conduct: Restraint, compliance, and internalization from infancy to the second year. *Child Development, 69*, 1378–1389. http://dx.doi.org/10.2307/1132272

Kopp, C. B., & Neufeld, S. J. (2003). Emotional development during infancy. In R. J. Davidson, K. R. Scherer, & H. H. Goldsmith (Eds.), *Handbook of affective sciences* (pp. 347–374). New York, NY: Oxford University Press.

Lengua, L. J., & Long, A. C. (2002). The role of emotionality and self-regulation in the appraisal-coping process: Tests of direct and moderating effects. *Journal of Applied Developmental Psychology, 23*, 471–493. http://dx.doi.org/10.1016/S0193-3973(02)00129-6

Li-Grining, C. P. (2007). Effortful control among low-income preschoolers in three cities: Stability, change, and individual differences. *Developmental Psychology, 43*, 208–221. http://dx.doi.org/10.1037/0012-1649.43.1.208

Metcalfe, J., & Mischel, W. (1999). A hot/cool-system analysis of delay of gratification: Dynamics of willpower. *Psychological Review, 106*, 3–19. http://dx.doi.org/10.1037/0033-295X.106.1.3

Mischel, W., Ebbesen, E. B., & Raskoff Zeiss, A. (1972). Cognitive and attentional mechanisms in delay of gratification. *Journal of Personality and Social Psychology, 21*, 204–218. http://dx.doi.org/10.1037/h0032198

Miyake, A., Friedman, N. P., Emerson, M. J., Witzki, A. H., Howerter, A., & Wager, T. D. (2000). The unity and diversity of executive functions and their contributions to complex "frontal lobe" tasks: A latent variable analysis. *Cognitive Psychology, 41*, 49–100. http://dx.doi.org/10.1006/cogp.1999.0734

Muris, P., van der Pennen, E., Sigmond, R., & Mayer, B. (2008). Symptoms of anxiety, depression, and aggression in non-clinical children: Relationships with self-report and performance-based measures of attention and effortful control. *Child Psychiatry and Human Development*, 39, 455–467. http://dx.doi.org/10.1007/s10578-008-0101-1

National Institute of Child Health and Human Development (NICHD) Early Child Care Research Network. (2003). Do children's attention processes mediate the link between family predictors and school readiness? *Developmental Psychology*, 39, 581–593. http://dx.doi.org/10.1037/0012-1649.39.3.581

Nelson, C. A., de Haan, M., & Thomas, K. M. (2006). *Neuroscience of cognitive development: The role of experience and the developing brain*. Hoboken, NJ: Wiley.

Olson, S. L., Bates, J. E., & Bayles, K. (1990). Early antecedents of childhood impulsivity: The role of parent–child interaction, cognitive competence, and temperament. *Journal of Abnormal Child Psychology*, 18, 317–334. http://dx.doi.org/10.1007/BF00916568

Olson, S. L., Schilling, E. M., & Bates, J. E. (1999). Measurement of impulsivity: Construct coherence, longitudinal stability, and relationship with externalizing problems in middle childhood and adolescence. *Journal of Abnormal Child Psychology*, 27, 151–165. http://dx.doi.org/10.1023/A:1021915615677

Prencipe, A., Kesek, A., Cohen, J., Lamm, C., Lewis, M. D., & Zelazo, P. D. (2011). Development of hot and cool executive function during the transition to adolescence. *Journal of Experimental Child Psychology*, 108, 621–637. http://dx.doi.org/10.1016/j.jecp.2010.09.008

Prencipe, A., & Zelazo, P. D. (2005). Development of affective decision making for self and other: Evidence for the integration of first- and third-person perspectives. *Psychological Science*, 16, 501–505.

Putnam, S. P., Gartstein, M. A., & Rothbart, M. K. (2006). Measurement of fine-grained aspects of toddler temperament: The early childhood behavior questionnaire. *Infant Behavior and Development*, 29, 386–401. http://dx.doi.org/10.1016/j.infbeh.2006.01.004

Reed, M. A., Pien, D. L., & Rothbart, M. K. (1984). Inhibitory self-control in preschool children. *Merrill-Palmer Quarterly*, 30, 131–147.

Rothbart, M. K., Ahadi, S. A., Hershey, K. L., & Fisher, P. (2001). Investigations of temperament at three to seven years: The Children's Behavior Questionnaire. *Child Development*, 72, 1394–1408. http://dx.doi.org/10.1111/1467-8624.00355

Rothbart, M. K., & Bates, J. E. (2006). Temperament. In N. Eisenberg, W. Damon, & R. M. Lerner (Eds.), *Handbook of child psychology: Vol. 3. Social, emotional, and personality development* (6th ed., pp. 99–166). Hoboken, NJ: Wiley.

Saarni, C. (1984). An observational study of children's attempts to monitor their expressive behavior. *Child Development*, 55, 1504–1513. http://dx.doi.org/10.2307/1130020

Schmeichel, B. J., Volokhov, R. N., & Demaree, H. A. (2008). Working memory capacity and the self-regulation of emotional expression and experience. *Journal of Personality and Social Psychology, 95*, 1526–1540. http://dx.doi.org/10.1037/a0013345

Shields, A., & Cicchetti, D. (1997). Emotion regulation among school-age children: The development and validation of a new criterion Q-sort scale. *Developmental Psychology, 33*, 906–916. http://dx.doi.org/10.1037/0012-1649.33.6.906

Smith, M., Hubbard, J. A., & Laurenceau, J. P. (2011). Profiles of anger control in second-grade children: Examination of self-report, observational, and physiological components. *Journal of Experimental Child Psychology, 110*, 213–226. http://dx.doi.org/10.1016/j.jecp.2011.02.006

Spinrad, T. L., Eisenberg, N., Cumberland, A., Fabes, R. A., Valiente, C., Shepard, S. A., . . . Guthrie, I. K. (2006). Relation of emotion-related regulation to children's social competence: A longitudinal study. *Emotion, 6*, 498–510. http://dx.doi.org/10.1037/1528-3542.6.3.498

Sulik, M. J., Huerta, S., Zerr, A. A., Eisenberg, N., Spinrad, T. L., Valiente, C., . . . Taylor, H. B. (2010). The factor structure of effortful control and measurement invariance across ethnicity and sex in a high-risk sample. *Journal of Psychopathology and Behavioral Assessment, 32*, 8–22. http://dx.doi.org/10.1007/s10862-009-9164-y

Thompson, R. A. (1994). Emotional regulation: A theme in search of definition. *Monographs of the Society for Research in Child Development, 59*(2–3), 25–52. http://dx.doi.org/10.2307/1166137

Valiente, C., Eisenberg, N., Smith, C. L., Reiser, M., Fabes, R. A., Losoya, S., . . . Murphy, B. C. (2003). The relations of effortful control and reactive control to children's externalizing problems: A longitudinal assessment. *Journal of Personality, 71*, 1171–1196. http://dx.doi.org/10.1111/1467-6494.7106011

Verstraeten, K., Vasey, M. W., Claes, L., & Bijttebier, P. (2010). The assessment of effortful control in childhood: Questionnaires and the Test of Everyday Attention for Children compared. *Personality and Individual Differences, 48*, 59–65. http://dx.doi.org/10.1016/j.paid.2009.08.016

White, J. L., Moffitt, T. E., Caspi, A., Bartusch, D. J., Needles, D. J., & Stouthamer-Loeber, M. (1994). Measuring impulsivity and examining its relationship to delinquency. *Journal of Abnormal Psychology, 103*, 192–205. http://dx.doi.org/10.1037/0021-843X.103.2.192

Willoughby, M., Kupersmidt, J., Voegler-Lee, M., & Bryant, D. (2011). Contributions of hot and cool self-regulation to preschool disruptive behavior and academic achievement. *Developmental Neuropsychology, 36*, 162–180. http://dx.doi.org/10.1080/87565641.2010.549980

Zelazo, P. D., Carlson, S. M., & Kesek, A. (2008). The development of executive function in childhood. In C. A. Nelson & M. Luciana (Eds.), *Handbook of cognitive developmental neuroscience* (2nd ed., pp. 553–574). Cambridge, MA: MIT Press.

Zelazo, P. D., Carter, A., Reznick, J. S., & Frye, D. (1997). Early development of executive function: A problem-solving framework. *Review of General Psychology, 1*, 198–226. http://dx.doi.org/10.1037/1089-2680.1.2.198

Zelazo, P. D., & Cunningham, W. (2007). Executive function: Mechanisms underlying emotion regulation. In J. Gross (Ed.), *Handbook of emotion regulation* (pp. 135–158). New York, NY: Guilford Press.

Zelazo, P. D., & Frye, D. (1998). Cognitive complexity and control: The development of executive function. *Current Directions in Psychological Science, 7*, 121–126. http://dx.doi.org/10.1111/1467-8721.ep10774761

Zhou, Q., Chen, S. H., & Main, A. (2012). Commonalities and differences in the study of children's effortful control and executive function; A call for an integrated model of self-regulation. *Child Development Perspectives, 6*, 112–121. http://dx.doi.org/10.1111/j.1750-8606.2011.00176.x

II

NEURODEVELOPMENT AND EXECUTIVE FUNCTION

6

INFANT COGNITIVE ABILITIES: POTENTIAL BUILDING BLOCKS OF LATER EXECUTIVE FUNCTIONS

SUSAN A. ROSE, JUDITH F. FELDMAN, AND JEFFERY J. JANKOWSKI

In this chapter, we present an overview of recent studies from our lab concerning several basic information-processing abilities that we have been examining in the first year of life. These studies point to the development and importance of early cognitive abilities as likely building blocks of later cognition, including executive functioning. Much of the work discussed is longitudinal, focusing on a group of preterm and full-term children that we have followed from early infancy. The preterm infants have served as a prototypic group at risk for later cognitive compromise. Although there is considerable evidence that children born prematurely often evidence intellectual and academic problems in later childhood (Allen, 2008; Aylward, 2002; Bhutta, Cleves, Casey, Cradock, & Anand, 2002; Botting, Powls, Cooke, & Marlow,

This research was funded in part by grants HD 13810 and HD 049494 from the National Institutes of Health. The authors are grateful to all the participants and their parents, and to Keisha Phillips for her invaluable help in testing children and scoring data.

http://dx.doi.org/10.1037/14797-007
Executive Function in Preschool-Age Children: Integrating Measurement, Neurodevelopment, and Translational Research, J. A. Griffin, P. McCardle, and L. S. Freund (Editors)

1998), these cognitive difficulties have generally gone undetected in infancy. By including infants at risk we hoped to both (a) elucidate the roots of later cognitive deficits in children born prematurely and (b) validate the cognitive nature of the infant measures.

The battery of infant tasks we have developed has been expanding over the years and now encompasses four cognitive domains—memory, processing speed, representational competence, and attention. Here we describe the tasks used to gauge performance in these domains in infancy and toddlerhood and show their sensitivity to risk and their predictive relations to later cognitive outcomes. The findings indicate that infant measures from these four domains are (a) sensitive to deficits associated with preterm birth, both in infancy (5, 7, and 12 months; Rose, Feldman, & Jankowski, 2001a, 2002, 2005a) and in toddlerhood (2 and 3 years old; Rose, Feldman, & Jankowski, 2009b); (b) show significant stability from the infant to the toddler period (Rose et al., 2009b); (c) predict general cognitive ability and language (Rose, Feldman, & Jankowski, 2007, 2009a; Rose, Feldman, Jankowski, & Van Rossem, 2005); and (d) mediate the effect of prematurity on later language and IQ (Rose, Feldman, & Jankowski, 2007; Rose, Feldman, Jankowski, & Van Rossem, 2005).

Finally, we speculate on how these basic aspects of information processing might also serve as the foundation of later executive functions and present preliminary findings to support this idea.

THE SAMPLE

The findings discussed here come primarily from work with a cohort of preterm and full-term infants who are enrolled in a prospective, longitudinal study of cognitive development. The original sample included 203 children (59 preterm infants and 144 full-term infants), born between February 1995 and July 1997. Preterm infants who were enrolled met the criteria of singleton birth, birth weight < 1,750 grams (g), gestational age < 37 weeks, and the absence of any obvious congenital, physical, or neurological abnormalities. For full-term infants, the criteria for study intake were birth weight > 2,500 g, gestational age of 38 to 42 weeks, 5-minute Apgar scores of 9 or 10, and uneventful pre- and perinatal circumstances. The children were followed through the first 3 years of life and seen at 5, 7, 12, 24, and 36 months.

Demographic factors were similar for preterm and full-term infants: About half the sample was male and a third first born. The sample was largely Black or Hispanic, with maternal education averaging slightly more than 13 years.

Preterm infants had an average birth weight of 1,107.9 g ($SD = 282.6$) and an average gestational age of 29.6 weeks ($SD = 2.9$). Of the preterm sample,

91.9% were very low birth weight (< 1,500 g) and 39.3% were extremely low birth weight (< 1,000 g); 34% were small-for-gestational age, about 50% had respiratory distress syndrome, and close to 50% had an intraventricular hemorrhage, mainly Grade I or II (Papile, Burstein, Burstein, & Koffler, 1978). Further details are presented in Rose et al. (2001a).

Visits of the preterm infants were targeted to corrected age, calculated from expected date of birth, with the result that they were, on average, 10.4 weeks older in postnatal age than the full-term infants.

INFORMATION-PROCESSING TASKS IN THE INFANT AND TODDLER PERIOD

The information-processing measures developed for infants (5, 7, and 12 months) and toddlers (24 and 36 months) assessed performance in four domains—memory, processing speed, representational competence, and attention—using a variety of tasks (see Exhibit 6.1). The tasks were made age-appropriate by shortening presentation and test times as the infants grew older, increasing the stringency of learning criteria, and in some instances, increasing stimulus complexity. The following descriptions summarize the essential characteristics of the tasks in each domain. More details on the infant versions can be found in the papers referenced with each task; more information on the toddler versions can be found in Rose et al. (2009b).

EXHIBIT 6.1
Information-Processing Abilities Assessed in Infants and Toddlers:
The Four Domains and Constituent Tasks

Memory
- Immediate recognition
- Delayed recognition
- Recall (elicited imitation)
- Short-term capacity (span)

Processing Speed
- Encoding speed (continuous familiarization)
- Psychomotor speed (RT; VExP)

Representational Competence
- Cross-modal transfer
- Anticipations (VExP)
- Object permanence
- Symbolic play

Attention
- Look duration
- Shift rate

Note. RT = reaction time; VExP = Visual Expectation Paradigm.

Memory

Immediate recognition was assessed with two tasks, one developed in our lab (the Rose; Rose et al., 2001a) and the other in Fagan's lab (the Fagan; Fagan & Sheperd, 1989). Both consist of a series of two-part trials in which a target (face or abstract pattern) is presented for familiarization and then the familiar target is paired with a novel one for test. A novelty score, defined as the percentage of total looking time on test directed toward the novel target, is computed on each trial; novelty scores are averaged across trials.

Delayed recognition was assessed by habituating the child to three objects sequentially (using a modified infant-controlled procedure; see Diamond, 1990) and then, after delays of 1, 3, or 5 minutes, pairing each habituated object, in turn, with a novel one. There were three problems at each of three delays. Novelty scores are calculated for each problem and averaged (Rose, Feldman, & Jankowski, 2004).

Recall memory was evaluated with an elicited imitation task (Bauer, 2002). Here, the child watched the examiner model a series of four different event sequences, one at a time. After a 15-minute delay, the child was given the props for each, in turn, and encouraged to reproduce the sequences. The child's score, based on the percentage of target actions reproduced for each event sequence, was averaged over sequences (Rose et al., 2005a).

Short-term capacity was assessed with a visual span task. Children were familiarized with a set of 1, 2, 3, or 4 objects. After all members of a set had been presented, recognition was tested by pairing each familiar object, in turn, with a novel one. Sets were presented in ascending order. Span length was measured by the highest number of items recognized (defined by a novelty score $\geq 55\%$) from all four spans (Rose, Feldman, & Jankowski, 2001b).

Processing Speed

Encoding speed, the rapidity of encoding target information, was assessed with the continuous familiarization task, in which a series of paired targets (faces) were presented, one of which changed from trial to trial while the other remained constant. Trials continued until the child showed a consistent preference for the new one or until all 36 trials had been presented (see Rose et al., 2002).

Psychomotor speed (reaction time [RT]), the time to orient to a stimulus, was assessed with Haith's Visual Expectation Paradigm (VExP; Haith, Hazan, & Goodman, 1988). Here targets appear briefly on a computer screen, to the left and right of midline, and the latency to look to each is measured. There were 10 baseline trials, in which targets appeared randomly, followed by 60 predictable trials, in which targets appeared in right-right-left (RRL) sequence. Mean RTs were analyzed (excluding RTs < 150 ms; Rose, Feldman, Jankowski, & Caro, 2002).

Representational Competence

Representational competence, referring to the ability to glean information about commonalties from experiences and represent them in some abstract way, was evaluated using tasks of cross-modal transfer, anticipation, object permanence, and symbolic play.

Cross-modal transfer was assessed with a tactual–visual task that required extracting information about shape by feeling an object and then recognizing it visually. Using the paired-comparison paradigm, tactual familiarization was followed by a test in which the previously felt object was presented visually alongside a new one (Rose & Feldman, 1995; Rose, Feldman, Futterweit, & Jankowski, 1997; Rose, Feldman, & Wallace, 1988; Rose, Gottfried, & Bridger, 1978). Novelty scores were computed for each problem and averaged over problems (Rose, Feldman, Wallace, & McCarton, 1991).

Anticipation, the ability to anticipate forthcoming events, was measured by the VExP task described above. Saccades to the upcoming stimulus were considered to be anticipatory if they were initiated before the stimulus could be perceived, that is, prior to or within 150 ms of onset, the minimal time thought to be required to initiate a saccade (Haith et al., 1988). To successfully anticipate stimulus onset the child had to abstract the RRL rule governing changes in location for the fast-paced sequence of pictures. Performance was scored for the number of trials with RTs $\leq$ 150 ms.

Object permanence (12 months only), which indicates the child's understanding that objects continue to exist when out of sight, was assessed with the Einstein Scale (Corman & Escalona, 1969). Here, the infant has to retrieve hidden objects as the number of possible hiding locations increases and displacements become more complex; performance was scored for the highest stage achieved.

Symbolic play (12 months only) requires imitating acts of increasing length, complexity, and symbolic content. It was assessed with an 18-level scale (based on the work of Damast, Tamis-LeMonda, & Bornstein, 1996; Tamis-LeMonda & Bornstein, 1990). Performance was scored for the highest level achieved.

Attention

Look duration, a measure of attentional efficiency (with short looks associated with better attention), was assessed using measures culled from the familiarization and test phases of the tests of visual recognition memory (the

Rose and the Fagan), the test phase of cross-modal transfer, and trials from the continuous familiarization task. A composite was formed by standardizing the scores on each task and then averaging them (Rose, Feldman, & Jankowski, 2004, 2005b). Shift rate, a measure of attentional efficiency and comparison behavior (with higher shift rates being associated with better attention), was assessed using measures available from all but one (the Fagan) of the tasks used for look duration. A composite was formed by standardizing the scores on each task and then averaging them (Rose et al., 2004, 2005b).

THUMBNAIL SKETCH OF MAJOR FINDINGS

Sensitivity to Risk

An overview of differences between preterm and full-term infants and toddlers is shown in Figure 6.1. The columns indicate the ages at which children were seen (5, 7, 12, 24, and 36 months); the rows indicate the four domains

Sensitivity to Risk					
Domain/Task	Age in Months				
	5	7	12	24	36
Memory					
Immediate recognition	√	√	√	√	√
Delayed recognition		√	√	√	√
Short-term capacity (span)	√	√	√	√	√
Recall (elicited imitation)			√	√	√
Processing Speed					
Encoding speed (continuous familiarization)	√	√	√	√	√
Psychomotor speed (RT; VExP)	√	√	√	√	√
Attention					
Look duration	√	√	√	√	√
Shift rate	√	√	√	√	√
Representational Competence					
Cross-modal transfer		√	√	√	√
Anticipations (VExP)	√	√	√	√	√
Object permanence			√		
Symbolic play			√		

Figure 6.1. The sensitivity of infant and toddler information processing to risk: preterm/full-term differences. Checks indicate tasks given. Shaded cells indicate preterm/full-term deficits. RT = reaction time; VExP = Visual Expectation Paradigm.

and the tasks used to assess each. Checkmarks indicate the age at which specific tasks were administered. Finally, tasks on which there were significant differences between preterm and full-term are indicated by shading in the box.

As can be seen, preterm infants and toddlers showed deficits in all four domains. In infancy, they showed poorer immediate recognition memory and poorer recall, were slower at encoding new information, had poorer attention (as indexed by longer looks and fewer shifts), and showed deficits in object permanence and symbolic play (Rose, Feldman, & Jankowski, 2001a, 2002, 2003a, 2003b, 2005a; Rose, Feldman, Jankowski, & Caro, 2002; Rose, Feldman, Wallace, & McCarton, 1989, 1991). In toddlerhood, comparable deficits were evident (Rose et al., 2009b). Thus, preterm infants showed no catch-up over the first 3 years of life but instead showed persistent deficits in immediate recognition, recall, encoding speed, and attention.

Stability

Cross-age stability from infancy to toddlerhood is shown in Table 6.1. The correlations shown here are based on composites, combined across groups, and partialed for birth status. (The correlations are combined because they were similar for both groups. Birth status was partialed to avoid any inflation due to mean differences.) The infancy scores were created by averaging scores from 7 and 12 months; toddler scores were created by averaging measures from 24 and 36 months.

TABLE 6.1
Stability of Information Processing From Infancy to Toddlerhood

Information-processing measures	R
Memory	
Immediate recognition	.33***
Delayed recognition	.29***
Short-term capacity (span)	.11
Recall (elicited imitation)	.26***
Processing Speed	
Encoding speed (continuous familiarization)	.20**
Psychomotor speed (RT; VExP)	.35***
Attention	
Look duration	.37***
Shift rate	.33***
Representational Competence	
Cross-modal transfer	.18*
Anticipations (VExP)	.25***

Note. The 7- and 12-month scores were averaged to create the infant scores; the 24- and 36-month scores were averaged to create the toddler scores. $N = 159–200$. Birth status was partialed from all scores. RT = reaction time; VExP = Visual Expectation Paradigm.
*$p \leq .05$ **$p \leq .01$ ***$p \leq .001$

As can be seen in Table 6.1, with the exception of short-term capacity, all cross-age correlations from infancy to toddlerhood were significant, ranging from .18 to .37, with a median correlation of about .30. There was no indication of the discontinuities that had been posited by much of the earlier literature (e.g., Piaget, 1962). On the contrary, the results indicate that a measurable degree of continuity prevails for information-processing abilities over the first 3 years of life. These findings are consistent with the notion that a wide variety of elementary information-processing abilities emerge very early and endure to form the basis of more mature cognition.

Prediction

As can be seen in Table 6.2, a number of these elementary abilities were related to global cognitive outcome, as indexed by the Mental Development Index (MDI) from the Scales of Infant Development (Bayley, 1993). The MDI score used here is a composite, created by averaging scores obtained at 24 and 36 months. Parallel results were obtained with infant and toddler predictors.

TABLE 6.2
Toddler MDI: Predicted From Infant and Toddler Information Processing

	Predicting toddler MDI	
Information-processing measures	From infancy r	From toddlerhood r
Memory		
Immediate recognition	.33***	.41***
Delayed recognition	.20**	.24***
Short-term capacity (span)	.09	.01
Recall (elicited imitation)	.29***	.44***
Processing Speed		
Encoding speed (continuous familiarization)	−.18*	−.23**
Psychomotor speed (RT; VExP)	−.05	−.12
Attention		
Look duration	−.07	−.12
Shift rate	.14†	.06
Representational Competence		
Cross-modal transfer	.35***	.30***
Anticipations (VExP)	−.12	−.01
Object permanence	.26***	—
Symbolic play	.21**	—

Note. The 7- and 12-month scores were averaged to create the infant scores; the 24- and 36-month scores were averaged to create the toddler scores. $N = 162$–170 for column 1, and $N = 153$–170 for column 2. Birth status was partialed from all scores. MDI = Mental Development Index; RT = reaction time; VExP = Visual Expectation Paradigm.
†$p ≤ 0.10$ *$p ≤ .05$ **$p ≤ .01$ ***$p ≤ .001$

In both cases, immediate and delayed recognition, recall memory, encoding speed, and cross-modal transfer all related to toddler MDI, with correlations ranging from .20 to .44 (Rose, Feldman, & Jankowski, 2009b). Simultaneous multiple regressions showed that the set of infant measures accounted for 29% of the variance in toddler MDI, with toddler measures accounting for 42% of the variance. Thus, these aspects of information processing, known to form the backbone of general cognitive ability at later ages, are already serving as the drivers of general cognitive ability at these early ages.

It is noteworthy that the same three early abilities—immediate recognition memory, recall, and cross-modal transfer—contributed independently to the prediction of MDI in both infancy and toddlerhood. The finding that the individual measures accounted for variance independently of each other is in line with earlier factor analyses showing that the infant measures were tapping discrete abilities (Rose et al., 2004, 2005b).

Table 6.3 shows that many of the infant measures affect not only later MDI but also later receptive language. Language was assessed at 36 months with the Peabody Picture Vocabulary Test—Revised (PPVT–R), Form L

TABLE 6.3
Three-Year Receptive Language (PPVT-R): Predicted From Infant
and Toddler Information Processing

Information-processing measures	Predicting 3-year receptive language	
	From infancy r	From toddlerhood r
Memory		
Immediate recognition	.20*	.27***
Delayed recognition	.24**	.24**
Short-term capacity (span)	.01	−.13
Recall (elicited imitation)	.28***	.27**
Processing Speed		
Encoding speed (continuous familiarization)	−.09	−.21**
Psychomotor speed (RT; VExP)	−.08	−.06
Attention		
Look duration	−.04	−14
Shift rate	.12	.04
Representational Competence		
Cross-modal transfer	.32***	.35***
Anticipations (VExP)	−.01	.00
Object permanence	.30***	—
Symbolic play	.21**	—

Note. The 7- and 12-month scores were averaged to create the infant scores; the 24- and 36-month scores were averaged to create the toddler scores. N = 159–200. Birth status was partialed from all scores. PPVT-R = Peabody Picture Vocabulary Test—Revised; RT = reaction time; VExP = Visual Expectation Paradigm.
*$p \le .05$ **$p \le .01$ ***$p \le .001$

(Dunn & Dunn, 1981). As can be seen, infant measures of immediate and delayed recognition, recall, and representational competence predicted 3-year receptive language, with significant correlations ranging from .20 to .35 (see also Rose, Feldman, & Jankowski, 2009a). Again, the information-processing measures predictive from toddlerhood were largely the same as those predictive from infancy. It was also noteworthy that the information-processing abilities predicted 3-year PPVT independently of a number of other factors strongly associated with language development, including (a) birth status; (b) earlier (12-month) language, indexed by performance on the short form of the MacArthur Communicative Developmental Inventory (Words and Gestures; Fenson et al., 2000); and (c) earlier (12-month) mental development, as indexed by the MDI (Rose et al., 2009a).

Table 6.4 shows that a number of the same infant and toddler measures also predicted expressive language at 3 years. Expressive language was indexed by verbal fluency, where children named as many things as possible in each of three categories: (a) things to eat, (b) animals, and (c) things that make noise. Performance on verbal fluency, like that on the PPVT, was predicted

TABLE 6.4
Three-Year Expressive Language (Verbal Fluency): Predicted From Infant and Toddler Information Processing

| Information-processing measures | Predicting 3-year expressive language | |
	From infancy r	From toddlerhood r
Memory		
Immediate recognition	.17*	.33***
Delayed recognition	.11	.11
Short-term capacity (span)	.15†	−.01
Recall (elicited imitation)	.11	.21*
Processing Speed		
Encoding speed (continuous familiarization)	−.18*	−.16†
Psychomotor speed (RT; VExP)	−.01	−.19
Attention		
Look duration	−.15†	−.09
Shift rate	.15†	.05
Representational Competence		
Cross-modal transfer	.26**	.30***
Anticipations (VExP)	−.05	.04
Object permanence	.22*	—
Symbolic play	.22*	—

Note. The 7- and 12-month scores were averaged to create the infant scores; the 24- and 36-month scores were averaged to create the toddler scores. $N = 159–200$. Birth status was partialed from all scores. RT = reaction time; VExP = Visual Expectation Paradigm.
†$p ≤ 0.10$ *$p ≤ .05$ **$p ≤ .01$ ***$p ≤ .001$

by the infant measures independent of birth status, 12-month language, and the 12-month MDI.

Overall then, it appears that a number of basic cognitive processes that can be identified in infancy contribute to the growth of early global abilities, receptive language, and expressive language. These findings are in line with the contention that language skill rests on a domain-general foundation and support the idea that early-appearing information-processing skills have broad implications for later cognitive function.

Mediation: A Developmental Cascade

We have proposed a developmental cascade model that shows how the basic abilities are linked to the more global ones. The model involves a sequence of effects in which more elementary cognitive processes influence more complex ones, which, in turn, influence still more complex and more general abilities. We have used this model to examine the relation of infant information-processing abilities to one another and their role in mediating the differences between preterm and full-term infants in later MDI. Using structural equation modeling (SEM) and 7-month information-processing measures, we initially tested a model that made two key assumptions:

- Infant information-processing abilities mediate the relation of prematurity to later cognition.
- Attention and speed are elementary abilities that influence more complex ones, such as memory and representational competence.

Thus, the model specified that risk → elementary abilities → complex abilities → MDI. This model fit quite well (Rose, Feldman, Jankowski, & Van Rossem, 2005). As shown in Figure 6.2, the 7-month information-processing abilities entirely accounted for the differences between preterm and full-term found in MDI at 2 years, χ^2 (14) = 18.53, p = .20, root mean square error of approximation = .03. That is, the direct path from birth status to MDI was no longer significant (as indicated by the dotted line). Thus, the preterm infants' poorer information processing imposes constraints on the level of intellectual growth achieved by toddlerhood. And—as hypothesized—there was evidence for a cascade of effects from birth status to the more elementary abilities (speed and attention), to the abilities posited to be more complex (memory and representational competence). The model fit was similar when MDI at 3 years was used as the outcome measure.

Whereas the model was fit using 7-month measures of information processing, a comparable model fit when 12-month measures were substituted (Rose, Feldman, Jankowski, & Van Rossem, 2008). Moreover, this same cascade of abilities was recently found at 11 years, in a longitudinal follow-up of this sample, using an entirely different set of tasks to index performance in

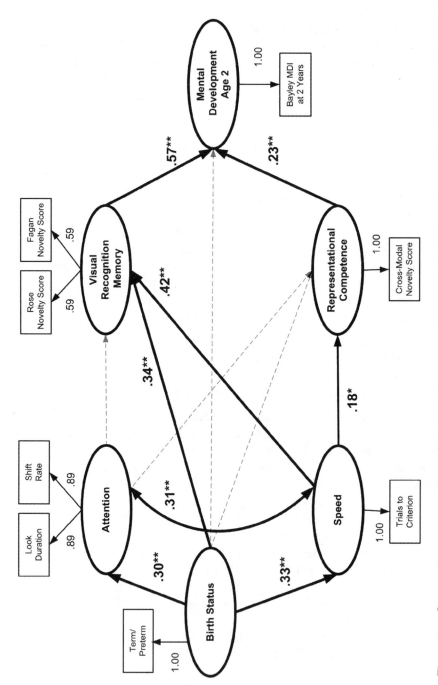

Figure 6.2. Structural equation model of the cascade of effects from prematurity and infant information processing at 7 months to 2-year Mental Development Index (MDI). Ovals represent latent variables; rectangles represent manifest variables. Birth status is coded in a binary manner: 1 for full-term and 0 for preterm. Single-headed arrows represent path coefficients; double-headed arrows represent correlations. Standardized coefficients for all paths are shown, with significant paths indicated by solid lines and nonsignificant paths by broken lines.
*p ≤ .05 **p ≤ .01

the four domains (Rose, Feldman, Jankowski, & Van Rossem, 2011). Again, these information-processing abilities were found to entirely account for differences between preterm and full-term at 11 years on global outcome, here indexed by full-scale Wechsler Intelligence Scale for Children–IV IQ (Wechsler, 2003).

INFANT INFORMATION PROCESSING: THE ROOTS OF PRESCHOOL EXECUTIVE FUNCTION?

We have seen that basic information-processing abilities can be assessed within the first year of life, and we have presented some evidence suggesting that they form the roots of later, more global abilities—MDI, IQ, and language. Three lines of evidence support the possibility that infant information-processing abilities may also underpin, or provide the foundation for, executive functioning.

First, studies of older children and adults have found that at least two of the abilities we assessed in infants and toddlers—processing speed and attention—are driving forces behind more global abilities, including executive functioning (Fry & Hale, 1996; Kail, 2007; Kail & Salthouse, 1994; Luck & Vogel, 1997; Rose, Feldman, & Jankowski, 2011; Salthouse, 1996). A number of these studies have found that age-related differences in speed and/or attention account for age-related differences in more complex cognitive abilities, including working memory, shifting, and inhibition.

Second, as noted earlier, a number of infant and toddler information-processing abilities were related to verbal fluency, an ability often considered to reflect complex executive functioning (Jurado & Rosselli, 2007). Specifically, we found that infant recognition memory, encoding speed, and representational competence were each significantly correlated with 3-year verbal fluency, which we had conceptualized as a measure of expressive language. To the extent that verbal fluency also reflects executive functioning, the relation of infant abilities to 3-year verbal fluency supports that notion that infant information processing underpins executive functioning.

Third, findings from the 11-year follow-up of this cohort provide even more compelling evidence that infant information-processing skills form the basis of later executive functions. This follow-up included not only 11-year counterparts of the infant measures but also measures of the three executive functions considered foundational by Miyake—working memory, inhibition, and shifting. Two of the findings are relevant here:

- Using SEM and a latent variable analysis, we established that there was significant continuity for all four domains, from infancy to preadolescence. Performance in each domain fit cascading models of this form: infant abilities → toddler abilities → 11-year abilities. Thus, abilities shown to affect executive functions in more mature individuals were found to be anchored in infancy (Rose, Feldman, Jankowski, & Van Rossem, 2012). These findings of continuity extend earlier work (Rose et al., 1997; Rose, Feldman, Futterweit, & Jankowski, 1998) and provide evidence that the nonverbal methods and simplified tasks that are the hallmark of infant testing serve as important harbingers of their more adultlike counterparts.

- Some of these infant abilities also appear to be related to later executive functions in much the same way as their more mature counterparts are. Specifically, infant and toddler measures from two domains—processing speed and memory—correlated significantly with 11-year latent factor scores of two executive functions—working memory and shifting (Rose, Feldman, & Jankowski, 2012). These findings are consistent with the idea that infant abilities set limitations on the growth of executive functioning.

Overall then, there is growing reason to believe that (a) basic information-processing abilities are involved in executive functions and (b) the origin of the basic abilities driving executive functions can be traced to infancy.

REFERENCES

Allen, M. C. (2008). Neurodevelopmental outcomes of preterm infants. *Current Opinion in Neurology, 21,* 123–128. http://dx.doi.org/10.1097/WCO.0b013e3282f88bb4

Aylward, G. P. (2002). Cognitive and neuropsychological outcomes: More than IQ scores. *Mental Retardation and Developmental Disabilities Research Reviews, 8,* 234–240. http://dx.doi.org/10.1002/mrdd.10043

Bauer, P. J. (2002). Long-term recall memory: Behavioral and neuro-developmental changes in the first two years of life. *Current Directions in Psychological Science, 11,* 137–141. http://dx.doi.org/10.1111/1467-8721.00186

Bayley, N. (1993). *The Bayley Scales of Infant Development.* San Antonio, TX: Psychological Corporation.

Bhutta, A. T., Cleves, M. A., Casey, P. H., Cradock, M. M., & Anand, K. J. S. (2002). Cognitive and behavioral outcomes of school-aged children who were born preterm: A meta-analysis. *JAMA, 288,* 728–737. http://dx.doi.org/10.1001/jama.288.6.728

Botting, N., Powls, A., Cooke, R. W. I., & Marlow, N. (1998). Cognitive and educational outcome of very-low-birthweight children in early adolescence. *Developmental Medicine & Child Neurology, 40*, 652–660. http://dx.doi.org/10.1111/j.1469-8749.1998.tb12324.x

Corman, H. H., & Escalona, S. K. (1969). Stages of sensorimotor development: A replication study. *Merrill-Palmer Quarterly, 15*, 351–361.

Damast, A. M., Tamis-LeMonda, C. S., & Bornstein, M. H. (1996). Mother–child play: Sequential interactions and the relation between maternal beliefs and behaviors. *Child Development, 67*, 1752–1766. http://dx.doi.org/10.2307/1131729

Diamond, A. (1990). Rate of maturation of the hippocampus and the developmental progression of children's performance on the delayed nonmatching to sample and visual paired comparison tasks. In A. Diamond (Ed.), *Development and neural bases of higher cognitive functions: Vol. 608. Annals of the New York Academy of Sciences* (pp. 394–426). New York, NY: Academic Press.

Dunn, L. M., & Dunn, L. M. (1981). *Peabody Picture Vocabulary Test—Revised (PPVT–R)*. Circle Pines, MN: American Guidance Service.

Fagan, J. F., & Sheperd, P. (1989). *The Fagan Test of Infant Intelligence*. Cleveland, OH: Infantest Corp.

Fenson, L., Pethick, S., Renda, C., Cox, J. L., Dale, P. S., & Reznick, J. S. (2000). Short-form versions of the MacArthur Communicative Developmental Inventories. *Applied Psycholinguistics, 21*, 95–115. http://dx.doi.org/10.1017/S0142716400001053

Fry, A. F., & Hale, S. (1996). Processing speed, working memory, and fluid intelligence: Evidence for a developmental cascade. *Psychological Science, 7*, 237–241. http://dx.doi.org/10.1111/j.1467-9280.1996.tb00366.x

Haith, M. M., Hazan, C., & Goodman, G. S. (1988). Expectation and anticipation of dynamic visual events by 3.5-month-old babies. *Child Development, 59*, 467–479. http://dx.doi.org/10.2307/1130325

Jurado, M. B., & Rosselli, M. (2007). The elusive nature of executive functions: A review of our current understanding. *Neuropsychology Review, 17*, 213–233. http://dx.doi.org/10.1007/s11065-007-9040-z

Kail, R. V. (2007). Longitudinal evidence that increases in processing speed and working memory enhance children's reasoning. *Psychological Science, 18*, 312–313. http://dx.doi.org/10.1111/j.1467-9280.2007.01895.x

Kail, R. V., & Salthouse, T. A. (1994). Processing speed as a mental capacity. *Acta Psychologica, 86*, 199–225. http://dx.doi.org/10.1016/0001-6918(94)90003-5

Luck, S. J., & Vogel, E. K. (1997). The capacity of visual working memory for features and conjunctions. *Nature, 390*, 279–281. http://dx.doi.org/10.1038/36846

Papile, L. A., Burstein, J., Burstein, R., & Koffler, H. (1978). Incidence and evolution of subependymal and intraventricular hemorrhage: A study of infants with birth weights less than 1,500 gm. *The Journal of Pediatrics, 92*, 529–534. http://dx.doi.org/10.1016/S0022-3476(78)80282-0

Piaget, J. (1962). The relation of affectivity to intelligence in the mental development of the child. *Bulletin of the Menninger Clinic, 26,* 129–137.

Rose, S. A., & Feldman, J. F. (1995). Prediction of IQ and specific cognitive abilities at 11 years from infancy measures. *Developmental Psychology, 31,* 685–696. http://dx.doi.org/10.1037/0012-1649.31.4.685

Rose, S. A., Feldman, J. F., Futterweit, L. R., & Jankowski, J. J. (1997). Continuity in visual recognition memory: Infancy to 11 years. *Intelligence, 24,* 381–392. http://dx.doi.org/10.1016/S0160-2896(97)90067-2

Rose, S. A., Feldman, J. F., Futterweit, L. R., & Jankowski, J. J. (1998). Continuity in tactual–visual cross-modal transfer: Infancy to 11 years. *Developmental Psychology, 34,* 435–440.

Rose, S. A., Feldman, J. F., & Jankowski, J. J. (2001a). Attention and recognition memory in the first year of life: A longitudinal study of preterm and full-term infants. *Developmental Psychology, 37,* 135–151. http://dx.doi.org/10.1037/0012-1649.37.1.135

Rose, S. A., Feldman, J. F., & Jankowski, J. J. (2001b). Visual short-term memory in the first year of life: Capacity and recency effects. *Developmental Psychology, 37,* 539–549. http://dx.doi.org/10.1037/0012-1649.37.4.539

Rose, S. A., Feldman, J. F., & Jankowski, J. J. (2002). Processing speed in the first year of life: A longitudinal study of preterm and full-term infants. *Developmental Psychology, 38,* 895–902. http://dx.doi.org/10.1037/0012-1649.38.6.895

Rose, S. A., Feldman, J. F., & Jankowski, J. J. (2003a). The building blocks of cognition. *The Journal of Pediatrics, 143*(Suppl.), 54–61. http://dx.doi.org/10.1067/S0022-3476(03)00402-5

Rose, S. A., Feldman, J. F., & Jankowski, J. J. (2003b). Infant visual recognition memory: Independent contributions of speed and attention. *Developmental Psychology, 39,* 563–571. http://dx.doi.org/10.1037/0012-1649.39.3.563

Rose, S. A., Feldman, J. F., & Jankowski, J. J. (2004). Dimensions of cognition in infancy. *Intelligence, 32,* 245–262. http://dx.doi.org/10.1016/j.intell.2004.01.004

Rose, S. A., Feldman, J. F., & Jankowski, J. J. (2005a). Recall memory in the first three years of life: A longitudinal study of preterm and term children. *Developmental Medicine & Child Neurology, 47,* 653–659. http://dx.doi.org/10.1111/j.1469-8749.2005.tb01049.x

Rose, S. A., Feldman, J. F., & Jankowski, J. J. (2005b). The structure of infant cognition at 1 year. *Intelligence, 33,* 231–250. http://dx.doi.org/10.1016/j.intell.2004.11.002

Rose, S. A., Feldman, J. F., & Jankowski, J. J. (2007). Developmental aspects of visual recognition memory in infancy. In L. M. Oakes & P. J. Bauer (Eds.), *Short- and long-term memory in infancy and early childhood* (pp. 153–178). New York, NY: Oxford University Press.

Rose, S. A., Feldman, J. F., & Jankowski, J. J. (2009a). A cognitive approach to the development of early language. *Child Development, 80*, 134–150. http://dx.doi.org/10.1111/j.1467-8624.2008.01250.x

Rose, S. A., Feldman, J. F., & Jankowski, J. J. (2009b). Information processing in toddlers: Continuity from infancy and persistence of preterm deficits. *Intelligence, 37*, 311–320. http://dx.doi.org/10.1016/j.intell.2009.02.002

Rose, S. A., Feldman, J. F., & Jankowski, J. J. (2011). Modeling a cascade of effects: The role of speed and executive functioning in preterm/full-term differences in academic achievement. *Developmental Science, 14*, 1161–1175. http://dx.doi.org/10.1111/j.1467-7687.2011.01068.x

Rose, S. A., Feldman, J. F., & Jankowski, J. J. (2012). Implications of infant cognition for executive functions at age 11. *Psychological Science, 23*, 1345–1355. http://dx.doi.org/10.1177/0956797612444902

Rose, S. A., Feldman, J. F., Jankowski, J. J., & Caro, D. M. (2002). A longitudinal study of visual expectation and reaction time in the first year of life. *Child Development, 73*, 47–61. http://dx.doi.org/10.1111/1467-8624.00391

Rose, S. A., Feldman, J. F., Jankowski, J. J., & Van Rossem, R. (2005). Pathways from prematurity and infant abilities to later cognition. *Child Development, 76*, 1172–1184. http://dx.doi.org/10.1111/j.1467-8624.2005.00842.x-i1

Rose, S. A., Feldman, J. F., Jankowski, J. J., & Van Rossem, R. (2008). A cognitive cascade in infancy: Pathways from prematurity to later mental development. *Intelligence, 36*, 367–378. http://dx.doi.org/10.1016/j.intell.2007.07.003

Rose, S. A., Feldman, J. F., Jankowski, J. J., & Van Rossem, R. (2011). Basic information processing abilities at 11 years account for deficits in IQ associated with preterm birth. *Intelligence, 39*, 198–209. http://dx.doi.org/10.1016/j.intell.2011.03.003

Rose, S. A., Feldman, J. F., Jankowski, J. J., & Van Rossem, R. (2012). Information processing from infancy to 11 years: Continuities and prediction of IQ. *Intelligence, 40*, 445–457. http://dx.doi.org/10.1016/j.intell.2012.05.007

Rose, S. A., Feldman, J. F., & Wallace, I. F. (1988). Individual differences in infants' information processing: Reliability, stability, and prediction. *Child Development, 59*, 1177–1197. http://dx.doi.org/10.2307/1130482

Rose, S. A., Feldman, J. F., Wallace, I. F., & McCarton, C. M. (1989). Infant visual attention: Relation to birth status and developmental outcome during the first five years. *Developmental Psychology, 25*, 560–576. http://dx.doi.org/10.1037/0012-1649.25.4.560

Rose, S. A., Feldman, J. F., Wallace, I. F., & McCarton, C. (1991). Information processing at one year: Relation to birth status and developmental outcome during the first five years. *Developmental Psychology, 27*, 723–737. http://dx.doi.org/10.1037/0012-1649.27.5.723

Rose, S. A., Gottfried, A. W., & Bridger, W. H. (1978). Cross-modal transfer in infants: Relationship to prematurity and socio-economic background. *Developmental Psychology, 14*, 643–652. http://dx.doi.org/10.1037/0012-1649.14.6.643

Salthouse, T. A. (1996). The processing-speed theory of adult age differences in cognition. *Psychological Review, 103*, 403–428. http://dx.doi.org/10.1037/0033-295X.103.3.403

Tamis-LeMonda, C. S., & Bornstein, M. H. (1990). Language, play, and attention at one year. *Infant Behavior and Development, 13*, 85–98. http://dx.doi.org/10.1016/0163-6383(90)90007-U

Wechsler, D. (2003). *The Wechsler Intelligence Scale for Children, Fourth Edition*. San Antonio, TX: Psychological Corporation.

7

PSYCHOBIOLOGY OF EXECUTIVE FUNCTION IN EARLY DEVELOPMENT

MARTHA ANN BELL AND KIMBERLY CUEVAS

Well-regulated attention and memory processes are critical to optimal cognitive development (Bell & Deater-Deckard, 2007; Calkins & Bell, 2010; Rothbart, Sheese, Rueda, & Posner, 2011). Although we know that from infancy into early childhood nearly all children show dramatic improvements in cognitive processes, the etiology of individual differences in this developmental progression is poorly understood. Current theory postulates that biopsychosocial mechanisms are most likely involved and, in particular, that optimal development of self-regulated cognition is promoted not only by certain complements of genes associated with frontal lobe architecture and

Much of our research highlighted in this chapter was supported by grants HD049878 and HD043057 from the Eunice Kennedy Shriver National Institute of Child Health and Human Development (NICHD). The content of this manuscript is solely the responsibility of the authors and does not necessarily represent the official views of the NICHD or the National Institutes of Health. Some of our research in this chapter was supported by a Small Grant Award and a Millennium Grant Award from the College of Arts and Sciences at Virginia Tech.

http://dx.doi.org/10.1037/14797-008
Executive Function in Preschool-Age Children: Integrating Measurement, Neurodevelopment, and Translational Research, J. A. Griffin, P. McCardle, and L. S. Freund (Editors)

development but also by co-occurring socialization experiences within the family (Rueda, Posner, & Rothbart, 2004; Sameroff, 2010).

The result of the interactions of these various biopsychosocial processes is that all young children do not improve in their cognitive control abilities at the same rate (Diamond, Prevor, Callender, & Druin, 1997). Thus, even among a group of normally developing children, there may be great variability in cognitive behaviors and in brain electrical activity measures of maturation and task performance (Bell, 2001; Bell & Fox, 1992; Cuevas & Bell, 2010, 2011). Other factors, such as child temperament or parenting, may affect developmental trajectories in cognitive development because they may alter child brain structure and/or functioning (Bernier, Carlson, & Whipple, 2010; Colombo & Saxon, 2002; Diamond & Amso, 2008).

In this chapter we highlight our research on individual differences in cognitive development. The specific cognitive processes we study are the executive functions (EFs). As evidenced by the contents of this volume, developmental scientists use many different definitions of EF to study cognitive development during the preschool years. We begin by giving the definition of EF that we use in our research program. Next, we introduce our longitudinal study on early EF development by focusing on our psychobiology conceptual framework. Then, we discuss our findings on brain electrophysiology and EFs as well as highlight our research on temperament and parenting correlates of these developing cognitive processes. We end by noting a series of questions that we ponder as we study developmental changes in EFs across major developmental transitions.

OUR DEFINITION OF EXECUTIVE FUNCTIONS

EFs are a set of higher order cognitive processes responsible for organizing and coordinating behavior to perform complex goal-related actions, especially in nonroutine situations (Banich, 2009; Diamond, 2002; Miyake et al., 2000). The prefrontal cortex is the central brain area involved in the core EFs of working memory, inhibitory control, and cognitive flexibility. These core EFs subserve more complex EFs such as problem solving, reasoning, and planning (Diamond & Lee, 2011). Many different models describe the components of EF and various opinions as to whether EF operates as a unitary construct or whether its subcomponents should be examined in isolation, especially depending on the developmental period under investigation (Garon, Bryson, & Smith, 2008; Miyake et al., 2000; Roberts & Pennington, 1996; Wiebe, Espy, & Charak, 2008). Our conceptualization of EF aligns with Roberts and Pennington's interactive framework focused on the core processes of working memory and inhibitory control (Morasch, Raj, & Bell, 2013).

In a nutshell, working memory processes are required for producing and performing correct responses and inhibitory control is necessary for suppressing interfering dominant responses (Roberts & Pennington, 1996). Although working memory and inhibitory control can be considered independently to characterize specific aspects of cognitive regulation (Luna, Garver, Urban, Lazar, & Sweeney, 2004), there is evidence that these cognitive processes often work together to support goal-driven behavior (Roberts & Pennington, 1996; Wolfe & Bell, 2004, 2007b). Roberts and Pennington (1996) conceptualized an interactive, dual-component process of working memory and inhibitory control that functions distinctly from either process in isolation. We have conceptualized this interactive skill (which we call WMIC—working memory inhibitory control) as cognitive control (Morasch et al., 2013; Wolfe & Bell, 2004, 2007a), a critical component of self-regulation (Bell & Deater-Deckard, 2007). As we describe our research on EFs, it will be apparent that we conceptualize our laboratory tasks as incorporating both working memory and inhibitory control components.

OUR LONGITUDINAL STUDY OF DEVELOPMENT OF EXECUTIVE FUNCTION

Our study of EF is focused on understanding processes involved in the development of these higher order cognitive behaviors and fundamental relationships between behavior and biology. The premise of our work is that the foundations of EF skills are found in infancy and early childhood (Roberts & Pennington, 1996). Infants and young children readily perform tasks requiring working memory and inhibitory control (Cuevas & Bell, 2010; Diamond et al., 1997; Morasch & Bell, 2011; Wolfe & Bell, 2004, 2007b). Furthermore, it is well accepted by cognitive neuroscientists that changes in cognition and the brain occur concurrently, although caution must be taken in interpreting these simultaneous developments as being causally linked (Casey, Tottenham, Liston, & Durston, 2005). Other factors, such as infant or child temperament or parenting, may affect these developmental trajectories (Bell & Calkins, 2012; Ruff & Rothbart, 1996; Wolfe & Bell, 2007b). Our study uses a developmental psychobiology framework to examine individual differences in the development of EF behaviors from infancy through early childhood. Our biological components, which we discuss in this chapter, include brain electrical activity and temperament. Parenting behaviors are measured during mother–child interactions.

We are collecting five waves of data across three developmental periods: infancy (5 and 10 months), toddlerhood (24 months), and the preschool years (36 and 48 months). We have thus far focused mainly on cross-sectional aspects of our dataset (e.g., Cuevas, Swingler, Bell, Marcovitch, & Calkins, 2012; Diaz & Bell, 2011; Morasch & Bell, 2011), although we are beginning to report some short-term longitudinal data (e.g., Cuevas, Bell, Marcovitch, & Calkins, 2012; Morasch & Bell, 2012; Smith & Bell, 2010) as well as some longer term findings (Cuevas, Hubble, & Bell, 2012).

The work we are conducting is critical for understanding cognitive development. First, with our completed dataset, we will be able to characterize trajectories of normal development. Characterization of normal trajectories is essential for understanding and interpreting less-than-optimal developmental pathways. Second, several studies by other research groups are focused solely on preschool EF. Our longitudinal data include infancy and toddler developmental periods. As such, our work is beginning to fill critical gaps in our scientific knowledge base regarding normal trajectories of cognitive development.

The comparability of working memory tasks for infants, toddlers, and preschool children is, of course, a concern for any longitudinal study that assesses participants across major periods of early development. We are using developmentally appropriate tasks and next we detail the task requirements at each time period. These cognitive requirements are comparable, with only the task response requiring different modalities (oculomotor for infants and toddlers, verbal for early childhood).

OUR EXECUTIVE FUNCTION TASKS

As part of our longitudinal investigation of EF development from infancy through early childhood, we have used a battery of age-appropriate tasks that recruit working memory and inhibitory control processes. Here, we briefly describe some of the working memory and inhibitory control tasks that we have used to examine brain–behavior relations during EF processes. Although the focus of this volume is on EFs in preschoolers, we also review relevant infant and toddler data from our studies. A developmental framework permits the examination of age-related changes in brain–behavior relations that presumably underlie changes in corresponding EF processes. Furthermore, only a few studies have examined the psychophysiological correlates of working memory and inhibitory control processes in preschoolers; thus, an analysis of brain–behavior relations at earlier points in development is informative as the foundation for examinations of these associations in preschoolers.

Infants

The A-not-B task, a variant of the Delayed Response task, has been used to examine working memory and inhibitory control during infancy

(Diamond, 1985). In it, infants must remember where a reward is hidden and inhibit a previously rewarded response. The A-not-B task includes three phases: (1) infants watch as a desirable object is hidden in one of two locations; (2) their gaze to the hidden object is broken during the delay period; and (3) infants are asked, "Where's the toy?" After infants correctly find the object on two same-side (A) trials, the hiding location is switched. The A-not-B error occurs when infants fail to find the object on reversal (B) trials. We use an incremental delay procedure to examine individual differences in emerging EFs. If infants are successful on reversal trials with a minimal delay between hiding and searching, then the delay for the next set of trials is increased by 2-second intervals until infants respond incorrectly on two out of three reversal trials at a given delay. The presumption is that working memory and inhibitory control processes are increasingly taxed as the delay interval is increased.

The reaching response required by the traditional version of the A-not-B task is inappropriate for biobehavioral examinations of EFs because associated motor artifacts impede analysis of cortical processing. To obtain corresponding psychophysiological data during executive processing, we use the looking A-not-B task. Previous research has found that performance on the looking and reaching versions of the A-not-B task is equivalent by 8 to 9 months of age (Bell & Adams, 1999; Cuevas & Bell, 2010) and concluded that performance differences earlier in development are related to the maturation of the motor response (i.e., reaching) rather than differences in the cognitive skills recruited during task performance. The looking A-not-B task permits examination of the emergence of EFs prior to the onset of coordinated reaching. We have used the looking A-not-B task with 5- to 10-month-old infants (e.g., Bell & Adams, 1999; Cuevas & Bell, 2011; Cuevas, Bell, et al., 2012), and our behavioral measures of interest are the total proportion of correct responses and the ordinal scale score (i.e., level of A-not-B competence).

Toddlers

We also use a modified version of the looking A-not-B task that includes invisible displacement to examine working memory and inhibitory control in 24-month-olds (Diamond et al., 1997; Morasch & Bell, 2011). In this version, toddlers watch as (1) a ball is displayed and hidden in a cup at a central location; (2) the cup (with the ball inside) is shifted to one side; and (3) an opaque barrier is placed in front of the cup. Next, a 5-second delay is implemented, during which the toddlers' gaze to cup location is broken and the experimenter places a second cup behind the barrier. Finally, the barrier is removed and toddlers are asked, "Where's the ball?" If toddlers look at the correct location on two same-side (A) trials, then the hiding location is reversed (B). Task administration ceases when toddlers respond incorrectly on two reversal trials. The behavioral measure of interest is total proportion of correct responses.

Preschoolers

At 3 and 4 years of age, a variety of EF tasks have been used to examine brain–behavior relations: Day-Night, Mommy-Me, Yes-No, Hand Game, and Forward Digit Span. The majority of this research has used tasks that recruit both working memory and inhibitory control processes. The Day-Night Stroop-like task (Gerstadt, Hong, & Diamond, 1994) requires children to say "day" when shown a picture of a moon and "night" when shown a picture of the sun. Thus, children must inhibit their prepotent response (i.e., to say the name of picture) and use working memory to remember the task rules. Our lab has developed two variants of the Day-Night task (i.e., Mommy-Me task, Yes-No task) to obtain additional psychophysiological data associated with EF processes (Cuevas, Hubble, & Bell, 2012; Wolfe & Bell, 2004). For the Yes-No task, children are instructed to say "yes" when the researcher shakes her head left-to-right (i.e., a nonverbal indication of "no") and to say "no" when the researcher nods her head up and down (i.e., a nonverbal indication of "yes"). Likewise, for the Mommy-Me task, preschoolers are required to say "mommy" when shown a picture of themselves and "me" when shown a picture of their mother. Some children, however, are more likely to provide nonverbal than verbal responses. Luria's Hand Game (Luria, Pribram, & Homskaya, 1964) is a nonverbal variant of the aforementioned tasks that has been adapted for use with children (Hughes, 1996). In our version of the hand game, children are instructed to make a fist when the researcher places her hand flat on the table and to place a flattened hand on the table when the researcher makes a fist. Finally, the Forward Digit Span task primarily requires working memory (Espy & Bull, 2005), but there is also the potential of proactive interference from previous trials. Preschoolers are asked to repeat lists of single-digit numbers beginning with a 2-digit trial and continuing for a total of two 2-, 3-, and 4-digit trials. For each of these tasks, total proportion correct is our performance measure.

BRAIN ELECTROPHYSIOLOGY ASSOCIATED WITH EXECUTIVE FUNCTIONS

In this section, we discuss the electrophysiological correlates of EF from infancy through early childhood. The electroencephalogram (EEG) is one of the most preferred brain-imaging techniques for use with developmental populations because of its noninvasive procedures, relative resistance to motor artifacts, comparatively inexpensive cost, and precise temporal resolution (i.e., milliseconds; Casey & de Haan, 2002). The EEG measures the electrical activity on the scalp, which is interpreted to be indicative of underlying cortical activity (i.e., the summation of postsynaptic potentials). The activity at a particular scalp location, however, also includes electrical activity originating from spatially distant locations. Thus, the spatial resolution of EEG is constrained by limited spatial sampling (i.e., the number of electrodes), the distorting effects of the skull and skin, and imperfect signal-to-noise ratios (Pizzagalli, 2007). Although other imaging techniques, such as functional magnetic resonance imaging (fMRI), have superior spatial resolution, these techniques are currently incompatible for use with young children and their temporal resolution does not permit real-time assessment of cognitive processes.

Developmental EEG researchers typically analyze either specific fluctuations of the EEG waveform on the order of milliseconds (i.e., event-related potentials [ERPs]) or frequency-dependent changes in neural activity and synchrony on the order of seconds to minutes (e.g., EEG power, EEG coherence). In our lab, we are interested in changes in EEG as a function of ongoing cognitive processing required by our EF tasks, and we analyze changes in 6 to 9 Hz EEG power and coherence throughout infancy, toddlerhood, and early childhood. We chose this band because research indicates that (a) the majority of EEG activity falls within this frequency range during this developmental period (Bell & Fox, 1992; Marshall, Bar-Haim, & Fox, 2002) and (b) this band is functionally related to executive processes during this developmental period (see below). Unless otherwise specified, all findings reported below are for the 6 to 9 Hz frequency band.

EEG power represents the neural activity (i.e., excitability of a group of neurons) at a given scalp location and EEG coherence represents the functional connectivity between two electrodes sites (i.e., measure of neural synchrony). EEG power and coherence, however, are independent measures; coherence, unlike power, is not affected by arousal, state changes, or opening or closing of the eyes. In the following section, we discuss two types of EEG power and coherence findings in relation to EF development: resting baseline and cognitive activity. Resting baseline measures provide information about the organization and activation of the brain when not involved in active cognitive processing and are often associated with brain maturation. EEG activity during cognitive processing, on the other hand, provides information about changes in brain activation and organization when involved in mental activity. Task-related changes in EEG measures are considered indicative of cognitive processing (e.g., Klimesch, Doppelmayr, Schimke, & Ripper, 1997; Sauseng, Klimesch, Schabus, & Doppelmayr, 2005). Thus, both baseline and task measures potentially provide useful information about EF development as well as individual differences in EFs.

Infants

We are interested in the psychophysiological correlates of the A-not-B task during infancy because (a) task performance recruits working memory and inhibitory control processes and (b) lesion research with adult and infant nonhuman primates has indicated that task performance is mediated by the dorsolateral prefrontal cortex (Diamond, 1990; Diamond & Goldman-Rakic, 1989). Although the frontal cortex exhibits protracted development until early adulthood, the EEG findings presented in this section reveal that the frontal cortex is intricately linked to task processing and performance during infancy.

Prior to the development of the looking A-not-B task, we found that baseline measures of frontal and occipital EEG power and frontal-posterior EEG coherence were related to reaching A-not-B performance between 7 and 12 months of age (Bell & Fox, 1992, 1997). Thus, it seemed likely that power and coherence measures would also be informative when recorded during executive processing (i.e., looking A-not-B task). Our research findings support this notion. Between 5 and 10 months of age, infants exhibit task-related increases in EEG power at all or most electrode sites (Bell, 2001, 2002; Bell & Wolfe, 2007; Cuevas & Bell, 2011; Cuevas, Bell, et al., 2012). Likewise, 8-month-olds display task-related decreases in frontal EEG coherence for multiple electrode pairs (Bell & Wolfe, 2007; Cuevas, Raj, & Bell, 2012). Longitudinal research, however, has revealed that task-related changes in frontal coherence become more localized by 10 months of age (i.e., medial frontal–posterior; Cuevas, Bell, et al., 2012). Together, these findings suggest that increases in neural activity and decreases in frontal synchrony (i.e., differentiation of function between frontal and other cortical areas) are associated with executive processing during infancy.

By 8 months of age, infants exhibit vast differences in A-not-B performance (Bell & Adams, 1999). It seemed likely that if baseline EEG measures were associated with task performance (Bell & Fox, 1992, 1997), then task-related changes in EEG measures would also be related to task performance. We have used multiple analytical techniques (i.e., within- and between-subjects, regression, multivariate analysis of variance) to examine changes in EEG measures as a function of task performance (i.e., level of working memory and inhibitory control) and task difficulty. Within-subjects analyses have revealed that 8-month-olds exhibit higher power (6–9 Hz) and frontal coherence (10–13 Hz) during trials with correct as opposed to incorrect responses (Bell, 2002; Cuevas, Raj, & Bell, 2012). Likewise, 10-month-olds display increases in frontal coherence during trials that require increased inhibitory process (i.e., same-side versus reversal trials; Cuevas, Swingler, et al., 2012). Thus, it appears that relatively higher levels of neural activity are associated with successful executive processing, and relatively higher levels of frontal synchrony (i.e., integration of function between frontal and other cortical areas) are indicative of successful executive processing as well as additional executive processing demands.

Our within-subjects findings are consistent with evidence from between-subjects comparisons of 8-month-olds with low and high executive processing skills (i.e., A-not-B performance). Infants in high-performance groups exhibited task-related increases in EEG coherence (medial frontal-parietal electrode pairs) and power (frontal pole, medial frontal, parietal, occipital electrodes), whereas infants in low-performance groups displayed task-related decreases in EEG coherence (medial frontal-parietal and frontal pole-medial frontal electrode pairs) and no task-related changes in EEG power (Bell, 2001, 2012). Thus, these results confirm that task-related increases in neural activity and frontal synchrony are associated with relatively higher levels of executive processing skills. Finally, regression analyses reveal that EEG power and coherence measures account for variability in executive processing skills by 8 months of age, when there is a high level of variability in A-not-B performance. Specifically, we have found that (a) EEG power and coherence measures fail to account for variability in task performance at 5 months of age (Cuevas, Bell, et al., 2012); (b) medial frontal-medial parietal coherence is a unique predictor of 8-month task performance (Bell, 2012); and (c) medial and lateral frontal EEG power are unique predictors of 10-month task performance (Cuevas, Bell, et al., 2012). In sum, these findings confirm that EEG power and coherence are informative regarding individual differences in executive processing during infancy and indicate that individual differences in executive processing are related to frontal cortical activity and synchrony.

Toddlers

Relatively little is known about brain–behavior relations during toddlerhood. In fact, Diamond (2002) has stated that less is known about frontal functioning between 1 and 3 years than in any other developmental period. Here, we report two relatively recent frontal findings during toddlerhood. In an examination of high-frequency (i.e., gamma; 31 to 50 Hz) EEG activity, Benasich, Gou, Choudhury, and Harris (2008) found that 24-month-olds' frontal power during a resting baseline was positively correlated to parental ratings of two executive processes: inhibitory control and attention shifting. They postulated that the emergence of gamma activity may be essential to the optimal development of cognitive functions, such as EFs. Our research has also revealed associations between frontal EEG power and maternal ratings of inhibitory control (i.e., Early Childhood Behavior Questionnaire; Putnam, Gartstein, & Rothbart, 2006) at 24 months of age (Morasch & Bell, 2011).

Our approach, however, was very different. We collected maternal-reported measures of inhibitory control and laboratory-based measures of executive processes (i.e., A-not-B with invisible displacement). We found that toddlers' task performance and concurrent task-related changes in lateral frontal EEG power accounted for unique variance in maternal-reported measures of inhibitory control (Morasch & Bell, 2011). Together, these findings suggest that baseline and executive-related frontal EEG activity are strongly related to parent-reported measures of EF. A decade after Diamond's (2002) initial call for frontal research during toddlerhood, a significant gap remains in our understanding of frontal functioning during this developmental period.

Preschoolers

Neuropsychological research with brain-damaged adults (e.g., frontal lesions; Luria et al., 1964) and fMRI research with typically developing older children and typical adults (e.g., Durston et al., 2002; Klingberg, Forssberg, & Westerberg, 2002) have provided evidence that the frontal cortex is intricately linked to performance on tasks requiring executive processes. Accordingly, the tasks that are used to examine EFs during the preschool years are hypothesized to involve the frontal cortex (e.g., Diamond et al., 1997). Few studies, however, have used psychophysiological methods to test this hypothesis. ERP research with preschoolers has used a task that requires inhibitory processes (i.e., Go/No-Go), but this task was used to examine emotion regulation as opposed to executive processes (Lewis, Todd, & Honsberger, 2007; Todd, Lewis, Meusel, & Zelazo, 2008). In this section, we review EEG research that was designed specifically for the investigation of preschoolers' brain–behavior relations during executive processing. These findings provide initial evidence of frontal activation during executive processing in preschoolers and reveal that frontal activation is also associated with preschoolers' executive task performance. When possible, we also highlight age-related changes in brain–behavior associations during executive processing.

We begin by describing longitudinal changes in the EEG correlates of executive processing from infancy to early childhood (Bell & Wolfe, 2007). A subset of our original sample of 8-month-olds (i.e., A-not-B task participants) returned to the laboratory when they were 4.5 years old to participate in two EF tasks (Day-Night and Yes-No). We combined preschoolers' EEG from the two tasks and examined whether preschoolers would exhibit similar task-related changes in EEG power and coherence during executive processing. Preschoolers exhibited task-related increases in medial frontal power and medial frontal-posterior coherence (Bell & Wolfe, 2007). This pattern is very different than that displayed during infancy: widespread task-related increases in EEG power and widespread task-related decreases in frontal EEG coherence.

Thus, it appears that task-related increases in neural activity become localized to frontal cortical areas during early childhood. Likewise, there is a shift from widespread decreases in frontal synchrony (i.e., differentiation of function between frontal and other cortical areas) to increases in frontal-posterior synchrony (i.e., integration in function between frontal and posterior areas). We conclude that developmental changes in behavioral measures of executive processes (i.e., EF task performance) are associated with corresponding qualitative changes in the frontal cortical activity and synchrony.

As was found during infancy, there is variability in preschoolers' performance on EF tasks (e.g., Wolfe & Bell, 2004). A comparison of 4.5-year-olds with high and low executive task performance (i.e., Day-Night, Yes-No) revealed that children in the high-performance group had greater baseline and task EEG power values (medial frontal, lateral frontal, temporal) than did children in the low-performance group (Wolfe & Bell, 2004). Higher overall levels of EEG power are considered indicative of greater brain maturation (Bell, 1998), which would correspond with the executive task performance differences exhibited by the two groups. Furthermore, this pattern of findings is different than during infancy when there were differences in baseline-to-task changes but not in overall power values (Bell, 2001). However, 4.5-year-olds exhibited localized, as compared with widespread, task-related changes in EEG power, and thus different patterns of change in performance-based groups are likely related to qualitative differences in executive processing and corresponding frontal activity.

The majority of individual differences examinations of brain–behavior relations during the preschool years have used regression techniques to determine whether frontal EEG measures account for variance in executive task performance. By 3 years of age, task-related changes in frontal power accounted for unique variance in preschoolers' performance on the Hand Game task (Watson & Bell, 2013). Likewise, 3.5-, 4-, and 4.5-year-olds' executive performance (i.e., Day-Night, Yes-No) was accounted for (i.e., unique variance, group membership) by corresponding task-related changes in frontal EEG power (Wolfe & Bell, 2004, 2007a, 2007b). Only one study, however, has examined whether measures of frontal neural synchrony (i.e., EEG coherence) are related to preschoolers' executive processing (Swingler, Willoughby, & Calkins, 2011). In this study, 4-year-olds participated in a battery of EF tasks (i.e., Working Memory Span, Pick the Picture, Spatial Conflict Arrows, Something's the Same, Silly Sounds Stroop, Animal Go/No-Go) while continuous EEG was recorded. Although task-related power values failed to predict executive task performance, task-related frontal coherence values were significantly related to task performance (Swingler et al., 2011). These findings highlight the importance of analyzing multiple measures of brain–behavior relations during executive processing. There is consistent evidence that frontal measures of executive processing are indicative of variability in preschoolers' executive task performance.

The transition to school is a significant early childhood event that is associated with new challenges for children's EF skills. We recently examined whether preschoolers' frontal EEG measures were predictive of their future (as opposed to concurrent) EF skills (Cuevas, Hubble, & Bell, 2012). Specifically, 4-year-olds participated in the Forward Digit Span and Mommy-Me tasks while EEG was recorded, and we contacted the children's mothers after their first year in school (i.e., at 6 years of age, after kindergarten) and asked them to complete the Behavior Rating Inventory of Executive Function (Preschool Version [BRIEF-P]; Gioia, Espy, & Isquith, 2003). The BRIEF-P is a parental-report assessment of children's EFs (e.g., working memory, inhibitory control, shifting). We found that 4-year-olds' task performance and task-related changes in frontal EEG power accounted for unique variance in maternal ratings of EF at 6 years of age. Although future investigations examining predictive relations between frontal activity and future executive task performance (as opposed to maternal ratings of EF) are necessary, these findings provide initial evidence that frontal activity associated with executive processing at one age is predictive of future EFs. These findings highlight that frontal activity is intricately linked to individual differences in EF skills.

Summary

Electrophysiological measures have provided substantial evidence of frontal cortical involvement in executive processing as well as individual differences in EF skills from infancy through early childhood. During this developmental period, however, there are qualitative shifts in neural activity and frontal synchrony (i.e., EEG power and coherence) during executive processing. We posit that the aforementioned shifts in neural activity and synchrony reflect the maturation of frontal structures and pathways essential for EF performance and correspond with developmental shifts in EFs skills. Additional brain–behavior research during toddlerhood is essential to understanding the precise timing of qualitative shifts in frontal functioning.

CONTRIBUTORS TO INDIVIDUAL DIFFERENCES IN EXECUTIVE FUNCTION

Diamond has noted the dramatic improvements in executive abilities across infancy and early childhood and hypothesized about the associated development of certain brain systems (Diamond, 1990, 2002). Yet, as we noted earlier in this chapter, children do not improve in their EF abilities at the same rate (Bell & Fox, 1992; Diamond, 1985). Our research program includes an investigation of two constructs that have been theoretically and empirically linked with the development of EFs: child temperament and parenting.

Child Temperament

Rothbart and Bates (2006) defined *temperament* as biologically based individual differences in emotional reactivity and the emergence of self-regulation of that reactivity beginning late in the first year of life. The emergence of these early regulatory processes is facilitated by the development of executive attention, which may have implications for cognitive development as well (Bush, Luu, & Posner, 2000; Ruff & Rothbart, 1996). We have proposed that this attentional regulation is related to the cognitive control infants and young children begin to exhibit on EF tasks (Bell & Deater-Deckard, 2007; Bell, Greene, & Wolfe, 2010; Bell & Wolfe, 2004).

Indeed, individual differences associated with executive attention are the focus of Engle's model of working memory (Engle, Kane, & Tulholski, 1999; Kane & Engle, 2002). Engle and colleagues consider these individual differences to be a characteristic of the individual person and not the result of experience. In this respect, executive attention is conceptually similar to temperament, especially during early infancy, because temperament is considered to be a characteristic of the individual infant (Rothbart & Bates, 2006). We have detailed elsewhere the intricate conceptual, empirical, and biological links between executive attention and the working memory aspect of EF (Bell & Deater-Deckard, 2007). In short, we and others conceptualize the executive attention system and the accompanying frontal lobe architecture of the anterior cingulate cortex as the critical link between EFs and developing self-regulation (Bell & Deater-Deckard, 2007; Calkins & Marcovitch, 2010; Rothbart, Ellis, & Posner, 2004).

In addition to links between working memory and executive attention, it may also be that inhibitory control processes associated with EF behaviors are similar to inhibitory control behaviors associated with executive attention aspects of temperament. Indeed, the definition of EF inhibitory control we noted earlier in this chapter (i.e., the suppression of interfering dominant responses so that a correct response can be given; Roberts & Pennington, 1996) is very similar to the definition of temperament-based inhibitory control (i.e., the capacity to plan and to suppress inappropriate approach responses under instructions). This conceptual similarity may be at the heart of at least three recent calls in the developmental literature for conceptual clarity for the constructs of cognitive-based EF, temperament-based effortful control, and overall self-regulation (Liew, 2012; McClelland & Cameron, 2012; Zhou, Chen, & Main, 2012). Many researchers use these terms interchangeably, leading to debate over underlying components of these constructs (McClelland & Cameron, 2012). We agree that clarity is warranted and emphasize that we see EF inhibitory control and temperament inhibitory control as sharing some neurological underpinnings, especially with respect to the executive attention component associated with both. Our definitions of each term focus on both the overlapping and separable natures of these constructs and current and future findings from our work can help elucidate these conceptual conundrums.

For example, using Rothbart's Child Behavior Questionnaire (CBQ; Rothbart, Ahadi, Hershey, & Fisher, 2001), we demonstrated positive correlations between performance on the Day-Night and Yes-No EF tasks and parent-rated attention focusing and inhibitory control aspects of temperament (Wolfe & Bell, 2004, 2007b). We also reported a negative correlation between EF performance and the anger/frustration scale of the CBQ, suggesting that children who perform better on the EF tasks also have a greater ability to regulate their negative emotions.

Surprising to us, we discovered very different EF–temperament linkages for infants. For a group of 8-month-old infants, we noted that children rated by their parents as high on activity level or high on distress to limitations (as measured by Rothbart's Infant Behavior Questionnaire; Rothbart, 1981) had better performance on the A-not-B EF task (Bell, 2012) than did infants rated lower on distress and activity level. This unexpected finding may mean that these infants require more parental support in the development of their attentional skills to help alleviate distress, a result that may lead to enhanced cognitive skills as infants get older if that support from the parent is appropriate and sensitive (Ruff & Rothbart, 1996). This finding is what first led us to consider the rather commonsense notion that parental behavior may be essential for optimal development of EFs (Colombo & Saxon, 2002). This conjecture deserves further attention and we currently are investigating this notion with our longitudinal study.

Parenting

We are specifically focused on the mechanisms by which early parenting can affect later EF outcomes. We propose that the effects of parenting on the development of EFs occur via brain development, but empirical evidence for parenting having an effect on children's brain development typically has focused on rodents (see review by Barrett & Fleming, 2011) or on maltreated children (see reviews by Belsky & de Haan, 2011; Hughes, 2011). However, maltreatment is not the only contributor to less-than-optimal brain development. The dopamine system of the prefrontal cortex can be affected by environmental variations, which are not as extreme as maltreatment (Diamond,

2011). We know of no data demonstrating how normal variations in parenting can affect brain development and subsequent aspects of EF. However, Bernier and colleagues recently reported data from a community sample demonstrating that sensitive mothering during infancy was associated with better EF performance in toddlerhood (Bernier et al., 2010) and preschool (Matte-Gagné & Bernier, 2011). These researchers suggested that responsive maternal behaviors during infancy may promote later child EFs through neurological development of the frontal lobes.

Using data from a subsample of the children in our current longitudinal study, we have provided preliminary evidence for Bernier and colleagues' proposal (Kraybill & Bell, 2013). We showed that infant frontal EEG at 10 months and maternal positive affect during interactions with her infant at 10 months predicted child EF performance (15% of variance) on a battery of laboratory tasks at age 4. Furthermore, when we used the same infant variables to predict postkindergarten EF, as reported by the parent using the BRIEF-P, we also explained 15% of the variance in age 6 general EF. Although the BRIEF was designed to accompany clinical assessments of dysfunctions in EF, it also provides researchers with a measure of children's EF skills as exhibited in a range of situations that they encounter on a daily basis (Gioia, Isquith, Guy, & Kenworthy, 2000). When we looked at the subscales of the BRIEF-P for our sample, infant frontal EEG and maternal positive affect at 10 months accounted for 15% of the variance in both working memory and emotional control subscales of the BRIEF-P at age 6. They also accounted for 12% of the variance in the attentional shifting subscale. These findings support the suggestion by Bernier and colleagues (2010) that responsive maternal behavior during infancy may promote cognitive control later in childhood via neurological development of the frontal lobes.

CRITICAL QUESTIONS FOR THE STUDY OF PRESCHOOL EXECUTIVE FUNCTION

Our program of research on individual differences in the development of early EF is contributing important information to the developmental literature. At the same time, we see our work as raising several critical questions for the study of EFs in preschool children. First, our longitudinal study follows children from infancy to toddlerhood to preschool years, crossing two major developmental transitions. We have struggled with this question: What types of EF tasks are informative across major developmental transitions? We have approached this issue by focusing on the cognitive requirements of the tasks because we are unaware of a task that can be accomplished by children as young as 5 months and as old as 48 months (except see Espy, Kaufmann,

McDiarmid, & Glisky, 1999, for using A-not-B with preschool children). By focusing on cognitive requirements rather than actual tasks, we have shown positive correlations in EF task performance from one lab visit to the next (Wolfe, Zhang, Kim-Spoon, & Bell, 2014).

Next, we have briefly noted in this chapter the lack of conceptual clarity between EF-based inhibitory control and temperament-based inhibitory control. Although not among the tasks we have focused on here, we have sometimes conceptualized classic temperament tasks (i.e., Crayon Delay, Tongue Task, Simon Says) as EF tasks. Thus, we have struggled, along with some other researchers in the field (e.g., McClelland & Cameron, 2012), with questions similar to our second query: Should we differentiate between cognitive inhibitory control EF tasks and more temperament inhibitory control tasks? Do they measure similar or different aspects of control? As we have noted in this chapter, there are compelling neurobiological reasons for viewing these two constructs as similar, and our program of research is designed to take advantage of linkages between cognitive-based and temperament-based emotion processes (Bell & Calkins, 2012; Morasch & Bell, 2012). We will continue to consider these issues and how to best conceptualize cognition–emotion linkages (Calkins & Bell, 2010).

Finally, we are intrigued by recent indications of parenting influences on typically developing EFs. Thus, our final question is: How can we best capture parental influences on higher order cognitive processes? There is strong evidence that adverse environments have detrimental effects on neurophysiology and resulting cognitive outcomes (Belsky & de Haan, 2011; Hughes, 2011). Bernier and colleagues (2010) and Colombo and Saxon (2002) have intriguing hypotheses that parenting can affect the neurobiology of typically developing infants. When and how to measure this important influence on cognitive outcomes should be an important focus in future EF research.

REFERENCES

Banich, M. T. (2009). Executive function: The search for an integrated account. *Current Directions in Psychological Science, 18,* 89–94. http://dx.doi.org/10.1111/j.1467-8721.2009.01615.x

Barrett, J., & Fleming, A. S. (2011). Annual research review: All mothers are not created equal: Neuronal and psychobiological perspectives on mothering and the importance of individual differences. *Journal of Child Psychology and Psychiatry, 52,* 368–397.

Bell, M. A. (1998). The ontogeny of the EEG during infancy and childhood: Implications for cognitive development. In B. Garreau (Ed.), *Neuroimaging in child neuropsychiatric disorders* (pp. 97–111). Berlin, Germany: Springer-Verlag.

Bell, M. A. (2001). Brain electrical activity associated with cognitive processing during a looking version of the A-not-B task. *Infancy, 2*, 311–330. http://dx.doi.org/10.1207/S15327078IN0203_2

Bell, M. A. (2002). Power changes in infant EEG frequency bands during a spatial working memory task. *Psychophysiology, 39*, 450–458. http://dx.doi.org/10.1111/1469-8986.3940450

Bell, M. A. (2012). A psychobiological perspective on working memory performance at 8 months of age. *Child Development, 83*, 251–265. http://dx.doi.org/10.1111/j.1467-8624.2011.01684.x

Bell, M. A., & Adams, S. E. (1999). Comparable performance on looking and reaching version of the A-not-B task at 8 months of age. *Infant Behavior and Development, 22*, 221–235. http://dx.doi.org/10.1016/S0163-6383(99)00010-7

Bell, M. A., & Calkins, S. D. (2012). Attentional control and emotion regulation in early development. In M. I. Posner (Ed.), *Cognitive neuroscience of attention* (2nd ed., pp. 322–330). New York, NY: Guilford Press.

Bell, M. A., & Deater-Deckard, K. (2007). Biological systems and the development of self-regulation: Integrating behavior, genetics, and psychophysiology. *Journal of Developmental and Behavioral Pediatrics, 28*, 409–420. http://dx.doi.org/10.1097/DBP.0b013e3181131fc7

Bell, M. A., & Fox, N. A. (1992). The relations between frontal brain electrical activity and cognitive development during infancy. *Child Development, 63*, 1142–1163. http://dx.doi.org/10.2307/1131523

Bell, M. A., & Fox, N. A. (1997). Individual differences in object permanence performance at 8 months: Locomotor experience and brain electrical activity. *Developmental Psychobiology, 31*, 287–297. http://dx.doi.org/10.1002/(SICI)1098-2302(199712)31:4<287::AID-DEV6>3.0.CO;2-N

Bell, M. A., Greene, D. R., & Wolfe, C. D. (2010). Psychobiological mechanisms of cognition–emotion integration in early development. In S. D. Calkins & M. A. Bell (Eds.), *Child development at the intersection of emotion and cognition* (pp. 115–132). Washington, DC: American Psychological Association.

Bell, M. A., & Wolfe, C. D. (2004). Emotion and cognition: An intricately bound developmental process. *Child Development, 75*, 366–370.

Bell, M. A., & Wolfe, C. D. (2007). Changes in brain functioning from infancy to early childhood: Evidence from EEG power and coherence working memory tasks. *Developmental Neuropsychology, 31*, 21–38.

Belsky, J., & de Haan, M. (2011). Annual research review: Parenting and children's brain development: The end of the beginning. *Journal of Child Psychology and Psychiatry, 52*, 409–428. http://dx.doi.org/10.1111/j.1469-7610.2010.02281.x

Benasich, A. A., Gou, Z., Choudhury, N., & Harris, K. D. (2008). Early cognitive and language skills are linked to resting frontal gamma power across the first three years. *Behavioural Brain Research, 195*, 215–222. http://dx.doi.org/10.1016/j.bbr.2008.08.049

Bernier, A., Carlson, S. M., & Whipple, N. (2010). From external regulation to self-regulation: Early parenting precursors of young children's executive functioning. *Child Development, 81*, 326–339. http://dx.doi.org/10.1111/j.1467-8624.2009.01397.x

Bush, G., Luu, P., & Posner, M. I. (2000). Cognitive and emotional influences in anterior cingulate cortex. *Trends in Cognitive Sciences, 4*, 215–222.

Calkins, S. D., & Bell, M. A. (Eds.). (2010). *Child development at the intersection of emotion and cognition*. Washington, DC: American Psychological Association.

Calkins, S. D., & Marcovitch, S. (2010). Emotion regulation and executive functioning in early development: Mechanisms of control supporting adaptive functioning. In S. D. Calkins & M. A. Bell (Eds.), *Child development at the intersection of emotion and cognition* (pp. 37–57). Washington, DC: American Psychological Association.

Casey, B. J., & de Haan, M. (2002). Introduction: New methods in developmental science. *Developmental Science, 5*, 265–267. http://dx.doi.org/10.1111/1467-7687.00365

Casey, B. J., Tottenham, N., Liston, C., & Durston, S. (2005). Imagine the developing brain: What have we learned about cognitive development? *Trends in Cognitive Sciences, 9*, 104–110.

Colombo, J., & Saxon, T. F. (2002). Infant attention and the development of cognition: Does the environment moderate continuity? In H. E. Fitzgerald, K. H. Karraker, & T. Luster (Eds.), *Infant development: Ecological perspectives* (pp. 35–60). Washington, DC: Garland Press.

Cuevas, K., & Bell, M. A. (2010). Developmental progression of looking and reaching performance on the A-not-B task. *Developmental Psychology, 46*, 1363–1371. http://dx.doi.org/10.1037/a0020185

Cuevas, K., & Bell, M. A. (2011). EEG and ECG from 5 to 10 months of age: Developmental changes in baseline activation and cognitive processing during a working memory task. *International Journal of Psychophysiology, 80*, 119–128. http://dx.doi.org/10.1016/j.ijpsycho.2011.02.009

Cuevas, K., Bell, M. A., Marcovitch, S., & Calkins, S. D. (2012). EEG and heart rate measures of working memory at 5 and 10 months of age. *Developmental Psychology, 77*, 8–16.

Cuevas, K., Hubble, M., & Bell, M. A. (2012). Early childhood predictors of post-kindergarten executive function: Behavior, parent-report, and psychophysiology. *Early Education and Development, 23*, 59–73. http://dx.doi.org/10.1080/10409289.2011.611441

Cuevas, K., Raj, V., & Bell, M. A. (2012). Functional connectivity and infant spatial working memory: A frequency band analysis. *Psychophysiology, 49*, 271–280. http://dx.doi.org/10.1111/j.1469-8986.2011.01304.x

Cuevas, K., Swingler, M. M., Bell, M. A., Marcovitch, S., & Calkins, S. D. (2012). Measures of frontal functioning and the emergence of inhibitory control processes at 10 months of age. *Developmental Cognitive Neuroscience, 2*, 235–243. http://dx.doi.org/10.1016/j.dcn.2012.01.002

Diamond, A. (1985). Development of the ability to use recall to guide action, as indicated by infants' performance on AB. *Child Development, 56,* 868–883. http://dx.doi.org/10.2307/1130099

Diamond, A. (1990). The development and neural bases of memory function as indexed by the AB and delayed response tasks in human infants and infant monkeys. In A. Diamond (Ed.), *The development and neural bases of higher cognitive functions* (pp. 267–317). New York, NY: New York Academy of Sciences Press.

Diamond, A. (2002). Normal development of prefrontal cortex from birth to young adulthood: Cognitive functions, anatomy, and biochemistry. In D. Stuss & R. Knight (Eds.), *Principles of frontal lobe function* (pp. 466–503). New York, NY: Oxford University Press.

Diamond, A. (2011). Biological and social influences on cognitive control processes dependent on prefrontal cortex. *Progress in Brain Research, 189,* 319–339.

Diamond, A., & Amso, D. (2008). Contributions of neuroscience to our understanding of cognitive development. *Current Directions in Psychological Science, 17,* 136–141. http://dx.doi.org/10.1111/j.1467-8721.2008.00563.x

Diamond, A., & Goldman-Rakic, P. S. (1989). Comparison of human infants and rhesus monkeys on Piaget's AB task: Evidence for dependence on dorsolateral prefrontal cortex. *Experimental Brain Research, 74,* 24–40. http://dx.doi.org/10.1007/BF00248277

Diamond, A., & Lee, K. (2011). Interventions shown to aid executive function development in children 4 to 12 years old. *Science, 333,* 959–964. http://dx.doi.org/10.1126/science.1204529

Diamond, A., Prevor, M., Callender, G., & Druin, D. P. (1997). Prefrontal cortex cognitive deficits in children treated early and continuously for PKU. *Monographs of the Society for Research in Child Development, 62*(4), 1–208.

Diaz, A., & Bell, M. A. (2011). Information processing efficiency and regulation at five months. *Infant Behavior and Development, 34,* 239–247. http://dx.doi.org/10.1016/j.infbeh.2010.12.011

Durston, S., Thomas, K. M., Yang, Y., Ulug, A. M., Zimmerman, R. D., & Casey, B. J. (2002). A neural basis for the development of inhibitory control. *Developmental Science, 5,* F9–F16. http://dx.doi.org/10.1111/1467-7687.00235

Engle, R. W., Kane, M. J., & Tulholski, S. J. (1999). Individual differences in working memory capacity and what they tell us about controlled attention, general fluid intelligence, and functions of the prefrontal cortex. In A. Miyake & P. Shah (Eds.), *Models of working memory: Mechanisms of active maintenance and executive control* (pp. 102–134). New York, NY: Cambridge University Press.

Espy, K. A., & Bull, R. (2005). Inhibitory processes in young children and individual variation in short-term memory. *Developmental Neuropsychology, 28,* 669–688. http://dx.doi.org/10.1207/s15326942dn2802_6

Espy, K. A., Kaufmann, P. M., McDiarmid, M. D., & Glisky, M. L. (1999). Executive functioning in preschool children: Performance on A-not-B and other delayed response format tasks. *Brain and Cognition, 41,* 178–199. http://dx.doi.org/10.1006/brcg.1999.1117

Garon, N., Bryson, S. E., & Smith, I. M. (2008). Executive function in preschoolers: A review using an integrative framework. *Psychological Bulletin, 134,* 31–60. http://dx.doi.org/10.1037/0033-2909.134.1.31

Gerstadt, C. L., Hong, Y. J., & Diamond, A. (1994). The relationship between cognition and action: Performance of children 3½–7 years old on a Stroop-like day–night test. *Cognition, 53,* 129–153. http://dx.doi.org/10.1016/0010-0277(94)90068-X

Gioia, G. A., Espy, K. A., & Isquith, P. K. (2003). *Behavior Rating Inventory of Executive Function, Preschool Version (BRIEF-P).* Odessa, FL: Psychological Assessment Resources.

Gioia, G. A., Isquith, P. K., Guy, S. C., & Kenworthy, L. (2000). Behavior rating inventory of executive function. *Child Neuropsychology, 6,* 235–238. http://dx.doi.org/10.1076/chin.6.3.235.3152

Hughes, C. (1996). Control of action and thought: Normal development and dysfunction in autism: A research note. *Journal of Child Psychology and Psychiatry, 37,* 229–236. http://dx.doi.org/10.1111/j.1469-7610.1996.tb01396.x

Hughes, C. (2011). Changes and challenges in 20 years of research into the development of executive functions. *Infant and Child Development, 20,* 251–271. http://dx.doi.org/10.1002/icd.736

Kane, M. J., & Engle, R. W. (2002). The role of prefrontal cortex in working-memory capacity, executive attention, and general fluid intelligence: An individual differences perspective. *Psychonomic Bulletin & Review, 9,* 637–671. http://dx.doi.org/10.3758/BF03196323

Klimesch, W., Doppelmayr, M., Schimke, H., & Ripper, B. (1997). Theta synchronization and alpha desynchronization in a memory task. *Psychophysiology, 34,* 169–176. http://dx.doi.org/10.1111/j.1469-8986.1997.tb02128.x

Klingberg, T., Forssberg, H., & Westerberg, H. (2002). Increased brain activity in frontal and parietal cortex underlies the development of visuospatial working memory capacity during childhood. *Journal of Cognitive Neuroscience, 14,* 1–10. http://dx.doi.org/10.1162/089892902317205276

Kraybill, J. H., & Bell, M. A. (2013). Infancy predictors of preschool and postkindergarten executive function. *Developmental Psychobiology, 55,* 530–538. http://dx.doi.org/10.1002/dev.21057

Lewis, M. D., Todd, R. M., & Honsberger, M. J. M. (2007). Event-related potential measures of emotion regulation in early childhood. *Neuroreport, 18,* 61–65. http://dx.doi.org/10.1097/WNR.0b013e328010a216

Liew, J. (2012). Effortful control, executive functions, and education: Bringing self-regulatory and socio-emotional competencies to the table. *Child Development Perspectives, 6,* 105–111. http://dx.doi.org/10.1111/j.1750-8606.2011.00196.x

Luna, B., Garver, K. E., Urban, T. A., Lazar, N. A., & Sweeney, J. A. (2004). Maturation of cognitive processes from late childhood to adulthood. *Child Development, 75,* 1357–1372. http://dx.doi.org/10.1111/j.1467-8624.2004.00745.x

Luria, A. R., Pribram, K. H., & Homskaya, E. D. (1964). An experimental analysis of the behavioral disturbance produced by a left frontal arachnoidal endothelioma (meningioma). *Neuropsychologia, 2,* 257–280. http://dx.doi.org/10.1016/0028-3932(64)90034-X

Marshall, P. J., Bar-Haim, Y., & Fox, N. A. (2002). Development of the EEG from 5 months to 4 years of age. *Clinical Neurophysiology, 113,* 1199–1208. http://dx.doi.org/10.1016/S1388-2457(02)00163-3

Matte-Gagné, C., & Bernier, A. (2011). Prospective relations between maternal autonomy support and child executive functioning: Investigating the mediating role of child language ability. *Journal of Experimental Child Psychology, 110,* 611–625. http://dx.doi.org/10.1016/j.jecp.2011.06.006

McClelland, M. M., & Cameron, C. E. (2012). Self-regulation in early childhood: Improving conceptual clarity and developing ecologically valid measures. *Child Development Perspectives, 6,* 136–142. http://dx.doi.org/10.1111/j.1750-8606.2011.00191.x

Miyake, A., Friedman, N. P., Emerson, M. J., Witzki, A. H., Howerter, A., & Wager, T. D. (2000). The unity and diversity of executive functions and their contributions to complex "frontal lobe" tasks: A latent variable analysis. *Cognitive Psychology, 41,* 49–100. http://dx.doi.org/10.1006/cogp.1999.0734

Morasch, K. C., & Bell, M. A. (2011). The role of inhibitory control in behavioral and physiological expressions of toddler executive function. *Journal of Experimental Child Psychology, 108,* 593–606. http://dx.doi.org/10.1016/j.jecp.2010.07.003

Morasch, K. C., & Bell, M. A. (2012). Self-regulation of negative affect at 5 and 10 months. *Developmental Psychobiology, 54,* 215–221. http://dx.doi.org/10.1002/dev.20584

Morasch, K. C., Raj, V. R., & Bell, M. A. (2013). The development of cognitive control from infancy through childhood. In D. Reisberg (Ed.), *Oxford handbook of cognitive psychology* (pp. 989–999). New York, NY: Oxford.

Pizzagalli, D. A. (2007). Electroencephalography and high-density electrophysiological source localization. In J. T. Cacioppo, L. G. Tassinary, & G. G. Berntson (Eds.), *Handbook of psychophysiology* (3rd ed., pp. 56–84). Cambridge, England: Cambridge University Press. http://dx.doi.org/10.1017/CBO9780511546396.003

Putnam, S. P., Gartstein, M. A., & Rothbart, M. K. (2006). Measurement of fine-grained aspects of toddler temperament: The Early Childhood Behavior Questionnaire. *Infant Behavior and Development, 29,* 386–401. http://dx.doi.org/10.1016/j.infbeh.2006.01.004

Roberts, R. J., Jr., & Pennington, B. F. (1996). An interactive framework for examining prefrontal cognitive processes. *Developmental Neuropsychology, 12,* 105–126. http://dx.doi.org/10.1080/87565649609540642

Rothbart, M. K. (1981). Measurement of temperament in infancy. *Child Development, 52,* 569–578.

Rothbart, M. K., Ahadi, S. A., Hershey, K. L., & Fisher, P. (2001). Investigations of temperament at three to seven years: The Children's Behavior Questionnaire. *Child Development, 72,* 1394–1408. http://dx.doi.org/10.1111/1467-8624.00355

Rothbart, M. K., & Bates, J. E. (2006). Temperament. In N. Eisenberg (Vol. Ed.), & W. Damon & R. M. Lerner (Eds.), *Handbook of child psychology: Vol. 3. Social, emotional, and personality development* (6th ed., pp. 99–166). Hoboken, NJ: Wiley.

Rothbart, M. K., Ellis, L. K., & Posner, M. I. (2004). Temperament and self-regulation. In R. F. Baumeister & K. D. Vohs (Eds.), *Handbook of self-regulation: Research, theory, and applications* (pp. 357–370). New York, NY: Guilford Press.

Rothbart, M. K., Sheese, B. E., Rueda, M. R., & Posner, M. I. (2011). Developing mechanisms of self-regulation in early life. *Emotion Review, 3,* 207–213. http://dx.doi.org/10.1177/1754073910387943

Rueda, M. R., Posner, M. I., & Rothbart, M. K. (2004). Attentional control and self-regulation. In R. F. Baumeister & K. D. Vohs (Eds.), *Handbook of self-regulation: Research, theory, and applications* (pp. 283–300). New York, NY: Guilford Press.

Ruff, H. A., & Rothbart, M. K. (1996). *Attention in early development: Themes and variations.* New York, NY: Oxford.

Sameroff, A. (2010). A unified theory of development: A dialectic integration of nature and nurture. *Child Development, 81,* 6–22. http://dx.doi.org/10.1111/j.1467-8624.2009.01378.x

Sauseng, P., Klimesch, W., Schabus, M., & Doppelmayr, M. (2005). Fronto-parietal EEG coherence in theta and upper alpha reflect central executive functions of working memory. *International Journal of Psychophysiology, 57,* 97–103. http://dx.doi.org/10.1016/j.ijpsycho.2005.03.018

Smith, C. L., & Bell, M. A. (2010). Stability in infant frontal asymmetry as a predictor of toddlerhood internalizing and externalizing behaviors. *Developmental Psychobiology, 52,* 158–167. http://dx.doi.org/10.1002/dev.20427

Swingler, M. M., Willoughby, M. T., & Calkins, S. D. (2011). EEG power and coherence during preschoolers' performance of an executive function battery. *Developmental Psychobiology, 53,* 771–784. http://dx.doi.org/10.1002/dev.20588

Todd, R. M., Lewis, M. D., Meusel, L.-A., & Zelazo, P. D. (2008). The time course of social–emotional processing in early childhood: ERP responses to facial affect and personal familiarity in a Go-NoGo task. *Neuropsychologia, 46,* 595–613. http://dx.doi.org/10.1016/j.neuropsychologia.2007.10.011

Watson, A. J., & Bell, M. A. (2013). Individual differences in inhibitory control skills at three years of age. *Developmental Neuropsychology, 38,* 1–21. http://dx.doi.org/10.1080/87565641.2012.718818

Wiebe, S. A., Espy, K. A., & Charak, D. (2008). Using confirmatory factor analysis to understand executive control in preschool children: I. Latent structure. *Developmental Psychology, 44,* 575–587. http://dx.doi.org/10.1037/0012-1649.44.2.575

Wolfe, C. D., & Bell, M. A. (2004). Working memory and inhibitory control in early childhood: Contributions from physiology, temperament, and language. *Developmental Psychobiology, 44,* 68–83. http://dx.doi.org/10.1002/dev.10152

Wolfe, C. D., & Bell, M. A. (2007a). Sources of variability in working memory in early childhood: A consideration of age, temperament, language, and brain electrical activity. *Cognitive Development, 22,* 431–455. http://dx.doi.org/10.1016/j.cogdev.2007.08.007

Wolfe, C. D., & Bell, M. A. (2007b). The integration of cognition and emotion during infancy and early childhood: Regulatory processes associated with the development of working memory. *Brain and Cognition, 65,* 3–13. http://dx.doi.org/10.1016/j.bandc.2006.01.009

Wolfe, C. D., Zhang, J., Kim-Spoon, J., & Bell, M. A. (2014). A longitudinal perspective on the association between cognition and temperamental shyness. *International Journal of Behavioral Development, 38,* 266–276. http://dx.doi.org/10.1177/0165025413516257

Zhou, Q., Chen, S. H., & Main, A. (2012). Commonalities and differences in the research on children's effortful control and executive function: A call for an integrated model of self-regulation. *Child Development Perspectives, 6,* 112–121. http://dx.doi.org/10.1111/j.1750-8606.2011.00176.x

8

IMAGING EXECUTIVE FUNCTIONS IN TYPICALLY AND ATYPICALLY DEVELOPED CHILDREN

TZIPI HOROWITZ-KRAUS, SCOTT K. HOLLAND, AND LISA S. FREUND

As described in the earlier chapters of this volume, executive functions (EFs) encompass a wide spectrum of self-regulatory controls during cognitive, social, and emotional functioning including inhibition, shifting, self-regulation, planning, and categorizing. Clinicians and researchers have been struggling to find a single test to evaluate EFs. Most of the available tests and batteries are based on parent- or teacher-report questionnaires, which can be useful but are vulnerable to subjective report. Neuroimaging tools that examine brain structure and function associated with EF skills can provide information about the neural substrates of EF. This information may lead to identification of more objective brain signatures of EF and how those signatures change throughout development. In this chapter we review current neuroimaging and electrophysiological data relating to EFs in children. Childhood, particularly preschool age, is considered a critically important

http://dx.doi.org/10.1037/14797-009
Executive Function in Preschool-Age Children: Integrating Measurement, Neurodevelopment, and Translational Research, J. A. Griffin, P. McCardle, and L. S. Freund (Editors)

period for development of EFs, so we focus our review on this age group. We then examine the application of brain assessment methods to the study of EF deficits in different learning and learning-related disorders of childhood.

WHAT CONTROLS EXECUTIVE FUNCTIONS?

More than a decade has passed since Monsell (1996) pointed out what he called an "embarrassing zone of almost total ignorance" (p. 93) relating to the absence of research in the area of higher cognition and EFs. Since then, an enormous number of cognitive and physiological studies have been performed to link EFs to their anatomic locations in the brain using neurophysiologic and neuroimaging methods. From this effort, the prefrontal cortex (PFC) emerges as the brain area most commonly associated with EFs, in particular its lateral regions (see Duncan & Owen, 2000). This cortical area comprises about 25% of the human cerebral cortex and is relatively large in humans compared with other primates (Preuss, 2000). The PFC is thought to be the main conductor of human cognition, emotion, and behavior and is well defined as the brain area involved in higher order cognitive abilities (Bechara, Damasio, Damasio, & Anderson, 1994).

The development of the PFC begins in infancy and matures well into adulthood. It reaches its maturity between the ages of 26 and 30 (Sowell, Thompson, Holmes, Jernigan, & Toga, 1999). This maturation is characterized by a regression in gray matter and an increase in myelination (Lenroot & Giedd, 2006), suggesting an increase in synaptic interconnectivity. Cognitive studies show that these physiological changes in the PFC are associated with an improvement in EFs (see Diamond, 2002, for a review).

In general, the PFC can be divided into three main parts based on anatomical and physiological findings: (a) the dorsolateral prefrontal cortex (DLPFC), the superior and middle frontal gyri of the PFC located in Brodmann areas (BAs) 9, 46, 9/46, 8, 10; (b) the orbitofrontal cortex (BAs 12, 13); and (c) ventrolateral areas (BAs 44, 45, 47/12). The DLPFC seems to be associated with cognitive functioning whereas the ventral and orbital areas are more active in response to emotional stimuli (Dias, Robbins, & Roberts, 1996; Liotti & Tucker, 1995).

The core EFs are basic cognitive abilities that enable everyday behavior, such as inhibition, working memory (WM), and attention shifting. Complex abilities include higher order thinking and problem solving. Numerous studies have tried to define the subcomponents that comprise the EFs using ability-specific tasks. Using a single test to evaluate several EF components (e.g., the Wisconsin Card Sorting Test [WCST], the Stroop task, and the Tower of London/Hanoi tasks) makes it difficult to evaluate EF abilities separately.

EFs can also be assessed by questionnaires that result in a single score for global EF (e.g., Behavior Rating Inventory of Executive Function [BRIEF]; Conners, 1989; Gioia, Isquith, Guy, & Kenworthy, 2000). However, the questionnaires are usually administered to parents, teachers, and sometimes directly to the child, so they may not provide a truly objective measure. Also in use are written and computerized test batteries that break EF into its subcomponents and provide a general EF score, such as the Delis-Kaplan Executive Function System (Delis, Kaplan, & Kramer, 2001) and the Cambridge Neuropsychological Test Automated Battery (CANTAB; Cambridge Cognition, 2012). However, such batteries are often fatiguing for young children and can possibly result in an underestimate of the child's true abilities. It is difficult to find a single, objective behavioral test that both examines EFs as a whole and reliably identifies EF subcomponents.

EXECUTIVE FUNCTIONS IN CHILDREN AND PRESCHOOLERS

The development of EFs is relatively accelerated in preschoolers and young children. For example, Diamond (2002) described the development of inhibition and WM from 6–8 to 11–12 months with a gradual improvement in inhibition in 1 to 3 years and improvement in WM and planning from preschool to kindergarten age (Best, Miller, & Jones, 2009). This development is correlated with anatomical and physiological changes of the PFC. Growth in length of dendritic branches of pyramidal neurons in layer III of the DLPFC has been shown to occur at the age of 7.5 to 12 months (Koenderink, Uylings, & Mrzljak, 1994). There is also an unequal gray matter loss in different subregions of the PFC in this age (Sowell et al., 2003), starting from the orbitofrontal cortex (OFC), followed by the ventro-lateral PFC (VLPFC) and the DLPFC (Gogtay et al., 2004). This loss of gray matter is thought to reflect the elimination of unnecessary or unused neurons and their connections.

Development of EFs in childhood is required for the acquisition of reading and writing and associated with greater academic success and intelligence scores (Damasio, 1994). EFs also set the basis for normal social relations and understanding of the other (Hughes & Ensor, 2007). According to developmental studies, well-developed EFs in preschoolers facilitate a crucial social understanding that another person's inner state can affect that person's behavior (i.e., theory of mind; Hughes, 1998). Therefore, it is important to assess EFs using a reliable tool at an early age.

One of the first imaging studies to report correlation between brain anatomy and a variety of EFs (planning, selective attention, and inhibition) identified an association between abnormal cerebral white matter among neonates born preterm and their EF abilities in preschool (Woodward, Clark, Pritchard, Anderson, & Inder, 2011). The identified white matter abnormalities could be a possible anatomic marker for impaired EFs and used as an early red flag for a variety of future problems, but the abnormalities themselves cannot differentiate between the different EFs, which would be important for specific early intervention.

Timing is an important factor when dealing with interventions to augment EFs or reverse their abnormal development. Preschoolers can benefit from such interventions and even transfer the training outcomes to other modalities. For example, domain transfer was examined in a study of preschoolers (4–5 years old) trained separately on either visuospatial WM or inhibition-based training programs (Thorell, Lindqvist, Bergman Nutley, Bohlin, & Klingberg, 2009). Following 5 weeks of training, the group that trained on WM abilities improved in spatial and verbal WM and demonstrated transfer effects to increased attention span. Conversely, the group that trained on inhibition ability showed improved inhibitory control (on the specific trained task) but did not show transfer to other modalities or other inhibitory tasks. These findings highlight the problem in defining and characterizing EF as a single ability rather than one composed of many different subcomponents. Some of these components develop early in life and might benefit broadly from training, and others develop relatively late without generalizing after training.

IMAGING EXECUTIVE FUNCTIONS

The vague definition of EFs is mostly due to the number of the subcomponents of EFs and their interactions with each other. The behavioral tasks used to assess EFs typically measure accuracy rates and reaction times. The advantage of various types of neuroimaging tools lies in the ability to provide information about cognitive circuits involved in each task in order to separate the different EFs that are involved in a given task.

Performance of a cognitive task requires neuronal activation, which is essentially an electric signal. This signal can be measured on the scalp using an electroencephalogram (EEG). The EEG enables measurement of voltage fluctuations following a cognitive response to a given stimulus. These potentials are averaged in order to amplify the signal-to-noise ratio of the neuronal activation. This signal can be observed in several ways. The first is by measuring the evoked response potentials (ERPs); an ERP is a stereotyped electrical signal evoked in a known location and time frame in response to an externally administered stimulus (Dawson, 1950). Frequency analysis of the ERP signal over a scalp region can provide information about the change in frequency during the task. The ERP is characterized by (a) its polarity (positive or negative); (b) its amplitude (measured in µV); and (c) its latency or timing after the stimulus (measured in milliseconds). Because of the excellent temporal resolution of the EEG used for recording ERPs (on the order of milliseconds), the detected signal can divide the cognitive process for a given task into its underlying components. For example, there are EEG methods to partition out signals associated with the WM process into encoding of stimuli features, processing of the stimuli into a meaningful perception, and temporary storage for manipulation or use of the stimuli information. However, the EEG signal is based on scalp recordings and therefore the localization of the source of the ERP signals is not precise (on the order of 1 centimeter [cm]).

Functional magnetic resonance imaging (fMRI) uses a different physical property of activated neurons. One of the characteristics of activated neuronal cells is an increase in oxygen consumption and a concomitant increase in blood flow (hemodynamic response). This response results in a change in blood flow when neurons are activated compared with a baseline condition when the neurons are not activated. This comparison is called blood-oxygen-level-dependent contrast (Kwong et al., 1992; Ogawa, Lee, Nayak, & Glynn, 1990). These changes in brain activation can be measured by fMRI. Several repetitions of stimulus presentation are needed to obtain sufficient signal to noise in the fMRI signal for reliable detection of neuronal activation. The fMRI technology can provide information about the activation or deactivation of specific brain regions with high spatial resolution (on the order of 1 millimeter [mm]). Most tasks, or even resting-state conditions that do not include an external stimuli, involve the activation of several brain areas (networks). With fMRI, the strength of connectivity between several brain regions of interest can be examined. However, the hemodynamic response reaches its peak only after 4 to 6 seconds from the moment of stimulus presentation, limiting the temporal resolution of fMRI to the order of seconds, which is not adequate to monitor direction or timing of information flow in brain networks.

Another tool that can be used to examine activation patterns of cortical regions is functional near-infrared spectroscopy (fNIRS; Villringer & Chance, 1997). This tool measures oxygenated blood in activated brain areas by using infrared waves (800 to 2500 nanometers [nm]). One advantage of fNIRS is the fact that it is less sensitive to motion than are EEG and fMRI. The hardware for image acquisition is portable, another major advantage over fMRI, particularly in studies involving infants. For example, fNIRS has been used to map developmental changes in activation of the PFC in children between the ages of 3 and 4 years while engaged in a cognitive shifting task (Moriguchi & Hiraki, 2011).

However, fNIRS does not provide as accurate spatial resolution as does fMRI or as precise temporal resolution as does EEG.

Mapping EFs into their corresponding brain areas and characterizing them by means of voltage intensity and time can deepen researchers' understanding as to the cognitive components of each executive task and enable tracking of the developmental changes in a given EF. These measures can also serve as biomarkers to assist in assessing and locating the effect of interventions.

IMAGING OF EXECUTIVE FUNCTIONS IN PRESCHOOLERS AND SCHOOL-AGE CHILDREN

Mapping the trajectory of EF development by examining trends in neuroimaging test results alone is challenging. There are often differences between the tasks that are used with preschoolers and those used with older children to examine the same ability because of physiological and cognitive differences as well as young children's varying abilities to comply with testing demands. Existing studies report that preschoolers activate primarily the lateral PFC when performing EF tasks. In contrast, school-age children activate primarily the dorsal part of the PFC for many of the same tasks. The gradual development from preschool to kindergarten age in EFs, especially in inhibition (see Diamond, 2002), might contribute to the increased activation of the DLPFC in children. The physiological direction of myelination in the developing brain is from inferior to superior and from central to anterior and posterior, so the frontal lobes are myelinated last (original work by Yakovlev & Lecours, 1967; for more recent work, see Giedd et al., 2009). This pattern of myelination development might point to the specialization of the DLPFC in tasks that examine EFs. However, in light of the limited amount of neuroimaging data available from studies in preschoolers, this conclusion is somewhat speculative. It is interesting that despite extensive use of the behavioral versions of the Wisconsin Card Sorting Test (WCST) and Tower of London and Tower of Hanoi tasks in children, limited imaging studies have used these tasks even though these tasks have been used widely in adult imaging research. The absence of neuroimaging data from these well-validated tasks in children might be due to the complexity and the long administration time of these tasks, which are problematic for imaging studies in children.

Table 8.1 provides a comprehensive summary of neuroimaging and electrophysiological studies of EFs in preschool-age children. Table 8.2 reviews the relevant imaging studies that examined EFs in typically developed school-age children. The tables summarize the EF subdomain tested, the type of task used,

TABLE 8.1
Imaging Studies of Executive Control Among Preschoolers

Executive ability	Task	Tool	Age	Findings	Reference
Attention	Attention Network task	EEG	64.7 ± 3.2 months	Larger negative amplitude 485 and 540 ms following stimulus presentation in the anterior frontal area	Rueda et al., 2004
Working memory	Spatial Item Recognition	NIRS	66.5 ± 6.2 months	Changes in oxy and de-oxy Hb in left and right PFC	Tsujii, Yamamoto, Ohira, Takahashi, & Watanabe, 2010
	Spatial Matching-to-Sample task	NIRS (optical topography)	70.3 ± 8.21 months	Increase in oxy-Hb in the lateral PFC. Decrease in oxy-Hb also occurred along the task	Kuwajima & Sawaguchi, 2010
	Item Recognition task	NIRS (optical topography)	69.7 ± 6.7 (5–6) years	Activation of the lateral PFC	Tsujimoto, Yamamoto, Kawaguchi, Koizumi, & Sawaguchi, 2004
	A-not-B task	EEG	8 (8–8.75) months	Increase in 6–9 Hz power values relative to baseline across the entire scalp	Bell & Wolfe, 2007
	Day-Night Stroop-like task	EEG	4.5 years old (52–56 months)	Increase in 6–9 Hz power values relative to baseline at medial frontal areas only	Bell & Wolfe, 2007
	Pick a Picture (self-ordered pointing task)	EEG	3.5–4.5 years	(a) Increased coherence from baseline to task at the left prefrontal and medial frontal site pairs (FP1/F3) and (b) decreased coherence at the analogous right hemisphere prefrontal and medial frontal site pairs (FP2/F4) and of the right medial frontal and lateral frontal site pairs (F4/F8) were associated with increased performance on the task.	Swingler, Willoughby, & Calkins, 2011

(continues)

TABLE 8.1
Imaging Studies of Executive Control Among Preschoolers   *(Continued)*

Executive ability	Task	Tool	Age	Findings	Reference
Inhibition	Animal Go/No-Go task	EEG	3.5–4.5 years	Same as above	Swingler et al., 2011
	Silly Sounds Stroop	EEG	3.5–4.5 years	Same as above	Swingler et al., 2011
	Spatial conflict errors (after Simon task)	EEG	3.5–4.5 years	Same as above	Swingler et al., 2011
Shifting	Something's the Same (after Flexible Item Selection task)	EEG	3.5–4.5 years	Same as above	Swingler et al., 2011
	Dimensional Change Card Sort	NIRS	68.3 ± 3 (61–74) months 41.3 ± 3.8 (37–47) months	Increase in oxy-Hb in right and left inferior prefrontal areas (channels 6, 7, 15, 17, 18) during preswitch and postswitch Increase in oxy-Hb in preswitch in right (channels 6, 9) and left (15) inferior prefrontal. Postswitch increase in oxy-Hb in right (channel 6) and left (channel 17) in the prefrontal region	Moriguchi & Hiraki, 2009 Moriguchi & Hiraki, 2009
Monitoring	Prize Guessing Game	EEG	4–5 years	Similar feedback-related negativity amplitude following positive and negative feedback as measured in frontal brain regions	Mai et al., 2011
	A videotape of puppets that presented correct or erroneous arithmetic problems	EEG	6–9 months	An increase in α and θ band in frontal areas (Fcz electrode) was observed for incorrect versus correct arithmetic problems	Berger, Tzur, & Posner, 2006

Note. EEG = electroencephalogram; fNIRS = functional near-infrared spectroscopy; PFC = prefrontal cortex; Hb = hemoglobin.

TABLE 8.2

Imaging Studies of Executive Functions Among School-Age Children

Executive ability	Task	Tool	Age	Findings	Reference
Attention	Attention Network task	fMRI	10.1 (8–12) years	For altering attention: activation of the right middle occipital cortex and right STG. For reorienting: activation of the left SFG, right occipito-temporal gyrus and right occipito-temporal gyrus. For the conflict condition: activation of the left middle frontal gyrus, right STG, and right and left occipital gyri	Konrad et al., 2005
WM	Spatial N-back	fMRI	9.6 (8–10) years	For the heavy load condition, activation of the right SFG (BA 8), right dorsolateral PFC (BA 10/46), right superior parietal cortex and bilateral inferior parietal cortex (decreased activation of ventral PFC)	Thomas et al., 1999
	Memory Guided task	fMRI + eye movement device	11.2 ± 1.3 (10–13) and 15.7 ± 1.2 (14–17) years	For the overload condition, activation of the left precuneus (BA 7), right inferior precentral sulcus (BA 6), left anterior cingulate (BA 24), right anterior cingulate (BA 33), left and right caudate, right caudate tail, left anterior insula, right anterior insula, left and right thalamus, left MTG (BA 21), right MTG (BA 22), left STG (BA 22), right STG (BA 13/22), left inferior parietal temporal gyrus (BA 37), right and left fusiform (BA 37), and left and right lateral cerebellum	Scherf, Sweeney, & Luna, 2006
	Verbal WM task	fMRI	9.8 (7.2–11.9) years	For the overload condition, activation of the frontal areas: middle (right BA 6/32/9, right BA 46), inferior (left BA 47/13), superior (left BA 10). Parietal: precuneus (right and left BA 7); subcortex: insula and inferior (right BA 47/13/45); occipital: lingual (left BA 18/19, right BA 18/19/23/17)	Thomason et al., 2008

(continues)

TABLE 8.2
Imaging Studies of Executive Functions Among School-Age Children *(Continued)*

Executive ability	Task	Tool	Age	Findings	Reference
	Spatial WM task	fMRI	9.8 (7.2–11.9) years	For the overload condition, the activated regions were limbic system: cingulate cortex (left BA 24/32/6); occipital lobe: lingual (left BA 18/19, right BA 19/18); cerebellum: posterior lobe (right pyramis); subcortex: left insula	Thomason et al., 2008
	Categorical N-Back	fMRI	6.1 ± 0.5 (5.11–6.6) years	The activated regions for the overload condition: bilateral premotor cortex (BA 6), ACC (BA 24), superior parietal cortex (BA 7), insula and caudate regions (BA 13), superior temporal region (BA 22), posterior cerebral vermal lobuli VII, posterior lateral hemisphere (R>L), and inferior frontal cortex (BA 44/45)	Ciesielski, Lesnik, Savoy, Grant, & Ahlfors, 2006
			10.1 ± 0.45 (9.10–10.5) years	The activated regions for the overload condition: premotor cortex (BA 6), putamen/insula (BA 13), superior/inferior parietal regions (BA 40/7), middle PFC (BA 9), anterior cingulate gyrus (BA 24), inferior PFC (BA 44/45), and the inferior/ventral temporal region (BA 37) and cerebellar hemisphere (Cruss II)	Ciesielski et al., 2006
	Verbal-Visual Sternberg	fMRI	9 ± 1.35 (7–10) years	Recruiting only of the left ventral PFC cortex for the heavy load condition. Other activated regions in the task: left inferior frontal gyrus (BA 47/9), left middle frontal gyrus (BA 9), left SFG (BA 10), left precentral gyrus (BA 6).	O'Hare, Lu, Houston, Bookheimer, & Sowell, 2008
	Digit Span	EEG	7–10.99 years	Better performance was associated with smaller N2 amplitude. The assumed OFC generator was left localized among poor performers.	Lamm, Zelazo, & Lewis, 2006

	Task	Method	Age	Findings	Reference
Inhibition	Go/No-go	fMRI	10.8 (8–13) years	Activated regions for the no-go condition: pre-SMA, right and left occipital lobe (BA 19), right DLPFC (BA 9/10), right temporoparietal junction (BA 22/42), right cerebellum, right putamen	Suskauer et al., 2008
		EEG	6–7 years old	For no-go trials: an increased N200 in fronto-parietal electrodes and decreased P300 in parietal areas (compared with 19–23 and 9–10 years old)	Jonkman, 2006
		fMRI	9.92 (7–12) years	No-go versus go condition: activation of both dorsolateral and orbitofrontal cortices: anterior cingulate (BAs 24, 32), inferior frontal (BAs 45, 47), middle frontal (BAs 9, 10, 46), orbital frontal (BA 11), superior frontal (BAs 6, 8)	Casey et al., 1997
	Flanker task	fMRI	9.2 ± 1.3 years	Activation of the left inferior frontal gyrus (BA 45), left insula (BA 6), left precentral gyrus (BA 4), right precentral gyrus (BA 4) left caudate nucleus, midbrain, and left midtemporal gyrus BA (37/21)	Vaidya et al., 2005
	Stroop	fMRI	10.16 (7.66–11.96) years	For the Stroop effect: activation of the left and right anterior cingulate gyri (BA 24/32), the left MFG and SFG (BA 6/9/45), left occipitoparietal regions and the lingual gyrus (BA 18/19), precuneus (BA 31/7), and the cuneus (BA 17)	Adleman et al., 2002
		Event-related fNIRS	10.4 ± 1.9 (7–13) years	Left lateral PFC (electrodes FC3 and F7)	Schroeter, Zysset, Wahl, & von Cramon, 2004
		EEG	7–10.99 years	Better performance was associated with smaller N200 amplitude. The assumed OFC generator was left localized among poor performers.	Lamm et al., 2006

(continues)

TABLE 8.2

Imaging Studies of Executive Functions Among School-Age Children   *(Continued)*

Executive ability	Task	Tool	Age	Findings	Reference
	Anti-saccade task	fMRI	10.9 ± 1.5 (8–13) years	Decreased superior marginal gyrus and increase in basal ganglia, IPS, superior sulcus, FEF, lateral cerebellum, DLPFC, dentate nucleus	Luna & Sweeney, 2001
Combined WM and inhibition	Computerized test that combines a visual N-back WM paradigm with a visual go/no-go inhibitory	fMRI	12.2 ± 3.5 years	For the increased WM load: greater frontal (BAs 10, 5, 11) and orbitofrontal/putamen (BA 9)	Krivitzky et al., 2011
Shifting	Rule Switching task	fMRI	9.5 (8–11) years	Following negative relative to positive feed-back: lateral OFC, ACC, dorsolateral PFC, medial PFC/ACC, and superior parietal cortex	Crone, Zanolie, Van Leijenhorst, Westenberg, & Rombouts, 2008
	Rule Switching task	fMRI	10.1 (8–12) years	Bivalent rule > univalent rule: left ventral lateral PFC (BAs 44, 45), bilateral insula (BA 13), pre-SMA and SMA (BA 6)	Crone et al., 2008
	Switch task for children (Day-Night paradigm)	fMRI	6.8 ± 0.5 years	Switch > nonswitch: Frontal areas: right SFG (BA 10/11), left SFG (BA 6), left MFG (BA 46/10), left postcentral gyrus (BA 4/48). Temporal areas: right STG (BA 48), right MTG (BA 20), right inferior temporal gyrus (BA 37). Left hippocampus. Left inferior parietal lobe (40).	Dibbets, Bakker, & Jolles, 2006

Category	Task	Method	Age	Findings	Reference
	A version of the WCST	fMRI	7–14 years	For the shifting condition, an activation of the right insula. For the extradimension vs. the intradimension shift, there was an activation of the right ventrolateral frontal area (BA 10).	Taylor, Donner, & Pang, 2012
	WCST	EEG	8 years	Activation of the right frontal scalp	Bell, Wolfe, & Adkins, 2007
	DCCS	fMRI	12.2 (11–13) years	Switch related to a higher activation of the superior parietal cortex (BA 40), dorsolateral prefrontal cortex (BA 9), inferior frontal junction (BAs 6, 9), presupplementary motor (BA 6) regions. A laterality was found with higher activation in the right superior frontal sulcus.	Morton, Bosma, & Ansari, 2009
Flexibility	DCCS	EEG	10.2 (9–11) years	Cue resulted in an evoked late frontal negativity, which was greater for switch trials relative to repeated trials. Stimulus revealed a frontocentral N2 whose amplitude was greater for bivalent than univalent stimuli.	Waxer & Morton, 2011
Decision making and error monitoring	Nonlinguistic Go/No-Go	EEG	7.9 ± 52 (7–8) years	Errors in different ages: latency of ERN in frontal areas was shorter than for adults. Smaller ERN than adolescents (13–14) and adults (23–24).	Wiersema, van der Meere, & Roeyers, 2007
	Flanker task	EEG	7–18 years	Errors in different ages: smaller ERN amplitudes at age 10 for girls and 13 for boys and then increase along adulthood (19–25 yrs old).	Davies, Segalowitz, & Gavin, 2004
	Reading	EEG	13.17 ± 0.64 years	Reading errors in different ages: smaller ERNs than adults (age 25.7 ± 3.72)	Horowitz-Kraus & Breznitz, 2011
	Attention Network Test	EEG	4–8 years	Incongruent versus congruent effect resulted in a larger frontal N2 only among children older than 6 years old and correlated with poor performance.	Buss, Dennis, Brooker, & Sippel, 2011

(continues)

TABLE 8.2

Imaging Studies of Executive Functions Among School-Age Children   *(Continued)*

Executive ability	Task	Tool	Age	Findings	Reference
Conflict monitoring	Iowa Gambling task	EEG	7–10.99 years	Better performance was associated with smaller N2 amplitude. The assumed OFC generator was left localized among poor performers.	Lamm et al., 2006
Reward	Delay Discounting task	EEG	7–10.99 years	Better performance was associated with larger N2 amplitude. The assumed OFC generator was left localized among poor performers.	Lamm et al., 2006
Fluency	Verb Generation task	fMRI	11.5 ± 1.68 (9–14) years	Verb generation (as opposed to repetition) activated the left inferior frontal gyrus (BA 45/47), premotor cortex (BA 6), and left middle temporal gyri.	Vannest et al., 2010
Reasoning	Visual Propositional Analogy task (after the Kaufman Brief Intelligence Test, 2nd ed.)	fMRI	9.87 ± 2.09 (6–13) years	Left rostrolateral PFC and right ventrolateral PFC and right superior parietal lobule (BA 7).	Wright, Matlen, Baym, Ferrer, & Bunge, 2008
Planning	Tower of London	fMRI	13.70 ± 2.85 (8.7–18.8) years	Planning vs. control condition resulted in the activation of the frontal area: left and right premotor area (BAs 6, 8), left middle frontal gyrus (BAs 9, 10) and right middle frontal gyrus (BAs 9, 10), left inferior frontal gyrus (BA 44). Parietal lobe: left precuneus (BA 7, 40) and right precuneus (BAs 7, 40, 19), left and right insular cortex, and left caudate nucleus.	Huyser, Veltman, Wolters, de Haan, & Boer, 2010

Note. fMRI = functional magnetic resonance imaging; WM = working memory; PFC = prefrontal cortex; BA = Brodmann area; MTG = medial temporal gyrus; STG = superior temporal gyrus; OFC = orbitofrontal cortex; SMA = supplementary motor area; DLPFC = dorsolateral prefrontal cortex; EEG = electroencephalogram; MFG = medial frontal gyrus; SFG = superior frontal gyrus; fNIRS = functional near-infrared spectroscopy; IPS = intraparietal sulcus; FEF = frontal eye field; ACC = anterior cingulate cortex; WCST = Wisconsin Card Sorting Test; DCCS = Dimensional Change Card Sort; ERN = error-related negativity.

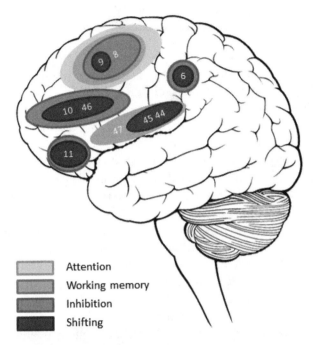

Attention
Working memory
Inhibition
Shifting

Figure 8.1. An estimation of the brain areas which are involved in attention, working memory, inhibition, and shifting (according to the data from Table 8.2). Numbers refer to Brodmann areas (Brodmann & Garey, 2010).

the neuroimaging modality used to examine brain activity, and the age range examined, along with the main findings and the key references. Figure 8.1 provides an illustration of the anatomical locations referring to the EFs described in Table 8.2.

IMAGING EXECUTIVE FUNCTION IN ATYPICALLY DEVELOPING CHILDREN

As very young children mature, more complex learning is required and more complex learning requires greater EF capacity. Learning new concepts, new facts, and new strategies for problem solving requires attention, memory, and correct integration of new information into the existing knowledge base. Research to date has shown that learning disabilities are associated with differences in how the brain processes information. To date, several imaging studies have examined EFs in children with learning- and learning-related disabilities. Following is a review of studies using neuroimaging to examine EFs in selected atypical pediatric populations, focusing on specific EF domains, the corresponding anatomical structures, and the brain activation patterns that characterize each disorder. Although no research on EFs in atypical populations has focused exclusively on very young children, understanding the brain correlates that are specific to EF deficits in learning-related disabilities among older, elementary school-age children may lead to earlier identification of disabilities, earlier interventions, and neural-based outcome measures.

Individuals with attention-deficit/hyperactivity disorder (ADHD) suffer from excessive inattention, impulsivity, and hyperactivity starting in childhood and persisting into adolescence and adulthood (Faraone, Sergeant, Gillberg, & Biederman, 2003). ADHD prevalence among school-age children in the United States and Europe is estimated at 3% to 7% (American Psychiatric Association, 2000). Some children with ADHD share a dominant deficit in attention, others exhibit hyperactivity, and some have a combination of both. In school, these symptoms are manifested by inability to sit still in class, answering questions before they have been completed, difficulties in organization, and frequent misplacing of materials or equipment. Because of fluctuations in attention, children with ADHD can have difficulties in extended seatwork or listening to an entire lesson without a break.

Children with ADHD often suffer from a deficit in EFs. Behavioral studies have demonstrated difficulties in inhibition (age 9.21 ± 1.51; Castellanos & Tannock, 2002; Marzocchi et al., 2008), sustained attention, response variability, WM, temporal processing (Castellanos & Tannock, 2002), time perception (Nicolson, Fawcett, & Dean, 1995), and planning and flexibility (Marzocchi et al., 2008). Social development is also reported to be affected, with more conflicts with peers and fewer romantic relationships (Fischer & Barkley, 2006). Large-scale imaging studies conducted in an attempt to find an anatomical marker for ADHD report that children with ADHD differ from normal peers in (a) smaller total brain volumes; (b) reduced volumes of the cerebral hemispheres, cerebellar vermis, and right caudate nucleus (Castellanos et al., 2002; Mackie et al., 2007; Valera, Faraone, Murray, & Seidman, 2007); and (c) decreased bilateral cortical folding (Wolosin, Richardson, Hennessey, Denckla, & Mostofsky, 2009).

Functional brain studies report that children with ADHD exhibit (a) slower function of the brain regions involved in the cognitive-attention network (e.g., cingulo-frontal-parietal network; Bush, 2011) and (b) a default-mode (resting-state) network that responds differently to a stimulus demanding attention compared with that of typically developing controls (Sonuga-Barke & Castellanos, 2007; Weissman, Roberts, Visscher, & Woldorff, 2006). The default-mode network is thought to support generalized, nonspecific cognition during rest but in children with ADHD, the network appears to intrude into periods of task-specific cognition, resulting in fluctuations in attention.

Characterization of brain activation patterns of children with ADHD performing tasks specific to EF reveals conflicting outcomes. Decreased activation of the DLPFC (Booth et al., 2005; Bush et al., 2008; Epstein et al., 2007), VLPFC (Epstein et al., 2007), OFC, anterior PFC, and anterior cingulate cortex (Booth et al., 2005) have been reported for children with ADHD, whereas other research describes opposite results (Durston, 2003). Decreased frontal activity in inhibitory tasks has also been reported (Bush et al., 2008; Rubia, Smith, Brammer, Toone, & Taylor, 2005; Zang et al., 2005). The attention network task is associated with increased activation of the VLPFC (Konrad, Neufang, Fink, & Herpertz-Dahlmann, 2007), whereas a WM task results in a decreased VLPFC activation in subjects with ADHD when memory load is heavy (Sheridan, Hinshaw, & D'Esposito, 2007). Decreased DLPFC activation is also found for spatial WM (Silk et al., 2005).

Error monitoring is the ability to detect errors in one's responses during a task. It can be measured electrophysiologically by the error-related negativity (ERN) component, which is present on error trials in choice reaction-time experiments. The ERN has been found to be impaired in children with attention deficits (Liotti, Pliszka, Perez, Kothmann, & Woldorff, 2005). The reduced ERN activity in children with ADHD appears to arise from a midline structure, the dorsal anterior cingulate cortex, which suggests a global deficit in cognitive control (Liotti et al., 2005).

Imaging data confirm that individuals with ADHD, compared with typical controls, have decreased brain activation or different patterns of brain activation when engaged in tasks requiring EFs, especially in frontal areas. Although brain areas in addition to the frontal lobe are involved in EF tasks, the results generally connect deficits in EFs with differences in frontal brain activity in patients with ADHD when compared with controls. These differences in brain activity may be due to fluctuations in attention (a common phenotype among patients with ADHD). The diagnosis of ADHD, however, is not synonymous with EF deficits. A recent study compared children with ADHD with and without EF deficits to specify the effect of EF deficits from the primary symptoms of the ADHD diagnosis (Lambek et al., 2010). A main finding of the study was that children with ADHD and EF deficits had significantly lower IQs than did children with ADHD without EF deficits, but did not differ in behavioral or school functioning domains. Thus, children with ADHD and EF deficits are not just at the more impaired tail of an ADHD spectrum of impairment but are a distinct subcategory of the ADHD diagnosis (Lambek et al., 2010).

Dyslexia is a language-based disability that specifically impairs a person's ability to read. Its prevalence is 5% to 10% in school-age children (American Psychiatric Association, 2000). Dyslexia continues into adulthood despite remedial interventions and exposure to written language. Although the main deficit in dyslexia is phonological processing (the ability to detect and manipulate sounds that make up words), it is a multifaceted disorder (Kinsbourne, Rufo, Gamzu, Palmer, & Berliner, 1991; National Institute of Neurological Disorders and Stroke, 2011). Therefore, it is not surprising that those studying brain functional and physiological abnormalities among subjects with dyslexia have reported diverse findings: (a) dominant right hemisphere and (b) decreased activation in the left hemisphere in reading (Masutto, Bravar, & Fabbro, 1994); (c) a decrease in white-matter volume (Eliez et al., 2000); and (d) abnormal symmetry in the PFC (Hynd, Semrud-Clikeman, Lorys, Novey, & Eliopulos, 1990). Individuals with dyslexia also exhibit EF deficits with increases in task demands (Brosnan et al., 2002; Pennington & Ozonoff, 1996). Individuals with dyslexia have deficits in planning and organizing (Condor, Anderson, & Saling, 1995), inhibition, WM (Brosnan et al., 2002), engagement of attention (Ruffino et al., 2010; Shaywitz & Shaywitz, 2008), and focus of attention (Facoetti et al., 2003), as well as problems with goal setting (Goldberg, Higgins, Raskind, & Herman, 2003). The ability to demonstrate mental flexibility while problem solving has been reported in some studies to be intact among those with dyslexia (Barkley, Grodzinsky, & DuPaul, 1992; Nyden, Gillberg, Hjelmquist, & Heiman, 1999) whereas another found flexibility to be impaired (Helland & Asbjørnsen, 2000). Another study reported that mental flexibility may be delayed in those with dyslexia but may improve with age (Snow, 1998). Error monitoring deficits are also demonstrated in both the nonverbal (Burgio-Murphy et al., 2007) and linguistic domains (Horowitz-Kraus & Breznitz, 2011). The same study showed that children with dyslexia exhibited smaller ERN amplitudes following a reading error than did control subjects, which suggests that a deficit in error detection in reading might contribute to the erroneous reading pattern in dyslexia (Horowitz-Kraus, 2011).

The cognitive performance of individuals with dyslexia is generally slower and less accurate than that of controls (Breznitz & Misra, 2003). ERPs are particularly helpful in identifying speed of processing deficits and irregularities in processing among individuals. Several abnormalities in frontally distributed ERP components have been observed among children with dyslexia. For example, differences in attention (later N100; Lehmkuhle, Garzia, Turner, Hash, & Baro, 1993), memory (smaller P600; Key, Dove, & Maguire, 2005), and inhibition tasks with later N200 (Fawcett et al., 1993) and smaller and later P300 (Taroyan, Nicolson, & Fawcett, 2007) have been reported.

A recent fMRI study found that adolescents and young adults with dyslexia exhibited connectivity abnormalities during a WM task in the executive frontoparietal network, which appears to be associated with a need for increased time in processing and memory maintenance of verbal stimuli. Compared with controls, those with dyslexia also showed decreased activation of the DLPFC and of the posterior parietal regions in a verbal WM task, regions associated with general EF deficits (Wolf et al., 2010). Another fMRI study supported the finding of difficulties in WM in individuals with dyslexia by showing a decrease in activation in the right inferior prefrontal gyrus and left superior parietal lobule with increases in memory load during a phonological WM task (Beneventi, Tønnessen, Ersland, & Hugdahl, 2010).

Besides the well-documented reading difficulties, children with dyslexia suffer from social and emotional problems that might be linked to underlying EF deficits (Goldberg et al., 2003). If there is a component of attention or inhibition deficit in dyslexia, even if a secondary one, such a deficit can contribute to social impairment and the ability to overcome it in adulthood. Unlike those for ADHD, intervention programs for dyslexia usually focus on reading alone. In light of the potential for interpersonal difficulties, an executive component intervention in the context of social functioning could be important to include in interventions for those with dyslexia.

Dyscalculia is a difficulty in fluent numerical computation and number sense, which cannot be attributed to a sensory deficit, low IQ, or educational deprivation (Butterworth, 2005). It affects 3.5% to 6.5% of school-age children. EFs linked to mathematical ability include inhibition, switching, inference, and WM (Bull & Scerif, 2001). Indeed, children with dyscalculia have exhibited difficulties in most of these EF subdomains: verbal WM (Rubinsten & Henik, 2009), attention (Shalev, Auerbach, & Gross-Tsur, 1995), inhibition (Censabella & Noël, 2007), and switching among types of cognitive routines (such as switching between addition and subtraction; Bull & Scerif, 2001).

Differences in EF components deficits might affect the child's math performance in different ways. For example, a WM deficit might impair simple and complex calculation, but a switching deficit could affect complex calculations and equations. In light of a distinct pattern of performance observed among children with math disability, Wilson and Dehaene (2007) suggested that there are two subgroups of individuals with developmental dyscalculia: one that shares a specific deficit in verbal WM and another that is characterized by attention deficit. Brain imaging studies have not yet supported this assumption (Wilson & Dehaene, 2007).

fMRI studies show that the course of arithmetic development in typically developing children involves a decrease in frontal lobe activation and an increase in activity within parietal regions (Ansari, Garcia, Lucas, Hamon, & Dhital, 2005; Kucian et al., 2006; Rivera, Reiss, Eckert, & Menon, 2005). In contrast, children with dyscalculia have less than expected activity in both frontal and parietal regions (Kucian et al., 2006). On the other hand, a recent fMRI meta-analysis found that children with dyscalculia had increased activation of the superior frontal regions and left posterior gyrus when making simple number classifications (Kaufmann, Wood, Rubinsten, & Henik, 2011). These conflicting reports suggest that in some cases children with dyscalculia may try to engage compensatory mechanisms to solve arithmetic problems and therefore display more diffuse brain activation than do controls, depending on the specific task.

Research has progressed enormously from the days when children with dyscalculia were classified as having math anxiety to the point where the disorder can be characterized by patterns of cortical activity during math processing, but this is still true only on a group level. Using such cortical patterns as a diagnostic criterion for an individual child with math disability is not yet possible and must wait until neuroimaging research with much larger, more representative populations with dyscalculia can be conducted.

Written language disorder (dysgraphia) is a combination of difficulties in the ability to compose written text. These deficits are manifested by illegible handwriting, letter shape distortion, dysfluent writing, spelling errors, and difficulty in writing expressive ideas, none of which is the consequence of reading difficulties or oral language disabilities (American Psychiatric Association, 2000). Its prevalence is 6.9% to 14.7% of all school-age children (Katusic, Colligan, Weaver, & Barbaresi, 2009). Children with written language disorder have been reported to exhibit poor EFs, especially inhibition and attention deficits (Berninger & Richards, 2010); attention deficits appear to be related specifically to poor spelling (Thomson et al., 2005).

Imaging studies of children with written language disorder are quite limited and mostly focused on the activation of frontal brain regions. Children with written language disorder differed in activation of the left posterior cingulate, calcarine, and bilateral precuneus, measured in an orthographic coding task using fMRI (Richards, Berninger, & Fayol, 2009).

Richards, Berninger, Stock, et al. (2009) found the frontal lobe, in general, to be the main indicator in differentiating poor from good writers: A finger sequencing task resulted in the activation of nine frontal or cingulate regions. They also found longitudinal correlations between behavioral measures of handwriting, spelling, and the activation of several frontal brain regions often associated with EFs (right superior frontal, right middle frontal, right inferior frontal orbital, and left middle cingulate).

Writing is a highly complex human ability and employs a large number of EFs. In their model, Berninger and Richards (2010) described how inhibition, switching and sustained attention, fluent retrieval of words and ideas from memory, monitoring the process, and a successful translation from phoneme representation to the corresponding grapheme together result in written output. It is clear that written language disorder is not just a motor problem, so it is appropriate to examine the other components of this model in future studies. fNIRS may turn out to be the best neuroimaging modality for this application because it can measure brain activity during the writing process itself without a restriction on subject motion or the need for an unnatural environment.

EXECUTIVE FUNCTIONS AS AN UNDERLYING FACTOR FOR LEARNING AND LEARNING-RELATED DISORDERS?

Learning disabilities and learning-related disorders present with variable symptoms and with variable levels of cortical connectivity. These disorders are better explained by a multiple-deficit rather than by a single-deficit model (Pennington, 2006). The common denominator of the learning disorders discussed above is impaired frontal activity, mostly involving deficits in attention, inhibition, and WM. These EF deficits interact with disorder-specific deficits that can vary in severity. Can the severity of executive dysfunction or the number of impaired EF subcomponents account for the severity of the disorder? A possible technique to address this question is to examine individuals who are unable to compensate for their disorder. Studies show that those who can compensate for their learning disabilities differ in general cognitive abilities (faster speed of processing and better performance on WM measures) from their peers who cannot compensate (Horowitz-Kraus & Breznitz, 2011; Shaywitz et al., 2003). Important questions to consider are whether well-developed EFs can improve the ability to compensate for a learning disability and whether learning is always mediated by EFs in a top-down process.

FROM IMAGING TO VISION

Assessment of EFs in preschoolers is gaining recognition as a valuable marker for current and future cognitive and socioemotional performance. A critical time window for executive development may well be before age 3 and therefore early assessment is crucial (Anderson et al., 2010). Training and optimizing EFs at this age could be particularly beneficial (Diamond & Lee, 2011), especially because it can facilitate school readiness with transference to math and reading abilities (Blair & Razza, 2007). One of the major challenges in this field is to develop better assessment tools to guide such interventions. This is particularly true for imaging-based methods.

The field of imaging is now trending toward an approach that merges different imaging tools to provide a broader spectrum of information on a given phenotype (e.g., merging EEG and fMRI data that provide high-quality temporal and spatial resolution). A recent report from a large, multisite, multimodal MRI study of typically developing children from 3 to 20 years of age demonstrated that brain development can be best specified by multidimensional measures of brain anatomy (Brown et al., 2012). This study used a composite metric of morphology, diffusivity (diffusion tensor imaging), and signal intensity to model the typical course of biological brain maturity that was more accurate in identification of a child's age than any single imaging modality alone and was more accurate than other biologically based metrics. It may well be that this type of approach will aid in identifying brain biomarkers, and their developmental course, that can serve as a biological metric of EFs in both typically and atypically developing children, even at a very young age.

Intact EFs enable the acquisition of reading, writing, and mathematical abilities, which are the platform for gaining knowledge. The importance of EFs extends even beyond academic skills given that creativity was also found to be related to frontal brain areas (Arden, Chavez, Grazioplene, & Jung, 2010). So that all children can have an equal chance for success, more sophisticated ways to evaluate and to facilitate EFs need to be developed. Neuroimaging clearly has a role in this activity.

REFERENCES

Adleman, N. E., Menon, V., Blasey, C. M., White, C. D., Warsofsky, I. S., Glover, G. H., & Reiss, A. L. (2002). A developmental fMRI study of the Stroop Color–Word task. *NeuroImage, 16*, 61–75. http://dx.doi.org/10.1006/nimg.2001.1046

American Psychiatric Association. (2000). *Diagnostic and statistical manual of mental disorders* (4th ed., text rev.). Washington, DC: Author.

Anderson, V., Spencer-Smith, M., Coleman, L., Anderson, P., Williams, J., Greenham, M., . . . Jacobs, R. (2010). Children's executive functions: Are they poorer after very early brain insult? *Neuropsychologia, 48*, 2041–2050. http://dx.doi.org/10.1016/j.neuropsychologia.2010.03.025

Ansari, D., Garcia, N., Lucas, E., Hamon, K., & Dhital, B. (2005). Neural correlates of symbolic number processing in children and adults. *Neuroreport, 16*, 1769–1773. http://dx.doi.org/10.1097/01.wnr.0000183905.23396.f1

Arden, R., Chavez, R. S., Grazioplene, R., & Jung, R. E. (2010). Neuroimaging creativity: A psychometric view. *Behavioural Brain Research, 214*, 143–156. http://dx.doi.org/10.1016/j.bbr.2010.05.015

Barkley, R. A., Grodzinsky, G., & DuPaul, G. J. (1992). Frontal lobe functions in attention-deficit disorder with and without hyperactivity: A review and research report. *Journal of Abnormal Child Psychology, 20*, 163–188. http://dx.doi.org/10.1007/BF00916547

Bechara, A., Damasio, A. R., Damasio, H., & Anderson, S. W. (1994). Insensitivity to future consequences following damage to human prefrontal cortex. *Cognition, 50*, 7–15. http://dx.doi.org/10.1016/0010-0277(94)90018-3

Bell, M. A., & Wolfe, C. D. (2007). Changes in brain functioning from infancy to early childhood: Evidence from EEG power and coherence working memory tasks. *Developmental Neuropsychology, 31,* 21–38. http://dx.doi.org/10.1207/s15326942dn3101_2

Bell, M. A., Wolfe, C. D., & Adkins, D. R. (2007). Frontal lobe development during infancy and childhood. In D. J. Coch, K. W. Fischer, & G. Dawson (Eds.), *Human behavior learning and the developing brain: Typical development* (pp. 247–276). New York, NY: Guilford Press.

Beneventi, H., Tønnessen, F. E., Ersland, L., & Hugdahl, K. (2010). Working memory deficit in dyslexia: Behavioral and fMRI evidence. *International Journal of Neuroscience, 120,* 51–59. http://dx.doi.org/10.3109/00207450903275129.

Berger, A., Tzur, G., & Posner, M. I. (2006). Infant brains detect arithmetic errors. *Proceedings of the National Academy of Sciences of the United States of America, 103,* 12649–12653. http://dx.doi.org/10.1073/pnas.0605350103

Berninger, V., & Richards, T. (2010). Inter-relationships among behavioral markers, genes, brain, and treatment in dyslexia and dysgraphia. *Future Neurology, 5,* 597–617. http://dx.doi.org/10.2217/fnl.10.22

Best, J. R., Miller, P. H., & Jones, L. L. (2009). Executive functions after age 5: Changes and correlates. *Developmental Review, 29,* 180–200. http://dx.doi.org/10.1016/j.dr.2009.05.002

Blair, C., & Razza, R. P. (2007). Relating effortful control, executive function, and false belief understanding to emerging math and literacy ability in kindergarten. *Child Development, 78,* 647–663. http://dx.doi.org/10.1111/j.1467-8624.2007.01019.x

Booth, J. R., Burman, D. D., Meyer, J. R., Lei, Z., Trommer, B. L., Davenport, N. D., ... Mesulam, M. M. (2005). Larger deficits in brain networks for response inhibition than for visual selective attention in attention-deficit/hyperactivity disorder (ADHD). *Journal of Child Psychology and Psychiatry, 46,* 94–111. http://dx.doi.org/10.1111/j.1469-7610.2004.00337.x

Breznitz, Z., & Misra, M. (2003). Speed of processing of the visual–orthographic and auditory–phonological systems in adult dyslexics: The contribution of "asynchrony" to word recognition deficits. *Brain and Language, 85,* 486–502.

Brodmann, K., & Garey, L. J. (2010). *Brodmann's: Localization in the cerebral cortex.* New York, NY: Springer.

Brosnan, M., Demetre, J., Hamill, S., Robson, K., Shepherd, H., & Cody, G. (2002). Executive functioning in adults and children with developmental dyslexia. *Neuropsychologia, 40,* 2144–2155. http://dx.doi.org/10.1016/S0028-3932(02)00046-5

Brown, T. T., Kuperman, J. M., Chung, Y., Erhart, M., McCabe, C., Hagler, D. J., Jr., ... Dale, A. M. (2012). Neuroanatomical assessment of biological maturity. *Current Biology, 22,* 1693–1698. http://dx.doi.org/10.1016/j.cub.2012.07.002

Bull, R., & Scerif, G. (2001). Executive functioning as a predictor of children's mathematics ability: Inhibition, switching, and working memory. *Developmental Neuropsychology, 19,* 273–293. http://dx.doi.org/10.1207/S15326942DN1903_3

Burgio-Murphy, A., Klorman, R., Shaywitz, S. E., Fletcher, J. M., Marchione, K. E., Holahan, J., . . . Shaywitz, B. A. (2007). Error-related event-related potentials in children with attention-deficit/hyperactivity disorder, oppositional defiant disorder, reading disorder, and math disorder. *Biological Psychology, 75,* 75–86. http://dx.doi.org/10.1016/j.biopsycho.2006.12.003

Bush, G. (2011). Cingulate, frontal, and parietal cortical dysfunction in attention-deficit/hyperactivity disorder. *Biological Psychiatry, 69,* 1160–1167. http://dx.doi.org/10.1016/j.biopsych.2011.01.022

Bush, G., Spencer, T. J., Holmes, J., Shin, L. M., Valera, E. M., Seidman, L. J., . . . Biederman, J. (2008). Functional magnetic resonance imaging of methylphenidate and placebo in attention-deficit/hyperactivity disorder during the multisource interference task. *Archives of General Psychiatry, 65,* 102–114. http://dx.doi.org/10.1001/archgenpsychiatry.2007.16

Buss, K. A., Dennis, T. A., Brooker, R. J., & Sippel, L. M. (2011). An ERP study of conflict monitoring in 4–8-year-old children: Associations with temperament. *Developmental Cognitive Neuroscience, 1,* 131–140. http://dx.doi.org/10.1016/j.dcn.2010.12.003

Butterworth, B. (2005). The development of arithmetical abilities. *Journal of Child Psychology and Psychiatry, 46,* 3–18. http://dx.doi.org/10.1111/j.1469-7610.2004.00374.x

Cambridge Cognition. (2012). CANTAB [Computer software]. Retrieved from http://www.cambridgecognition.com/?gclid=COT198rL27ECFQcQNAodqSMA1Q

Casey, B. J., Trainor, R. J., Orendi, J. L., Schubert, A. B., Nystrom, L. E., Giedd, J. N., . . . Rapoport, J. L. (1997). A developmental functional MRI study of prefrontal activation during performance of a Go-No-Go task. *Journal of Cognitive Neuroscience, 9,* 835–847. http://dx.doi.org/10.1162/jocn.1997.9.6.835

Castellanos, F. X., Lee, P. P., Sharp, W., Jeffries, N. O., Greenstein, D. K., Clasen, L. S., . . . Rapoport, J. L. (2002). Developmental trajectories of brain volume abnormalities in children and adolescents with attention-deficit/hyperactivity disorder. *JAMA, 288,* 1740–1748. http://dx.doi.org/10.1001/jama.288.14.1740

Castellanos, F. X., & Tannock, R. (2002). Neuroscience of attention-deficit/hyperactivity disorder: The search for endophenotypes. *Nature Reviews Neuroscience, 3,* 617–628. http://dx.doi.org/10.1038/nrn896

Censabella, S., & Noël, M. P. (2007). The inhibition capacities of children with mathematical disabilities. *Child Neuropsychology, 14,* 1–20. http://dx.doi.org/10.1080/09297040601052318

Ciesielski, K. T., Lesnik, P. G., Savoy, R. L., Grant, E. P., & Ahlfors, S. P. (2006). Developmental neural networks in children performing a categorical N-Back task. *NeuroImage, 33,* 980–990. http://dx.doi.org/10.1016/j.neuroimage.2006.07.028

Condor, A., Anderson, V., & Saling, A. (1995). Do reading disabled children have planning problems? *Developmental Neuropsychology, 11,* 485–502. http://dx.doi.org/10.1080/87565649509540633

Conners, C. K. (1989). *Conners' Rating Scales manual.* North Tonawanda, NY: Multi-Health Systems.

Crone, E. A., Zanolie, K., Van Leijenhorst, L., Westenberg, P. M., & Rombouts, S. A. (2008). Neural mechanisms supporting flexible performance adjustment during development. *Cognitive, Affective, & Behavioral Neuroscience, 8,* 165–177. http://dx.doi.org/10.3758/CABN.8.2.165

Damasio, A. R. (1994). *Descartes' error: Emotion, reason, and human brain.* New York, NY: Grosset/Putnam.

Davies, P. L., Segalowitz, S. J., & Gavin, W. J. (2004). Development of error-monitoring event-related potentials in adolescents. *Annals of the New York Academy of Sciences, 1021,* 324–328. http://dx.doi.org/10.1196/annals.1308.039

Dawson, G. D. (1950). Cerebral responses to nerve stimulation in man. *British Medical Bulletin, 6,* 326–329.

Delis, D. C., Kaplan, E., & Kramer, J. H. (2001). *Delis-Kaplan Executive Function System (D-KEFS).* San Antonio, TX: Pearson.

Diamond, A. (2002). Normal development of prefrontal cortex from birth to young adulthood: Cognitive functions, anatomy, and biochemistry. In D. T. Stuss & R. T. Knight (Eds.), *Principles of frontal lobe function* (pp. 466–503). http://dx.doi.org/10.1093/acprof:oso/9780195134971.001.0001

Diamond, A., & Lee, K. (2011). Interventions shown to aid executive function development in children 4 to 12 years old. *Science, 333,* 959–964. http://dx.doi.org/10.1126/science.1204529

Dias, R., Robbins, T. W., & Roberts, A. C. (1996). Dissociation in prefrontal cortex of affective and attentional shifts. *Nature, 380,* 69–72. http://dx.doi.org/10.1038/380069a0

Dibbets, P., Bakker, K., & Jolles, J. (2006). Functional MRI of task switching in children with specific language impairment (SLI). *Neurocase, 12,* 71–79. http://dx.doi.org/10.1080/13554790500507032

Duncan, J., & Owen, A. M. (2000). Common regions of the human frontal lobe recruited by diverse cognitive demands. *Trends in Neurosciences, 23,* 475–483. http://dx.doi.org/10.1016/S0166-2236(00)01633-7

Durston, S. (2003). A review of the biological bases of ADHD: What have we learned from imaging studies? *Mental Retardation and Developmental Disabilities Research Review, 9,* 184–195. http://dx.doi.org/10.1002/mrdd.10079

Eliez, S., Rumsey, J. M., Giedd, J. N., Schmitt, J. E., Patwardhan, A. J., & Reiss, A. L. (2000). Morphological alteration of temporal lobe gray matter in dyslexia: An MRI study. *Journal of Child Psychology and Psychiatry, 41,* 637–644. http://dx.doi.org/10.1111/1469-7610.00650

Epstein, J. N., Casey, B. J., Tonev, S. T., Davidson, M. C., Reiss, A. L., Garrett, A., . . . Spicer, J. (2007). ADHD- and medication-related brain activation effects in concordantly affected parent–child dyads with ADHD. *Journal of Child Psychology and Psychiatry, 48,* 899–913. http://dx.doi.org/10.1111/j.1469-7610.2007.01761.x

Facoetti, A., Lorusso, M. L., Paganoni, P., Cattaneo, C., Galli, R., & Mascetti, G. G. (2003). The time course of attentional focusing in dyslexic and normally reading children. *Brain and Cognition, 53,* 181–184. http://dx.doi.org/10.1016/S0278-2626(03)00105-2

Faraone, S. V., Sergeant, J., Gillberg, C., & Biederman, J. (2003). The worldwide prevalence of ADHD: Is it an American condition? *World Psychiatry, 2,* 104–113.

Fawcett, A. J., Chattopadhyay, A. K., Kandler, R. H., Jarratt, J. A., Nicolson, R. I., & Proctor, M. (1993). Event-related potentials and dyslexia. *Annals of the New York Academy of Sciences, 682,* 342–345. http://dx.doi.org/10.1111/j.1749-6632.1993.tb22988.x

Fischer, M., & Barkley, R. (2006). Young adult outcomes of children with hyperactivity: Leisure, financial, and social activities. *International Journal of Disability, Development and Education, 53,* 229–245. http://dx.doi.org/10.1080/10349120600716182

Giedd, J. N., Lalonde, F. M., Celano, M. J., White, S. L., Wallace, G. L., Lee, N. R., & Lenroot, R. K. (2009). Anatomical brain magnetic resonance imaging of typically developing children and adolescents. *Journal of the American Academy of Child & Adolescent Psychiatry, 48,* 465–470. http://dx.doi.org/10.1097/CHI.0b013e31819f2715

Gioia, G. A., Isquith, P. K., Guy, S. C., & Kenworthy, L. E. (2000). *Behavior Rating Inventory of Executive Function (BRIEF): Professional manual.* Lutz, FL: Psychological Assessment Resources.

Gogtay, N., Giedd, J. N., Lusk, L., Hayashi, K. M., Greenstein, D., Vaituzis, A. C., . . . Thompson, P. M. (2004). Dynamic mapping of human cortical development during childhood through early adulthood. *Proceedings of the National Academy of Sciences of the United States of America, 101,* 8174–8179. http://dx.doi.org/10.1073/pnas.0402680101

Goldberg, R. J., Higgins, H. L., Raskind, M. H., & Herman, K. L. (2003). Predictors of success in individuals with learning disabilities: A qualitative analysis of a 20-year longitudinal study. *Learning Disabilities Research & Practice, 18,* 222–236. http://dx.doi.org/10.1111/1540-5826.00077

Helland, T., & Asbjørnsen, A. (2000). Executive functions in dyslexia. *Child Neuropsychology, 6,* 37–48. http://dx.doi.org/10.1076/0929-7049(200003)6:1;1-B;FT037

Horowitz-Kraus, T. (2011). Does development affect the error-related negativity of impaired and skilled readers? An ERP study. *Developmental Neuropsychology, 36,* 914–932. http://dx.doi.org/10.1080/87565641.2011.606415

Horowitz-Kraus, T., & Breznitz, Z. (2011). Reaction time and accuracy in erroneous v. correct responses among dyslexic and regular readers: From letters to sentences. *Dyslexia, 17,* 72–84. http://dx.doi.org/10.1002/dys.417

Hughes, C. (1998). Executive function in preschoolers links with theory of mind and verbal ability. *British Journal of Developmental Psychology, 16,* 233–253. http://dx.doi.org/10.1111/j.2044-835X.1998.tb00921.x

Hughes, C., & Ensor, R. (2007). Executive function and theory of mind: Predictive relations from ages 2 to 4. *Developmental Psychology, 43,* 1447–1459. http://dx.doi.org/10.1037/0012-1649.43.6.1447

Huyser, C., Veltman, D. J., Wolters, L. H., de Haan, E., & Boer, F. (2010). Functional magnetic resonance imaging during planning before and after cognitive–behavioral therapy in pediatric obsessive–compulsive disorder. *Journal of the American Academy of Child & Adolescent Psychiatry, 49,* 1238–1248. http://dx.doi.org/10.1016/j.jaac.2010.08.007

Hynd, G. W., Semrud-Clikeman, M., Lorys, A. R., Novey, E. S., & Eliopulos, D. (1990). Brain morphology in developmental dyslexia and attention-deficit disorder/hyperactivity. *Archives of Neurology, 47,* 919–926. http://dx.doi.org/10.1001/archneur.1990.00530080107018

Jonkman, L. M. (2006). The development of preparation, conflict monitoring, and inhibition from early childhood to young adulthood: A Go/NoGo ERP study. *Brain Research, 1097,* 181–193. http://dx.doi.org/10.1016/j.brainres.2006.04.064

Katusic, S. K., Colligan, R. C., Weaver, A. L., & Barbaresi, W. J. (2009). The forgotten learning disability: Epidemiology of written-language disorder in a population-based birth cohort (1976–1982), Rochester, Minnesota. *Pediatrics, 123,* 1306–1313. http://dx.doi.org/10.1542/peds.2008-2098

Kaufmann, L., Wood, G., Rubinsten, O., & Henik, A. (2011). Meta-analyses of developmental fMRI studies investigating typical and atypical trajectories of number processing and calculation. *Developmental Neuropsychology, 36,* 763–787. http://dx.doi.org/10.1080/87565641.2010.549884

Key, A. P., Dove, G. O., & Maguire, M. J. (2005). Linking brainwaves to the brain: An ERP primer. *Developmental Neuropsychology, 27,* 183–215. http://dx.doi.org/10.1207/s15326942dn2702_1

Kinsbourne, M., Rufo, D. T., Gamzu, E., Palmer, R. L., & Berliner, A. K. (1991). Neuropsychological deficits in adults with dyslexia. *Developmental Medicine & Child Neurology, 33,* 763–775. http://dx.doi.org/10.1111/j.1469-8749.1991.tb14960.x

Koenderink, M. J., Uylings, H. B., & Mrzljak, L. (1994). Postnatal maturation of the layer III pyramidal neurons in the human prefrontal cortex: A quantitative Golgi analysis. *Brain Research, 653,* 173–182. http://dx.doi.org/10.1016/0006-8993(94)90387-5

Konrad, K., Neufang, S., Fink, G. R., & Herpertz-Dahlmann, B. (2007). Long-term effects of methylphenidate on neural networks associated with executive attention in children with ADHD: Results from a longitudinal functional MRI study. *Journal of the American Academy of Child & Adolescent Psychiatry, 46,* 1633–1641. http://dx.doi.org/10.1097/chi.0b013e318157cb3b

Konrad, K., Neufang, S., Thiel, C. M., Specht, K., Hanisch, C., Fan, J., . . . Fink, G. R. (2005). Development of attentional networks: An fMRI study with children and adults. *NeuroImage, 28*, 429–439. http://dx.doi.org/10.1016/j.neuroimage.2005.06.065

Krivitzky, L. S., Roebuck-Spencer, T. M., Roth, R. M., Blackstone, K., Johnson, C. P., & Gioia, G. (2011). Functional magnetic resonance imaging of working memory and response inhibition in children with mild traumatic brain injury. *Journal of the International Neuropsychological Society, 17*, 1143–1152. http://dx.doi.org/10.1017/S1355617711001226

Kucian, K., Loenneker, T., Dietrich, T., Dosch, M., Martin, E., & von Aster, M. (2006). Impaired neural networks for approximate calculation in dyscalculic children: A functional MRI study. *Behavioral and Brain Functions, 2*, 31. http://dx.doi.org/10.1186/1744-9081-2-31

Kuwajima, M., & Sawaguchi, T. (2010). Similar prefrontal cortical activities between general fluid intelligence and visuospatial working memory tasks in preschool children as revealed by optical topography. *Experimental Brain Research, 206*, 381–397. http://dx.doi.org/10.1007/s00221-010-2415-z

Kwong, K. K., Belliveau, J. W., Chesler, D. A., Goldberg, I. E., Weisskoff, R. M., Poncelet, B. P., . . . Turner, R. (1992). Dynamic magnetic resonance imaging of human brain activity during primary sensory stimulation. *Proceedings of the National Academy of Sciences of the United States of America, 89*, 5675–5679. http://dx.doi.org/10.1073/pnas.89.12.5675

Lambek, R., Tannock, R., Dalsgaard, S., Trillingsgaard, A., Damm, D., & Thomsen, P. H. (2010). Validating neuropsychological subtypes of ADHD: How do children with and without an executive function deficit differ? *Journal of Child Psychology and Psychiatry, 51*, 895–904. http://dx.doi.org/10.1111/j.1469-7610.2010.02248.x

Lamm, C., Zelazo, P. D., & Lewis, M. D. (2006). Neural correlates of cognitive control in childhood and adolescence: Disentangling the contributions of age and executive function. *Neuropsychologia, 44*, 2139–2148. http://dx.doi.org/10.1016/j.neuropsychologia.2005.10.013

Lehmkuhle, S., Garzia, R. P., Turner, L., Hash, T., & Baro, J. A. (1993). A defective visual pathway in children with reading disability. *The New England Journal of Medicine, 328*, 989–996. http://dx.doi.org/10.1056/NEJM199304083281402

Lenroot, R. K., & Giedd, J. N. (2006). Brain development in children and adolescents: Insights from anatomical magnetic resonance imaging. *Neuroscience and Biobehavioral Reviews, 30*, 718–729. http://dx.doi.org/10.1016/j.neubiorev.2006.06.001

Liotti, M., Pliszka, S. R., Perez, R., Kothmann, D., & Woldorff, M. G. (2005). Abnormal brain activity related to performance monitoring and error detection in children with ADHD. *Cortex, 41*, 377–388. http://dx.doi.org/10.1016/S0010-9452(08)70274-0

Liotti, M., & Tucker, D. M. (1995). Emotion in asymmetric corticolimbic networks. In R. J. Davidson & K. H. Hugdahl, *Brain asymmetry* (pp. 389–423). Cambridge, MA: MIT Press.

Luna, B., & Sweeney, J. A. (2001). Studies of brain and cognitive maturation through childhood and adolescence: A strategy for testing neurodevelopmental hypotheses. *Schizophrenia Bulletin, 27,* 443–455. http://dx.doi.org/10.1093/oxfordjournals.schbul.a006886

Mackie, S., Shaw, P., Lenroot, R., Pierson, R., Greenstein, D. K., Nugent, T. F., III, . . . Rapoport, J. L. (2007). Cerebellar development and clinical outcome in attention-deficit/hyperactivity disorder. *The American Journal of Psychiatry, 164,* 647–655. http://dx.doi.org/10.1176/ajp.2007.164.4.647

Mai, X., Tardif, T., Doan, S. N., Liu, C., Gehring, W. J., & Luo, Y. J. (2011). Brain activity elicited by positive and negative feedback in preschool-aged children. *PLoS ONE, 6,* e18774. http://dx.doi.org/10.1371/journal.pone.0018774

Marzocchi, G. M., Oosterlaan, J., Zuddas, A., Cavolina, P., Geurts, H., Redigolo, D., . . . Sergeant, J. A. (2008). Contrasting deficits on executive functions between ADHD and reading disabled children. *Journal of Child Psychology and Psychiatry, 49,* 543–552. http://dx.doi.org/10.1111/j.1469-7610.2007.01859.x

Masutto, C., Bravar, L., & Fabbro, F. (1994). Neurolinguistic differentiation of children with subtypes of dyslexia. *Journal of Learning Disabilities, 27,* 520–526. http://dx.doi.org/10.1177/002221949402700807

Monsell, S. (1996). *Control of mental processes.* Hove, England: Erlbaum.

Moriguchi, Y., & Hiraki, K. (2009). Neural origin of cognitive shifting in young children. *Proceedings of the National Academy of Sciences of the United States of America, 106,* 6017–6021. http://dx.doi.org/10.1073/pnas.0809747106

Moriguchi, Y., & Hiraki, K. (2011). Longitudinal development of prefrontal function during early childhood. *Developmental Cognitive Neuroscience, 1,* 153–162. http://dx.doi.org/10.1016/j.dcn.2010.12.004

Morton, J. B., Bosma, R., & Ansari, D. (2009). Age-related changes in brain activation associated with dimensional shifts of attention: An fMRI study. *NeuroImage, 46,* 249–256. http://dx.doi.org/10.1016/j.neuroimage.2009.01.037

National Institute of Neurological Disorders and Stroke. (2011). NINDS dyslexia information page. Retrieved from http://www.ninds.nih.gov/disorders/dyslexia/dyslexia.htm

Nicolson, R. I., Fawcett, A. J., & Dean, P. (1995). Time estimation deficits in developmental dyslexia: Evidence of cerebellar involvement. *Proceedings of the Royal Society B: Biological Sciences, 259,* 43–47. http://dx.doi.org/10.1098/rspb.1995.0007

Nyden, A., Gillberg, C., Hjelmquist, E., & Heiman, M. (1999). Executive function/attention deficits in boys with Asperger syndrome attention disorder and reading/writing disorder. *Autism, 3,* 213–228.

Ogawa, S., Lee, T. M., Nayak, A. S., & Glynn, P. (1990). Oxygenation-sensitive contrast in magnetic resonance image of rodent brain at high magnetic fields.

Magnetic Resonance in Medicine, 14, 68–78. http://dx.doi.org/10.1002/mrm.1910140108

O'Hare, E. D., Lu, L. H., Houston, S. M., Bookheimer, S. Y., & Sowell, E. R. (2008). Neurodevelopmental changes in verbal working memory load-dependency: An fMRI investigation. *NeuroImage, 42,* 1678–1685. http://dx.doi.org/10.1016/j.neuroimage.2008.05.057

Pennington, B. F. (2006). From single to multiple deficit models of developmental disorders. *Cognition, 101,* 385–413. http://dx.doi.org/10.1016/j.cognition.2006.04.008

Pennington, B. F., & Ozonoff, S. (1996). Executive functions and developmental psychopathology. *Journal of Child Psychology and Psychiatry, 37,* 51–87. http://dx.doi.org/10.1111/j.1469-7610.1996.tb01380.x

Preuss, T. M. (2000). What's human about the human brain? In M. S. Gazzaniga (Ed.), *The new cognitive neurosciences* (2nd ed., pp. 1219–1234). Cambridge, MA: MIT Press.

Richards, T., Berninger, V., & Fayol, M. (2009). FMRI activation differences between 11-year-old good and poor spellers' access in working memory to temporary and long-term orthographic representations. *Journal of Neurolinguistics, 22,* 327–353. http://dx.doi.org/10.1016/j.jneuroling.2008.11.002

Richards, T. L., Berninger, V. W., Stock, P., Altemeier, L., Trivedi, P., & Maravilla, K. (2009). Functional magnetic resonance imaging sequential-finger movement activation differentiating good and poor writers. *Journal of Clinical and Experimental Neuropsychology, 31,* 967–983. http://dx.doi.org/10.1080/13803390902780201

Rivera, S. M., Reiss, A. L., Eckert, M. A., & Menon, V. (2005). Developmental changes in mental arithmetic: Evidence for increased functional specialization in the left inferior parietal cortex. *Cerebral Cortex, 15,* 1779–1790. http://dx.doi.org/10.1093/cercor/bhi055

Rubia, K., Smith, A. B., Brammer, M. J., Toone, B., & Taylor, E. (2005). Abnormal brain activation during inhibition and error detection in medication-naive adolescents with ADHD. *The American Journal of Psychiatry, 162,* 1067–1075. http://dx.doi.org/10.1176/appi.ajp.162.6.1067

Rubinsten, O., & Henik, A. (2009). Developmental dyscalculia: Heterogeneity might not mean different mechanisms. *Trends in Cognitive Sciences, 13,* 92–99. http://dx.doi.org/10.1016/j.tics.2008.11.002

Rueda, M. R., Fan, J., McCandliss, B. D., Halparin, J. D., Gruber, D. B., Lercari, L. P., & Posner, M. I. (2004). Development of attentional networks in childhood. *Neuropsychologia, 42,* 1029–1040. http://dx.doi.org/10.1016/j.neuropsychologia.2003.12.012

Ruffino, M., Trussardi, A. N., Gori, S., Finzi, A., Giovagnoli, S., Menghini, D., . . . Facoetti, A. (2010). Attentional engagement deficits in dyslexic children. *Neuropsychologia, 48,* 3793–3801.

Scherf, K. S., Sweeney, J. A., & Luna, B. (2006). Brain basis of developmental change in visuospatial working memory. *Journal of Cognitive Neuroscience, 18,* 1045–1058.

Schroeter, M. L., Zysset, S., Wahl, M., & von Cramon, D. Y. (2004). Prefrontal activation due to Stroop interference increases during development—An event-related fNIRS study. *NeuroImage, 23,* 1317–1325. http://dx.doi.org/10.1016/j.neuroimage.2004.08.001

Shalev, R. S., Auerbach, J., & Gross-Tsur, V. (1995). Developmental dyscalculia behavioral and attentional aspects: A research note. *Journal of Child Psychology and Psychiatry, 36,* 1261–1268. http://dx.doi.org/10.1111/j.1469-7610.1995.tb01369.x

Shaywitz, S. E., & Shaywitz, B. A. (2008). Paying attention to reading: The neurobiology of reading and dyslexia. *Developmental and Psychopathology, 20,* 1329–1349. http://dx.doi.org/10.1017/S0954579408000631

Shaywitz, S. E., Shaywitz, B. A., Fulbright, R. K., Skudlarski, P., Mencl, W. E., Constable, R. T., . . . Gore, J. C. (2003). Neural systems for compensation and persistence: Young adult outcome of childhood reading disability. *Biological Psychiatry, 54,* 25–33. http://dx.doi.org/10.1016/S0006-3223(02)01836-X

Sheridan, M. A., Hinshaw, S., & D'Esposito, M. (2007). Efficiency of the prefrontal cortex during working memory in attention-deficit/hyperactivity disorder. *Journal of the American Academy of Child & Adolescent Psychiatry, 46,* 1357–1366. http://dx.doi.org/10.1097/chi.0b013e31812eecf7

Silk, T., Vance, A., Rinehart, N., Egan, G., O'Boyle, M., Bradshaw, J. L., & Cunnington, R. (2005). Fronto-parietal activation in attention-deficit/hyperactivity disorder, combined type: Functional magnetic resonance imaging study. *British Journal of Psychiatry, 187,* 282–283. http://dx.doi.org/10.1192/bjp.187.3.282

Snow, J. H. (1998). Developmental patterns and use of the Wisconsin Card Sorting Test for children and adolescents with learning disabilities. *Child Neuropsychology, 4,* 89–97. http://dx.doi.org/10.1076/chin.4.2.89.3180

Sonuga-Barke, E. J., & Castellanos, F. X. (2007). Spontaneous attentional fluctuations in impaired states and pathological conditions: A neurobiological hypothesis. *Neuroscience and Biobehavioral Reviews, 31,* 977–986. http://dx.doi.org/10.1016/j.neubiorev.2007.02.005

Sowell, E. R., Thompson, P. M., Holmes, C. J., Jernigan, T. L., & Toga, A. W. (1999). In vivo evidence for post-adolescent brain maturation in frontal and striatal regions. *Nature Neuroscience, 2,* 859–861. http://dx.doi.org/10.1038/13154

Sowell, E. R., Thompson, P. M., Welcome, S. E., Henkenius, A. L., Toga, A. W., & Peterson, B. S. (2003). Cortical abnormalities in children and adolescents with attention-deficit/hyperactivity disorder. *The Lancet, 362,* 1699–1707. http://dx.doi.org/10.1016/S0140-6736(03)14842-8

Suskauer, S. J., Simmonds, D. J., Caffo, B. S., Denckla, M. B., Pekar, J. J., & Mostofsky, S. H. (2008). fMRI of intrasubject variability in ADHD: Anomalous premotor activity with prefrontal compensation. *Journal of the American Academy of Child & Adolescent Psychiatry, 47*, 1141–1150. http://dx.doi.org/10.1097/CHI.0b013e3181825b1f

Swingler, M. M., Willoughby, M. T., & Calkins, S. D. (2011). EEG power and coherence during preschoolers' performance of an executive function battery. *Developmental Psychobiology, 53*, 771–784. http://dx.doi.org/10.1002/dev.20588

Taroyan, N. A., Nicolson, R. I., & Fawcett, A. J. (2007). Behavioral and neurophysiological correlates of dyslexia in the continuous performance task. *Clinical Neurophysiology, 118*, 845–855. http://dx.doi.org/10.1016/j.clinph.2006.11.273

Taylor, M. J., Donner, E. J., & Pang, E. W. (2012). fMRI and MEG in the study of typical and atypical cognitive development. *Clinical Neurophysiology, 42*, 19–25. http://dx.doi.org/10.1016/j.neucli.2011.08.002

Thomas, K. M., King, S. W., Franzen, P. L., Welsh, T. F., Berkowitz, A. L., Noll, D. C., . . . Casey, B. J. (1999). A developmental functional MRI study of spatial working memory. *NeuroImage, 10*, 327–338. http://dx.doi.org/10.1006/nimg.1999.0466

Thomason, M. E., Race, E., Burrows, B., Whitfield-Gabrieli, S., Glover, G. H., & Gabrieli, J. D. E. (2008). Development of spatial and verbal working memory capacity in the human brain. *Journal of Cognitive Neuroscience, 21*, 316–332.

Thomson, J. B., Chenault, B., Abbott, R. D., Raskind, W. H., Richards, T., Aylward, E., & Berninger, V. W. (2005). Converging evidence for attentional influences on the orthographic word form in child dyslexics. *Journal of Neurolinguistics, 18*, 93–126. http://dx.doi.org/10.1016/j.jneuroling.2004.11.005

Thorell, L. B., Lindqvist, S., Bergman Nutley, S., Bohlin, G., & Klingberg, T. (2009). Training and transfer effects of executive functions in preschool children. *Developmental Science, 12*, 106–113. http://dx.doi.org/10.1111/j.1467-7687.2008.00745.x

Tsujii, T., Yamamoto, E., Ohira, T., Takahashi, T., & Watanabe, S. (2010). Antihistamine effects on prefrontal cortex activity during working memory process in preschool children: A near-infrared spectroscopy (NIRS) study. *Neuroscience Research, 67*, 80–85. http://dx.doi.org/10.1016/j.neures.2010.01.010

Tsujimoto, S., Yamamoto, T., Kawaguchi, H., Koizumi, H., & Sawaguchi, T. (2004). Prefrontal cortical activation associated with working memory in adults and preschool children: An event-related optical topography study. *Cerebral Cortex, 14*, 703–712. http://dx.doi.org/10.1093/cercor/bhh030

Vaidya, C. J., Bunge, S. A., Dudukovic, N. M., Zalecki, C. A., Elliott, G. R., & Gabrieli, J. D. (2005). Altered neural substrates of cognitive control in childhood ADHD: Evidence from functional magnetic resonance imaging. *The American Journal of Psychiatry, 162*, 1605–1613. http://dx.doi.org/10.1176/appi.ajp.162.9.1605

Valera, E. M., Faraone, S. V., Murray, K. E., & Seidman, L. J. (2007). Meta-analysis of structural imaging findings in attention-deficit/hyperactivity disorder. *Biological Psychiatry, 61,* 1361–1369. http://dx.doi.org/10.1016/j.biopsych.2006.06.011

Vannest, J., Rasmussen, J., Eaton, K. P., Patel, K., Schmithorst, V., Karunanayaka, P., . . . Holland, S. (2010). FMRI activation in language areas correlates with verb generation performance in children. *Neuropediatrics, 41,* 235–239. http://dx.doi.org/10.1055/s-0030-1267982

Villringer, A., & Chance, B. (1997). Noninvasive optical spectroscopy and imaging of human brain function. *Trends in Neurosciences, 20,* 435–442. http://dx.doi.org/10.1016/S0166-2236(97)01132-6

Waxer, M., & Morton, J. B. (2011). Multiple processes underlying dimensional change card sort performance: A developmental electrophysiological investigation. *Journal of Cognitive Neuroscience, 23,* 3267–3279. http://dx.doi.org/10.1162/jocn_a_00038

Weissman, D. H., Roberts, K. C., Visscher, K. M., & Woldorff, M. G. (2006). The neural bases of momentary lapses in attention. *Nature Neuroscience, 9,* 971–978. http://dx.doi.org/10.1038/nn1727

Wiersema, J. R., van der Meere, J. J., & Roeyers, H. (2007). Developmental changes in error monitoring: An event-related potential study. *Neuropsychologia, 45,* 1649–1657. http://dx.doi.org/10.1016/j.neuropsychologia.2007.01.004

Wilson, A. J., & Dehaene, S. (2007). Number sense and developmental dyscalculia. In D. Coch, G. Dawson, & K. W. Fischer (Eds.), *Human behavior, learning, and the developing brain: Atypical development* (pp. 212–238). New York, NY: Guilford Press.

Wolf, R. C., Sambataro, F., Lohr, C., Steinbrink, C., Martin, C., & Vasic, N. (2010). Functional brain network abnormalities during verbal working memory performance in adolescents and young adults with dyslexia. *Neuropsychologia, 48,* 309–318. http://dx.doi.org/10.1016/j.neuropsychologia.2009.09.020

Wolosin, S. M., Richardson, M. E., Hennessey, J. G., Denckla, M. B., & Mostofsky, S. H. (2009). Abnormal cerebral cortex structure in children with ADHD. *Human Brain Mapping, 30,* 175–184. http://dx.doi.org/10.1002/hbm.20496

Woodward, L. J., Clark, C. A., Pritchard, V. E., Anderson, P. J., & Inder, T. E. (2011). Neonatal white matter abnormalities predict global executive function impairment in children born very preterm. *Developmental Neuropsychology, 36,* 22–41. http://dx.doi.org/10.1080/87565641.2011.540530

Wright, S. B., Matlen, B. J., Baym, C. L., Ferrer, E., & Bunge, S. A. (2008). Neural correlates of fluid reasoning in children and adults. *Frontiers in Human Neuroscience, 1,* 1–8.

Yakovlev, P. I., & Lecours, A.-R. (1967). The myelogenetic cycles of regional maturation of the brain. In A. Minkowski (Ed.), *Regional development of the brain in early life* (pp. 3–70). Oxford, England: Blackwell Scientific.

Zang, Y. F., Jin, Z., Weng, X. C., Zhang, L., Zeng, Y. W., Yang, L., . . . Faraone, S. V. (2005). Functional MRI in attention-deficit/hyperactivity disorder: Evidence for hypofrontality. *Brain & Development, 27,* 544–550. http://dx.doi.org/10.1016/j.braindev.2004.11.009

9

DEVELOPMENT OF SELECTIVE SUSTAINED ATTENTION: THE ROLE OF EXECUTIVE FUNCTIONS

ANNA FISHER AND HEIDI KLOOS

Whereas the definition of executive function (EF) remains nonstandardized and somewhat diffuse, one of the EF components, attention, is a multifaceted construct that also notoriously lacks a commonly agreed-upon definition. Nonetheless, there is widespread agreement that attention is central to human performance. Several subfunctions of attention are commonly distinguished, including alerting (i.e., achieving high sensitivity to incoming stimuli), orienting (i.e., selecting information from sensory input), and executive (or endogenous) attention (i.e., monitoring and resolving cognitive conflict and directing cognitive resources on a volitional basis; Colombo & Cheatham, 2006; Posner & Petersen, 1990; Posner & Rothbart, 2007). Some theories of attention also include maintenance (i.e., sustaining attention) as a separate subfunction (Kahneman, 1973), although others consider it as a part of the alerting

Preparation of this chapter was supported in part by grant number 1R03HD060086-01A1 from the Eunice Kennedy Shriver National Institute of Child Health and Human Development to Anna Fisher and by grant number NSF DRL #723638 from the National Science Foundation to Heidi Kloos.

http://dx.doi.org/10.1037/14797-010
Executive Function in Preschool-Age Children: Integrating Measurement, Neurodevelopment, and Translational Research, J. A. Griffin, P. McCardle, and L. S.Freund (Editors)

function (Posner & Petersen, 1990; Posner & Rothbart, 2007) or EF (Colombo & Cheatham, 2006).

The focus of this chapter is the type of attention that is both selective (as opposed to divided over multiple tasks) and sustained (i.e., extended over time as opposed to extremely brief, as in visual search, which can typically be accomplished in several hundred milliseconds). Selective sustained attention, which has also been referred to as *focused attention* in the infancy literature (e.g., Colombo & Cheatham, 2006; Oakes, Kannass, & Shaddy, 2002; Ruff & Rothbart, 2001; Tellinghuisen, Oakes, & Tjebkes, 1999), is the ability to maintain focus on a single object, task, or sensory channel for an extended period. It is a crucially important ability that has been implicated in learning across development—from the crib to the classroom and beyond (e.g., Kupietz & Richardson, 1978; Oakes et al., 2002). As Oakes et al. (2002) put it, "if attention were constantly reoriented to every new event, it would be difficult . . . to learn about any single object or event" (p. 1644). This chapter reviews extant research on the development of selective sustained attention and discusses research opportunities in furthering an understanding of this important ability.

THEORETICAL PERSPECTIVES ON SELECTIVE SUSTAINED ATTENTION

Ruff and Rothbart (2001) proposed that selective sustained attention is subserved by two systems that are anatomically and neurally separate: the orienting system and the executive control system. These two systems are said to have different maturation schedules, with the orienting system maturing during infancy and the executive control system following a protracted maturational schedule that extends into adolescence (Diamond, 2002; Luna, 2009; Posner & Rothbart, 2007). Therefore, the orienting system is assumed to subserve selective sustained attention early in life, whereas the executive control system becomes increasingly important later in development.

Orienting in infants is often characterized as stimulus driven or automatic (i.e., driven by exogenous factors), rather than participant-driven or voluntary (i.e., driven by endogenous factors). That is to say, the locus of attention in newborns and young infants is determined largely by the properties of the stimulus, such as its frequency and duration for auditory stimuli, and intensity, degree of curvature, and brightness for visual stimuli (Bornstein, 1990; Ruff & Rothbart, 2001). This lack of intentionally guided attention is furthermore illustrated by the phenomenon called *obligatory looking*: Once a visual stimulus grabs attention, 1- to 2-month-old infants often find it difficult to disengage attention, and unlimited exposure to attention-grabbing stimuli may result in prolonged looking ending in considerable distress (Colombo,

2001; Stechler & Latz, 1966). Obligatory looking diminishes after 2 months of age, suggesting development of some degree of control over disengagement of attention. In a similar manner, control over engagement of attention also develops during the first months of life. For example, unlike 4-month-old infants, 6-month-olds are capable of both reactionary saccades (saccades in response to the appearing target) and anticipatory saccades (saccades to the anticipated location of a yet invisible target; S. P. Johnson, Amso, & Slemmer, 2003).

According to Ruff and Rothbart (2001), periods of selective sustained attention in early infancy are "a prolongation of the orienting response, sustained as long as the object retains some novelty" (p. 114). As a consequence, early in life, sustained attention is at its maximum when objects are novel; termination of sustained attention is particularly likely if there is competition from another novel object or event (Richards, 1988).

There is general agreement in the literature that between 9 and 12 months of age many cognitive processes, including selective sustained attention, gradually come "under control of both systems rather than one" (Ruff & Rothbart, 2001, p. 117; see also Colombo & Cheatham, 2006; Diamond, 2006; Oakes et al., 2002). There is also agreement that the ability to sustain attention in a voluntary fashion is supported by higher order cognitive functions that are typically characterized as EFs, namely inhibition and working memory. It has been argued that sustaining attention to an object or a task requires inhibition of orienting to irrelevant objects and events (Colombo & Cheatham, 2006; Kane & Engle, 2002; Ruff & Rothbart, 2001). Inhibition is traditionally considered one of the core EFs (e.g., Miyake et al., 2000; although see MacLeod, Dodd, Sheard, Wilson, & Bibi, 2003, for divergent arguments), and persistent correlations between level of inhibitory control and sustained attention have been documented in children as well as adults (Barkley, 1997; Hrabok, Kerns, & Müller, 2007; Reck & Hund, 2011).

Working memory, another of the core EFs, is also considered to be a key component in the ability to voluntarily sustain attention (Colombo & Cheatham, 2006; Kane & Engle, 2002): One needs to maintain an active representation of a goal to organize behavior to achieve this goal. However, Colombo and Cheatham (2006) also argued that the linkages between selective sustained attention and memory are bidirectional, as memory "can serve as a basis for the distribution of attentional resources" and "sustained allocation of attention to a stimulus allows for the establishment of an enduring memory trace" (p. 300).

Functional neuroimaging data provide support to the proposal that the orienting and executive systems of attention involve distinct anatomical regions (Colombo & Cheatham, 2006; Fan, McCandliss, Fossella, Flombaum, & Posner, 2005; Posner & Rothbart, 2007). In humans, brain injury to the posterior parietal lobe, superior colliculus, or lateral pulvinar nucleus of the thalamus impairs the ability to shift attention covertly (i.e., in the absence of shifting one's eyes; Posner & Petersen, 1990). However, injury to each of these brain regions impairs orienting in different ways. Specifically, damage to the posterior parietal lobe produces the greatest impairment in the ability to disengage attention from target stimuli contralateral to the side of the lesion. In contrast, progressive deterioration in the superior colliculus leads to a deficit in the ability to shift attention, regardless of whether attention was first engaged elsewhere or not. Yet a different pattern is found in patients with lesions of the thalamus, who exhibit difficulties in engaging attention to target stimuli contralateral to the side of the lesion (Posner & Petersen, 1990).

The executive control system is traditionally associated with the prefrontal cortex (PFC) and anterior cingulate gyrus (e.g., Diamond, 2002; Miller & Cohen, 2001; Posner & Rothbart, 2007). PFC damage has long been known to produce profound deficits in goal-directed behavior. Patients with prefrontal damage exhibit difficulties in classic tasks assessing EF, such as Stroop, Wisconsin Card Sorting Test, and Tower of London (Miller & Cohen, 2001). With regard to its maturation, the PFC is said to undergo "one of the longest periods of development of any brain region, taking over two decades to reach full maturity" (Diamond, 2002, p. 466). Evidence for protracted maturation of the PFC comes from the postmortem studies of myelination, examination of resting levels of glucose metabolism, and studies of synaptogenesis and gray matter reduction (for a review, see Casey, Giedd, & Thomas, 2000).

Studies of chemical modulation of attention networks are often carried out on alert animals that can perform a variety of attention tasks after being injected with various neuromodulators. Chemical modulation in the brain regions associated with the orienting network has been linked to the neurotransmitter acetylcholine (for a review, see Davidson & Marrocco, 2000). For example, blocking cholinergic receptors with scopolamine, an anticholinergic drug, impairs orienting and sustained attention in rhesus monkeys and rats (Callahan, Kinsora, Harbaugh, Reeder, & Davis, 1993; Jones & Higgins, 1995). A reduction in cholinergic neurotransmission through selective lesions in monkeys and rats similarly leads to impairment in orienting but not in learning or working memory (Chiba, Bushnell, Oshiro, & Gallagher, 1999; Voytko et al., 1994). Finally, direct injections of scopolamine into the lateral intraparietal area of rhesus monkeys have been shown to produce dose-dependent increases in reaction times and decreases in accuracy during visual orienting tasks (Davidson & Marrocco, 2000).

In contrast, chemical modulation in the PFC is linked to the neurotransmitter dopamine. For example, local injections of selective dopamine antagonists into the PFC in rhesus monkeys led to dose-dependent increases of error rates and reaction time on working memory tasks but not on control tasks (Sawaguchi & Goldman-Rakic, 1991); similar findings have been obtained in rats (Seamans, Floresco, & Phillips, 1998). Furthermore, when infant rhesus monkeys show improvement in performance on several tasks thought to involve the PFC, there is also a concomitant increase in the level of dopamine and density of dopamine receptors in their PFC (for a review, see Diamond, 2002). In human infants, reduced dopamine level in the PFC is associated with reduced level of performance on tasks requiring working memory and response inhibition (Diamond, Briand, Fossella, & Gehlbach, 2004; Diamond, Prevor, Callender, & Druin, 1997).

Finally, several recent neuroimaging and genetic studies have established linkages between specific genes, neurotransmitters, and attention networks (for review, see Posner & Rothbart, 2007). Many genes exhibit variants, or polymorphisms, which are relatively high in frequency. These polymorphisms are thought to lead to different efficiency of cholinergic and dopaminergic modulation, and in turn to individual differences in performance on attention tasks. Several studies have linked specific genes and gene polymorphisms to modulation of orienting through acetylcholine, and executive control through dopamine (Diamond et al., 2004; Parasuraman, Greenwood, Kumar, & Fossella, 2005).

Summary

Overall, selective sustained attention is commonly thought to be subserved by two distinct systems of attention, the orienting system and the executive system. Neuroimaging and neurophysiological studies suggest that these systems involve distinct anatomical regions and different maturation schedules. Specifically, the executive system (subserved by the PFC and anterior cingulate gyrus) is thought to follow a more protracted maturational schedule than does the orienting system (subserved by the posterior parietal lobe, superior colliculus, and lateral pulvinar nucleus of the thalamus). Neuroimaging and genetic studies indicate that these two systems also involve distinct chemical modulators, with the executive system being linked to dopamine and the orienting system to acetylcholine.

SELECTIVE SUSTAINED ATTENTION ACROSS THE LIFESPAN

Characterizing selective sustained attention at different points in development often involves drastically different research paradigms. Therefore, this part of the chapter is organized around different types of measures that have been used to study selective sustained attention from infancy to adulthood.

Looking-Based Measurement of Selective Sustained Attention

This section summarizes research on selective sustained attention that is based on, or involves to a large degree, measures of looking behavior. Looking has been traditionally used to investigate different aspects of visual attention across the lifespan (for reviews, see Colombo, 2001; Henderson & Ferreira, 2004; Just & Carpenter, 1976), and there is evidence that visual attention and saccadic eye movements rely on the same neural mechanisms (Corbetta et al., 1998). Furthermore, looking is sometimes used as a behavioral measure of auditory attention as well (e.g., Reisberg, 1978; Saffran, Aslin, & Newport, 1996; Spelke, 1976).

Ample evidence suggests that selective sustained attention is present in young infants, including newborns. For example, when newborns (averaging less than 40 minutes after birth at the moment of testing) are presented with moving schematic face-like images and scrambled images (containing the same features as the face-like stimuli), newborns turn their head and eyes to track both kinds of stimuli, although more so for the face-like images (Goren, Sarty, & Wu, 1975; M. H. Johnson, Dziurawiec, Ellis, & Morton, 1991). The findings resulting from this paradigm are usually presented in terms of degree of head and eye rotation rather than duration of visual attention; however, on the basis of the reported results it is possible to estimate that newborns can sustain attention to face-like stimuli for up to 9 seconds (mean reported eye rotation was approximately 45 degrees and stimuli were moved at 5 degrees per second; M. Johnson et al., 1991).

Measuring infants' looking and heart rate, Richards and colleagues (e.g., Richards, 1987; see also Casey & Richards, 1988) identified different attentional states in 2- to 6-month-old infants, including preattention, orienting, sustained attention, and attention termination. In this paradigm, animated stimuli (e.g., a Sesame Street recording or a series of sequentially appearing and disappearing concentric squares) were presented to infants on a TV monitor. Results indicated that rapid heart-rate deceleration accompanied initial orienting to a stimulus; slower heart rate was maintained throughout the sustained attention phase and heart rate returned to baseline level when attention was terminated (for a review, see Richards, 2003). Such changes in heart rate show that selective sustained attention to dynamic events in 2- to 6-month-old infants can last from 2 up to 120 seconds, with duration of sustained attention influenced by the state of an infant during testing, stimulus novelty and complexity, and individual differences.

With regard to static two-dimensional images, a steady age-related decrease in looking duration was found during the first 6 months of life (Colombo & Cheatham, 2006). This decrease is traditionally attributed to improved efficiency of processing with development: The more efficiently an infant can encode the features of an object or event, the shorter looking duration is required to do so. This possibility is supported by negative correlations between duration of looking early in the first year of life and later cognitive outcomes (i.e., IQ and language development; for a review, see Bornstein, 1990).

However, it has also been shown that between approximately 6 months and 3 years of age duration of looking to static images steadily increases (Colombo & Cheatham, 2006). Furthermore, beyond age 1, the correlations between looking duration and cognitive outcomes are positive, such that longer looking predicts better learning (Dixon & Salley, 2006), problem solving (Kannass & Colombo, 2007), and better cognitive outcomes later in development (Lawson & Ruff, 2004).

Colombo and Cheatham (2006) suggested that nonlinear changes in looking duration during infancy provide support for the hypothesized shift in the locus of attentional control. In particular, they suggested that the U-shaped curve of looking duration in infancy stems from a change in the processes underlying selective sustained attention—from reflexive (or endogenous) to voluntary (or exogenous). According to this proposal, whereas initial decrease in looking duration over the first 6 months of life likely reflects improved encoding efficiency, the increase in looking duration over the next 3 years likely reflects "the ability to voluntarily sustain or maintain attention to an object, either in response to the object's properties or to some short-term goal" (Colombo & Cheatham, 2006, p. 294).

There has also been reported a developmental increase in duration of looking at a blank screen in anticipation of a rewarding stimulus. Goldman, Shapiro, and Nelson (2004) developed a computerized measure of sustained attention for toddlers and young children—the Early Childhood Vigilance Task (ECVT). In this task children need to look at a computer screen in the absence of stimuli to view interesting stimuli (e.g., moving cartoon characters) when they appear: The better able children are to sustain attention to the blank screen in 5- to 15-second intervals between cartoons, the more likely they are to view the short cartoons when they appear on the screen. Children are videotaped during the task and their looking is later analyzed to determine the total duration of time they spent looking toward the computer screen. With a sample of 12- to 46-month-old children, Goldman et al. (2004) found a significant age-related increase in total looking toward the screen on the ECVT.

Play-Based Measurement of Selective Sustained Attention

Developmental studies of selective sustained attention often use elaborate coding schemes to determine the attentional state of a participant, typically during free play. The coding schemes commonly distinguish between selective sustained (or focused) attention and casual attention. Selective sustained attention is measured by coding a child's direction of gaze and behavior, including facial expressions that are intent or show concentration or interest (e.g., knitted brows, lip biting); minimal extraneous body movement; postural enclosure of the object, or leaning toward the object while looking at it (Choudhury & Gorman, 2000; Oakes et al., 2002; Ruff & Capozzoli, 2003; Ruff & Rothbart, 2001; Tellinghuisen, Oakes, & Tjebkes, 1999). Studies that used coding schemes similar to the one described above point to a steady increase in duration of selective sustained attention, from approximately 2 minutes in 21-month-old infants to 4 minutes in 2- and 3-year-old children, and to over 9 minutes in 5- and 6-year-olds (Choudhury & Gorman, 2000; Ruff & Lawson, 1990; Sarid & Breznitz, 1997).

Being in the state of selective sustained attention has been shown to affect children's responses to environmental distracters. For example, following an episode of distraction, children were more likely to return to the interrupted activity if they were in a state of selective sustained attention than if they were in a state of casual attention (Oakes & Tellinghuisen, 1994). Furthermore, infants and children take longer to orient to environmental distracters when in a state of selective sustained attention (Lansink & Richards, 1997; Oakes et al., 2002; Oakes & Tellinghuisen, 1994). For example, Oakes et al. (2002) presented 6- to 9-month-old infants with target events that consisted of colorful multipart toys. As infants investigated the toy, distracter events were presented in the periphery on a computer monitor. Distracters consisted of visual–auditory compounds (i.e., colored blinking rectangles accompanied by a beeping sound) and were presented until infants visually fixated on them. Latencies to orient to a distracter were longer when infants were in a state of selective sustained attention and target events were novel. Richards (1987) similarly showed that latency to orient to a distracter is greater if the distracter is presented during the maximum heart rate deceleration (i.e., the sustained attention phase to the target stimulus) compared with distracter presentation during heart rate acceleration (i.e., return to baseline, which marks termination of selective sustained attention).

Performance-Based Measurement of Selective Sustained Attention

Beyond infancy and toddlerhood, one of the most widely used tests of selective sustained attention is the Continuous Performance Test (CPT; Rosvold, Mirsky, Sarason, Bransome, & Beck, 1956[1]). The CPT was originally

---

[1] Several commercial versions of this task have been developed (e.g., Conners' CPT: Conners, 2002; Gordon Diagnostic System: Gordon, 1983; Test of Variables of Attention: Greenberg & Waldmant, 1993). Note however, that there are many versions and modifications of the CPT, with some versions being referred to by other names (e.g., Picture Selection task; Akshoomoff, 2002).

developed as a screening tool for brain damage but is widely used today in research on sustained attention. Topics include attention in neurotypical adults (e.g., Davies & Parasuraman, 1982; Nuechterlein, Parasuraman, & Jiang, 1983), attention in typically developing children (e.g., Akshoomoff, 2002; Corkum, Byrne, & Ellsworth, 1995), attention in patients with attention-deficit/hyperactivity disorder (ADHD; e.g., Barkley, 1990; Kerns & Rondeau, 1998), and attention in patients with schizophrenia (e.g., Cornblatt & Keilp, 1994; Nuechterlein & Dawson, 1984).

The core feature of the CPT is that participants are presented with a continuous stream of stimuli consisting of infrequently appearing targets and frequently appearing nontargets (usually numbers or letters). The typical duration ranges from 5 to 40 minutes, with shorter durations often used with younger participants. Participants have to respond to targets (usually via a button press) and withhold responses to nontarget stimuli. Originally performance on the CPT was measured in terms of commission errors (false alarms), omission errors (misses), and reaction time; however, signal detection indices d' (sensitivity) and β (response criterion) have become increasingly popular (Davies & Parasuraman, 1982).

A variety of factors were found to affect performance on the CPT (for extensive reviews, see Ballard, 1996; Riccio, Reynolds, & Lowe, 2001; Riccio, Waldrop, Reynolds, & Lowe, 2001). Depending on the version of the test, they include (a) the ratio of targets to nontargets; (b) the presentation rate; (c) the type of target event (e.g., target event can be defined as letter X in the X-CPT version or as letter X preceded by a different letter, such as A, in the AX-CPT version); (d) the modality in which the task is administered (i.e., visual vs. auditory); (e) demographics (primarily age, although some effects of education level and gender have been observed; Chen, Hsiao, Hsiao, & Hwu, 1998); (f) whether clinical symptoms are present (i.e., the diagnosis of ADHD, schizophrenia, and, more recently, specific language impairment; Spaulding, Plante, & Vance, 2008); (g) environmental factors (e.g., noise and temperature); and (h) the person's physiological state (e.g., amount of sleep; intake of caffeine, glucose, alcohol, or medication). Summarizing these effects is beyond the scope of this chapter, particularly given the many different versions of the CPT; instead we concentrate on the typical patterns of performance in neurotypical populations.

The core CPT pattern with adults is a decrease in performance over time, usually referred to as *vigilance decrement*. Vigilance decrement in CPT typically occurs for relatively long task durations; however, under certain conditions (e.g., detection of perceptually degraded stimuli), decrements in performance can occur after less than 10 minutes of performing the task (Nuechterlein et al., 1983). Standard versions of the CPT have been successfully used with children starting from approximately 5 to 6 years of age (e.g., Edley & Knopf, 1987; Gordon, Thomason, & Cooper, 1990). However, the task was deemed inappropriate for younger children, primarily because of long task durations and possible unfamiliarity with letters and numbers.

Corkum et al. (1995) created the first adaptation of the CPT that closely paralleled the adult versions. In their version, letters and numbers were substituted for pictures of familiar objects (e.g., ice cream, sun, pig, lollipop), task duration was reduced to 9 minutes, rate of presentation of stimuli was decreased to allow for longer viewing time and a longer response window, and a training phase was included to familiarize children with the task. Despite these changes, 50% of 3-year-olds failed to complete the task. Performance of the 3-year-old children who completed the task was significantly below that of 4- and 5-year-olds in terms of both misses and false alarms; in addition, younger children spent more time looking away from the computer screen during the task than did older children. Indeed, vigilance decrement was observed in all three age groups for omission errors, with the slope of the decrement being steeper for younger children.

Based on the results reported by Corkum et al. (1995), successive studies using the CPT with preschool-age children further reduced the task duration to 5 minutes (Akshoomoff, 2002; Kerns & Rondeau, 1998). With the reduced task duration, almost all children were able to complete the task, although Akshoomoff (2002) found that nearly half of the children below 4.5 years of age did not reach the performance criterion for inclusion in data analyses (i.e., at least 50% hits and less than 20% false alarms). Overall, developmental studies indicate a clear age-related improvement in CPT performance from preschool age until adolescence (Akshoomoff, 2002; Annett, Bender, Gordon, & the Childhood Asthma Management Program Research Group, 2007; Corkum et al., 1995; Cornblatt, Risch, Faris, Friedman, & Erlenmeyer-Kimling, 1988; Kerns & Rondeau, 1998) and decreased performance with aging (e.g., Chen et al., 1998).

Summary

In infancy, development of selective sustained attention follows a U-shaped pattern, characterized by initial decrease in looking duration at static images until approximately 6 months of age, and subsequent increase in looking over the next 3 years. Beyond the first year of life, all paradigms used to investigate selective sustained attention (i.e., looking-based, play-based, and performance-based paradigms) indicate improvement in this ability from infancy to adulthood, with marked gains during the preschool years. Performance-based measures also indicate a decline in selective sustained attention in the course of aging.

Despite much progress made in the study of development of selective sustained attention, important issues remain, including several conceptual issues and the need to advance the methodological toolbox. Addressing these issues will ultimately allow a more precise specification of the coordination of the two systems supporting selective sustained attention at different points in development.

Conceptual Issues

Whenever multiple tasks are used to assess the purportedly same psychological process, it is important to understand whether these different tasks tap into the same process. With regard to selective sustained attention, at least two important differences between the paradigms are used with younger and older participants. The first critical difference is that looking-based and play-based measures are self-paced and allow children to stay on task until they lose interest, whereas predetermined task durations are used in the CPT. It is possible that this difference taps into the distinction between controlled and automatic processes: Looking- and play-based measures may be well suited to assess selective attention sustained in an automatic stimulus-driven fashion and CPT may be well suited to assess selective attention sustained in a controlled fashion. However, caution is needed when adopting this interpretation of task differences. Although infants indeed sustain attention to an object or activity for as long as it maintains some level of novelty, research reviewed earlier in this chapter indicates that toddlers and preschoolers clearly have some degree of control over how their attention is allocated and maintained. Therefore, as Ruff and Rothbart (2001) pointed out, the differences uncovered by different paradigms may stem not only from the differences in the locus of control of attention but also from the differences in the degree to which the task is motivating to participants of different ages. One could argue that executive control is needed precisely when the task or activity is not intrinsically motivating but needs to be performed nonetheless. This argument, however, poses a new problem, because executive control is often defined as "the ability to orchestrate thought and action in accordance with internal goals" (Miller & Cohen, 2001, p. 167). Intrinsic motivation is by definition driven by the participants' intentions (although it can interact with the properties of the outside world). Further research is needed to clarify the relationship among selective sustained attention, motivation, and executive control.

The second important difference is that in looking- and play-based measures of selective sustained attention, participants actively engage in an activity when the measurement is taken, whereas in the CPT participants spend a significant proportion of the time in preparation for action—often referred to as *vigilance*. Therefore, it is not at all clear whether the two kinds of paradigms measure the same kind of process. Both sustained attention and vigilance refer to attentional processes unfolding over time. However, unlike vigilance, which involves maintaining an alert state, sustained attention refers to active engagement with a particular activity for a period of time. The vast majority of researchers use the term *sustained attention* interchangeably with the term *vigilance*, which is problematic if the two processes are distinct, and this possibility was recently raised by Egeland and Kovalik-Gran (2010). In a recent study, these researchers examined the factor structure of the commercial Conners' CPT (Conners, 2002) in a clinical sample of participants with compromised subfunctions of attention. The scores loaded onto five different factors, identified as focusing, hyperactivity–impulsivity, sustained attention, mental control, and vigilance. Egeland and Kovalik-Gran (2010) concluded that the CPT assesses "not only sustained attention, as we are accustomed to think, but also other aspects of attention" (p. 343). With regard to the distinction between vigilance and sustained attention, Egeland and Kovalik-Gran summarized it as a "differentiation between a fall in vigilance when driving on monotonous straight roads as opposed to fatigue because of a high activity level over time" (2010, p. 344).

Measurement Issues

As stated above, the CPT is by far the most common measure of selective sustained attention from preschool age onward. This task was originally considered a relatively pure measure of selective sustained attention (Ballard, 1996). However, subsequent research highlighted that it is not clear to what degree the CPT measures selective sustained attention versus other aspects of performance. For example, there is a consistent relationship between CPT performance and academic readiness (Edley & Knopf, 1987), classroom inattentiveness (Kupietz & Richardson, 1978), and academic performance (Annett et al., 2007; Riccio, Reynolds, & Lowe, 2001). At the same time, CPT performance is correlated not only with academic success but also with general tests of intelligence, memory, and speed of processing (Annett et al., 2007; Gordon et al., 1990; Riccio, Reynolds, & Lowe, 2001). All of these factors are also known to correlate with academic achievement, so it is not clear what proportion of the variance in academic achievement is uniquely accounted for by CPT performance. More important, it is not clear to what extent general intelligence, memory, and speed of processing are reflected in CPT performance. Shalev, Ben-Simon, Mevorach, Cohen, and Tsal (2011) recently evaluated a new version of the CPT that is intended to minimize memory and perceptual components of the task. The results of this evaluation are promising; however, further evaluations are clearly needed, particularly with children and clinical populations.

Tapping multiple aspects of performance is not unique to the CPT: Many cognitive measurement tools, particularly those designed to study higher order processes, tap more than one aspect of performance—an issue that Miyake et al. (2000) referred to as the "task impurity problem." Miyake and colleagues offered the following solution to this problem in their research on the structure of EFs:

> We . . . carefully select multiple tasks that tap each target executive function, and examine the extent of unity or diversity of these three executive functions at the level of *latent variables* (i.e., what is shared among the multiple exemplar tasks for each executive function), rather than at the level of *manifest variables* (i.e., individual tasks). (p. 54)

Implementation of this elegant solution to the task impurity problem indicated that set shifting, information monitoring, and inhibition are separable but related functions.

Notice that attention maintenance was not included in Miyake et al.'s (2000) study, as it was not included in the majority of other similar analyses of the unity and diversity of EFs (for a review, see Garon, Bryson, & Smith, 2008). One reason for this omission could be that attention maintenance is not under the purview of executive control, although several theoretical proposals suggest otherwise (Colombo & Cheatham, 2006; Ruff & Rothbart, 2001). Another reason could be the relative paucity of tools for assessing selective sustained attention, which would make the central feature of Miyake et al.'s approach (i.e., selection of multiple tasks that putatively tap the same construct) impossible. In light of the suggested task impurity problem with regard to the CPT, an important direction for future research in this area is development of new measurement tools, particularly tools that are not based on the CPT paradigm. Below we briefly describe our research on developing a new developmentally sensitive paradigm—the Track-It task—for assessment of selective sustained attention in the visual domain.

In the Track-It task participants visually track a target moving among several distracters. All objects move along a random trajectory on a grid and participants are asked to report the last location visited by the target object before it disappears; in the studies briefly described below, each location was marked by a different cartoon character to facilitate reporting. Targets and distracters are randomly selected on each trial from a pool of unique objects (e.g., a red circle, a green diamond). At the onset of each trial the target is clearly marked by being encircled in red (see Figure 9.1; the circle disappears when the objects start moving).

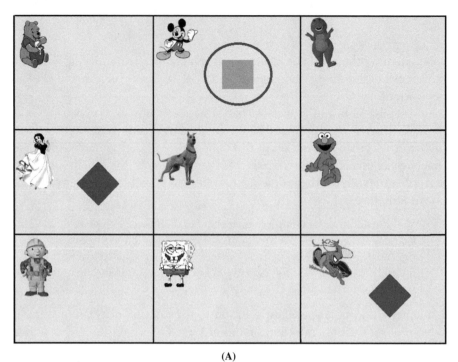

(A)

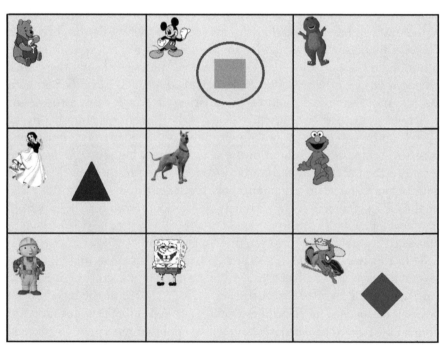

(B)

Figure 9.1. Example of the Track-It task in the Homogeneous Distracters condition (Panel A) and Heterogeneous Distracters condition (Panel B). Note that (a) in the experiment proper all target and distracter objects were presented in color and (b) the red circle marking the target object disappeared as soon as the objects began to move. From "Assessing Selective Sustained Attention in 3- to 5-year-old Children: Evidence From a New Paradigm," by A. Fisher, E. Thiessen, K. Godwin, H. Kloos, and J. Dickerson, 2013, *Journal of Experimental Child Psychology, 114,* p. 279. Copyright 2013 by Elsevier. Adapted with permission.

At the end of each trial, participants are asked to identify the target object. This memory check helps to discriminate between two possible reasons why a participant may fail to correctly report the location where the target object disappears. The first possibility is that a child may fail to actively maintain the representation of the specific object to be tracked; this would indicate working memory failure. The second possibility is that a child may track distracters for a part of the trial despite remembering which object was supposed to be watched; this would indicate the failure of selective sustained attention.

Empirical results based on the Track-It paradigm are partially described in Fisher, Thiessen, Godwin, Kloos, and Dickerson (2013), and we only briefly summarize them here. Three- to 5-year-old children were presented with the task, with minimum trial duration set at 10 seconds. There were two experimental conditions. In the Homogeneous Distracters condition there were two distracters, which were identical to each other and different from the target; in the Heterogeneous Distracters condition, the two distracters were different from each other and from the target (see Figure 9.1). The target objects were expected to be more distinct, and thus more salient, in the Homogeneous Distracters condition. All children were presented with these conditions in counterbalanced order.

We predicted that performance in the Heterogeneous Distracters condition should reflect the contribution of predominantly endogenous factors, as children were engaged in a task that was not intrinsically motivating and the task provided no contextual support that could benefit performance (i.e., target objects were not more salient than distracters). In the Homogeneous Distracters condition each target object was unique and likely more salient than distracters. Thus, performance in this condition was expected to reflect the contributions of both endogenous factors (e.g., completing a task that is not intrinsically motivating) and exogenous factors (e.g., higher saliency of target objects compared with distracters). The difference in performance between these conditions was expected to reflect the unique contribution of exogenous factors to performance on this task at different points in development.

It is important to note that manipulating saliency of the target objects within the same paradigm allowed us to addresses the concern raised by Ruff and Rothbart (2001) regarding the interpretation of findings as reflecting exogenous or endogenous locus of attentional control. Any differences in performance observed between conditions could not be due to greater motivation to perform one task versus another, as all children performed the same task. Differences in tracking performance could arise from differences in memory demands, but memory performance was equivalent in both conditions (see Figure 9.2): Memory accuracy was lower in 3-year-olds than in both older age

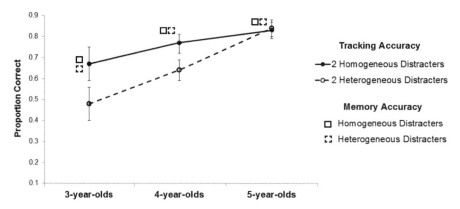

Figure 9.2. Tracking and memory accuracy on the Track-It task reported in Fisher et al. (2013). From "Assessing Selective Sustained Attention in 3- to 5-Year-Old Children: Evidence From a New Paradigm," by A. Fisher, E. Thiessen, K. Godwin, H. Kloos, and J. Dickerson, 2013, *Journal of Experimental Child Psychology, 114,* p. 282. Copyright 2013 by Elsevier. Adapted with permission.

groups. However, there were no differences in memory performance between the Homogeneous and Heterogeneous Distracters conditions in any age group. Furthermore, memory performance was equivalent in 4- and 5-year-old children. Despite equivalent memory performance, there were substantial differences in tracking accuracy in the two experimental conditions in younger children, with greater accuracy in the Homogeneous than in the Heterogeneous Distracters condition (Figure 9.2).

Follow-up experiments indicated that some parametric manipulations (e.g., removing background images) decrease task difficulty and thus make it possible to extend the task to younger children, and other parametric manipulations (e.g., increasing the number of distracters and the grid size) increase the task difficulty and thus make it possible to extend the task to older children. Test–retest reliability of this task has been relatively high in our initial testing ($r = .80$).

Overall, our research indicates that the Track-It task is developmentally sensitive, has good parametric properties, allows dissociating memory failures from attention failures, and makes it possible to estimate the contribution of exogenous and endogenous factors to maintaining selective attention within the same paradigm. Although these initial results are promising, clearly further research is needed to evaluate this new paradigm as well as develop other paradigms for investigating selective sustained attention and its underlying mechanisms.

CONCLUSION

Selective sustained attention is an important cognitive process that has been implicated in both successful learning and performance. Several theoretical accounts suggest that in early infancy sustaining selective attention is subserved by the orienting system, and beyond infancy by the executive control system. Ample empirical evidence has accumulated to support the role of the orienting system in selective sustained attention; however, there is less direct evidence for the role of the executive control system and very little is known about the coordination of these two systems in the course of development. Last, several conceptual issues and measurement issues in the study of selective sustained attention remain to be addressed in future research.

REFERENCES

Akshoomoff, N. (2002). Selective attention and active engagement in young children. *Developmental Neuropsychology, 22,* 625–642. http://dx.doi.org/10.1207/S15326942DN2203_4

Annett, R. D., Bender, B. G., Gordon, M., & the Childhood Asthma Management Program Research Group. (2007). Relating children's attentional capabilities to intelligence, memory, and academic achievement: A test of construct specificity in children with asthma. *Child Neuropsychology, 13,* 64–85. http://dx.doi.org/10.1080/09297040600770779

Ballard, J. C. (1996). Computerized assessment of sustained attention: A review of factors affecting vigilance performance. *Journal of Clinical and Experimental Neuropsychology, 18,* 843–863. http://dx.doi.org/10.1080/01688639608408307

Barkley, R. A. (1990). *Attention-deficit/hyperactivity disorder: A handbook for diagnosis and treatment.* New York, NY: Guilford Press.

Barkley, R. A. (1997). Behavioral inhibition, sustained attention, and executive functions: Constructing a unifying theory of ADHD. *Psychological Bulletin, 121,* 65–94. http://dx.doi.org/10.1037/0033-2909.121.1.65

Bornstein, M. H. (1990). Attention in infancy and the prediction of cognitive capacities in childhood. In J. T. Enns (Ed.), *Advances in psychology: Vol. 69. Development of attention: Research and theory* (pp. 3–19). Amsterdam, Netherlands: Elsevier Science. http://dx.doi.org/10.1016/S0166-4115(08)60448-3

Callahan, M. J., Kinsora, J. J., Harbaugh, R. E., Reeder, T. M., & Davis, R. E. (1993). Continuous ICV infusion of scopolamine impairs sustained attention of rhesus monkeys. *Neurobiology of Aging, 14,* 147–151. http://dx.doi.org/10.1016/0197-4580(93)90090-X

Casey, B. J., Giedd, J. N., & Thomas, K. M. (2000). Structural and functional brain development and its relation to cognitive development. *Biological Psychology,* *54,* 241–257. http://dx.doi.org/10.1016/S0301-0511(00)00058-2

Casey, B. J., & Richards, J. E. (1988). Sustained visual attention in young infants measured with an adapted version of the visual preference paradigm. *Child Development, 59,* 1514–1521. http://dx.doi.org/10.2307/1130666

Chen, W. J., Hsiao, C. K., Hsiao, L. L., & Hwu, H. G. (1998). Performance of the Continuous Performance Test among community samples. *Schizophrenia Bulletin, 24,* 163–174. http://dx.doi.org/10.1093/oxfordjournals.schbul.a033308

Chiba, A. A., Bushnell, P. J., Oshiro, W. M., & Gallagher, M. (1999). Selective removal of cholinergic neurons in the basal forebrain alters cued target detection. *Neuro-Report, 10,* 3119–3123. http://dx.doi.org/10.1097/00001756-199909290-00044

Choudhury, N., & Gorman, K. (2000). The relationship between sustained attention and cognitive performance in 17–24-month-old children. *Infant and Child Development, 9,* 127–146. http://dx.doi.org/10.1002/1522-7219(200009)9:3< 127::AID-ICD225>3.0.CO;2-5

Colombo, J. (2001). The development of visual attention in infancy. *Annual Review of Psychology, 52,* 337–367. http://dx.doi.org/10.1146/annurev.psych.52.1.337

Colombo, J., & Cheatham, C. L. (2006). The emergence and basis of endogenous attention in infancy and early childhood. In R. Kail (Ed.), *Advances in child development and behavior* (Vol. 34, pp. 283–322). Oxford, England: Academic Press. http://dx.doi.org/10.1016/S0065-2407(06)80010-8

Conners, C. K. (2002). *Conners' continuous performance test.* Toronto, Ontario, Canada: Multi-Health System.

Corbetta, M., Akbudak, E., Conturo, T. E., Snyder, A. Z., Ollinger, J. M., Drury, H. A., . . . Shulman, G. L. (1998). A common network of functional areas for attention and eye movements. *Neuron, 21,* 761–773. http://dx.doi.org/10.1016/ S0896-6273(00)80593-0

Corkum, V., Byrne, J. M., & Ellsworth, C. (1995). Clinical assessment of sustained attention in preschoolers. *Child Neuropsychology, 1,* 3–18. http://dx.doi. org/10.1080/09297049508401338

Cornblatt, B. A., & Keilp, J. G. (1994). Impaired attention, genetics, and the pathophysiology of schizophrenia. *Schizophrenia Bulletin, 20,* 31–46. http://dx.doi. org/10.1093/schbul/20.1.31

Cornblatt, B. A., Risch, N. J., Faris, G., Friedman, D., & Erlenmeyer-Kimling, L. (1988). The continuous performance test, identical pairs version (CPT-IP): I. New findings about sustained attention in normal families. *Psychiatry Research, 26,* 223–238.

Davidson, M. C., & Marrocco, R. T. (2000). Local infusion of scopolamine into intraparietal cortex slows covert orienting in rhesus monkeys. *Journal of Neurophysiology, 83,* 1536–1549.

Davies, D. R., & Parasuraman, R. (1982). *The psychology of vigilance*. London, England: Academic Press.

Diamond, A. (2002). Normal development of prefrontal cortex from birth to young adulthood: Cognitive functions, anatomy, and biochemistry. In D. T. Stuss & R. T. Knight (Eds.), *Principles of frontal lobe function* (pp. 466–503). London, England: Oxford University Press. http://dx.doi.org/10.1093/acprof:oso/9780195134971.003.0029

Diamond, A. (2006). The early development of executive functions. In E. Bialystok & F. Craik (Eds.), *Lifespan cognition: Mechanisms of change* (pp. 7–95). New York, NY: Oxford University Press. http://dx.doi.org/10.1093/acprof:oso/9780195169539.003.0006

Diamond, A., Briand, L., Fossella, J., & Gehlbach, L. (2004). Genetic and neurochemical modulation of prefrontal cognitive functions in children. *The American Journal of Psychiatry, 161*, 125–132. http://dx.doi.org/10.1176/appi.ajp.161.1.125

Diamond, A., Prevor, M. B., Callender, G., & Druin, D. P. (1997). Prefrontal cortex cognitive deficits in children treated early and continuously for PKU. *Monographs of the Society for Research in Child Development, 62*, i–v, 1–208. http://dx.doi.org/10.2307/1166208

Dixon, W. E., Jr., & Salley, B. J. (2006). "Shhh! We're tryin' to concentrate": Attention and environmental distracters in novel word learning. *The Journal of Genetic Psychology: Research and Theory on Human Development, 167*, 393–414. http://dx.doi.org/10.3200/GNTP.167.4.393-414

Edley, R. S., & Knopf, I. J. (1987). Sustained attention as a predictor of low academic readiness in a preschool population. *Journal of Psychoeducational Assessment, 5*, 340–352. http://dx.doi.org/10.1177/073428298700500404

Egeland, J., & Kovalik-Gran, I. (2010). Measuring several aspects of attention in one test: The factor structure of Conners's continuous performance test. *Journal of Attention Disorders, 13*, 339–346. http://dx.doi.org/10.1177/1087054708323019

Fan, J., McCandliss, B. D., Fossella, J., Flombaum, J. I., & Posner, M. I. (2005). The activation of attentional networks. *NeuroImage, 26*, 471–479. http://dx.doi.org/10.1016/j.neuroimage.2005.02.004

Fisher, A., Thiessen, E., Godwin, K., Kloos, H., & Dickerson, J. (2013). Assessing selective sustained attention in 3- to 5-year-old children: Evidence from a new paradigm. *Journal of Experimental Child Psychology, 114*, 275–294. http://dx.doi.org/10.1016/j.jecp.2012.07.006

Garon, N., Bryson, S. E., & Smith, I. M. (2008). Executive function in preschoolers: A review using an integrative framework. *Psychological Bulletin, 134*, 31–60.

Goldman, D. Z., Shapiro, E. G., & Nelson, C. A. (2004). Measurement of vigilance in 2-year-old children. *Developmental Neuropsychology, 25*, 227–250. http://dx.doi.org/10.1207/s15326942dn2503_1

Gordon, M. (1983). *The Gordon Diagnostic System*. New York, NY: DeWitt.

Gordon, M., Thomason, D., & Cooper, S. (1990). To what extent does attention affect K-ABC scores? *Psychology in the Schools, 27*, 144–147. http://dx.doi.org/10.1002/1520-6807(199004)27:2<144::AID-PITS2310270209>3.0.CO;2-G

Goren, C. C., Sarty, M., & Wu, P. Y. (1975). Visual following and pattern discrimination of face-like stimuli by newborn infants. *Pediatrics, 56*, 544–549.

Greenberg, L. M., & Waldmant, I. D. (1993). Developmental normative data on the test of variables of attention (T.O.V.A.). *Journal of Child Psychology and Psychiatry, 34*, 1019–1030. http://dx.doi.org/10.1111/j.1469-7610.1993.tb01105.x

Henderson, J. M., & Ferreira, F. (2004). Scene perception for psycholinguists. In J. M. Henderson & F. Ferreira (Eds.), *The interface of language, vision, and action: Eye movements and the visual world* (pp. 1–51). New York, NY: Psychology Press.

Hrabok, M., Kerns, K. A., & Müller, U. (2007). The vigilance, orienting, and executive attention networks in 4-year-old children. *Child Neuropsychology, 13*, 408–421. http://dx.doi.org/10.1080/13825580600977224

Johnson, M. H., Dziurawiec, S., Ellis, H., & Morton, J. (1991). Newborns' preferential tracking of face-like stimuli and its subsequent decline. *Cognition, 40*, 1–19. http://dx.doi.org/10.1016/0010-0277(91)90045-6

Johnson, S. P., Amso, D., & Slemmer, J. A. (2003). Development of object concepts in infancy: Evidence for early learning in an eye-tracking paradigm. *Proceedings of the National Academy of Sciences of the United States of America, 100*, 10568–10573. http://dx.doi.org/10.1073/pnas.1630655100

Jones, D. N., & Higgins, G. A. (1995). Effect of scopolamine on visual attention in rats. *Psychopharmacology, 120*, 142–149. http://dx.doi.org/10.1007/BF02246186

Just, M. A., & Carpenter, P. A. (1976). Eye fixations and cognitive processes. *Cognitive Psychology, 8*, 441–480. http://dx.doi.org/10.1016/0010-0285(76)90015-3

Kahneman, D. (1973). *Attention and effort.* Englewood Cliffs, NJ: Prentice-Hall.

Kane, M. J., & Engle, R. W. (2002). The role of prefrontal cortex in working-memory capacity, executive attention, and general fluid intelligence: An individual-differences perspective. *Psychonomic Bulletin & Review, 9*, 637–671. http://dx.doi.org/10.3758/BF03196323

Kannass, K. N., & Colombo, J. (2007). The effects of continuous and intermittent distractors on cognitive performance and attention in preschoolers. *Journal of Cognition and Development, 8*, 63–77. http://dx.doi.org/10.1080/15248370709336993

Kerns, K. A., & Rondeau, L. (1998). Development of a continuous performance test for preschool children. *Journal of Attention Disorders, 2*, 229–238. http://dx.doi.org/10.1177/108705479800200403

Kupietz, S. S., & Richardson, E. (1978). Children's vigilance performance and inattentiveness in the classroom. *The Journal of Child Psychology and Psychiatry, 19*, 145–154. http://dx.doi.org/10.1111/j.1469-7610.1978.tb00455.x

Lansink, J. M., & Richards, J. E. (1997). Heart rate and behavioral measures of attention in 6-, 9-, and 12-month-old infants during object exploration. *Child Development, 68*, 610–620. http://dx.doi.org/10.2307/1132113

Lawson, K. R., & Ruff, H. A. (2004). Early attention and negative emotionality predict later cognitive and behavioral function. *International Journal of Behavioral Development, 28*, 157–165. http://dx.doi.org/10.1080/01650250344000361

Luna, B. (2009). Developmental changes in cognitive control through adolescence. *Advances in Child Development and Behavior, 37*, 233–278. http://dx.doi.org/10.1016/S0065-2407(09)03706-9

MacLeod, C. M., Dodd, M. D., Sheard, E. D., Wilson, D. E., & Bibi, U. (2003). In opposition to inhibition. In B. H. Ross (Ed.), *The psychology of learning and motivation* (Vol. 43, pp. 163–214). San Diego, CA: Academic Press.

Miller, E. K., & Cohen, J. D. (2001). An integrative theory of prefrontal cortex function. *Annual Review of Neuroscience, 24*, 167–202. http://dx.doi.org/10.1146/annurev.neuro.24.1.167

Miyake, A., Friedman, N. P., Emerson, M. J., Witzki, A. H., Howerter, A., & Wager, T. D. (2000). The unity and diversity of executive functions and their contributions to complex "frontal lobe" tasks: A latent variable analysis. *Cognitive Psychology, 41*, 49–100. http://dx.doi.org/10.1006/cogp.1999.0734

Nuechterlein, K. H., & Dawson, M. E. (1984). Information processing and attentional functioning in the developmental course of schizophrenic disorders. *Schizophrenia Bulletin, 10*, 160–203. http://dx.doi.org/10.1093/schbul/10.2.160

Nuechterlein, K. H., Parasuraman, R., & Jiang, Q. (1983). Visual sustained attention: Image degradation produces rapid sensitivity decrement over time. *Science, 220*, 327–329. http://dx.doi.org/10.1126/science.6836276

Oakes, L. M., Kannass, K. N., & Shaddy, D. J. (2002). Developmental changes in endogenous control of attention: The role of target familiarity on infants' distraction latency. *Child Development, 73*, 1644–1655. http://dx.doi.org/10.1111/1467-8624.00496

Oakes, L. M., & Tellinghuisen, D. J. (1994). Examining in infancy: Does it reflect active processing? *Developmental Psychology, 30*, 748–756. http://dx.doi.org/10.1037/0012-1649.30.5.748

Parasuraman, R., Greenwood, P. M., Kumar, R., & Fossella, J. (2005). Beyond heritability: Neurotransmitter genes differentially modulate visuospatial attention and working memory. *Psychological Science, 16*, 200–207. http://dx.doi.org/10.1111/j.0956-7976.2005.00804.x

Posner, M. I., & Petersen, S. E. (1990). The attention system of the human brain. *Annual Review of Neuroscience, 13*, 25–42. http://dx.doi.org/10.1146/annurev.ne.13.030190.000325

Posner, M. I., & Rothbart, M. K. (2007). Research on attention networks as a model for the integration of psychological science. *Annual Review of Psychology, 58*, 1–23. http://dx.doi.org/10.1146/annurev.psych.58.110405.085516

Reck, S. G., & Hund, A. M. (2011). Sustained attention and age predict inhibitory control during early childhood. *Journal of Experimental Child Psychology, 108*, 504–512. http://dx.doi.org/10.1016/j.jecp.2010.07.010

Reisberg, D. (1978). Looking where you listen: Visual cues and auditory attention. *Acta Psychologica, 42,* 331–341. http://dx.doi.org/10.1016/0001-6918(78)90007-0

Riccio, C. A., Reynolds, C. R., & Lowe, P. A. (2001). *Clinical applications of continuous performance tests.* New York, NY: Wiley.

Riccio, C. A., Waldrop, J. J., Reynolds, C. R., & Lowe, P. (2001). Effects of stimulants on the continuous performance test (CPT): Implications for CPT use and interpretation. *The Journal of Neuropsychiatry and Clinical Neurosciences, 13,* 326–335. http://dx.doi.org/10.1176/jnp.13.3.326

Richards, J. E. (1987). Infant visual sustained attention and respiratory sinus arrhythmia. *Child Development, 58,* 488–496. http://dx.doi.org/10.2307/1130525

Richards, J. E. (1988). Heart rate offset responses to visual stimuli in infants from 14 to 26 weeks of age. *Psychophysiology, 25,* 278–291. http://dx.doi.org/10.1111/j.1469-8986.1988.tb01243.x

Richards, J. E. (2003). The development of visual attention and the brain. In De Haan & Johnson (Eds.), *The cognitive neuroscience of development* (pp. 73–78). East Sussex, England: Psychology Press.

Rosvold, H. E., Mirsky, A. F., Sarason, I., Bransome, E. D., Jr., & Beck, L. L. (1956). A continuous performance test of brain damage. *Journal of Consulting Psychology, 20,* 343–350. http://dx.doi.org/10.1037/h0043220

Ruff, H. A., & Capozzoli, M. C. (2003). Development of attention and distractibility in the first 4 years of life. *Developmental Psychology, 39,* 877–890. http://dx.doi.org/10.1037/0012-1649.39.5.877

Ruff, H. A., & Lawson, K. R. (1990). Development of sustained, focused attention in young children during free play. *Developmental Psychology, 26,* 85–93.

Ruff, H., & Rothbart, M. K. (2001). *Attention in early development.* New York, NY: Oxford University Press. http://dx.doi.org/10.1093/acprof:oso/9780195136326.001.0001

Saffran, J. R., Aslin, R. N., & Newport, E. L. (1996). Statistical learning by 8-month-old infants. *Science, 274,* 1926–1928. http://dx.doi.org/10.1126/science.274.5294.1926

Sarid, M., & Breznitz, Z. (1997). Developmental aspects of sustained attention among 2- to 6-year-old children. *International Journal of Behavioral Development, 21,* 303–312. http://dx.doi.org/10.1080/016502597384884

Sawaguchi, T., & Goldman-Rakic, P. S. (1991). D1 dopamine receptors in prefrontal cortex: Involvement in working memory. *Science, 251,* 947–950. http://dx.doi.org/10.1126/science.1825731

Seamans, J. K., Floresco, S. B., & Phillips, A. G. (1998). D1 receptor modulation of hippocampal-prefrontal cortical circuits integrating spatial memory with executive functions in the rat. *The Journal of Neuroscience, 18,* 1613–1621.

Shalev, L., Ben-Simon, A., Mevorach, C., Cohen, Y., & Tsal, Y. (2011). Conjunctive Continuous Performance Task (CCPT)—a pure measure of sustained attention. *Neuropsychologia, 49,* 2584–2591. http://dx.doi.org/10.1016/j.neuropsychologia.2011.05.006

Spaulding, T. J., Plante, E., & Vance, R. (2008). Sustained selective attention skills of preschool children with specific language impairment: Evidence for separate attentional capacities. *Journal of Speech, Language, and Hearing Research, 51,* 16–34. http://dx.doi.org/10.1044/1092-4388(2008/002)

Spelke, E. (1976). Infants' intermodal perception of events. *Cognitive Psychology, 8,* 553–560. http://dx.doi.org/10.1016/0010-0285(76)90018-9

Stechler, G., & Latz, E. (1966). Some observations on attention and arousal in the human infant. *Journal of the American Academy of Child Psychiatry, 5,* 517–525. http://dx.doi.org/10.1016/S0002-7138(09)62098-7

Tellinghuisen, D. J., Oakes, L. M., & Tjebkes, T. L. (1999). The influence of attentional state and stimulus characteristics on infant distractibility. *Cognitive Development, 14,* 199–213. http://dx.doi.org/10.1016/S0885-2014(99)00002-7

Voytko, M. L., Olton, D. S., Richardson, R. T., Gorman, L. K., Tobin, J. R., & Price, D. L. (1994). Basal forebrain lesions in monkeys disrupt attention but not learning and memory. *The Journal of Neuroscience, 14,* 167–186.

III

EXECUTIVE FUNCTION AND TRANSLATIONAL RESEARCH ON RISK AND PREVENTION

10

PRESCHOOL EXECUTIVE FUNCTIONS IN THE CONTEXT OF FAMILY RISK

MEGAN M. McCLELLAND, LESLIE D. LEVE, AND KATHERINE C. PEARS

The transition from preschool to formal schooling is an exciting and important milestone for young children. Although many young children navigate this transition with ease, a substantial group of children experience difficulty with the demands of more structured school settings compared with relatively less structured preschool classrooms (McClelland, Morrison, & Holmes, 2000; Rimm-Kaufman, Pianta, & Cox, 2000). This issue has garnered enormous attention as parents, teachers, and policymakers strive to help children appropriately manage their thoughts, feelings, and behavior while navigating increasingly demanding academic environments. Recently, children's executive function (EF) has been identified as key to the development of these skills and to a successful transition to formal schooling. Laying the foundation for strong EF is important for a range of children's outcomes, including social and academic success (McClelland, Acock, & Morrison, 2006; Moffitt et al., 2011). Of significant concern is research documenting

http://dx.doi.org/10.1037/14797-011
Executive Function in Preschool-Age Children: Integrating Measurement, Neurodevelopment, and Translational Research, J. A. Griffin, P. McCardle, and L. S. Freund (Editors)

that many young children, and especially those growing up in the context of family risk, lack strong EF and start school significantly behind their peers (Evans & Rosenbaum, 2008; Lengua, 2009; Mistry, Benner, Biesanz, Clark, & Howes, 2010; Sektnan, McClelland, Acock, & Morrison, 2010).

In this chapter, we discuss the importance of early EF for children experiencing family and contextual risk. We first discuss conceptual issues including the components of EF (cognitive or attentional flexibility, working memory, and inhibitory control), which are especially relevant for academic achievement from childhood to early adulthood. We next review research highlighting how growing up in the context of risk, including contextual, familial, prenatal, or genetic risk, can impede the development of EF. We then discuss recent studies documenting the compensatory effects of strong EF for children experiencing early risk, including such adverse environmental contexts as economic adversity or maltreatment and placement in foster care. Finally, we conclude with suggestions regarding future research directions.

CONCEPTUAL ISSUES

EF includes cognitive processes of set shifting (or cognitive or attentional flexibility), working memory, and inhibitory control (Carlson, Zelazo, & Faja, 2013; Garon, Bryson, & Smith, 2008). EF forms the foundation for children's ability to self-regulate; researchers from a variety of disciplines use terms such as *self-regulation* (McClelland, Ponitz, Messersmith, & Tominey, 2010), *behavioral regulation* (McClelland et al., 2007; Ponitz, McClelland, Matthews, & Morrison, 2009), *effortful control* (Liew, McTigue, Barrois, & Hughes, 2008; Valiente, Lemery-Chalfant, & Swanson, 2010), and *executive function* (Blair, Zelazo, & Greenberg, 2005; Carlson, 2005; Carlson et al., 2013) to refer to similar skills. In this chapter, we use the term *executive function* because our interests lie in how these processes work together to help children regulate their emotions, cognitions, and behavior (McClelland et al., 2010). Several studies have also demonstrated that these cognitive aspects of EF are especially relevant for academic achievement and help children function successfully in classroom settings (Blair & Diamond, 2008; Blair & Razza, 2007; McClelland et al., 2007; Ponitz et al., 2009).

EXECUTIVE FUNCTION AND ACADEMIC ACHIEVEMENT

A number of studies have shown that EF is important for academic success from preschool through college, even after accounting for important variables like initial achievement levels and children's intelligence (Blair &

Razza, 2007; Breslau et al., 2009; McClelland et al., 2007; McClelland, Acock, Piccinin, Rhea, & Stallings, 2013). For example, one study found that children's attention (one aspect of EF) at 5 to 6 years of age predicted higher reading and math achievement between kindergarten and early adolescence (Duncan et al., 2007). In another study, teacher ratings of attention problems at age 6 significantly predicted math and reading achievement at age 17 after controlling for background variables, including child IQ (Breslau et al., 2009). Finally, results of a recent study indicated that children with strong attention-span persistence at age 4 (as rated by parents) had 49% greater odds of completing college by age 25. Moreover, the majority of the relationship between attention-span persistence at age 4 and college completion was direct and not significantly mediated by math or reading skills at age 7 or age 21. Attention-span persistence at age 4 also predicted reading skills and math skills at age 21 after controlling for early achievement, parent education, vocabulary level, and gender (McClelland, Acock, Piccinin, Rhea, & Stallings, 2013). Similar relations between EF and achievement have also been found cross-culturally with young children from Asian (Wanless, McClelland, Acock, et al., 2011) and European (von Suchodoletz, Trommsdorff, Heikamp, Wieber, & Gollwitzer, 2009; von Suchodoletz et al., 2013) countries. Together, this research suggests that EF is vital for children to do well academically and may be a key ingredient for understanding, and intervening with, children who are at risk for academic difficulties.

HOW RISK CAN IMPEDE THE DEVELOPMENT OF EXECUTIVE FUNCTION

Although research points to significant relations between EF and achievement, it is likely that these relations are complex and influenced by the context in which young children live (Blair & Raver, 2012). In this section, we review research on children's EF in four areas of family risk: contextual risk, parenting factors, prenatal influences, and genetic influences.

Mounting evidence suggests that children growing up in the context of family risk have significant difficulty with EF and that risk factors such as poverty and ethnic minority status predict lower EF and achievement in young children (Blair, 2010; Blair & Raver, 2012; Evans & Rosenbaum, 2008; Lengua, 2009; Mistry et al., 2010; Sektnan et al., 2010). Other research finds evidence for cumulative risk on children's EF. In one study, children from low-income families began prekindergarten with significantly lower EF than did their peers. Moreover, English-speaking children from low-income families exhibited a faster rate of EF growth than did English-language learners from low-income families. Although disadvantaged English-speaking children caught up to their more economically advantaged peers by the end of kindergarten on EF, disadvantaged English-language learners did not (Wanless, McClelland, Tominey, & Acock, 2011).

There is also evidence that economic disadvantage may be a key factor in predicting poorer EF in young minority children (Evans & Rosenbaum, 2008). In one study, Latino children from poor but not middle-class families demonstrated weaker aspects of EF (Galindo & Fuller, 2010). Research also shows that children with weak EF are likely to have increased problems at higher levels of contextual risk, such as living in a dangerous neighborhood, suggesting that these relations for children are complex and transactional (Lengua, 2009).

In addition to contextual risk, a number of studies have examined the complex relations between aspects of parenting, children's EF, and school readiness. This research suggests that parents who are autonomy-supporting (Bernier, Carlson, & Whipple, 2010) and positively engaged with their children (Rhoades, Greenberg, Lanza, & Blair, 2011; Robinson, Burns, & Davis, 2009) in the first few years have children with stronger EF. In contrast, research has generally found that more parental control is detrimental to the development of EF (Eddy, Leve, & Fagot, 2001; Karreman, van Tuijl, van Aken, & Dekovic, 2006). For example, one study found that controlling and coercive parenting was related to lower EF (measured as self-control) through a child's aggressive behavior (Walker & MacPhee, 2011). In addition, studies have found that children in foster care, who are likely to have experienced harsh or neglectful parenting, have poorer EF than do their peers (Lewis, Dozier, Ackerman, & Sepulveda-Kozakowski, 2007; Pears & Fisher, 2005).

Research has also demonstrated that other aspects related to parenting, such as the quality of the home learning environment, are important predictors of strong EF in young children (Mistry et al., 2010; NICHD Early Child Care Research Network, 2003). For example, in one study, early exposure to family risk in infancy was related to lower EF (called self-regulation), problem behavior, and lower achievement through continued exposure to risk in preschool, less language stimulation, and lower maternal warmth (Mistry et al., 2010).

A third way in which family risk may affect children's EF is through prenatal or perinatal events that may impact the early development of infants' neurobiological development. For example, children whose mothers engage in substance use during pregnancy have an increased likelihood of having EF deficits, with studies of preschoolers through adolescents indicating that individuals with fetal alcohol syndrome or effects make more perseverative errors and show impairments in planning, response inhibition, abstract thinking, and cognitive flexibility (Kodituwakku, Handmaker, Cutler, Weathersby, & Handmaker, 1995; Kopera-Frye, Dehaene, & Streissguth, 1996; Mattson,

Goodman, Caine, Delis, & Riley, 1999; Noland et al., 2003). These deficits remain even when IQ scores are controlled (Connor, Sampson, Bookstein, Barr, & Streissguth, 2000), suggesting that prenatal alcohol exposure might produce selective effects on the prefrontal cortex, a brain region involved in the development of EF. Prenatal exposure to tobacco (Huijbregts, Warren, de Sonneville, & Swaab-Barneveld, 2008), marijuana (Fried, 2002; Fried & Smith, 2001), and cocaine (Espy, Kaufmann, & Glisky, 1999) has also been linked to deficits in children's EF. In addition, pregnancy and perinatal birthing complications have been shown to affect EF. For example, a study of preterm infants without disability and age-matched full-term infants indicated that the preterm infants performed more poorly on EF tasks that measured working memory, inhibition of distraction, and planning, as compared with the full-term infants (Sun, Mohay, & O'Callaghan, 2009). Other studies comparing preterm and full-term infants showed similar EF deficits among preterm infants (e.g., Rose, Feldman, & Jankowski, 2009), adding to the consistent literature demonstrating the effects of prenatal and perinatal adverse experiences on young children's EF.

Fourth, behavioral and molecular genetic studies have indicated that EF is highly heritable, with 40% to 80% of the variance in young children's EF accounted for by genetic influences (Groot, de Sonneville, Stins, & Boomsma, 2004; Lemery-Chalfant, Doelger, & Goldsmith, 2008; Polderman et al., 2007). Adverse genetic influences can be considered as another early family risk mechanism that predisposes young children to EF difficulties. Two primary methodologies have been used to examine genetic influences on EF: behavior genetic studies (twin or adoption studies) and candidate gene studies. Twin studies have shown that more than half of the variance in children's EF is due to genetic influences (Polderman et al., 2007). Candidate gene studies have shown an association between specific polymorphisms such as catechol-O-methyltransferase and prefrontal cortex–based EFs (Goldberg & Weinberger, 2004). Both common genetic factors and specific genetic influences have been suggested to underlie the various components of EF task performance (Friedman et al., 2008). Further, adoption studies have suggested that genetic influences on aspects of EF such as memory function (Plomin & DeFries, 1985) and attention (Leve et al., 2010) are present as early as infancy.

Such studies also indicate the interactive influences of contextual and genetic risk factors on children's EF, with one adoption study showing that infants demonstrated weaker attention regulation only in the context of having a rearing mother who exhibited anxious and depressive symptoms and having inherited genetic risk for attentional deficits (Leve et al., 2010). Conversely, those infants with inherited genetic risk who lived in an adoptive family home environment where the mother did not evidence depression or anxiety did not show attention regulation difficulties, suggesting the potent role of the family environment in offsetting genetic risk.

Together, this research suggests that growing up in the context of risk—be it contextual, familial, prenatal, or genetic—can set the stage for a negative cycle where children experiencing factors such as poverty, minority status, poor parenting, prenatal adversity, inherited risk for EF difficulties, or maternal depression enter school with poorer EF, have difficulty in the classroom and on academic tasks, have teachers who find them challenging, and, as a result, gradually disengage from school and learning early in elementary school (Blair & Diamond, 2008).

THE IMPORTANCE OF COMPENSATORY PROCESSES FOR CHILDREN EXPERIENCING EARLY RISK FOR EXECUTIVE FUNCTION DIFFICULTIES

Accumulating research also suggests that EF is an important compensatory factor for children experiencing early risk (Obradović, 2010; Sektnan et al., 2010) and that poor outcomes for children might be offset by interventions to improve EF (Pears, Fisher, Bruce, Kim, & Yoerger, 2010). That is, not all children who experience early risk will develop difficulties. In this section, we review studies describing compensatory processes whereby children exposed to contextual and familial risks continue to develop strong EF skills which, in turn, contribute to positive outcomes.

Evidence from several studies suggests that EF is an individual characteristic related to resilience among youth exposed to early contextual risks. For example, one study found that EF (measured as effortful control) significantly predicted resiliency in a sample of children exposed to contextual adversity—namely homelessness. This study found that homeless children experiencing substantial cumulative risk had significantly lower EF but also found that children with one standard deviation higher EF were more than five times as likely to be identified as resilient compared with children with lower EF (Obradović, 2010). Similar results were also found in a recent study using data from the National Institute of Child Health and Human Development Study of Early Child Care and Youth Development (Sektnan et al., 2010). Results indicated that the contextual risks of minority status, low income, or low maternal education were significantly related to lower reading, math, and vocabulary achievement in first grade. However, higher maternal education was associated with higher first-grade achievement through higher EF at 54 months and in kindergarten. Fewer periods of maternal depressive symptoms between birth and 54 months were also associated with higher child achievement indirectly through higher early EF.

The Sektnan et al. (2010) study also explored how different patterns of risk and regulation were related to achievement. Regardless of the presence of a risk factor, children with stronger EF had stronger achievement than did children with weaker EF. For example, children with stronger EF scored 15 points higher on math in first grade, 11 points higher on early reading, and nearly 7 points higher on vocabulary than did children facing multiple risk factors with weaker EF. As might be expected, children with multiple risk factors fared worse academically compared with children with fewer risk factors, and as the number of risk factors increased, children scored significantly lower on reading, math, and vocabulary outcomes. However, for children with the same number of risk factors, those with strong EF did better academically than did children with low EF.

Studies of children exposed to maltreatment and subsequent placement in foster care have also shown evidence of compensatory effects on children's EF. A number of studies have shown that young children in foster care have poorer EF than do their nonmaltreated counterparts (Lewis et al., 2007; Pears, Fisher, et al., 2010), presumably as a result of their maltreatment and early adverse experiences. For example, in a sample of maltreated preschool-age children in foster care and a comparison sample of nonmaltreated, same-age children from comparable socioeconomic backgrounds, the children in foster care showed poorer EF across a host of dimensions, including visuospatial processing memory, cognitive performance, and language (Pears & Fisher, 2005). In addition, several factors were associated with deficits in EF in this sample, including experiences of neglect or emotional abuse and having been exposed to a greater number of maltreatment types.

However, despite the risk context that foster children have experienced and the poorer overall EF within this group, studies suggest that not all children in foster care will go on to show low academic competence. A study that followed maltreated foster children and nonmaltreated community children across kindergarten and first grade suggested that EF (measured as inhibitory control) could be an important mediating mechanism in reducing the effects of maltreatment and foster care placement on young children's outcomes (Pears, Fisher, et al., 2010). Specifically, this study found that EF fully mediated the associations between early adversity (as characterized by maltreatment and foster care placement) and academic competence during kindergarten and first grade. In addition, children's EF skills also mediated associations between early adversity and children's socioemotional competence. This finding suggests a possible compensatory role for EF not only in relation to academic performance but also in terms of children's social adjustment. Another study with this foster care sample suggested further benefits of EF on young children's social relations, with EF having a negative association with the problematic social behavior of indiscriminate friendliness (the willingness to approach and interact with unfamiliar adults in a familiar fashion; Pears, Bruce, Fisher, & Kim, 2010). These results replicate and extend studies of nonfoster youth that similarly suggest the positive benefits of EF on academic and social functioning during the transition to school (e.g., Blair & Razza, 2007; McClelland et al., 2007).

Together, these results suggest that even when children are exposed to contextual and familial risks, those with strong self-regulation have better school and social adjustment outcomes than do those with poorer regulatory skills. This finding provides promise for the development of interventions that target EF skills as a means of improving school and social adjustment outcomes.

CONCLUSION

A strong body of evidence supports the notion that children's EF is an important predictor of academic success and social competence throughout childhood and into early adulthood (Blair & Razza, 2007; McClelland et al., 2013; Ponitz et al., 2009). Being able to listen and pay attention, persist on tasks, remember instructions, and demonstrate inhibitory control clearly helps children do better in learning environments and on academic achievement. Research also suggests that children growing up in the context of risk have significant difficulty with EF (Blair, 2010; Mistry et al., 2010; Obradović, 2010; Pears, Bruce, et al., 2010; Wanless, McClelland, Tominey, & Acock, 2011). Moreover, relations between EF and risk for young children are likely complex and transactional (Lengua, 2009). Thus, growing up in the context of risk—be it contextual, familial, prenatal, or genetic—can set the stage for a negative cycle where these children enter school with poorer EF, have difficulty in the classroom and on academic tasks, and have teachers who find them challenging, and, as a result, they may gradually disengage and be more likely to fail in school (Blair & Diamond, 2008).

However, research also suggests that EF is an important compensatory factor for children experiencing early risk (Obradović, 2010; Pears, Fisher, et al., 2010; Sektnan et al., 2010) and that compensatory factors may help offset familial or genetic risks (Leve et al., 2010). Even when children experience multiple risk factors, those with stronger EF have better achievement outcomes than do those with weaker regulatory skills. Thus, strengthening EF may be an effective way to help children at risk succeed in school and have positive social relations with their peers and teachers.

As discussed in other chapters in this volume, interventions targeting children's EF skills may be especially important. For example, preschool programs such as Tools of the Mind focus on social, emotional, and EF skills in addition to literacy and math. Research suggests that program participation is related to significant improvement in children's EF (Diamond, Barnett, Thomas, & Munro, 2007) and social behavior (Barnett et al., 2008). Other examples are the Promoting Alternative Thinking Strategies (PATHS) and the Head Start REDI (Research-Based, Developmentally Informed) interventions (Bierman, Domitrovich, et al., 2008), which focus on social–emotional skills and EF. Children participating in these interventions have been rated as being more socially competent compared with children in the control group (Domitrovich, Cortes, & Greenberg, 2007) and also show significant improvements in EF skills (Bierman, Nix, Greenberg, Blair, & Domitrovich, 2008).

In addition to intervention effects on behavioral indices of EF, there is preliminary evidence that interventions targeting family risk contexts may also produce changes at the biological level, as examined using electrophysiological measures of EF. One family-based preventive intervention for preschool-age maltreated children in foster care collected event-related potential measures while children performed a Flanker task. Following the intervention, children who had been randomly assigned to the foster care intervention condition showed more effective response monitoring during the Flanker task as compared with children who had been assigned to the foster care services-as-usual condition (Bruce, McDermott, Fisher, & Fox, 2009). That is, children in the intervention condition were more sensitive to feedback (as measured by the amplitudes of the N1, P2, and feedback-related negativity) and slowed their response rate after committing errors and receiving negative feedback about those errors. Conversely, children in the foster care services-as-usual condition did not adjust their rate of response after negative feedback. This study provides preliminary evidence that effective interventions that improve EF at the behavioral level may also be producing change at the neurobiological level.

There is less evidence demonstrating the efficacy of EF interventions to improve academic achievement, but some research is emerging. For example, a large study examining the efficacy of the Chicago School Readiness Project found that the intervention not only improved low-income preschool children's EF skills but also improved vocabulary, letter-naming, and math skills over the preschool year (Raver et al., 2011). In addition, children's EF was found to partially mediate the relation between being in the intervention and their early achievement (Raver et al., 2011). The Kids in Transition to School Program is another intervention focusing on social–emotional skills, EF, and academic achievement with foster children. Research on the effectiveness of this program has shown that participating children had significantly higher levels of EF and early literacy skills than did nonparticipating children (Pears et al., 2013; Pears, Kim, Healey, Yoerger, & Fisher, 2014). Finally, a recent study found that participation in a series of preschool games focusing on attentional flexibility, working memory, and inhibitory control was significantly related to improved EF skills over the school year for children starting the year with low EF. Children in the intervention also showed significant improvement in letter–word identification compared with children in the control group (Tominey & McClelland, 2011). Together, recent research on interventions targeting EF indicates that such programs can strengthen social–emotional skills, EF, and academic achievement, especially in the short term (see Bryck & Fisher, 2012, for a review of EF intervention studies). Examining the long-term effectiveness of such interventions is an important avenue for future research.

FUTURE DIRECTIONS

Our discussion of children's EF in the context of family risk leads us to consider a number of questions and future directions for the field. First, it is important to continue clarifying concepts, definitions, and terminology in the field of EF because doing so has major implications for how our work is translated and disseminated. Second, it is critical to examine the complex relations between EF and different indices of success for children at risk. A number of effective interventions are now available, but information about specificity is still lacking. For example, it is unclear which groups of children benefit the most from what type of intervention, how much intervention is needed for different groups, and whether interventions produce change at the neurobiological as well as the behavioral level. Other important questions that remain to be answered include the following: What are the key ingredients in effective interventions for different groups of children? In school settings, how and to what extent do teachers play a role in children's EF development? Do effective EF interventions demonstrate sustained effects? Researchers have begun to address some of these questions, but much more remains to be done.

The field also needs to continue to improve the measurement of EF skills in young children—especially the development of measures that are reliable, ecologically valid, and valid for different groups of children. Such measures must also work for a broad age range of children. There are strong measures of achievement and other cognitive skills, but similarly strong measures of EF are needed, at both the behavioral and brain activity level, that are reliable and sensitive to change over time.

We are making some progress in this area. For example, the NIH Toolbox has developed brief measures of EF for use between the ages of 3 and 85 (Zelazo et al., 2013). Another recent measure that has proven effective is the Head-Toes-Knees-Shoulders task, which assesses attentional flexibility, working memory, and inhibitory control. The task is quick and easy to administer, is reliable and valid with diverse groups of children, and predicts achievement levels and gains in preschool and kindergarten in the United States and a number of other countries (McClelland et al., 2007; Ponitz et al., 2009; Wanless, McClelland, Acock, et al., 2011). This and similar measures may hold promise for being translated into tools that accurately screen children for early intervention based on their performance and family risk factors. School administrators, teachers, and parents are especially interested in reliable, valid, and easy-to-administer screening tools to accurately identify children at risk before they enter formal schooling. More of this type of translational research is strongly needed in the field.

In summary, there is clear evidence that the family risk context negatively affects children's EF capacities. Factors such as economic stress, harsh parenting, prenatal exposure to substances, and inherited genetic risk have each been shown to predict decreased EF capacities in young children. In addition, these family risk factors likely interact with one another to create a cascade of negative influences on the development of strong EF skills. However, not all children who experience family risks have poor academic and social outcomes. As discussed earlier, one possible mechanism underlying this resilience is strong EF skills—numerous studies have shown that children with strong EF do significantly better socially and academically than do children with poorer EF, even when such children have experienced high or chronic family risk. Therefore, interventions that improve children's EF hold the promise not only of improving children's long-term social and academic adjustment, but also of generating a cost savings to society through the eventual reduction of educational and social service supports for children.

REFERENCES

Barnett, W. S., Jung, K., Yarosz, D. J., Thomas, J., Hornbeck, A., Stechuk, R., & Burns, S. (2008). Educational effects of the Tools of the Mind curriculum: A randomized trial. *Early Childhood Research Quarterly, 23,* 299–313. http://dx.doi.org/10.1016/j.ecresq.2008.03.001

Bernier, A., Carlson, S. M., & Whipple, N. (2010). From external regulation to self-regulation: Early parenting precursors of young children's executive functioning. *Child Development, 81,* 326–339. http://dx.doi.org/10.1111/j.1467-8624.2009.01397.x

Bierman, K. L., Domitrovich, C. E., Nix, R. L., Gest, S. D., Welsh, J. A., Greenberg, M. T., . . . Gill, S. (2008). Promoting academic and social–emotional school readiness: The Head Start REDI program. *Child Development, 79,* 1802–1817. http://dx.doi.org/10.1111/j.1467-8624.2008.01227.x

Bierman, K. L., Nix, R. L., Greenberg, M. T., Blair, C., & Domitrovich, C. E. (2008). Executive functions and school readiness intervention: Impact, moderation, and mediation in the Head Start REDI program. *Development and Psychopathology, 20,* 821–843. http://dx.doi.org/10.1017/S0954579408000394

Blair, C. (2010). Stress and the development of self-regulation in context. *Child Development Perspectives, 4,* 181–188. http://dx.doi.org/10.1111/j.1750-8606.2010.00145.x

Blair, C., & Diamond, A. (2008). Biological processes in prevention and intervention: The promotion of self-regulation as a means of preventing school failure. *Development and Psychopathology, 20,* 899–911. http://dx.doi.org/10.1017/S0954579408000436

Blair, C., & Raver, C. C. (2012). Child development in the context of adversity: Experiential canalization of brain and behavior. *American Psychologist, 67,* 309–318. http://dx.doi.org/10.1037/a0027493

Blair, C., & Razza, R. P. (2007). Relating effortful control, executive function, and false belief understanding to emerging math and literacy ability in kindergarten. *Child Development, 78,* 647–663. http://dx.doi.org/10.1111/j.1467-8624.2007.01019.x

Blair, C., Zelazo, P. D., & Greenberg, M. T. (2005). The measurement of executive function in early childhood. *Developmental Neuropsychology, 28,* 561–571. http://dx.doi.org/10.1207/s15326942dn2802_1

Breslau, J., Miller, E., Breslau, N., Bohnert, K., Lucia, V., & Schweitzer, J. (2009). The impact of early behavior disturbances on academic achievement in high school. *Pediatrics, 123,* 1472–1476. http://dx.doi.org/10.1542/peds.2008-1406

Bruce, J., McDermott, J. M., Fisher, P. A., & Fox, N. A. (2009). Using behavioral and electrophysiological measures to assess the effects of a preventive intervention: A preliminary study with preschool-aged foster children. *Prevention Science, 10,* 129–140. http://dx.doi.org/10.1007/s11121-008-0115-8

Bryck, R. L., & Fisher, P. A. (2012). Training the brain: Practical applications of neural plasticity from the intersection of cognitive neuroscience, developmental psychology, and prevention science. *American Psychologist, 67,* 87–100. http://dx.doi.org/10.1037/a0024657

Carlson, S. M. (2005). Developmentally sensitive measures of executive function in preschool children. *Developmental Neuropsychology, 28,* 595–616. http://dx.doi.org/10.1207/s15326942dn2802_3

Carlson, S. M., Zelazo, P. D., & Faja, S. (2013). Executive function. In P. D. Zelazo (Ed.), *The Oxford handbook of developmental psychology: Vol. 1. Body and mind* (pp. 706–743). New York, NY: Oxford University Press. http://dx.doi.org/10.1093/oxfordhb/9780199958450.013.0025

Connor, P. D., Sampson, P. D., Bookstein, F. L., Barr, H. M., & Streissguth, A. P. (2000). Direct and indirect effects of prenatal alcohol damage on executive function. *Developmental Neuropsychology, 18,* 331–354. http://dx.doi.org/10.1207/S1532694204Connor

Diamond, A., Barnett, W. S., Thomas, J., & Munro, S. (2007). Preschool program improves cognitive control. *Science, 318,* 1387–1388. http://dx.doi.org/10.1126/science.1151148

Domitrovich, C. E., Cortes, R. C., & Greenberg, M. T. (2007). Improving young children's social and emotional competence: A randomized trial of the preschool "PATHS" curriculum. *The Journal of Primary Prevention, 28*, 67–91. http://dx.doi.org/10.1007/s10935-007-0081-0

Duncan, G. J., Dowsett, C. J., Claessens, A., Magnuson, K., Huston, A. C., Klebanov, P., . . . Japel, C. (2007). School readiness and later achievement. *Developmental Psychology, 43*, 1428–1446. http://dx.doi.org/10.1037/0012-1649.43.6.1428

Eddy, J. M., Leve, L. D., & Fagot, B. I. (2001). Coercive family processes: A replication and extension of Patterson's coercion model. *Aggressive Behavior, 27*, 14–25. http://dx.doi.org/10.1002/1098-2337(20010101/31)27:1<14::AID-AB2>3.0.CO;2-2

Espy, K. A., Kaufmann, P. M., & Glisky, M. L. (1999). Neuropsychologic function in toddlers exposed to cocaine in utero: A preliminary study. *Developmental Neuropsychology, 15*, 447–460. http://dx.doi.org/10.1080/87565649909540761

Evans, G. W., & Rosenbaum, J. (2008). Self-regulation and the income-achievement gap. *Early Childhood Research Quarterly, 23*, 504–514. http://dx.doi.org/10.1016/j.ecresq.2008.07.002

Fried, P. A. (2002). Conceptual issues in behavioral teratology and their application in determining long-term sequelae of prenatal marijuana exposure. *The Journal of Child Psychology and Psychiatry, 43*, 81–102. http://dx.doi.org/10.1111/1469-7610.00005

Fried, P. A., & Smith, A. M. (2001). A literature review of the consequences of prenatal marijuana exposure. An emerging theme of a deficiency in aspects of executive function. *Neurotoxicology and Teratology, 23*, 1–11. http://dx.doi.org/10.1016/S0892-0362(00)00119-7

Friedman, N. P., Miyake, A., Young, S. E., Defries, J. C., Corley, R. P., & Hewitt, J. K. (2008). Individual differences in executive functions are almost entirely genetic in origin. *Journal of Experimental Psychology: General, 137*, 201–225. http://dx.doi.org/10.1037/0096-3445.137.2.201

Galindo, C., & Fuller, B. (2010). The social competence of Latino kindergartners and growth in mathematical understanding. *Developmental Psychology, 46*, 579–592. http://dx.doi.org/10.1037/a0017821

Garon, N., Bryson, S. E., & Smith, I. M. (2008). Executive function in preschoolers: A review using an integrative framework. *Psychological Bulletin, 134*, 31–60. http://dx.doi.org/10.1037/0033-2909.134.1.31

Goldberg, T. E., & Weinberger, D. R. (2004). Genes and the parsing of cognitive processes. *Trends in Cognitive Sciences, 8*, 325–335. http://dx.doi.org/10.1016/j.tics.2004.05.011

Groot, A. S., de Sonneville, L. M. J., Stins, J. F., & Boomsma, D. I. (2004). Familial influences on sustained attention and inhibition in preschoolers. *The Journal of Child Psychology and Psychiatry, 45*, 306–314. http://dx.doi.org/10.1111/j.1469-7610.2004.00222.x

Huijbregts, S. C., Warren, A. J., de Sonneville, L. M. J., & Swaab-Barneveld, H. (2008). Hot and cool forms of inhibitory control and externalizing behavior in children of mothers who smoked during pregnancy: An exploratory study. *Journal of Abnormal Child Psychology, 36*, 323–333. http://dx.doi.org/10.1007/s10802-007-9180-x

Karreman, A., van Tuijl, C., van Aken, M. A. G., & Dekovic, M. (2006). Parenting and self-regulation in preschoolers: A meta-analysis. *Infant and Child Development, 15*, 561–579. http://dx.doi.org/10.1002/icd.478

Kodituwakku, P. W., Handmaker, N. S., Cutler, S. K., Weathersby, E. K., & Handmaker, S. D. (1995). Specific impairments in self-regulation in children exposed to alcohol prenatally. *Alcoholism: Clinical and Experimental Research, 19*, 1558–1564. http://dx.doi.org/10.1111/j.1530-0277.1995.tb01024.x

Kopera-Frye, K., Dehaene, S., & Streissguth, A. P. (1996). Impairments of number processing induced by prenatal alcohol exposure. *Neuropsychologia, 34*, 1187–1196. http://dx.doi.org/10.1016/0028-3932(96)00043-7

Lemery-Chalfant, K., Doelger, L., & Goldsmith, H. H. (2008). Genetic relations between effortful and attentional control and symptoms of psychopathology in middle childhood. *Infant and Child Development, 17*, 365–385. http://dx.doi.org/10.1002/icd.581

Lengua, L. J. (2009, January). Effortful control in the context of socioeconomic and psychosocial risk. APA *Psychological Science Agenda, 23*(1). Retrieved from http://www.apa.org/science/about/psa/2009/01/lengua.aspx

Leve, L. D., Kerr, D. C. R., Shaw, D., Ge, X., Neiderhiser, J. M., Scaramella, L. V., . . . Reiss, D. (2010). Infant pathways to externalizing behavior: Evidence of Genotype × Environment interaction. *Child Development, 81*, 340–356. http://dx.doi.org/10.1111/j.1467-8624.2009.01398.x

Lewis, E. E., Dozier, M., Ackerman, J., & Sepulveda-Kozakowski, S. (2007). The effect of placement instability on adopted children's inhibitory control abilities and oppositional behavior. *Developmental Psychology, 43*, 1415–1427. http://dx.doi.org/10.1037/0012-1649.43.6.1415

Liew, J., McTigue, E., Barrois, L., & Hughes, J. (2008). Adaptive and effortful control and academic self-efficacy beliefs on achievement: A longitudinal study of first through third graders. *Early Childhood Research Quarterly, 23*, 515–526. http://dx.doi.org/10.1016/j.ecresq.2008.07.003

Mattson, S. N., Goodman, A. M., Caine, C., Delis, D. C., & Riley, E. P. (1999). Executive functioning in children with heavy prenatal alcohol exposure. *Alcoholism: Clinical and Experimental Research, 23*, 1808–1815. http://dx.doi.org/10.1111/j.1530-0277.1999.tb04077.x

McClelland, M. M., Acock, A. C., & Morrison, F. J. (2006). The impact of kindergarten learning-related skills on academic trajectories at the end of elementary school. *Early Childhood Research Quarterly, 21*, 471–490. http://dx.doi.org/10.1016/j.ecresq.2006.09.003

McClelland, M. M., Acock, A. C., Piccinin, A., Rhea, S. A., & Stallings, M. C. (2013). Relations between preschool attention span-persistence and age 25 educational outcomes. *Early Childhood Research Quarterly, 28*, 314–324. http://dx.doi.org/10.1016/j.ecresq.2012.07.008

McClelland, M. M., Cameron, C. E., Connor, C. M., Farris, C. L., Jewkes, A. M., & Morrison, F. J. (2007). Links between behavioral regulation and preschoolers' literacy, vocabulary, and math skills. *Developmental Psychology, 43*, 947–959. http://dx.doi.org/10.1037/0012-1649.43.4.947

McClelland, M. M., Morrison, F. J., & Holmes, D. L. (2000). Children at-risk for early academic problems: The role of learning-related social skills. *Early Childhood Research Quarterly, 15*, 307–329. http://dx.doi.org/10.1016/S0885-2006(00)00069-7

McClelland, M. M., Ponitz, C. C., Messersmith, E., & Tominey, S. (2010). Self-regulation: The integration of cognition and emotion. In W. Overton (Vol. Ed.) & R. Lerner (Ed.), *Handbook of life-span human development: Vol. 1. Cognition, biology, and methods* (pp. 509–553). Hoboken, NJ: Wiley.

Mistry, R. S., Benner, A. D., Biesanz, J. C., Clark, S. L., & Howes, C. (2010). Family and social risk, and parental investments during the early childhood years as predictors of low-income children's school readiness outcomes. *Early Childhood Research Quarterly, 25*, 432–449. http://dx.doi.org/10.1016/j.ecresq.2010.01.002

Moffitt, T. E., Arseneault, L., Belsky, D., Dickson, N., Hancox, R. J., Harrington, H., . . . Caspi, A. (2011). A gradient of childhood self-control predicts health, wealth, and public safety. *Proceedings of the National Academy of Sciences of the United States of America, 108*, 2693–2698. http://dx.doi.org/10.1073/pnas.1010076108

National Institute of Child Health and Human Development Early Child Care Research Network. (2003). Do children's attention processes mediate the link between family predictors and school readiness? *Developmental Psychology, 39*, 581–593. http://dx.doi.org/10.1037/0012-1649.39.3.581

Noland, J. S., Singer, L. T., Arendt, R. E., Minnes, S., Short, E. J., & Bearer, C. F. (2003). Executive functioning in preschool-age children prenatally exposed to alcohol, cocaine, and marijuana. *Alcoholism: Clinical and Experimental Research, 27*, 647–656. http://dx.doi.org/10.1111/j.1530-0277.2003.tb04401.x

Obradović, J. (2010). Effortful control and adaptive functioning of homeless children: Variable-focused and person-focused analyses. *Journal of Applied Developmental Psychology, 31*, 109–117. http://dx.doi.org/10.1016/j.appdev.2009.09.004

Pears, K. C., Bruce, J., Fisher, P. A., & Kim, H. K. (2010). Indiscriminate friendliness in maltreated foster children. *Child Maltreatment, 15*, 64–75. http://dx.doi.org/10.1177/1077559509337891

Pears, K., & Fisher, P. A. (2005). Developmental, cognitive, and neuropsychological functioning in preschool-aged foster children: Associations with prior maltreatment and placement history. *Journal of Developmental and Behavioral Pediatrics, 26*, 112–122. http://dx.doi.org/10.1097/00004703-200504000-00006

Pears, K. C., Fisher, P. A., Bruce, J., Kim, H. K., & Yoerger, K. (2010). Early elementary school adjustment of maltreated children in foster care: The roles of inhibitory control and caregiver involvement. *Child Development, 81,* 1550–1564. http://dx.doi.org/10.1111/j.1467-8624.2010.01491.x

Pears, K. C., Fisher, P. A., Kim, H. K., Bruce, J., Healey, C. V., & Yoerger, K. (2013). Immediate effects of a school readiness intervention for children in foster care. *Early Education and Development, 24,* 771–791. http://dx.doi.org/10.1080/10409289.2013.736037

Pears, K. C., Kim, H. K., Healey, C., Yoerger, K., & Fisher, P. A. (2014). Improving child self-regulation and parenting in families of pre-kindergarten children with developmental disabilities and behavioral difficulties. *Prevention Science.* Advance online publication.

Plomin, R., & DeFries, J. C. (1985). A parent–offspring adoption study of cognitive abilities in early childhood. *Intelligence, 9,* 341–356. http://dx.doi.org/10.1016/0160-2896(85)90019-4

Polderman, T. J. C., Posthuma, D., de Sonneville, L. M. J., Stins, J. F., Verhulst, F. C., & Boomsma, D. I. (2007). Genetic analyses of the stability of executive functioning during childhood. *Biological Psychology, 76,* 11–20. http://dx.doi.org/10.1016/j.biopsycho.2007.05.002

Ponitz, C. C., McClelland, M. M., Matthews, J. S., & Morrison, F. J. (2009). A structured observation of behavioral self-regulation and its contribution to kindergarten outcomes. *Developmental Psychology, 45,* 605–619. http://dx.doi.org/10.1037/a0015365

Raver, C. C., Jones, S. M., Li-Grining, C., Zhai, F., Bub, K., & Pressler, E. (2011). CSRP's impact on low-income preschoolers' preacademic skills: Self-regulation as a mediating mechanism. *Child Development, 82,* 362–378. http://dx.doi.org/10.1111/j.1467-8624.2010.01561.x

Rhoades, B. L., Greenberg, M. T., Lanza, S. T., & Blair, C. (2011). Demographic and familial predictors of early executive function development: Contribution of a person-centered perspective. *Journal of Experimental Child Psychology, 108,* 638–662. http://dx.doi.org/10.1016/j.jecp.2010.08.004

Rimm-Kaufman, S. E., Pianta, R. C., & Cox, M. J. (2000). Teachers' judgments of problems in the transition to kindergarten. *Early Childhood Research Quarterly, 15,* 147–166. http://dx.doi.org/10.1016/S0885-2006(00)00049-1

Robinson, J. B., Burns, B. M., & Davis, D. W. (2009). Maternal scaffolding and attention regulation in children living in poverty. *Journal of Applied Developmental Psychology, 30,* 82–91. http://dx.doi.org/10.1016/j.appdev.2008.10.013

Rose, S. A., Feldman, J. F., & Jankowski, J. J. (2009). Information processing in toddlers: Continuity from infancy and persistence of preterm deficits. *Intelligence, 37,* 311–320. http://dx.doi.org/10.1016/j.intell.2009.02.002

Sektnan, M., McClelland, M. M., Acock, A., & Morrison, F. J. (2010). Relations between early family risk, children's behavioral regulation, and academic achievement. *Early Childhood Research Quarterly, 25,* 464–479. http://dx.doi.org/10.1016/j.ecresq.2010.02.005

Sun, J., Mohay, H., & O'Callaghan, M. (2009). A comparison of executive function in very preterm and term infants at 8 months corrected age. *Early Human Development, 85,* 225–230. http://dx.doi.org/10.1016/j.earlhumdev.2008.10.005

Tominey, S. L., & McClelland, M. M. (2011). Red light, purple light: Findings from a randomized trial using circle time games to improve behavioral self-regulation in preschool. *Early Education and Development, 22,* 489–519. http://dx.doi.org/10.1080/10409289.2011.574258

Valiente, C., Lemery-Chalfant, K., & Swanson, J. (2010). Prediction of kindergartners' academic achievement from their effortful control and emotionality: Evidence for direct and moderated relations. *Journal of Educational Psychology, 102,* 550–560. http://dx.doi.org/10.1037/a0018992

von Suchodoletz, A., Gestsdottir, S., Wanless, S. B., McClelland, M. M., Birgisdottir, F., Gunzenhauser, C., & Ragnarsdottir, H. (2013). Behavioral self-regulation and relations to emergent academic skills among children in Germany and Iceland. *Early Childhood Research Quarterly, 28,* 62–73. http://dx.doi.org/10.1016/j.ecresq.2012.05.003

von Suchodoletz, A., Trommsdorff, G., Heikamp, T., Wieber, F., & Gollwitzer, P. M. (2009). Transition to school: The role of kindergarten children's behavior regulation. *Learning and Individual Differences, 19,* 561–566. http://dx.doi.org/10.1016/j.lindif.2009.07.006

Walker, A. K., & MacPhee, D. (2011). How home gets to school: Parental control strategies predict children's school readiness. *Early Childhood Research Quarterly, 26,* 355–364. http://dx.doi.org/10.1016/j.ecresq.2011.02.001

Wanless, S. B., McClelland, M. M., Acock, A. C., Ponitz, C. C., Son, S. H., Lan, X., . . . Li, S. (2011). Measuring behavioral regulation in four societies. *Psychological Assessment, 23,* 364–378. http://dx.doi.org/10.1037/a0021768

Wanless, S. B., McClelland, M. M., Tominey, S. L., & Acock, A. C. (2011). The influence of demographic risk factors on children's behavioral regulation in prekindergarten and kindergarten. *Early Education and Development, 22,* 461–488. http://dx.doi.org/10.1080/10409289.2011.536132

Zelazo, P. D., Anderson, J. E., Richler, J., Wallner-Allen, K., Beaumont, J. L., & Weintraub, S. (2013). II. NIH Toolbox Cognition Battery (CB): Measuring executive function and attention. *Monographs of the Society for Research in Child Development, 78*(4), 16–33. http://dx.doi.org/10.1111/mono.12032

11

SOCIOECONOMIC STATUS AND THE DEVELOPMENT OF EXECUTIVE FUNCTION: BEHAVIORAL AND NEUROSCIENCE APPROACHES

GWENDOLYN M. LAWSON, CAYCE J. HOOK, DANIEL A. HACKMAN, AND MARTHA J. FARAH

Socioeconomic status (SES) exerts a powerful effect on cognitive development, as measured by intelligence and academic achievement. Executive function (EF) is one important facet of cognitive ability that appears to play a role in many real-world domains of success and well-being including general intellectual ability (e.g., Brydges, Reid, Fox, & Anderson, 2012) and academics (e.g., Bull, Espy, & Wiebe, 2008). For this reason, the relation between SES and EF has recently become a topic of intense research interest.

Here we review the relationship of childhood SES to behavioral and neural measures of EF, with particular focus on the preschool years. We also examine evidence for EF's role as a mediator between SES and differences in academic achievement by children with lower and higher SES. EF is a particularly promising candidate mediator of SES–achievement differences because it is associated with both SES and academic achievement.

http://dx.doi.org/10.1037/14797-012
Executive Function in Preschool-Age Children: Integrating Measurement, Neurodevelopment, and Translational Research, J. A. Griffin, P. McCardle, and L. S. Freund (Editors)

EF is reliant on the prefrontal cortex (PFC), which is highly plastic and undergoes a long period of postnatal development (e.g., Casey, Giedd, & Thomas, 2000). Given the importance of the PFC to EF, these characteristics suggest that EF may be particularly susceptible to influences of childhood experience in general and disparities between lower and higher SES environments in particular. Indeed, a growing body of behavioral and neural evidence, to be reviewed shortly, suggests that EF varies along socioeconomic gradients, showing stronger associations with SES than do many other neurocognitive systems (Hackman & Farah, 2009). EF in early childhood is highly predictive of later academic achievement (Blair & Diamond, 2008; Buckner, Mezzacappa, & Beardslee, 2009), suggesting that differences in EF in preschool and beyond may powerfully affect the life trajectories of children growing up in poverty.

Using the methods of cognitive neuroscience to investigate the relationships among environmental factors, developing EF, and disparities in academic achievement has the potential to address basic scientific questions about how the environment influences the development of EF. This work also has important societal applications. Identifying specific factors that mediate the relationship between SES and EF may help provide specific targets for interventions, potentially reducing the achievement gap that plays a critical role in reinforcing the intergenerational cycle of poverty. Here we review what is known about socioeconomic influences on EF development in the preschool and school years.

SOCIOECONOMIC STATUS AND EXECUTIVE FUNCTION: DEFINITIONAL CHALLENGES

What is SES? As the term itself implies, SES combines economic factors such as a person's income and material wealth with noneconomic characteristics such as social prestige and education (Adler & Rehkopf, 2008; Bradley & Corwyn, 2002). These factors correlate with a wide range of neighborhood and family characteristics, such as frequency of stressful life events, exposure to toxins and violence, school quality, and parental care (Bradley & Corwyn, 2002; Evans, 2004). Given the intercorrelated nature of these different factors, most researchers either combine income, education, and occupational status into a composite index of SES, or measure income or educational attainment alone with the assumption that any one will provide a serviceable estimate of the more complete set. This is the case for most of the studies reviewed here. However, because different aspects of SES likely play different roles in producing the life outcomes discussed here, different economic and social factors should be examined separately in the future (Braveman et al., 2005; Duncan & Magnuson, 2012).

EF is also a multifaceted construct, which is also conceptualized and operationalized differently by different researchers. Its components have been subdivided into (a) working memory, set shifting, and inhibition (by Miyake et al., 2000); (b) planning, response control, and attentional shifting (by Robbins, Weinberger, Taylor, & Morris, 1996); and (c) response initiation, task set, and self-monitoring (by Stuss & Alexander, 2007). Furthermore, there is reason to believe that the componential structure of EF may change over development (Isquith, Gioia, & Espy, 2004; Senn, Espy, & Kaufmann, 2004; Wiebe, Espy, & Charak, 2008). Although these issues add to the challenge of interpreting research results, they do not represent an insurmountable obstacle. As with the different approaches to assessing SES, which generally converge in finding SES differences in EF, different approaches to EF assessment generally converge in demonstrating SES differences.

BEHAVIORAL STUDIES OF SES AND EF IN CHILDREN

SES differences in EF can be observed as early as infancy. Performance on the A-not-B task is often considered one of the first measures of emerging EF and is believed to reflect frontal lobe maturation (Diamond, 2001). This task requires infants to search for a toy that they have watched the experimenter hide. After several trials in which the toy is hidden in one location, A, and the infant successfully retrieves it, the infant then watches the experimenter hide the toy in a new location, B. Retrieving the toy this time requires both working memory (to retain the location of the toy) and inhibitory control (to avoid habitually reaching for the old location). Lipina, Martelli, Vuelta, and Colombo (2005) compared performance on this task in 6- to 14-month-old Argentinian infants from homes with "satisfied" and "unsatisfied" basic needs (based on a composite score of parental education, occupation, dwelling, and overcrowding conditions). Results showed that infants from poor homes performed fewer consecutive correct responses and reached erroneously to location A more frequently than did those from more socioeconomically advantaged homes.

Several studies have found SES effects during the preschool years. In a study of 2-year-olds, Hughes and Ensor (2005) found that social disadvantage (as indicated by markers such as "family living in publicly funded housing" and "head of household unemployed") predicted poorer performance on a battery of EF tasks, including developmentally appropriate versions of working memory, set shifting, and inhibition tasks. SES disparities have also been found in tasks of goal-setting, cognitive flexibility, and working memory in 3- to 5-year-olds (Lipina, Martelli, Vuelta, Injoque-Ricle, & Colombo, 2004) and in measures of alerting and executive attention in 4- to 7-year-olds (Mezzacappa, 2004).

Studies of young children using latent EF factors derived from a number of EF tasks rather than the individual tasks themselves have also documented SES disparities. In a study that followed children between the ages of 4 and 6, Hughes, Ensor, Wilson, and Graham (2009) found that family income predicted mean levels of a single latent EF construct that supported performance on planning, inhibitory control, and working memory tasks. Similarly, demographic factors, including income-to-needs ratio and maternal education, have been found to predict performance on latent EF in a sample of 3-year-olds from predominantly low-income nonurban families (Blair et al., 2011; Rhoades, Greenberg, Lanza, & Blair, 2011). Although Wiebe et al. (2008) did not find an SES difference in mean levels of a latent EF construct in one sample of 2- to 6-year-olds, a second sample showed lower mean latent EF in children with lower SES as compared with their higher SES peers (Wiebe et al., 2011). In sum, SES differences can be found in very young children whether EF is operationalized as a single, latent factor or as individual tasks or domains.

Evidence suggests that early SES-related differences in EF persist throughout childhood. To highlight a few examples, there are SES disparities in fluency in children 5 to 14 years old (Ardila, Rosselli, Matute, & Guajardo, 2005), in a latent measure of working memory in children 10 to 18 years old (Hackman et al., 2014), and in working memory, inhibitory control, and cognitive flexibility in a sample of children 8 to 12 years old (Sarsour et al., 2011). Although not all studies find SES differences in all tasks of EF (e.g., Engel, Santos, & Gathercole, 2008; Waber et al., 2007), in some cases this may be due to rigorous exclusion criteria that result in samples with particularly healthy and able children of low SES.

How do the SES disparities in EF compare with SES disparities in other neurocognitive systems? We have addressed the neurocognitive profile of SES disparities in a series of studies, which indicate that EF is disproportionately, but not uniquely, affected by SES. In three studies of kindergarteners, first graders, and middle schoolers, batteries of tasks were administered assessing the prefrontal (executive), left perisylvian (language), medial temporal (memory), parietal (spatial cognition), and occipitotemporal (visual cognition) systems. The most robust differences between lower- and middle-income children were in language abilities and EF, particularly in the domains of working memory and cognitive control (Farah et al., 2006; Noble, McCandliss, & Farah, 2007; Noble, Norman, & Farah, 2005). This profile of differences suggests it is implausible that SES differences in EF arise as a result of differences in general factors such as motivation, comfort in the research environment, or task understanding, as it is unlikely that only certain neuropsychological domains would be influenced by such factors. Further support for this interpretation comes from more direct studies of the brain, particularly studies of brain structure.

NEUROSCIENCE STUDIES OF SES AND PREFRONTAL CORTICAL FUNCTION IN CHILDREN

To investigate SES disparities in brain development more directly, several research groups have used electrophysiological measures, which may reveal differences in cognitive processing even when no differences in behavioral measures are apparent (see Hackman & Farah, 2009). Baseline electroencephalogram (EEG) activity has been used to assess overall differences in resting brain function and can be used as a measure of brain maturation, particularly in regions subserving EF. In a longitudinal study of Mexican preschool children, Otero (1997) and Otero, Pliego-Rivero, Fernández, and Ricardo (2003) found differences in resting EEG patterns as a function of SES. The observed differences were consistent with a maturational lag in frontal areas among children with low SES.

Several recent studies have used event-related potential (ERP) measures of selective attention to examine SES differences in neural processing. These studies have shown SES differences in patterns of neural processing even when task performance does not differ between SES groups. In a study of children between the ages of 3 and 8 years, Stevens, Lauinger, and Neville (2009) examined the effects of maternal education level (a proxy for SES) on ERP measures of a selective auditory attention task. Children were presented two narrative stories simultaneously, one in each ear, and were cued to attend to one of the stories while ERPs to probe stimuli were recorded. There were no SES differences in ERP responses to probes in the attended channel, but children with low SES exhibited a higher amplitude response to the probes in the unattended channel, indicative of difficulty suppressing distracting stimuli. These reduced effects of selective attention were observed electrophysiologically despite similar behavioral performance between children with low SES and children with middle SES and provide direct evidence for socioeconomic differences in early stages of EF processing.

An analysis of brain structure using the National Institutes of Health (NIH) Magnetic Resonance Imaging (MRI) Study of Normal Brain Development's sample of children between 5 months and 4 years old found that early brain growth in frontal gray matter was more rapid among the children with higher SES scanned (Hanson et al., 2013). In a study focused on functional brain asymmetries for language in 5-year-olds, Raizada, Richards, Meltzoff, and Kuhl (2008) reported a borderline significant effect of SES on gray matter volume in the left inferior frontal gyrus, with higher SES associated with greater volume.

Additional neuroscience evidence concerning frontal lobe development and EF is available from older school-age children. D'Angiulli, Herdman, Stapells, and Hertzman (2008) found similar SES differences in selective attention using a task of nonspatial auditory selective attention. In this task, preadolescent children with lower and higher SES were instructed to attend to two types of tones but ignore two other types. The two SES groups showed equivalent accuracy and reaction time but different patterns of ERP waveform activity. Specifically, children with high SES showed significantly different ERP waveforms between attended (relevant) and unattended (irrelevant) stimuli, whereas children with low SES showed equivalent ERP responses to both types of stimuli. The authors interpreted these results as evidence that children with low SES made less use of selective attention, allocating greater attentional resources to the irrelevant stimuli than did their counterparts with high SES. In addition, a study of 7- to 12-year-old children used a simple target detection task, on which behavioral performance between SES groups did not differ, to measure the ERP response to task-relevant and task-irrelevant stimuli (Kishiyama, Boyce, Jimenez, Perry, & Knight, 2009). Children with low SES showed reduced extrastriate (P1 and N1) and novelty (N2) ERP responses relative to children with high SES, consistent with reduced recruitment of prefrontal attentional mechanisms among children with low SES. In a study combining ERP and spectral analysis of EEGs, D'Angiulli et al. (2012) replicated earlier findings of larger ERP attentional effects in children with higher SES as well as EEG indications of greater left frontal activity. Together, these electrophysiological studies extend the behavioral research summarized in the previous section by demonstrating that there may be SES-related differences in the degree to which specific neural systems are recruited during attentional processing even when there are no task performance differences.

Sheridan, Sarsour, Jutte, D'Esposito, and Boyce (2012) conducted the first functional magnetic resonance imaging (fMRI) study of SES and EF in 8- to 12-year-old children. Subjects with low SES and subjects with high SES performed a stimulus classification task using either a familiar, practiced classification rule or a novel rule. The latter requires resisting use of the more habitual rule and therefore places heavier demands on EF. Brain activation associated with the novel–familiar contrast was localized to several prefrontal regions and SES differences in activation were observed, most clearly in the right superior frontal gyrus.

A number of recent studies have measured structural differences in prefrontal areas among school-age children. In light of the lengthy and nonlinear patterns of structural brain development observed across childhood and adolescence (Gogtay et al., 2004), as well as the complexity of structure–function relations in cognitive development (Crone & Ridderinkhof, 2011), these findings provide context concerning SES differences in EF development, but they cannot be applied directly to understanding EF during the preschool years. In contrast to the findings already cited from Hanson and colleagues' (2013) analysis of growth trajectories in frontal volume over the preschool years, no SES difference has been observed in frontal lobe volume among the 4- to 18-year-old children from the NIH MRI Study of Normal Brain Development (Brain Development Cooperative Group, 2012; Lange, Froimowitz, Bigler, Lainhart, & Brain Development Cooperative Group, 2010). However, when the same data set was used to examine cortical thickness in subregions of the PFC and the anterior cingulate gyrus, children with lower SES were found to have thinner cortex in some regions (Lawson, Duda, Avants, Wu, & Farah, 2013). A small sample of 10-year-old children of diverse SES revealed volumetric differences in certain regions of the PFC, with lower SES associated with smaller volumes, and differences in PFC gyrification were also found as a function of SES (Jednoróg et al., 2012).

CANDIDATE MECHANISMS FOR THE DEVELOPMENT OF SES DISPARITIES IN EF

Although EF has been found to be a highly heritable trait (Friedman et al., 2008), a growing body of evidence suggests that environmental factors also influence developing EF (e.g., Hammond, Müller, Carpendale, Bibok, & Liebermann-Finestone, 2012; see also Deater-Deckard, 2014). Burrage et al. (2008) used the natural experiment of a school cutoff design, which compared cognitive abilities in children of approximately the same age with or without a year of schooling to show that school promoted EF. Participation in training programs has also been shown to improve EF performance (Diamond, Barnett, Thomas, & Munro, 2007; Jaeggi, Buschkuehl, Jonides, & Shah, 2011; Klingberg, 2010; but see Shipstead, Hicks, & Engle, 2012). The behavioral genetics evidence regarding a broader measure of cognitive development, IQ, suggest that whereas cognitive ability is highly heritable within a middle- or high-SES population, the environment accounts for the majority of IQ variance in impoverished families (Harden, Turkheimer, & Loehlin, 2007; Turkheimer, Haley, Waldron, D'Onofrio, & Gottesman, 2003).

What aspects of the environment might be responsible for SES disparities in EF? As observed earlier, SES is not a unitary construct but rather consists of multiple economic and social factors. Children growing up in poverty are more likely to be exposed to inadequate nutrition, violence, and toxins in their environment and are less likely to be spoken to in complex sentences, to be read to at home, or to be provided with a challenging curriculum in school (Bradley & Corwyn, 2002; Evans, 2004). Each of these factors has the potential to explain socioeconomic differences in the development of EF, making it challenging to determine the pathway through which poverty exerts its effects. Several proposed mediating pathways have received support from developmental psychology studies as well as from experiments with animal models (for a review, see Hackman, Farah, & Meaney, 2010).

One candidate mediating pathway by which SES may influence the development of EF is through the direct effect of stress on the developing brain. It has been well established that children with lower SES experience greater levels of environmental and psychosocial stressors (Bradley & Corwyn, 2002; Evans, 2004; Goodman, McEwen, Dolan, Schafer-Kalkhoff, & Adler, 2005) and show increased levels of the stress hormone cortisol (Evans, 2003; Lupien, King, Meaney, & McEwen, 2001). Chronically elevated levels of stress hormones may exert damaging effects on neural and other body systems (McEwen & Gianaros, 2011). Brain areas that are involved in the stress response, such as the PFC, may be particularly vulnerable to heightened levels of cortisol, implicating EF as a neurocognitive system that is particularly likely to be affected by chronic stress (Blair, 2010; Liston, McEwen, & Casey, 2009; Lupien, Maheu, Tu, Fiocco, & Schramek, 2007; McEwen & Gianaros, 2010). Sheridan and colleagues (2012) measured the rise of the stress hormone cortisol as a result of fMRI participation in their 8- to 12-year-old subjects and found that stress reactivity was related to both SES and prefrontal activation. More directly consistent with the stress account of the SES–EF relation are the findings of Evans and Schamberg (2009), who showed that elevated allostatic load in childhood mediated the effect of chronic, rural poverty on working memory in adolescence.

A related candidate mediating pathway focuses on the potential role of parental behavior in influencing developing EF. Lower household income tends to be associated with lower maternal responsivity, an effect that may be mediated by increased maternal stress among low-SES populations (Evans, Boxhill, & Pinkava, 2008). Research using animal models suggests that parental nurturance in infancy is critical in programming stress responsivity throughout the life span (Champagne & Curley, 2009; Meaney, Szyf, & Seckl, 2007). In humans, maternal engagement in early childhood is associated with greater cortisol reactivity (indicating more developed regulation of the hypothalamic–pituitary–adrenal axis), an effect that carries over until at least adolescence (Hackman et al., 2013). Parental care also influences basal cortisol in childhood (Blair et al., 2008; Gunnar & Quevedo, 2007). Similarly, salivary cortisol levels have been found to partially mediate the association between positive parenting measured at 7, 15, and 24 months and EF at 3 years (Blair et al., 2011). These findings suggest that early programming of the stress response may also occur in humans, potentially influencing cognitive development throughout the lifespan.

In addition to stress and parenting, cognitive stimulation also affects later EF. It has been well established that access to cognitively enriching materials varies with SES: Children below the poverty line have less access to reading materials and enriching learning activities (e.g., trips to a museum; Bradley, Corwyn, McAdoo, & Coll, 2001) and hear fewer words of speech

(Hart & Risley, 1992). Animal models of early experience have demonstrated that environmental complexity alters a wide range of neural outcomes, such as dendritic branching, gliogenesis, and synaptic density (Sale, Berardi, & Maffei, 2009; van Praag, Kempermann, & Gage, 2000), suggesting that cognitive stimulation may be one pathway through which SES affects the developing brain.

Several studies have investigated the role of these and other candidate mediating pathways in creating SES disparities in preschool EF. The quality of parent–child interactions, particularly during infancy, has been found to mediate SES effects on EF at 36 months of age (Blair et al., 2011; Rhoades et al., 2011). Other studies have found support for parental support of child autonomy (Bernier, Carlson, & Whipple, 2010) as well as parent scaffolding and family chaos (Bibok, Carpendale, & Müller, 2009; Hughes & Ensor, 2009) as important predictors of early childhood. The quality of home environment—including cognitive stimulation and parental nurturance—partially accounts for these disparities throughout childhood according to an analysis of data from the National Institute of Child Health and Human Development (NICHD) Study of Early Child Care and Youth Development (SECCYD; Hackman, Gallop, Evans, & Farah, 2015). This study used the longitudinal measures of EF, SES, and multiple potential mediators for the SES–EF relation to identify mediators of SES disparities in early childhood EF. This rich data set also made it possible to examine prospective mediators in relation to one another, reducing the problem of omitted variable bias that complicates the interpretation of many studies in this area. Specifically, when potential mediators are correlated with one another, and not all of them are measured, the finding that one factor statistically mediates the SES–cognition relation does not rule out the possibility that unmeasured correlated factors are the true causal mediators. In the NICHD SECCYD, although early childhood home environment and maternal sensitivity both emerged as significant mediators when raw, unadjusted mediators were tested individually or in combination with other candidate mediators, Hackman et al. (2015) found that only childhood home environment was a significant mediator after controlling for the correlation between maternal sensitivity and home environment. This finding provides strong evidence that the quality of the childhood home environment is a specific, dissociable pathway through which SES influences the development of early childhood EF.

SES, EF, AND ACADEMIC ACHIEVEMENT

One reason EF is an important topic within developmental psychology in general, and studies of SES and development in particular, is that it plays a role in school achievement. Current research is addressing the role of

EF in SES disparities in school readiness and academic performance. These disparities are evident at the earliest experiences of children in school or preschool and persist throughout the course of schooling (e.g., Bradley & Corwyn, 2002; Reardon, 2011).

EF would be expected to support school achievement for several reasons. It can enable students to focus on learning in the classroom, ignoring distractions from without (e.g., other students talking) or within (e.g., daydreaming or worrying). In addition, some academic subjects, particularly math, require information to be held in working memory and manipulated. Indeed, evidence is accumulating that EF does indeed support school achievement, from studies of early childhood school readiness (e.g., Alloway et al., 2005; Blair & Razza, 2007) to school performance throughout childhood and adolescence (Best, Miller, & Naglieri, 2011; St Clair-Thompson & Gathercole, 2006). Measures of EF performance during childhood and adolescence correlate strongly with concurrent measures of reading and math performance, as measured on standardized achievement tests (Best, Miller, & Naglieri, 2011; St Clair-Thompson & Gathercole, 2006). Furthermore, longitudinal studies have found that EF prospectively predicts academic achievement (e.g., Bull, Espy, & Wiebe, 2008; Mazzocco & Kover, 2007; Passolunghi, Vercelloni, & Schadee, 2007), even after controlling for prior measures of academic achievement (Welsh, Nix, Blair, Bierman, & Nelson, 2010).

Evidence for a causal relation between EF and academic achievement comes from intervention programs. Direct training of EF may boost academic achievement, although the literature is mixed (Titz & Karbach, 2014). More broadly based intervention programs for preschoolers produce gains in academic readiness partly through their impact on EF (Bierman et al., 2008; Raver et al., 2011).

Several studies have directly tested the hypothesis that EF mediates SES disparities in academic achievement in the earliest years of schooling. In the NICHD SECCYD, children's sustained attention and impulsivity were found to partially mediate the relationship between home environment quality and achievement at 54 months (NICHD Early Child Care Research Network, 2003). Another study using a sample of preschool children enrolled in either needs-based or private preschools found that EF partially mediated the relationship between SES group and achievement (Fitzpatrick, McKinnon, Blair, & Willoughby, 2014). Other studies using early childhood samples find that EF partially mediates the relationship between SES and math skill (Dilworth-Bart, 2012) and between SES and math and literacy achievement (Nesbitt, Baker-Ward, & Willoughby, 2013). Two more recent studies with older children indicate that EF continues to mediate at least certain aspects of academic achievement throughout the school years (Crook & Evans, 2014; Lawson & Farah, 2014).

CONCLUSION

What can we conclude about SES and EF in preschoolers, and what remains to be understood? It is clear that EF in the preschool years differs across levels of SES. As early as infancy, children's behavior indicates that higher SES is associated with more mature EF. Neuroscience research shows corresponding differences in the neural substrates of EF. The causes of these physical and psychological differences are not well understood, but certain factors seem likely to play a role. As noted earlier, life stress and parenting behavior are known to differ by SES. So do many aspects of the environment that provide or restrict opportunities to explore and learn.

Future research can extend the field's understanding of SES–EF relations in several ways. A better understanding of meditational processes, that is, the mechanisms by which childhood SES and EF are related, is needed to help prevent and redress the cognitive disadvantages of low SES children. In particular, a more detailed understanding of how and when mediators influence EF development would provide a valuable theoretical basis for the design of prevention and intervention programs. A number of approaches may be useful in addressing the question of causality. Natural experiments on EF development, such as the school cutoff design of Burrage et al. (2008), could incorporate measures of SES, and natural experiments on SES and child development, such as used by Costello, Compton, Keeler, and Angold (2003), could assess EF. In addition, intervention research represents an important opportunity to advance scientific understanding of the causal relations linking SES and EF, as well as a means to eventually improve the life chances of children with low SES.

We note that most research to date has involved samples of young children studied cross-sectionally. Longitudinal studies, measuring EF early and extending through adolescence and adulthood, would illuminate the ultimate scope and impact of the effects of preschool EF disparities. A longitudinal approach would also help identify sensitive periods, in which environmental factors associated with SES exert greater influence on EF. This knowledge would have important implications for the timing of interventions designed to improve EF among children at risk. To date, the evidence suggests that infancy through preschool may be such an important developmental epoch. With continued research, an understanding of the role of SES in EF development, as well as EF's contributions to myriad life outcomes, can be harnessed to improve the life chances and social mobility of children growing up in poverty.

REFERENCES

Adler, N. E., & Rehkopf, D. H. (2008). U.S. disparities in health: Descriptions, causes, and mechanisms. *Annual Review of Public Health, 29*, 235–252. http://dx.doi.org/10.1146/annurev.publhealth.29.020907.090852

Alloway, T. P., Gathercole, S. E., Adams, A. M., Willis, C., Eaglen, R., & Lamont, E. (2005). Working memory and phonological awareness as predictors of progress towards early learning goals at school entry. *British Journal of Developmental Psychology, 23*, 417–426. http://dx.doi.org/10.1348/026151005X26804

Ardila, A., Rosselli, M., Matute, E., & Guajardo, S. (2005). The influence of the parents' educational level on the development of executive functions. *Developmental Neuropsychology, 28*, 539–560. http://dx.doi.org/10.1207/s15326942dn2801_5

Bernier, A., Carlson, S. M., & Whipple, N. (2010). From external regulation to self-regulation: Early parenting precursors of young children's executive functioning. *Child Development, 81*, 326–339. http://dx.doi.org/10.1111/j.1467-8624.2009.01397.x

Best, J. R., Miller, P. H., & Naglieri, J. A. (2011). Relations between executive function and academic achievement from ages 5 to 17 in a large, representative national sample. *Learning and Individual Differences, 21*, 327–336. http://dx.doi.org/10.1016/j.lindif.2011.01.007

Bibok, M. B., Carpendale, J. I. M., & Müller, U. (2009). Parental scaffolding and the development of executive function. *New Directions for Child and Adolescent Development, 2009*(123), 17–34. http://dx.doi.org/10.1002/cd.233

Bierman, K. L., Domitrovich, C. E., Nix, R. L., Gest, S. D., Welsh, J. A., Greenberg, M. T., . . . Gill, S. (2008). Promoting academic and social–emotional school readiness: The Head Start REDI program. *Child Development, 79*, 1802–1817. http://dx.doi.org/10.1111/j.1467-8624.2008.01227.x

Blair, C. (2010). Stress and the development of self-regulation in context. *Child Development Perspectives, 4*, 181–188. http://dx.doi.org/10.1111/j.1750-8606.2010.00145.x

Blair, C., & Diamond, A. (2008). Biological processes in prevention and intervention: The promotion of self-regulation as a means of preventing school failure. *Development and Psychopathology, 20*, 899–911. http://dx.doi.org/10.1017/S0954579408000436

Blair, C., Granger, D. A., Kivlighan, K. T., Mills-Koonce, R., Willoughby, M., Greenberg, M. T., . . . Family Life Project Investigators. (2008). Maternal and child contributions to cortisol response to emotional arousal in young children from low-income, rural communities. *Developmental Psychology, 44*, 1095–1109. http://dx.doi.org/10.1037/0012-1649.44.4.1095

Blair, C., Granger, D. A., Willoughby, M., Mills-Koonce, R., Cox, M., Greenberg, M. T., . . . FLP Investigators. (2011). Salivary cortisol mediates effects of poverty and parenting on executive functions in early childhood. *Child Development, 82*, 1970–1984. http://dx.doi.org/10.1111/j.1467-8624.2011.01643.x

Blair, C., & Razza, R. P. (2007). Relating effortful control, executive function, and false belief understanding to emerging math and literacy ability in kindergarten. *Child Development, 78*, 647–663. http://dx.doi.org/10.1111/j.1467-8624.2007.01019.x

Bradley, R. H., & Corwyn, R. F. (2002). Socioeconomic status and child development. *Annual Review of Psychology, 53*, 371–399. http://dx.doi.org/10.1146/annurev.psych.53.100901.135233

Bradley, R. H., Corwyn, R. F., McAdoo, H. P., & Coll, C. G. (2001). The home environments of children in the United States Part I: Variations by age, ethnicity, and poverty status. *Child Development, 72*, 1844–1867. http://dx.doi.org/10.1111/1467-8624.t01-1-00382

Brain Development Cooperative Group. (2012). Total and regional brain volumes in a population-based normative sample from 4 to 18 years: The NIH MRI Study of Normal Brain Development. *Cerebral Cortex, 22*, 1–12. http://dx.doi.org/10.1093/cercor/bhr018

Braveman, P. A., Cubbin, C., Egerter, S., Chideya, S., Marchi, K. S., Metzler, M., & Posner, S. (2005). Socioeconomic status in health research: One size does not fit all. *JAMA, 294*, 2879–2888. http://dx.doi.org/10.1001/jama.294.22.2879

Brydges, C. R., Reid, C. L., Fox, A. M., & Anderson, M. (2012). A unitary executive function predicts intelligence in children. *Intelligence, 40*, 458–469. http://dx.doi.org/10.1016/j.intell.2012.05.006

Buckner, J. C., Mezzacappa, E., & Beardslee, W. R. (2009). Self-regulation and its relations to adaptive functioning in low income youths. *American Journal of Orthopsychiatry, 79*, 19–30. http://dx.doi.org/10.1037/a0014796

Bull, R., Espy, K. A., & Wiebe, S. A. (2008). Short-term memory, working memory, and executive functioning in preschoolers: Longitudinal predictors of mathematical achievement at age 7 years. *Developmental Neuropsychology, 33*, 205–228. http://dx.doi.org/10.1080/87565640801982312

Burrage, M. S., Ponitz, C. C., McCready, E. A., Shah, P., Sims, B. C., Jewkes, A. M., & Morrison, F. J. (2008). Age- and schooling-related effects on executive functions in young children: A natural experiment. *Child Neuropsychology, 14*, 510–524. http://dx.doi.org/10.1080/09297040701756917

Casey, B. J., Giedd, J. N., & Thomas, K. M. (2000). Structural and functional brain development and its relation to cognitive development. *Biological Psychology, 54*, 241–257. http://dx.doi.org/10.1016/S0301-0511(00)00058-2

Champagne, F. A., & Curley, J. P. (2009). Epigenetic mechanisms mediating the long-term effects of maternal care on development. *Neuroscience and Biobehavioral Reviews, 33*, 593–600. http://dx.doi.org/10.1016/j.neubiorev.2007.10.009

Costello, E. J., Compton, S. N., Keeler, G., & Angold, A. (2003). Relationships between poverty and psychopathology: A natural experiment. *JAMA, 290*, 2023–2029. http://dx.doi.org/10.1001/jama.290.15.2023

Crone, E. A., & Ridderinkhof, K. R. (2011). The developing brain: From theory to neuroimaging and back. *Developmental Cognitive Neuroscience, 1*, 101–109. http://dx.doi.org/10.1016/j.dcn.2010.12.001

Crook, S. R., & Evans, G. W. (2014). The role of planning skills in the income-achievement gap. *Child Development, 85,* 405–411. http://dx.doi.org/10.1111/cdev.12129

D'Angiulli, A., Herdman, A., Stapells, D., & Hertzman, C. (2008). Children's event-related potentials of auditory selective attention vary with their socioeconomic status. *Neuropsychology, 22,* 293–300. http://dx.doi.org/10.1037/0894-4105.22.3.293

D'Angiulli, A., Van Roon, P. M., Weinberg, J., Oberlander, T. F., Grunau, R. E., Hertzman, C., & Maggi, S. (2012). Frontal EEG/ERP correlates of attentional processes, cortisol and motivational states in adolescents from lower and higher socioeconomic status. *Frontiers in Human Neuroscience, 6,* 306.

Deater-Deckard, K. (2014). Family matters: Intergenerational and interpersonal processes of executive function and attentive behavior. *Current Directions in Psychological Science, 23,* 230–236. http://dx.doi.org/10.1177/0963721414531597

Diamond, A. (2001). Looking closely at infants' performance and experimental procedures in the A-not-B task. *Behavioral and Brain Sciences, 24,* 38–41. http://dx.doi.org/10.1017/S0140525X01253916

Diamond, A., Barnett, W. S., Thomas, J., & Munro, S. (2007). Preschool program improves cognitive control. *Science, 318,* 1387–1388. http://dx.doi.org/10.1126/science.1151148

Dilworth-Bart, J. E. (2012). Does executive function mediate SES and home quality associations with academic readiness? *Early Childhood Research Quarterly, 27,* 416–425. http://dx.doi.org/10.1016/j.ecresq.2012.02.002

Duncan, G. J., & Magnuson, K. (2012). Socioeconomic status and cognitive functioning: Moving from correlation to causation. *Wiley Interdisciplinary Reviews: Cognitive Science, 3,* 377–386. http://dx.doi.org/10.1002/wcs.1176

Engel, P. M. J., Santos, F. H., & Gathercole, S. E. (2008). Are working memory measures free of socioeconomic influence? *Journal of Speech, Language, and Hearing Research, 51,* 1580–1587. http://dx.doi.org/10.1044/1092-4388(2008/07-0210)

Evans, G. W. (2003). A multimethodological analysis of cumulative risk and allostatic load among rural children. *Developmental Psychology, 39,* 924–933. http://dx.doi.org/10.1037/0012-1649.39.5.924

Evans, G. W. (2004). The environment of childhood poverty. *American Psychologist, 59,* 77–92. http://dx.doi.org/10.1037/0003-066X.59.2.77

Evans, G., Boxhill, L., & Pinkava, M. (2008). Poverty and maternal responsiveness: The role of maternal stress and social resources. *International Journal of Behavioral Development, 32,* 232–237. http://dx.doi.org/10.1177/0165025408089272

Evans, G. W., & Schamberg, M. A. (2009). Childhood poverty, chronic stress, and adult working memory. *Proceedings of the National Academy of Sciences of the United States of America, 106,* 6545–6549. http://dx.doi.org/10.1073/pnas.0811910106

Farah, M. J., Shera, D. M., Savage, J. H., Betancourt, L., Giannetta, J. M., Brodsky, N. L., . . . Hurt, H. (2006). Childhood poverty: Specific associations with neurocognitive development. *Brain Research, 1110,* 166–174. http://dx.doi.org/10.1016/j.brainres.2006.06.072

Fitzpatrick, C., McKinnon, R. D., Blair, C. B., & Willoughby, M. T. (2014). Do preschool executive function skills explain the school readiness gap between advantaged and disadvantaged children? *Learning and Instruction, 30,* 25–31. http://dx.doi.org/10.1016/j.learninstruc.2013.11.003

Friedman, N. P., Miyake, A., Young, S. E., Defries, J. C., Corley, R. P., & Hewitt, J. K. (2008). Individual differences in executive functions are almost entirely genetic in origin. *Journal of Experimental Psychology: General, 137,* 201–225. http://dx.doi.org/10.1037/0096-3445.137.2.201

Gogtay, N., Giedd, J. N., Lusk, L., Hayashi, K. M., Greenstein, D., Vaituzis, A. C., . . . Thompson, P. M. (2004). Dynamic mapping of human cortical development during childhood through early adulthood. *Proceedings of the National Academy of Sciences of the United States of America, 101,* 8174–8179. http://dx.doi.org/10.1073/pnas.0402680101

Goodman, E., McEwen, B. S., Dolan, L. M., Schafer-Kalkhoff, T., & Adler, N. E. (2005). Social disadvantage and adolescent stress. *Journal of Adolescent Health, 37,* 484–492. http://dx.doi.org/10.1016/j.jadohealth.2004.11.126

Gunnar, M., & Quevedo, K. (2007). The neurobiology of stress and development. *Annual Review of Psychology, 58,* 145–173. http://dx.doi.org/10.1146/annurev.psych.58.110405.085605

Hackman, D. A., Betancourt, L. M., Brodsky, N. L., Kobrin, L., Hurt, H., & Farah, M. J. (2013). Selective impact of early parental responsivity on adolescent stress reactivity. *PLoS ONE, 8*(4), 1–9. http://dx.doi.org/10.1371/journal.pone.0058250

Hackman, D. A., Betancourt, L. M., Gallop, R., Romer, D., Brodsky, N. L., Hurt, H., & Farah, M. J. (2014). Mapping the trajectory of socioeconomic disparity in working memory: Parental and neighborhood factors. *Child Development, 85,* 1433–1445.

Hackman, D. A., & Farah, M. J. (2009). Socioeconomic status and the developing brain. *Trends in Cognitive Sciences, 13,* 65–73. http://dx.doi.org/10.1016/j.tics.2008.11.003

Hackman, D. A., Farah, M. J., & Meaney, M. J. (2010). Socioeconomic status and the brain: Mechanistic insights from human and animal research. *Nature Reviews Neuroscience, 11,* 651–659. http://dx.doi.org/10.1038/nrn2897

Hackman, D. A., Gallop, R., Evans, G. W., & Farah, M. J. (2015). Socioeconomic status and executive function: Developmental trajectories and mediation. *Developmental Science.* Advance online publication. http://dx.doi.org/10.1111/desc.12246

Hammond, S. I., Müller, U., Carpendale, J. I., Bibok, M. B., & Liebermann-Finestone, D. P. (2012). The effects of parental scaffolding on preschoolers' executive function. *Developmental Psychology, 48,* 271–281. http://dx.doi.org/10.1037/a0025519

Hanson, J. L., Hair, N., Shen, D. G., Shi, F., Gilmore, J. H., Wolfe, B. L., & Pollak, S. D. (2013). Family poverty affects the rate of human infant brain growth. *PLoS ONE*, 8(12), 1–9. http://dx.doi.org/10.1371/journal.pone.0080954

Harden, K. P., Turkheimer, E., & Loehlin, J. C. (2007). Genotype by environment interaction in adolescents' cognitive aptitude. *Behavior Genetics*, 37, 273–283. http://dx.doi.org/10.1007/s10519-006-9113-4

Hart, B., & Risley, T. (1992). American parenting of language-learning children: Persisting differences in family–child interactions observed in natural home environments. *Developmental Psychology*, 28, 1096–1105. http://dx.doi.org/10.1037/0012-1649.28.6.1096

Hughes, C. H., & Ensor, R. A. (2005). Executive function and theory of mind in 2-year-olds: A family affair? *Developmental Neuropsychology*, 28, 645–668. http://dx.doi.org/10.1207/s15326942dn2802_5

Hughes, C. H., & Ensor, R. A. (2009). How do families help or hinder the emergence of early executive function? *New Directions for Child and Adolescent Development*, 2009(123), 35–50. http://dx.doi.org/10.1002/cd.234

Hughes, C. H., Ensor, R. A., Wilson, A., & Graham, A. (2009). Tracking executive function across the transition to school: A latent variable approach. *Developmental Neuropsychology*, 35, 20–36. http://dx.doi.org/10.1080/87565640903325691

Isquith, P. K., Gioia, G. A., & Espy, K. A. (2004). Executive function in preschool children: Examination through everyday behavior. *Developmental Neuropsychology*, 26, 403–422. http://dx.doi.org/10.1207/s15326942dn2601_3

Jaeggi, S. M., Buschkuehl, M., Jonides, J., & Shah, P. (2011). Short- and long-term benefits of cognitive training. *Proceedings of the National Academy of Sciences of the United States of America*, 108, 10081–10086. http://dx.doi.org/10.1073/pnas.1103228108

Jednoróg, K., Altarelli, I., Monzalvo, K., Fluss, J., Dubois, J., Billard, C., . . . Ramus, F. (2012). The influence of socioeconomic status on children's brain structure. *PLoS ONE*, 7(8), 1–9. http://dx.doi.org/10.1371/journal.pone.0042486

Kishiyama, M. M., Boyce, W. T., Jimenez, A. M., Perry, L. M., & Knight, R. T. (2009). Socioeconomic disparities affect prefrontal function in children. *Journal of Cognitive Neuroscience*, 21, 1106–1115. http://dx.doi.org/10.1162/jocn.2009.21101

Klingberg, T. (2010). Training and plasticity of working memory. *Trends in Cognitive Sciences*, 14, 317–324. http://dx.doi.org/10.1016/j.tics.2010.05.002

Lange, N., Froimowitz, M. P., Bigler, E. D., Lainhart, J. E., & Brain Development Cooperative Group. (2010). Associations between IQ, total and regional brain volumes, and demography in a large normative sample of healthy children and adolescents. *Developmental Neuropsychology*, 35, 296–317. http://dx.doi.org/10.1080/87565641003696833

Lawson, G. M., Duda, J. T., Avants, B. B., Wu, J., & Farah, M. J. (2013). Associations between children's socioeconomic status and prefrontal cortical thickness. *Developmental Science*, 16, 641–652. http://dx.doi.org/10.1111/desc.12096

Lawson, G. M., & Farah, M. J. (2014, May). *Executive function as a mediator between SES and academic achievement throughout childhood.* Poster presented at the meeting of the Association for Psychological Science, San Francisco, CA.

Lipina, S. J., Martelli, M. I., Vuelta, B., & Colombo, J. A. (2005). Performance on the A-not-B task of Argentinian infants from unsatisfied and satisfied basic needs homes. *International Journal of Psychology, 39,* 49–60.

Lipina, S. J., Martelli, M. I., Vuelta, B. L., Injoque-Ricle, I., & Colombo, J. A. (2004). Poverty and executive performance in preschool pupils from Buenos Aires city (Republica Argentina). *Interdisciplinaria, 21,* 153–193.

Liston, C., McEwen, B. S., & Casey, B. J. (2009). Psychosocial stress reversibly disrupts prefrontal processing and attentional control. *Proceedings of the National Academy of Sciences of the United States of America, 106,* 912–917. http://dx.doi.org/10.1073/pnas.0807041106

Lupien, S. J., King, S., Meaney, M. J., & McEwen, B. S. (2001). Can poverty get under your skin? Basal cortisol levels and cognitive function in children from low and high socioeconomic status. *Development and Psychopathology, 13,* 653–676. http://dx.doi.org/10.1017/S0954579401003133

Lupien, S. J., Maheu, F., Tu, M., Fiocco, A., & Schramek, T. E. (2007). The effects of stress and stress hormones on human cognition: Implications for the field of brain and cognition. *Brain and Cognition, 65,* 209–237. http://dx.doi.org/10.1016/j.bandc.2007.02.007

Mazzocco, M. M. M., & Kover, S. T. (2007). A longitudinal assessment of executive function skills and their association with math performance. *Child Neuropsychology, 13,* 18–45. http://dx.doi.org/10.1080/09297040600611346

McEwen, B. S., & Gianaros, P. J. (2010). Central role of the brain in stress and adaptation: Links to socioeconomic status, health, and disease. *Annals of the New York Academy of Sciences, 1186,* 190–222. http://dx.doi.org/10.1111/j.1749-6632.2009.05331.x

McEwen, B. S., & Gianaros, P. J. (2011). Stress- and allostasis-induced brain plasticity. *Annual Review of Medicine, 62,* 431–445.

Meaney, M. J., Szyf, M., & Seckl, J. R. (2007). Epigenetic mechanisms of perinatal programming of hypothalamic–pituitary–adrenal function and health. *Trends in Molecular Medicine, 13,* 269–277. http://dx.doi.org/10.1016/j.molmed.2007.05.003

Mezzacappa, E. (2004). Alerting, orienting, and executive attention: Developmental properties and sociodemographic correlates in an epidemiological sample of young, urban children. *Child Development, 75,* 1373–1386. http://dx.doi.org/10.1111/j.1467-8624.2004.00746.x

Miyake, A., Friedman, N. P., Emerson, M. J., Witzki, A. H., Howerter, A., & Wager, T. D. (2000). The unity and diversity of executive functions and their contributions to complex "frontal lobe" tasks: A latent variable analysis. *Cognitive Psychology, 41,* 49–100. http://dx.doi.org/10.1006/cogp.1999.0734

Nesbitt, K. T., Baker-Ward, L., & Willoughby, M. T. (2013). Executive function mediates socioeconomic and racial differences in early academic achievement. *Early Childhood Research Quarterly, 28,* 774–783. http://dx.doi.org/10.1016/j.ecresq.2013.07.005

NICHD Early Child Care Research Network. (2003). Do children's attention processes mediate the link between family predictors and school readiness? *Developmental Psychology, 39,* 581–593. http://dx.doi.org/10.1037/0012-1649.39.3.581

Noble, K. G., McCandliss, B. D., & Farah, M. J. (2007). Socioeconomic gradients predict individual differences in neurocognitive abilities. *Developmental Science, 10,* 464–480. http://dx.doi.org/10.1111/j.1467-7687.2007.00600.x

Noble, K. G., Norman, M. F., & Farah, M. J. (2005). Neurocognitive correlates of socioeconomic status in kindergarten children. *Developmental Science, 8,* 74–87. http://dx.doi.org/10.1111/j.1467-7687.2005.00394.x

Otero, G. A. (1997). Poverty, cultural disadvantage, and brain development: A study of preschool children in Mexico. *Electroencephalography and Clinical Neurophysiology, 102,* 512–516. http://dx.doi.org/10.1016/S0013-4694(97)95213-9

Otero, G. A., Pliego-Rivero, F. B., Fernández, T., & Ricardo, J. (2003). EEG development in children with sociocultural disadvantages: A follow-up study. *Clinical Neurophysiology, 114,* 1918–1925. http://dx.doi.org/10.1016/S1388-2457(03)00173-1

Passolunghi, M. C., Vercelloni, B., & Schadee, H. (2007). The precursors of mathematics learning: Working memory, phonological ability, and numerical competence. *Cognitive Development, 22,* 165–184. http://dx.doi.org/10.1016/j.cogdev.2006.09.001

Raizada, R. D. S., Richards, T. L., Meltzoff, A., & Kuhl, P. K. (2008). Socioeconomic status predicts hemispheric specialisation of the left inferior frontal gyrus in young children. *NeuroImage, 40,* 1392–1401. http://dx.doi.org/10.1016/j.neuroimage.2008.01.021

Raver, C. C., Jones, S. M., Li-Grining, C., Zhai, F., Bub, K., & Pressler, E. (2011). CSRP's impact on low-income preschoolers' preacademic skills: Self-regulation as a mediating mechanism. *Child Development, 82,* 362–378. http://dx.doi.org/10.1111/j.1467-8624.2010.01561.x

Reardon, S. F. (2011). The widening academic achievement gap between the rich and the poor: New evidence and possible explanations. In R. Murnane & G. Duncan (Eds.), *Whither opportunity? Rising inequality and the uncertain life chances of low-income children* (pp. 91–113). New York, NY: Sage.

Rhoades, B. L., Greenberg, M. T., Lanza, S. T., & Blair, C. (2011). Demographic and familial predictors of early executive function development: Contribution of a person-centered perspective. *Journal of Experimental Child Psychology, 108,* 638–662. http://dx.doi.org/10.1016/j.jecp.2010.08.004

Robbins, T. W., Weinberger, D., Taylor, J. G., & Morris, R. G. (1996). Dissociating executive functions of the prefrontal cortex. *Philosophical Transactions of the*

Royal Society B: Biological Sciences, 351, 1463–1471. http://dx.doi.org/10.1098/rstb.1996.0131

Sale, A., Berardi, N., & Maffei, L. (2009). Enrich the environment to empower the brain. *Trends in Neurosciences, 32,* 233–239. http://dx.doi.org/10.1016/j.tins.2008.12.004

Sarsour, K., Sheridan, M., Jutte, D., Nuru-Jeter, A., Hinshaw, S., & Boyce, W. T. (2011). Family socioeconomic status and child executive functions: The roles of language, home environment, and single parenthood. *Journal of the International Neuropsychological Society, 17,* 120–132. http://dx.doi.org/10.1017/S1355617710001335

Senn, T. E., Espy, K. A., & Kaufmann, P. M. (2004). Using path analysis to understand executive function organization in preschool children. *Developmental Neuropsychology, 26,* 445–464. http://dx.doi.org/10.1207/s15326942dn2601_5

Sheridan, M. A., Sarsour, K., Jutte, D., D'Esposito, M., & Boyce, W. T. (2012). The impact of social disparity on prefrontal function in childhood. *PLoS ONE, 7*(4), 1–13. http://dx.doi.org/10.1371/journal.pone.0035744

Shipstead, Z., Hicks, K. L., & Engle, R. W. (2012). Cogmed working memory training: Does the evidence support the claims? *Journal of Applied Research in Memory and Cognition, 1,* 185–193. http://dx.doi.org/10.1016/j.jarmac.2012.06.003

St Clair-Thompson, H. L., & Gathercole, S. E. (2006). Executive functions and achievements in school: Shifting, updating, inhibition, and working memory. *The Quarterly Journal of Experimental Psychology, 59,* 745–759. http://dx.doi.org/10.1080/17470210500162854

Stevens, C., Lauinger, B., & Neville, H. (2009). Differences in the neural mechanisms of selective attention in children from different socioeconomic backgrounds: An event-related brain potential study. *Developmental Science, 12,* 634–646. http://dx.doi.org/10.1111/j.1467-7687.2009.00807.x

Stuss, D. T., & Alexander, M. P. (2007). Is there a dysexecutive syndrome? *Philosophical Transactions of the Royal Society B: Biological Sciences, 362,* 901–915. http://dx.doi.org/10.1098/rstb.2007.2096

Titz, C., & Karbach, J. (2014). Working memory and executive functions: Effects of training on academic achievement. *Psychological Research, 78,* 852–868. http://dx.doi.org/10.1007/s00426-013-0537-1

Turkheimer, E., Haley, A., Waldron, M., D'Onofrio, B., & Gottesman, I. I. (2003). Socioeconomic status modifies heritability of IQ in young children. *Psychological Science, 14,* 623–628. http://dx.doi.org/10.1046/j.0956-7976.2003.psci_1475.x

van Praag, H., Kempermann, G., & Gage, F. H. (2000). Neural consequences of environmental enrichment. *Nature Reviews Neuroscience, 1,* 191–198. http://dx.doi.org/10.1038/35044558

Waber, D. P., De Moor, C., Forbes, P. W., Almli, C. R., Botteron, K. N., Leonard, G., . . . Brain Development Cooperative Group. (2007). The NIH MRI study of normal brain development: Performance of a population-based sample of healthy children aged 6 to 18 years on a neuropsychological battery. *Journal of the International Neuropsychological Society, 13,* 729–746. http://dx.doi.org/10.1017/S1355617707070841

Welsh, J. A., Nix, R. L., Blair, C., Bierman, K. L., & Nelson, K. E. (2010). The development of cognitive skills and gains in academic school readiness for children from low-income families. *Journal of Educational Psychology, 102,* 43–53. http://dx.doi.org/10.1037/a0016738

Wiebe, S. A., Espy, K. A., & Charak, D. (2008). Using confirmatory factor analysis to understand executive control in preschool children: I. Latent structure. *Developmental Psychology, 44,* 575–587. http://dx.doi.org/10.1037/0012-1649.44.2.575

Wiebe, S. A., Sheffield, T., Nelson, J. M., Clark, C. A. C., Chevalier, N., & Espy, K. A. (2011). The structure of executive function in 3-year-olds. *Journal of Experimental Child Psychology, 108,* 436–452. http://dx.doi.org/10.1016/j.jecp.2010.08.008

12

ASSESSING DEVELOPMENTAL TRAJECTORIES OF EXECUTIVE FUNCTION IN LOW-INCOME, ETHNIC MINORITY PRESCHOOLERS: OPPORTUNITIES AND CHALLENGES

MARGARET O'BRIEN CAUGHY, MARGARET TRESCH OWEN,
AND JAMIE HURST DeLUNA

African American and Latino children in the United States experience disparities in virtually all domains of health and development. Between 2003 and 2005, the infant mortality rate among African American non-Latino infants (13.6 per 1,000 live births) was almost two and a half times the rate for European American non-Latino (5.7 per 1,000) or Mexican-origin Latino infants (5.5 per 1,000; U.S. Department of Health and Human Services, 2010). Although Latino infants, particularly those of Mexican

This research project is funded by the Eunice Kennedy Shriver National Institute of Child Health and Development (1R01HD058643-01A1). The authors would like to thank all members of the research team including home visitors Plaststilla Arnold, Carmen Gonzalez, Bunnoi McDaniel, and Clare Stevens; project management staff Melissa Amos, Adriana Baird, Piper Duarte, Caroline Mejias, Nazly Hasanizadeh, Ana-Maria Mata-Otero, Jerry Roberson, and Junie Strestha; and student interns Alexandra Abercrombie, Russell Ansley, Glenda Heisick, Cynthia Medina, June Ng'ang'a, Daisy Pena, and Helen Reyes. Without your tireless dedication, this project would not have been possible. We are also indebted to the Dallas families who welcomed us into their homes. Getting to know you and your children has enriched our lives.

http://dx.doi.org/10.1037/14797-013
Executive Function in Preschool-Age Children: Integrating Measurement, Neurodevelopment, and Translational Research, J. A. Griffin, P. McCardle, and L. S. Freund (Editors)

origin, experience more optimal birth outcomes, they experience disparities in other domains. According to the 2010 Pediatric Nutrition Surveillance Survey, Latino preschoolers had a rate of obesity 45% higher than the rate of obesity among European American non-Latino preschoolers and 52% higher than the rate among African American non-Latino preschoolers (Centers for Disease Control/National Center for Health Statistics, 2011). Overall, the parents of African American and Latino children are more likely to report that their child has experienced poor health (Braveman & Barclay, 2009; Flores, Olson, & Tomany-Korman, 2005).

A significant contributing factor to health disparities among African American and Latino children in the United States is the profound disparity in socioeconomic status present in American society. Over the past 30 years, the childhood poverty rate among African American and Latino children has been persistently two to three times the rate among European American non-Latino children (Williams, Mohammed, Leavell, & Collins, 2010). Furthermore, ethnic minority children are more likely to experience chronic poverty and to live in a neighborhood characterized by high poverty, high crime, and high levels of other physical and social incivilities (Acevedo-Garcia, Osypuk, McArdle, & Williams, 2008; Brooks-Gunn, Duncan, & Maritato, 1997; Caughy & Franzini, 2005).

There are also profound ethnic disparities in educational attainment. In 2006, 82.3% of African American adults in the United States had a high school degree and only 18.5% had a college degree (Williams et al., 2010). The rates of high school graduation are much lower among Latinos; only 60.3% of Latino adults have a high school degree or higher with the lowest proportion among Latinos of Mexican origin (53.9%). These rates are even lower in large, urban school districts serving large proportions of minority youth, with graduation rates for African American and Latino youth in many of the largest school districts in the country well below 40% (Freudenberg & Ruglis, 2007). Low educational attainment is a strong predictor of poor health in adulthood (Davey Smith et al., 1998), leading some to suggest that eliminating disparities in educational attainment has central importance for eliminating disparities in health (Freudenberg & Ruglis, 2007; Woolf, Johnson, Phillips, & Philipsen, 2007).

Disparities in academic achievement emerge early. When entering kindergarten, only half of Latino children could recognize letters compared with 75% of European American non-Latino children (Garcia & Gonzales, 2006). Approximately 34% of African American kindergarteners and 42% of Latino kindergarteners tested in the lowest quartile for reading skills compared with only 18% of European American non-Latino children (West, Denton, & Germino-Hausken, 2000). Comparable percentages for math were 39% and 40% in the lowest quartile for African Americans and Latinos, respectively, versus 18% for European-American non-Latino children. Duncan and Magnuson (2005) reported that African American and Latino kindergarteners in the Early Childhood Longitudinal Survey—Kindergarten cohort (ECLS-K) scored two thirds of a standard deviation lower in math and about a half a standard deviation lower in reading as compared with European American non-Latino kindergarteners.

THE CONTRIBUTION OF EXECUTIVE FUNCTION DEVELOPMENT TO DISPARITIES IN SCHOOL READINESS

Because of the strong continuities between a child's skills at school entry and achievement in middle school and high school, many have emphasized eliminating disparities in school readiness as critically important for eliminating disparities in academic achievement and high school completion (Entwisle, Alexander, & Olson, 2005; Kowaleski-Jones & Duncan, 1999; Morrison, Rimm-Kaufman, & Pianta, 2003; Pettit, Bates, & Dodge, 1997). Recently, there has been an increased emphasis in the research literature on the importance of child self-regulation skills for positive adjustment in kindergarten and early elementary school (Blair, 2002; Blair & Diamond, 2008; Lewit & Baker, 1995; McClelland et al., 2007; Miech, Essex, & Goldsmith, 2001; Rimm-Kaufman, Pianta, & Cox, 2000; Sektnan, McClelland, Acock, & Morrison, 2010). Blair (2002; Blair & Razza, 2007) has identified the development of metacognitive skills of executive function (EF), including working memory, attention shifting, and inhibitory control as the basis for self-regulated learning, characterized by planning, problem solving, and goal-directed activity.

Empirical evidence suggests that the development of EF skills and self-regulation is negatively influenced by socioeconomic and other contextual risk factors (Lengua, Honorado, & Bush, 2007; Mistry, Benner, Biesanz, Clark, & Howes, 2010; Sektnan et al., 2010) and as such, deficits in self-regulation may be a key factor in explaining ethnic disparities in school readiness and early academic achievement. Therefore, understanding EF skill development among low-income African American and Latino preschoolers is important for the development of effective early childhood interventions to reduce and eliminate disparities in school readiness. However, very little empirical data are available on the emergence and development of EF skills among low-income, ethnic minority preschoolers—the population at greatest risk for early school failure.

Garon, Bryson, and Smith (2008) reviewed the extant literature on the development of EF skills in preschool children. Very little longitudinal data on EF development are available for very young children. Garon et al. found that either researchers did not report the race/ethnicity of their samples or reported samples composed of 80% to 95% European-American non-Latino children. The only longitudinal studies of EF and self-regulation initiated before age 4 included virtually no ethnic minority children (Carlson, 2005; Kochanska, Coy, & Murray, 2001; Lengua et al., 2007), included only a very limited longitudinal follow-up component (Li-Grining, 2007; Spinrad et al., 2007), or did not include direct assessment of EF abilities (Raikes, Robinson, Bradley, Raikes, & Ayoub, 2007). The Family Life Project (FLP) has longitudinal EF data from direct assessment starting at age 36 months, and the sample is approximately 60% European American non-Latino and 40% African American and rural (Willoughby, Blair, Wirth, Greenberg, & The Family Life Project Investigators, 2010).

There is a significant need for more empirical data on the emergence of EF skills among low-income, ethnically diverse children. The Dallas Preschool Readiness Project (DPReP) was launched in 2009 with the primary aim of assembling a large cohort of ethnically diverse preschoolers to study longitudinally the emergence of EF and the relation of this developmental process to markers of school readiness. In the remainder of this chapter, we describe that project, report initial findings, and discuss the challenges of conducting longitudinal, community-based developmental research with this population.

DALLAS PRESCHOOL READINESS PROJECT

Participants in the DPReP were recruited through a wide range of community-based recruitment strategies including distribution of study information to organizations and agencies serving low-income communities such as Women, Infants, and Children (WIC) clinics, medical clinics, day-care centers, community recreational centers, and churches. Project staff also recruited participants directly by attending community fairs or frequenting other venues in low-income communities where families with young children are present such as parks or grocery stores. To be eligible for the study, the target child had to be between the ages of 29 and 31 months before the end of December 2010, have at least one parent who self-identified as African American or Latino, be living in a family with an income at or below 200% of the federal poverty level, and have been hospitalized for less than 1 week following birth. We recruited families who said they planned to remain in the Dallas–Fort Worth area for at least 1 year, and indeed very few had moved out of the city or country 1 year later, although many families changed residences and residential situations within their communities. A total of 404 children (186 girls) were enrolled in the study; their characteristics are displayed in Table 12.1. Approximately 55% of the children were Latino and 45% were African American non-Latino. African American children were significantly

TABLE 12.1

Characteristic of Dallas Preschool Readiness Study Sample (N = 404)

	African American (n = 182) n (%)	Latino (n = 222) n (%)	χ^2
Family income[a]			
< 50% federal poverty level	97 (61.8)	40 (19.3)	73.48***
50–99% federal poverty level	26 (16.6)	87 (42.0)	
100–149% federal poverty level	22 (14.0)	56 (27.1)	
150–200% federal poverty level	7 (4.5)	21 (10.1)	
>200% federal poverty level	5 (3.2)	3 (1.4)	
Child gender			
Boy	102 (56.0)	116 (52.3)	.58
Girl	80 (44.0)	106 (47.7)	
Primary caregiver relationship to child			
Mother	162 (89.0)	216 (97.3)	73.48***
Father	9 (4.9)	3 (1.4)	
Grandmother	11 (6.0)	2 (.9)	
Aunt or uncle	0 (0.0)	21 (10.1)	
Father/father-figure in household			
No	80 (44.0)	26 (11.7)	53.73***
Yes	102 (56.0)	196 (88.3)	
Latino families only Preferred language			
English		54 (24.3)	
Spanish		166 (74.8)	
Nativity			
U.S. born		59 (26.6)	
Foreign born		163 (73.4)	
Country of origin			
Mexico		156 (95.7)	
Central America		5 (3.1)	
South America		1 (0.0)	

[a]11 families who screened eligible reported income above the eligibility cutoff at the time of the home visit. Those with incomes >300% FPL were excluded from the sample, but the 8 between 200% and 300% FPL were retained.
***$p < .001$

more likely to be living in households below 50% of the federal poverty level and in households without a father present. Almost three quarters of the Latino primary caregivers in the sample were foreign born, with the vast majority of those being from Mexico. Approximately 80% of the children as well as 75% of the mothers in our Latino sample spoke primarily Spanish at the time of enrollment. Fathers or father-figures who were living in the home were eligible to participate in the study as well. A total of 321 children in the DPReP study had a father or father-figure residing in the home at Time 1, Time 2, or both. Of these, 252 (80%) participated in at least one data collection visit. Father participation was slightly higher among African American fathers (85%) compared with Latino fathers (76%).

Data Collection Procedures

Families were visited in their homes for the first time when the target child was 2.5 years old and for a second time approximately one year later. The average age of children at the time of the first assessment was 29.79 months ($SD = .63$, range 28–31 months). African American children were slightly older than Latino children at the time of the first home visit, 29.87 months ($SD = .69$) versus 29.73 months ($SD = .56$), t (402) = 2.31, $p < .05$. The average age at the time of the second assessment was 41.2 months ($SD = 1.26$, range 38–46). Of the 404 children who completed the assessment at age 2.5, 363 (90%) completed the second home visit 1 year later. The follow-up rate for Latino families (93%) was higher than the follow-up rate with African American families (86%).

Each home visit followed a similar format. One home visitor conducted an interview with the primary caregiver while the other home visitor completed the assessment activities with the target child. A semistructured interaction task for the primary caregiver and child was conducted about halfway through the child assessments to give the child a break and allow him or her more freedom to move around. If the father was available during the home visit, he was interviewed as well, and a similar semistructured interaction task was conducted with the father and target child. If the father was not available or the child seemed to be fatigued, the father data collection was scheduled for another time. All child assessment activities and the parent–child interaction tasks were video-recorded for subsequent coding. Families received a $50 incentive ($100 if the father participated) and a DVD copy of the home visit. Children received a developmentally appropriate book or toy as part of the Wrapped Gift task in the EF assessment battery.

Measures of Executive Function

For assessing self-regulation and EF skills, we chose a range of activities after extensive piloting to determine which tasks worked with this population and could be feasibly implemented in home settings under a wide range of conditions. Many were drawn from the work of others who have developed self-regulation batteries for young children (Cameron Ponitz et al., 2008; Carlson, 2005; Kochanska, Murray, & Harlan, 2000). The tasks we used at each of the two assessments points are displayed in Table 12.2. Tasks that

TABLE 12.2
Measures of Executive Function

30 months	42 months
Snack Delay	Snack Delay
Wrapped Gift/Wait for Bow	Wrapped Gift/Wait for Bow
Forbidden Toy	Mommy-Me
Shape Stroop	Heads & Toes
Mommy-Me	Dimensional Change Card Sort
Walk-a-Line Slowly	Memory Chocolates

were used at 30 months but not at 42 months were dropped to keep the entire home visit within a reasonable length (1.5–2 hours). Several tasks were used at 42 months but not 30 months because our pilot work suggested a floor effect at 30 months due to task difficulty. Because detailed descriptions of most of these tasks can be found elsewhere (Carlson, 2005; Garon et al., 2008; Kochanska et al., 2000), we will describe only the tasks that are less commonly used. Mommy-Me is a Stroop-like task developed by Bell and her colleagues (Bell, Hubble, & Morasch, 2010) in which children are presented with pictures of both themselves and their mothers. Children are instructed to point to the picture of themselves when told "point to mommy" and that they are to point to the picture of their mother when told "point to [child's name]." Memory Chocolates is a forward digit span test of working memory developed especially for this study. The child is presented with a heart-shaped plastic box that contains spaces for 12 differently shaped plastic chocolate candies with removable lids (Smart Snacks Hide 'n' Peek Chocolates by Learning Resources, http://www.learningresources.com). Only six of the plastic chocolate candies were used for the assessment at age 42 months. Under the lid of each chocolate is a sticker of one of six different animals: cat, elephant, fish, lion, rabbit, or horse. After naming and teaching trials, the child is asked to find one animal (e.g., "cat"), two animals (e.g., "cat", "fish"), and so on in a forward digit span-like memory test.

Scoring Procedures

EF tasks were scored using coding systems developed by others. Each of the four Snack Delay trials was coded on a 7-point scale reflecting if or when the child picked up the candy (0 = *ate candy before delay halfway point*; 6 = *waited until bell rang*), and the scores from the four trials were averaged. The Wrapped Gift/Wait for Bow task was coded for the nature of the child's peeking and nature of touching the gift as well as latencies to peek, touch, lift, and open the gift. These scores were standardized and averaged such that higher scores indicated greater self-regulation. Similarly, the Forbidden Toy task was coded for type of engagement and latency to engagement and these scores were standardized and averaged. The Shape Stroop and Mommy-Me tasks were coded in two different ways. First, following the same coding system used by Kochanska (Kochanska et al., 2000) and Carlson (2005), each trial was coded on a 3-point scale (0 = *incorrect*, 1 = *self-correct*, and 2 = *correct*), and the test trials were averaged. However, because only 31% of our sample at age 30 months were able to complete the naming and practice trials and make it to the test trials for Shape Stroop, and only 6% made it to the test trials for Mommy-Me, we followed the example of Bell and colleagues (2010) in coding the full range of child responses across the administration of the task. On each task, children were categorized into one of seven groups: refused, could not pass naming trials, naming trials correct, practice trials correct, one to two test trials correct, or three to four test trials correct.

Performance on Tasks in the DPReP Sample at 30 Months

In selecting EF tasks for DPReP, we looked to the literature to identify tasks that best discriminate individual differences in 2.5-year-olds. Carlson (2005) provided summary data on the average pass rates of more than 600 mostly middle-class European-American children from age 24 months to 6 years on a large variety of EF tasks. However, in the course of piloting the tasks with children in our target population, it was apparent that children were not able to complete the tasks at the same pass rates for children of similar ages reported in the literature. The discrepancy was more apparent in tasks involving attentional conflict, such as Stroop-like tasks, than in tasks requiring children to inhibit their impulses to touch a desired object. To examine more closely differences in performance on a task requiring inhibition to touch an attractive object, we compared performance of the children in the DPReP sample on the Wrapped Gift task with data reported by Kochanska, Murray, and Harlan (2000). Kochanska enrolled a sample of 112 children at age 9 months and reassessed them at 14, 22, and 33 months. The Snack Delay task was administered at 22 and 33 months. In Figure 12.1, we display a comparison in the latencies to peek during the wrapping phase as well as latencies to touch, lift, and open the gift during the Wait for Bow phase. Children in the 30-month DPReP sample peeked during the gift wrap phase of the task just about as quickly as the 22-month-olds did in Kochanska's sample. However, during the Wait for Bow phase, DPReP children waited the longest before touching the gift and waited an intermediate time before lifting and opening the gift as compared with the 22-month-olds and 33-month-olds in Kochanska's sample.

Performance differences between the DPReP and other samples of preschoolers on tasks that involved some form of attentional conflict were more striking. In Figure 12.2, we display the average test scores on the Shape Stroop

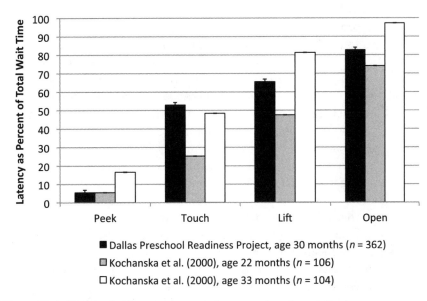

Figure 12.1. Wrapped gift performance in two samples of preschoolers.

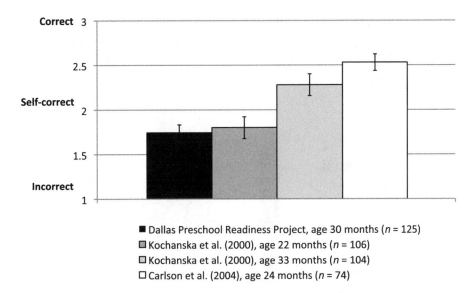

Figure 12.2. Average Shape Stroop scores in three samples of preschoolers.

task for our sample compared with data reported by Kochanska (Kochanska et al., 2000) and Carlson (Carlson, Mandell, & Williams, 2004). Kochanska et al. (2000) collected Shape Stroop data at both 22 and 33 months of age, whereas Carlson et al. (2004) collected Shape Stroop data at age 24 months only. Similar to the Kochanska et al. sample, Carlson et al.'s sample was overwhelmingly European American and middle class. As can be seen in the figure, the 30-month-old children in the DPReP sample performed most similarly to the 22-month-old children in Kochanska's sample and significantly poorer than did the Kochanska sample at age 33 months and the Carlson sample at age 24 months. What is also striking from the figure is that Shape Stroop test scores were available for only 125 (31%) of the DPReP sample at 30 months because the remainder of the children failed to successfully complete the naming and teaching trials of the task and therefore could not be tested. Kochanska et al. did not report whether any of the children in their sample failed to make it to the test trials, and Carlson et al. reported test data for over 90% of their participants. The much higher task failure rate among the DPReP children suggests that the mean test score overestimates the EF skills in this population because it fails to capture the full range of child performance on the task. To address this shortcoming of relying on the mean test score for those relatively few children who completed test trials, we followed the lead of Bell et al. (2010) and scored each child on a 7-point scale based on whether he or she refused, succeeded at the naming trials, succeeded at the teaching trials, or succeeded at the test trials. Children were grouped based on the highest category they achieved. A comparison in the performance between the two samples is displayed in Figure 12.3. Almost half of the DPReP sample either

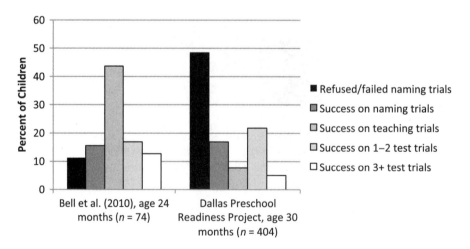

Figure 12.3. Shape Stroop performance in two samples of preschoolers.

refused (15.1%) or failed the preliminary naming trials (33.5%) for the task. The frequent inability of children in the DPReP sample to name the fruits used in the Shape Stroop test underscores the importance of stimuli selection when implementing EF assessments in diverse populations. Pictures of the stimuli used in our Shape Stroop (shown in Figure 12.4) were the same as those used in Bell's lab. Is it possible that children in our sample had less exposure to these fresh fruits, or was it an issue of not recognizing them in cartoon form? We examined whether there was a difference in naming success by child ethnicity, but the Latino children in our sample failed at the naming trials at the same rate (34%) as did the African American children in our sample (33%). The failure of the children in the DPReP sample to successfully name the fruits used in the Shape Stroop task raises questions regarding its validity as a measure of EF in this ethnically diverse, low-income sample, particularly at the age of 30 months.

As described above, we also administered a Stroop-like task developed by Bell et al. (2010) called Mommy-Me in which the stimuli were pictures of the child and his or her mother. A comparison of the performance of our sample of children with a sample of eighty-one 24-month-olds reported by Bell et al. (2010) indicated that Mommy-Me is a more difficult task than Shape Stroop, although Bell's sample of 24-month-olds still outperformed the 30-month-olds in our sample. Only 13.5% of the children in Bell's sample and 6.2% of the children in the DPReP sample made it to the test trials on Mommy-Me, compared with 29.6% and 30.9%, respectively, on the Shape Stroop task. It is interesting that none of the children in the DPReP sample failed the naming trials of the Mommy-Me task, which suggests that using stimuli that are familiar to the child (in this case, a picture of the child's mother and of the child) may be one way to overcome differences in familiarity with stimuli that might limit the validity of implementing other tasks with diverse populations. In addition, the lower success rates in both samples in the Mommy-Me task compared with Shape Stroop suggests that pointing to a picture of mommy is a stronger prepotent impulse than is pointing to a picture of a "baby" fruit.

Figure 12.4. Stimuli used in Shape Stroop task. Copyright Martha Ann Bell. Reprinted with permission.

CHALLENGES AND OPPORTUNITIES
IN CONDUCTING LONGITUDINAL RESEARCH
IN DIVERSE, LOW-INCOME COMMUNITIES

Collecting valid longitudinal data on the development of EF in ethnically diverse, low-income children is critically important not only for developing effective interventions but also for describing how developmental processes are similar or different across disparate populations. Developmental scientists, particularly those studying basic developmental processes in very young children, have relied on convenience samples of children from predominantly European-American middle-class families, with notable exceptions (Blair et al., 2011; Lengua et al., 2007; Li-Grining, 2007). A major hindrance to expanding the literature to include more ethnically diverse groups of children is that following such children longitudinally presents a number of challenges rarely discussed in empirical reports of study findings. In this section, we describe some of the challenges we have encountered in implementing the DPReP in hopes that this information can be helpful to others interested in working with similar populations.

Diverse and Changing Household Compositions

Many of the children in the DPReP sample lived in households that frequently did not fit neatly into one of our preconceived categories of household structure. Such situations were more common among our African American than our Latino participants. For example, we had several children for whom the primary caregiver was reported to be the mother but experiences in the field led staff to question this. In some situations, the child was living with the grandmother the majority of the time and the mother appeared to be visiting solely for the purpose of participating in the home visit. In other situations, the child moved between the mother's home and the homes of other adult relatives on a regular basis. In yet another situation, the biological father of the target child lived with the child and the child's mother for half the week and lived with his own parents the remainder of the week. Such fluid family structures and household boundaries are consistent with qualitative research on African American families that documents the utilization of extended kin as well as fictive kin networks in childrearing (Burton & Jarrett, 2000; Nobles, 1988; Stewart, 2007). This situation created practical challenges for scheduling, particularly during the summer months when movement between households was more frequent. One consequence was a lower follow-up rate in our African American sample (86%) compared with our Latino sample (93%).

Although Latino households in our sample were more stable over time, we encountered other, unanticipated challenges. Although the vast majority

(88%) of the Latino children in our study had a father living in the home at the time of the first home visit, the work situations of many of the Latino fathers made securing participation very difficult. Once we were in the field recruiting participants, we discovered a high number of Latino fathers were regularly traveling outside the city or even state for work, and we started recording more specifically how frequently the father was present in the home. Even Latino fathers who were not traveling to jobs often worked multiple jobs, especially during the spring and summer, and were infrequently at home and available to participate in a home visit. Furthermore, work schedules were unpredictable, and it frequently occurred that a home visitor would arrive at the home to discover the father had been called in to work at the last minute.

As a result of these challenges, we maintained maximum flexibility when completing father data collection. We had one team member, a native Spanish speaker and well known member of the Latino community in Dallas, who dedicated herself to completing father data collection. She scheduled visits with fathers at all hours of the day or night and every day of the week. Because of her connections in the Latino community, she was successful in convincing many fathers who were reluctant to be video-recorded to participate. (Generally speaking, we found African American fathers were much less resistant to participation than were Latino fathers in our sample, in part, we think, because they were more often not employed.) As a result, we were able to secure an unusually high rate of father participation as compared with other studies with similar populations of fathers.

Challenging Situations in the Home and Community

Any researcher who collects data in high-poverty neighborhoods has encountered a range of situations that present challenges to completing data collection activities, and the DPReP is no different in that regard. Although such instances were not frequent, research staff did encounter shootings while in the field or adult participants who were behaving or dressed inappropriately at the time of the home visit. It is important when hiring staff for a project such as this to hire individuals who are savvy about being in the community in terms of how they dress, how they act, and how they approach community residents.

As the first author of this chapter found in her work in Baltimore and we have found in our work in Dallas, having members of the community as part of the research team can be invaluable for ensuring the safety of research team members. Our team members who were familiar with the community could often anticipate problems before they arose. Throughout our fieldwork, we encourage our staff to rely on their instincts to dictate when it is safest to leave a situation without collecting data.

In addition, because our research team members who had ties to the community had long histories with their respective communities (both were mothers in their 40s), our research teams were able to connect with families in a way that supported recruitment and enhanced retention. Our research team members often knew other relatives of participating families, and being able to talk about these connections fostered a bond between the research team and family. These bonds were evident in rapport and scheduling calls, when families often asked if a particular team member would be attending the scheduled home visit. In such situations, the family might not agree to participate unless that particular team member was coming or if that individual could reassure the family firsthand about the team members who were scheduled to visit. Our research team has achieved an extraordinarily high retention rate with a population that is notoriously hard to track. We believe our experience underscores the importance of the relationship that is formed between the participant and the research team. Being sensitive to the bonds that participants form with particular research team members through all contacts with the family is critical for maintaining engagement and participation in the study.

Conditions in the homes can also present unique challenges for collecting valid EF data. Distractions during testing should be minimal so the child can focus on the task and perform to the best of his or her ability. However, many of the houses of the families in our study provided less than an ideal environment for data collection. Many families, especially the Latino families, were living with multiple families in the same residence. Some families were restricted to living in a single bedroom, for example, or were confined to a living area subdivided from a larger living area by hanging sheets. Ambient noise sometimes made hearing the recorded voices of participants difficult. During the summer of our follow-up visits, the Dallas area experienced record-breaking heat, with triple-digit temperatures every day for almost the entire summer. Many of our families could not afford the cost of air conditioning and turned off their units during the day, making home visits challenging to complete.

Despite the challenging conditions often encountered, we were encouraged by the positive reception our researchers received from many of the families who participated. The vast majority of parents in our study were very interested in how their child was developing and whether their child would be ready to enter school. For a number of families, our home visit was an important occasion for which parents took time off from work and other family members came to observe. Other challenges were presented, however, when additional family members, eager to witness the child's performance, added to the already overcrowded situation and sometimes interfered with the child's performance with verbal encouragement and prompts. The high level of engagement of families with our study was evident when a number of families, when contacted for the follow-up visit, agreed even though they had not realized they would receive a financial incentive for the second visit. In addition, when we contacted some families about the follow-up visit, we discovered they had been anticipating our visit by practicing the tasks with their child as seen on the DVD we had sent after the first home visit as a thank you gift. We consequently altered our follow-up procedure and omitted those tasks from the thank you DVD that could potentially be practiced based on viewing the DVD.

Our experience with many of the fathers in our study provided a picture that is in contradiction with commonly held perceptions of absent fathers in low-income, usually African American, households. Although a large proportion of the African American children in our sample (44%) did not have a father living in the household with them, many of the fathers who were there were exceptionally engaged with the research process. As stated previously, it was common to have a father take a day off work to be present at the home visit. In addition to the 5% of African American families and 1.4% of Latino families in which the father was the primary caregiver, we had a number of fathers who actively participated in all parts of the data collection including sitting next to the mother during her interview and providing additional information on the questions being asked. Our preliminary analyses of data from our 30-month home visit suggests that sensitive supportive fathering is uniquely associated with better EF performance, particularly for African American children. Although collecting data on fathers is challenging in a number of ways, our experience suggests that it is feasible and has the potential for adding invaluable information to our understanding of the factors contributing to the development of EF among low-income, ethnically diverse groups of young children.

CONCLUSION

Early childhood education intervention efforts such as Head Start that strive to tackle prevailing deficits in school achievement among low-income minority children in the United States have increasingly emphasized the importance of literacy and numeracy skills in their efforts to foster school readiness in low-income children. However, evidence points to the need to understand and support the young child's development more broadly. Growing evidence of the links between children's emerging EF skills and school achievement suggests that individual differences in these skills are important for processing and integrating information and regulating behavior in social interactions (Blair, 2002) and may be a source of ethnic disparities in school readiness and early academic achievement. Unfortunately, the bulk of what is known about the development of behavior regulation and EF among very young children comes from middle-income European American children, rather than from children at greatest risk for poor school achievement and health. A major purpose of the DPReP is to help remedy this general dearth of data on the development of these skills among low-income African American and Latino preschoolers.

The findings presented in this chapter pertaining to the self-regulation skills shown in our children in the first wave of planned longitudinal assessments indicate that deficits in fundamental EF skills of simple and more complex response inhibition that involves attention focusing and attention shifting start early in these low-income children. Comparisons made of early EF skills between our low-income African American and Latino preschoolers and published data based on similar measures of middle-class mostly European American preschoolers indicate considerable self-regulation skill deficits of approximately 8 months, or more than a 25% delay at the early age of 2.5 years. These early deficits in EF skills suggest that greater emphasis on targeting and supporting the development of these skills in low-income children at an early age may advance the effectiveness of early childhood interventions to improve school readiness and eliminate school achievement disparities.

Variations in the early emergence of these skills were also evident in this study's first step in assessing developmental trajectories of EF in low-income African American and Latino children. In these preschoolers who were 2.5 years of age when first assessed for EF skills, even the simple response inhibition tasks presented a considerable challenge for a majority of the children. Meaningful variations would have been obscured by floor effects had we measured EF skills only by enumerating correct responses, given the very few children who showed evidence of "passing" responses, particularly in the more complex response inhibition tasks. We thus advocate our approach, based on Bell's EF rating classifications (Bell et al., 2010), that measures task understanding and foundational skills involved in the assessment of EF, such as the ability to discriminate and name task stimuli (e.g., the pictured pieces of fruit).

Our 1-year follow-up of study families has demonstrated an extremely low attrition rate despite having a study population that included a large proportion of families at high risk whose lives are very unstable and mobile. Our success in tracking participants is largely due to enlisting data-collection home visitors who are a part of and know well the families' communities, demonstrating that a community-engaged approach can enhance the effectiveness of longitudinal studies with ethnically diverse low-income populations. We expect the study will yield a new understanding of the development of EF skills in the context of poverty and parent–child relationships, and the early results presented in this chapter are an important first step. It is our hope that this new knowledge will help shape effective supports for children's school readiness in ways that will serve to close the achievement gap that has been such a challenge to bridge.

REFERENCES

Acevedo-Garcia, D., Osypuk, T. L., McArdle, N., & Williams, D. R. (2008). Toward a policy-relevant analysis of geographic and racial/ethnic disparities in child health. *Health Affairs, 27,* 321–333. http://dx.doi.org/10.1377/hlthaff.27.2.321

Bell, M. A., Hubble, M., & Morasch, K. C. (2010, March). *Correlates of two different Stroop-like inhibitory control tasks for 24-month-olds.* Paper presented at the International Conference for Infant Studies, Baltimore, MD.

Blair, C. (2002). School readiness: Integrating cognition and emotion in a neurobiological conceptualization of children's functioning at school entry. *American Psychologist, 57,* 111–127. http://dx.doi.org/10.1037/0003-066X.57.2.111

Blair, C., & Diamond, A. (2008). Biological processes in prevention and intervention: The promotion of self-regulation as a means of preventing school failure. *Development and Psychopathology, 20,* 899–911. http://dx.doi.org/10.1017/S0954579408000436

Blair, C., Granger, D. A., Willoughby, M., Mills-Koonce, R., Cox, M., Greenberg, M. T., . . . FLP Investigators. (2011). Salivary cortisol mediates effects of poverty and parenting on executive functions in early childhood. *Child Development, 82,* 1970–1984. http://dx.doi.org/10.1111/j.1467-8624.2011.01643.x

Blair, C., & Razza, R. P. (2007). Relating effortful control, executive function, and false belief understanding to emerging math and literacy ability in kindergarten. *Child Development, 78,* 647–663. http://dx.doi.org/10.1111/j.1467-8624.2007.01019.x

Braveman, P., & Barclay, C. (2009). Health disparities beginning in childhood: A life-course perspective. *Pediatrics, 124*(Suppl. 3), S163–S175. http://dx.doi.org/10.1542/peds.2009-1100D

Brooks-Gunn, J., Duncan, G. J., & Maritato, N. (1997). Poor families, poor outcomes: The well-being of children and youth. In G. J. Duncan & J. Brooks-Gunn (Eds.), *Consequences of growing up poor* (pp. 1–17). New York, NY: Sage.

Burton, L. M., & Jarrett, R. L. (2000). In the mix, yet on the margins: The place of families in urban neighborhood and child development research. *Journal of Marriage and the Family, 62,* 1114–1135. http://dx.doi.org/10.1111/j.1741-3737.2000.01114.x

Cameron Ponitz, C. E., McClelland, M. M., Jewkes, A. M., Connor, C. M., Farris, C. L., & Morrison, F. J. (2008). Touch your toes! Developing a direct measure of behavioral regulation in early childhood. *Early Childhood Research Quarterly, 23,* 141–158. http://dx.doi.org/10.1016/j.ecresq.2007.01.004

Carlson, S. M. (2005). Developmentally sensitive measures of executive function in preschool children. *Developmental Neuropsychology, 28,* 595–616. http://dx.doi.org/10.1207/s15326942dn2802_3

Carlson, S. M., Mandell, D. J., & Williams, L. (2004). Executive function and theory of mind: Stability and prediction from ages 2 to 3. *Developmental Psychology, 40,* 1105–1122. http://dx.doi.org/10.1037/0012-1649.40.6.1105

Caughy, M. O., & Franzini, L. (2005). Neighborhood correlates of cultural differences in perceived effectiveness of parental disciplinary actions. *Parenting: Science and Practice, 5,* 119–151. http://dx.doi.org/10.1207/s15327922par0502_1

Centers for Disease Control/National Center for Health Statistics. (2011). 2010 Pediatric Nutrition Surveillance: Summary of trends in growth and anemia indicators by race/ethnicity. Children aged <5 years (Table 18D). Retrieved from http://www.cdc.gov/pednss/pednss_tables/pdf/national_table18.pdf

Davey Smith, G., Hart, C., Hole, D., MacKinnon, P., Gillis, C., Watt, G., . . . Hawthorne, V. (1998). Education and occupational social class: Which is the more important indicator of mortality risk? *Journal of Epidemiology and Community Health, 52,* 153–160. http://dx.doi.org/10.1136/jech.52.3.153

Duncan, G. J., & Magnuson, K. A. (2005). Can family socioeconomic resources account for racial and ethnic test score gaps? *The Future of Children, 15,* 35–54. http://dx.doi.org/10.1353/foc.2005.0004

Entwisle, D. R., Alexander, K. L., & Olson, L. S. (2005). First grade and educational attainment by age 22: A new story. *American Journal of Sociology, 110,* 1458–1502. http://dx.doi.org/10.1086/428444

Flores, G., Olson, L., & Tomany-Korman, S. C. (2005). Racial and ethnic disparities in early childhood health and health care. *Pediatrics, 115,* e183–e193. http://dx.doi.org/10.1542/peds.2004-1474

Freudenberg, N., & Ruglis, J. (2007). Reframing school dropout as a public health issue. *Preventing Chronic Disease: Public Health Research, Practice, and Policy, 4*(4), 1–11. Retrieved from http://www.cdc.gov/pcd/issues/2007/oct/pdf/07_0063.pdf

Garcia, E. E., & Gonzales, D. M. (2006). *Pre-K and Latinos: The foundation of America's future.* Washington, DC: Pre-K Now.

Garon, N., Bryson, S. E., & Smith, I. M. (2008). Executive function in preschoolers: A review using an integrative framework. *Psychological Bulletin, 134,* 31–60. http://dx.doi.org/10.1037/0033-2909.134.1.31

Kochanska, G., Coy, K. C., & Murray, K. T. (2001). The development of self-regulation in the first four years of life. *Child Development, 72,* 1091–1111. http://dx.doi.org/10.1111/1467-8624.00336

Kochanska, G., Murray, K. T., & Harlan, E. T. (2000). Effortful control in early childhood: Continuity and change, antecedents, and implications for social development. *Developmental Psychology, 36,* 220–232. http://dx.doi.org/10.1037/0012-1649.36.2.220

Kowaleski-Jones, L., & Duncan, G. J. (1999). The structure of achievement and behavior across middle childhood. *Child Development, 70,* 930–943. http://dx.doi.org/10.1111/1467-8624.00067

Lengua, L. J., Honorado, E., & Bush, N. R. (2007). Contextual risk and parenting as predictors of effortful control and social competence in preschool children. *Journal of Applied Developmental Psychology, 28,* 40–55. http://dx.doi.org/10.1016/j.appdev.2006.10.001

Lewit, E. M., & Baker, L. S. (1995). School readiness. *The Future of Children, 5,* 128–139. http://dx.doi.org/10.2307/1602361

Li-Grining, C. P. (2007). Effortful control among low-income preschoolers in three cities: Stability, change, and individual differences. *Developmental Psychology, 43,* 208–221. http://dx.doi.org/10.1037/0012-1649.43.1.208

McClelland, M. M., Cameron, C. E., Connor, C. M., Farris, C. L., Jewkes, A. M., & Morrison, F. J. (2007). Links between behavioral regulation and preschoolers' literacy, vocabulary, and math skills. *Developmental Psychology, 43,* 947–959. http://dx.doi.org/10.1037/0012-1649.43.4.947

Miech, R., Essex, M. J., & Goldsmith, H. (2001). Socioeconomic status and the adjustment to school: The role of self-regulation during early childhood. *Sociology of Education, 74,* 102–120. http://dx.doi.org/10.2307/2673165

Mistry, R. S., Benner, A. D., Biesanz, J. C., Clark, S. L., & Howes, C. (2010). Family and social risk, and parental investments during the early childhood years as predictors of low-income children's school readiness outcomes. *Early Childhood Research Quarterly, 25,* 432–449. http://dx.doi.org/10.1016/j.ecresq.2010.01.002

Morrison, E. F., Rimm-Kaufman, S., & Pianta, R. C. (2003). A longitudinal study of mother–child interactions at school entry and social and academic outcomes in middle school. *Journal of School Psychology, 41,* 185–200. http://dx.doi.org/10.1016/S0022-4405(03)00044-X

Nobles, W. W. (1988). African American family life: An instrument of culture. In H. P. McAdoo (Ed.), *Black families* (2nd ed., pp. 44–53). Beverly Hills, CA: Sage.

Pettit, G. S., Bates, J. E., & Dodge, K. A. (1997). Supportive parenting, ecological context, and children's adjustment: A 7-year longitudinal study. *Child Development, 68,* 908–923.

Raikes, H. A., Robinson, J. L., Bradley, R. H., Raikes, H. H., & Ayoub, C. C. (2007). Developmental trends in self-regulation among low-income toddlers. *Social Development, 16,* 128–149.

Rimm-Kaufman, S. E., Pianta, R. C., & Cox, M. J. (2000). Teachers' judgments of problems in the transition to kindergarten. *Early Childhood Research Quarterly, 15,* 147–166. http://dx.doi.org/10.1016/S0885-2006(00)00049-1

Sektnan, M., McClelland, M. M., Acock, A., & Morrison, F. J. (2010). Relations between early family risk, children's behavioral regulation, and academic achievement. *Early Childhood Research Quarterly, 25,* 464–479. http://dx.doi.org/10.1016/j.ecresq.2010.02.005

Spinrad, T. L., Eisenberg, N., Gaertner, B., Popp, T., Smith, C. L., Kupfer, A., . . . Hofer, C. (2007). Relations of maternal socialization and toddlers' effortful control to children's adjustment and social competence. *Developmental Psychology*, *43*, 1170–1186. http://dx.doi.org/10.1037/0012-1649.43.5.1170

Stewart, P. (2007). Who is kin? Family definition and African American families. *Journal of Human Behavior in the Social Environment*, *15*, 163–181. http://dx.doi.org/10.1300/J137v15n02_10

U.S. Department of Health and Human Services. (2010). About linked birth/infant death records 2003–2006. *CDC WONDER* [Online database]. Retrieved from http://wonder.cdc.gov/lbd-v2006.html

West, J., Denton, K., & Germino-Hausken, E. (2000). *America's kindergartners* (NCES Statistical Analysis Report 2000-070). Washington, DC: U.S. Department of Education.

Williams, D. R., Mohammed, S. A., Leavell, J., & Collins, C. (2010). Race, socioeconomic status, and health: Complexities, ongoing challenges, and research opportunities. *Annals of the New York Academy of Sciences*, *1186*, 69–101. http://dx.doi.org/10.1111/j.1749-6632.2009.05339.x

Willoughby, M. T., Blair, C. B., Wirth, R. J., Greenberg, M., & The Family Life Project Investigators. (2010). The measurement of executive function at age 3 years: Psychometric properties and criterion validity of a new battery of tasks. *Psychological Assessment*, *22*, 306–317. http://dx.doi.org/10.1037/a0018708

Woolf, S. H., Johnson, R. E., Phillips, R. L., Jr., & Philipsen, M. (2007). Giving everyone the health of the educated: An examination of whether social change would save more lives than medical advances. *American Journal of Public Health*, *97*, 679–683. http://dx.doi.org/10.2105/AJPH.2005.084848

13

PROMOTING THE DEVELOPMENT OF EXECUTIVE FUNCTIONS THROUGH EARLY EDUCATION AND PREVENTION PROGRAMS

KAREN L. BIERMAN AND MARCELA TORRES

Promoting executive function (EF) skills is currently a hot topic in early childhood education. EF refers to a complex set of cognitive regulatory processes, including working memory and attention control skills, that enable children to organize their thinking and behavior with increasing intentionality and flexibility (Barkley, 2001; Hughes & Graham, 2002). These skills develop rapidly during the preschool and early elementary years (ages 3 to 7) and provide a neural foundation to support school readiness, facilitating self-regulated behavior and academic learning (Blair, 2002; McClelland et al., 2007). At school entry, higher levels of EF skills promote accelerated literacy and math skills acquisition (Blair & Razza, 2007; Welsh, Nix, Blair, Bierman, & Nelson, 2010) and enhance the resilience of children who experience early adversity (e.g., reducing school difficulties among maltreated children; Pears, Fisher, Bruce, Kim, & Yoerger, 2010). EF development is often delayed among children growing up in poverty (Noble, McCandliss, & Farah, 2007),

http://dx.doi.org/10.1037/14797-014
Executive Function in Preschool-Age Children: Integrating Measurement, Neurodevelopment, and Translational Research, J. A. Griffin, P. McCardle, and L. S. Freund (Editors)

as are the learning behaviors that support academic achievement, as reflected in low levels of classroom engagement and elevated teacher-rated attention problems (Bodovski & Youn, 2011; McClelland et al., 2007).

Practitioners and policymakers alike have been intrigued by the possibility of strengthening early education and preventive interventions by targeting EF development demonstrated in recent developmental neuroscience research (Diamond & Lee, 2011). Most of the empirical research on preschool education has focused on learning in domain-specific content areas (e.g., emergent literacy and numeracy skills). In contrast, EF-focused interventions have targeted the development of domain-general skills that affect the pace and quality of children's learning capacity (e.g., attention control, memory, planning, persistence, problem solving). Promoting EF skills in early education and prevention programs may play a key role in reducing the substantial gaps in school readiness and later achievement that separate disadvantaged children from their more advantaged peers (Shonkoff & Phillips, 2000).

Yet, despite the excitement associated with EF-focused interventions, research evidence is sparse regarding what works to promote EF development and the impact these interventions have on social–emotional adjustment or academic progress in school. Only relatively recently have randomized controlled trials (RCTs) been undertaken using both direct assessments of EF skill acquisition and real-world measures of impact on child behavior and learning in school contexts. This chapter provides an overview of intervention research that has tackled the task of improving EFs and associated self-regulated learning skills, especially in the preschool and early elementary years. We focus on strategies that have strong scientific evidence of efficacy, as documented by randomized controlled trials, assess the current state of knowledge, and identify future directions for research and intervention program development and refinement. A wide array of intervention approaches is considered, grouped into those that focus on (a) direct training of EF skills, (b) improving teacher–child relationships and positive classroom contexts, (c) using play as a central context for intervention, (d) promoting social–emotional learning, or (e) using other promising approaches. In each section, the logic model describing the rationale for the approach is presented, along with studies assessing the impact of the approach.

DIRECT TRAINING AND PRACTICE

One straightforward approach to intervention has been to foster EF skills with repeated practice sessions on specific EF tasks. The logic model supporting this intervention approach is straightforward. Parallel to the usefulness of strength training in sports, the approach focuses on targeting growth of the neural circuits that support EF, with the hope that these stronger circuits will support more well-regulated attention and behavior (Posner, Sheese, Odludaş, & Tang, 2006).

In many cases, initial studies have demonstrated that practice improves performance on the specific tasks practiced and generalizes to closely related tasks (Klingberg, Forssberg, & Westerberg, 2002). The greater question for early education and prevention efforts is the extent to which gains on specific EF tasks generalize to improved performance on learning or behavioral tasks that use the targeted EF skills—that is, whether these gains support improved attention, behavior regulation, and achievement in the classroom context.

Training Working Memory

Two RCTs showed that direct training improved the working memory skills of grade-school children but provided only limited and mixed evidence regarding generalized impact on learning behavior and academic achievement. Both used the Cogmed computer program (Klingberg, 2001), which provides graduated practice on a set of working memory tasks, and compared outcomes with those of a control group that used the same program, set at the lowest level of challenge.

In the first study, outcomes for 44 of the 53 randomized participants (those who completed at least 20 days of training) revealed significant effects for treatment on an untrained working memory task as well as a set of broader tasks tapping other EF skills (attention inhibition, nonverbal reasoning), which were maintained at a 3-month follow-up (Klingberg et al., 2005). Parent ratings for 36 children (68% of the sample) also showed a significant reduction in attention-deficit/hyperactivity disorder (ADHD) symptoms, although teacher ratings did not.

The second RCT of Cogmed with grade-school children (ages 8–11) who had low pretest working memory randomized children at three schools to the treatment condition ($n = 22$) and children at three different schools to the control group ($n = 20$; Holmes, Gathercole, & Dunning, 2009). At postintervention and 6-month follow-up assessments, the intervention group showed significantly better performance on working memory tasks than did the control group. Although no intervention effects emerged on IQ measures, basic word reading, or math at the posttest, the intervention group had significantly higher scores than did the control group on mathematical reasoning at the 6-month follow-up (Holmes et al., 2009). These findings suggest potential effects of the intervention on academic learning, although a limitation of the design was that intervention and control conditions were administered in different schools, which might also have affected math learning.

Two additional RCTs examined training working memory skills in preschool children, each comparing this training with an alternative computer-based skill training program. Thorell, Lindqvist, Bergman Nutley, Bohlin, and Klingberg (2009) compared Cogmed training in visuospatial working memory ($n = 17$) with training in attention inhibition (go/no-go, stop-signal, and flanker tasks; $n = 18$). Children at two other preschools served as the control group ($n = 30$). Training included 15-minute sessions each day for 5 weeks. Compared with children at the control preschools, the children trained on working memory improved significantly on nontrained tests of spatial and verbal working memory but did not improve on measures of attention inhibition. In contrast, children trained on inhibition showed no significant improvements relative to the control group on either type of task. In a second preschool study including 112 children (ages 4.0–4.5), Bergman Nutley et al. (2011) compared the impact of Cogmed working memory training, training in nonverbal reasoning tasks, and a combination of working memory and nonverbal reasoning with a control group that used the combined program set to the lowest level of difficulty. Significant domain-specific effects were documented: Children showed improvements in the domain they trained on (working memory or nonverbal reasoning) but not the other domain. The combined condition appeared to work least well, likely due to the dilution in practice time for each kind of task. Unfortunately, neither of these studies included measures of classroom behavior or academic learning, leaving unanswered the question of whether EF skill gains have a generalized impact on school functioning.

Overall, these studies suggest that computerized training can enhance the working memory skills of children, including preschool children (see also the review by Morrison & Chein, 2011). However, the preschool studies show very specific effects on working memory, with a lack of generalized impact on related cognitive skills. In addition, evidence that the improvements in working memory generalize to promote learning engagement, attention control, or academic achievement in the classroom is currently lacking.

Training Attention Control

Attention training has also been evaluated as an intervention. Initial studies focused on grade-school children with ADHD. For example, Kerns, Eso, and Thomson (1999) randomly assigned children diagnosed with ADHD (ages 5–10) to a 16-session after-school program, where they played either games practicing attention control (e.g., sorting cards quickly into categories by color or picture or pressing a buzzer in response to a certain word; $n = 7$) or computer games ($n = 7$). At posttest, the intervention group outperformed the control group on measures of sustained attention, inhibitory control, mazes, and math efficiency (but not working memory). Intervention effects on teacher attention ratings were marginally significant. Although they are based on a very small sample, such findings galvanized efforts to examine the impact of attention training on younger children.

Focusing on normally developing 4-year-old ($n = 49$) and 6-year-old ($n = 24$) children, Rueda, Rothbart, McCandliss, Saccomanno, and Posner (2005) compared the impact of playing computer games designed to train attention control with doing nothing or watching children's movies. After 5 days of attentional training, the 4-year-old children in the intervention group showed significantly greater improvements than did those in the control group on the visual matrices of the Kaufman Brief Intelligence Test (Kaufman & Kaufman, 2004); however, the intervention–control group differences were not significant for the 6-year-olds. In addition, attention control, a central focus of the training, which was assessed using a flanker task, was not significantly improved relative to the control group at either age. No measures of classroom behavior or academic achievement were collected.

A particularly important study examining attention training in early elementary school was conducted by Rabiner, Murray, Skinner, and Malone (2010). This study used a more rigorous research design than did other direct training studies by (a) comparing computerized attention training with an alternative, potentially potent intervention (e.g., computerized academic tutoring) as well as with a wait-list control group; (b) using intent-to-treat analyses, rather than analyzing only those children who completed the training, thus avoiding selection biases; (c) randomizing to condition within school and using a nested design that accounted for teacher and school influences, rather than assigning schools to different conditions; (d) examining teacher ratings of classroom behavior and standardized achievement measures to assess the generalized impact of intervention on school progress; and (e) including a 6-month follow-up assessment. The sample included 77 first-grade students, selected on the basis of elevated teacher-rated inattention, randomly assigned to one of three after-school groups: the Captain's Log computerized attention training program ($n = 25$), the Destination Reading and Destination Math computerized tutoring programs ($n = 27$), or a wait-list control group ($n = 25$). Intervention sessions were held twice per week for 14 weeks. At posttreatment assessments, students who received any of the computerized trainings were more likely than wait-list controls to show significant improvements in teacher-rated attention skills. However, only students who received the computerized reading and math tutoring showed significant gains in reading fluency and improved teacher ratings of academic performance. No group differences were sustained at the second-grade follow-up assessment, although post hoc analyses suggested long-term benefits associated with intervention for children who had more serious attention problems at baseline. This study is important because it suggests that domain-specific training (i.e., computerized tutoring in reading and math) may be as beneficial as domain-general training (i.e., computerized attention training) at promoting growth in attention skills, but the domain-specific training has the added advantage of promoting achievement in the targeted domain (e.g., in this study, improving reading fluency). However, in this study, the impact on EF skills was not assessed directly.

Summary

Although these studies suggest that direct training of EF skills (working memory or attention inhibition) can promote skill acquisition in specific domains, the results are variable across studies. In addition, there is little evidence that this kind of training has effects that generalize to substantially affect school learning behavior or achievement (see also Owen et al., 2010). Rabiner et al.'s (2010) findings are particularly provocative because they suggest that other types of interventions might improve EF but have stronger academic relevance and more potential to close the school achievement gap than do those focused only on direct training of EF skills. For example, Siegler and Ramani (2008) found that they could significantly reduce the numerical knowledge gap shown by low-income preschool children relative to their advantaged peers by having them play a simple numerical board game over four 15-minute sessions. Playing games that substituted colors for numbers did not have this effect. Although Siegler and Ramani did not measure EF skills, their findings raise the question of whether selected math games might serve the dual purpose of improving numeracy understanding and fostering EF skill development.

IMPROVING TEACHER–CHILD RELATIONSHIPS AND POSITIVE CLASSROOM CLIMATES

A second approach to promoting EF skills in early education settings focuses on improving the quality of teacher–child interactions and providing more predictable, supportive, sensitive, and responsive classroom climates. The logic model for this intervention approach has roots in developmental research that suggests that high-quality early caregiving plays a key role in promoting EF development (Bernier, Carlson, Deschênes, & Matte-Gagné, 2012). In particular, sensitive, responsive caregiving, language stimulation, and adult support that fosters guided exploration of the social and physical environment (joint attention and scaffolding) have been implicated in the development of EF skills (Bernier et al., 2012; Lengua, Honorado, & Bush,

2007). Conversely, instability or nonresponsiveness in adult–child relationships associated with maternal depression, neglect, or exposure to violence predicts delays in EF development (Cicchetti, 2002; Lengua et al., 2007). The implication for early childhood education is that the provision of high-quality adult–child interactions and a predictable, supportive school context might facilitate EF development, particularly among children who have experienced early poverty or adversity.

The Incredible Years Teacher Training Program focuses specifically on improving the quality of teacher–student interactions and promoting positive classroom management strategies (Webster-Stratton, Reid, & Hammond, 2001). The intervention is delivered via monthly teacher workshops that involve the review of modeling videotapes, group discussion, practice assignments, and consultation provided in response to the ongoing program experiences of the participating teachers. Five core teaching skills are targeted: (a) supporting positive child behavior with specific, contingent attention, encouragement, and praise; (b) motivating learning effort and engagement with incentives and rewards; (c) preventing behavior problems by structuring the classroom effectively and planning for transitions; (d) decreasing inappropriate behavior with nonpunitive consequences (e.g., planned ignoring, time out); and (e) building positive relationships with students. Research by the developer demonstrated positive effects on teachers (e.g., increased use of praise, reduced levels of harsh and critical interactions in the classroom) and improvements in children's learning behavior (e.g., higher levels of learning engagement and on-task behavior) but did not include direct measures of child EF skills (Webster-Stratton et al., 2001).

More recently, however, the Incredible Years Teacher Training Program was incorporated by Raver and colleagues (2008) into the Chicago School Readiness Project (CSRP) in a study that included direct measures of EF skills as well as academic skill acquisition and classroom behavioral adjustment. The CSRP provided Head Start teachers with five 6-hour training sessions in the Incredible Years program. In addition, the program provided teachers with a mental health consultant, who met with them weekly to support their implementation of the Incredible Years classroom management skills and to provide emotional support for their own stress reduction. Mental health consultants also implemented individualized management plans for children displaying high levels of disruptive behavior in the classroom.

The CSRP was evaluated in the context of a cluster-randomized trial that included 35 Head Start classrooms (18 randomly assigned to receive treatment) and 543 children. Approximately 17 children (age 3 or 4) participated from each classroom. Analyses used an intent-to-treat model (to avoid selection biases associated with level of treatment participation) and hierarchical linear modeling that accounted for nesting of children in classrooms and classrooms in sites (Raudenbush & Bryk, 2002). The intervention had the expected impact on the quality of teacher–child interactions, with intervention teachers showing significantly higher levels of positive climate, teacher sensitivity, and positive behavior management than did the teachers in the usual-practice control group (Raver et al., 2008). In terms of the impact on child outcomes, significant intervention effects were documented on two EF measures that use attention and inhibitory control (Peg Tapping, Balance Beam), with an effect size of 0.37 (Raver et al., 2011). Examiners also rated children in the intervention condition as more focused and less distractible during the testing sessions relative to children in the control condition, $d = 0.43$. The intervention also had significant effects on academic learning (vocabulary scores, letter learning, math skills; Raver et al., 2011) and classroom behavior (lower levels of observed aggressive and disruptive behavior; Raver et al., 2009). Additional analyses suggested that the improved academic skills associated with the intervention were mediated largely by the intervention impact on improved EF (Raver et al., 2011).

This study suggests that improving the quality of teacher–child interactions in ways that provide more contingent positive support, reduce negative exchanges, and improve instructional support has benefits for EF skill development, child learning engagement, and academic achievement. The only caveat is that the Head Start programs that participated in this study were drawn from very-high-risk neighborhoods (selected for high neighborhood poverty and crime rates), and it is not yet clear whether a program focused on behavior management such as this one would have the same transformative impact in preschool programs serving children in lower risk neighborhoods with lower base rates of problem behavior in the classroom.

FOSTERING THE POWER OF PLAY

A third approach to early intervention is based on developmental research that suggests that sociodramatic play provides a particularly powerful context for the promotion of EF skills in early childhood (Blair & Diamond, 2008; Vygotsky, 1967). Young children begin to seek each other out for social play during the preschool years, forming their first friendships and taking great pleasure in cooperative and shared fantasy play with peers. To sustain friendly exchanges, children must learn to negotiate, cooperate, and compromise. To contribute to elaborated play, they must mentally represent and enact complementary social roles and social routines (Bodrova & Leong, 2007). Thus, interactions with peers motivate and support the development of the emotional and social skills that provide a foundation for effective social collaboration (empathy, cooperation, role coordination) and stimulate the development of the cognitive skills that underlie effective social exchange, including inhibitory control, perspective taking, and flexible problem solving (Bierman, Torres, Domitrovich, Welsh, & Gest, 2009). Indeed, Barkley (2001) postulated that the EF system evolved primarily to support advanced social collaboration skills and that sociodramatic play represents the primary natural context for its development. Pretend social play requires children to exercise all three of the core EF skills (Blair & Diamond, 2008); role-playing requires holding one's own character role and those of others in mind, exercising working memory; successful social play requires inhibiting behavioral impulses to act out of character and employing attentional set-shifting skills to flexibly adapt to unexpected changes in play scenarios. The elaborated play of older preschool children—including their ability to sustain synchronized, thematic play and negotiate turn taking and resource sharing—reflects their growing capacity to mentally represent and follow social scripts, while simultaneously tracking social exchange (Barkley, 2001). During the preschool years, collaborative play thus represents a context in which children are motivated to be effortful in their attempts to initiate and sustain engagement with peers, which in turn requires the application of working memory, inhibitory control, and attention set shifting in the service of emotion regulation and social collaboration.

A number of studies have documented significant correlations between the frequency and complexity of a child's sociodramatic play, particularly the use of symbolic representation in play, and concurrent measures of IQ, problem-solving skills, language acquisition, social competence, and self-regulation (see Hanline, Milton, & Phelps, 2008). In a short-term longitudinal study, Elias and Berk (2002) found that impulsive preschool children who engaged in higher levels of complex sociodramatic play with peers in the fall of the year showed improved self-regulated functioning in the spring. Solitary sociodramatic play was not associated with improved self-regulation, which suggests that the social interactive component of this play may be critical for its positive developmental influence on growth in self-regulation skills.

The use of sociodramatic play as a preschool intervention to promote social and cognitive skills was first tested empirically by Smilansky (1968), who examined the impact of teaching economically disadvantaged children how to engage in pretend play. Several quasi-experimental studies followed, with results that suggested that engaging children systematically in sociodramatic play might enhance their language, social interaction, and problem-solving skills (Rosen, 1974). One of the most well-designed of these studies was conducted by Saltz, Dixon, and Johnson (1977). Working with 146 low-income preschool children (ages 3–4.5) in an urban setting, they randomly assigned classrooms to four treatment conditions: (a) fantasy play (acting out fairy tales, such as *Three Billy Goats Gruff* or *Little Red Riding*

Hood), (b) sociodramatic play (acting out scenes from everyday life, such as trips to the grocery store or doctor's office), (c) listening to and discussing fairy tales, or (d) paper-and-pencil crafts and artwork. The interventions were conducted 15 minutes per day in the preschool context, 3 days per week, for about six months, by undergraduate students or research staff who worked with children in groups of three or four. The goal was to compare the effects of different kinds of sociodramatic play (e.g., using fantasy stories or real-life activities) with fantasy exposure that did not involve a social interaction component (listening and discussing the stories) and the artwork activity control. Over the course of the year, the two sociodramatic play conditions (fantasy or real-life enactment) as compared with nonplay conditions produced greater improvements on tests of vocabulary (Peabody Picture Vocabulary Test; Dunn & Dunn, 2007), delay of gratification (inhibiting the touch of a forbidden toy), and matching figures, suggesting a direct effect on EF skills associated with attention control.

More recently, sociodramatic play has been embedded as a central feature of a comprehensive preschool and early elementary school curriculum, Tools of the Mind (Tools; Bodrova & Leong, 2007). In Tools, teachers are taught how to introduce and support complex dramatic play themes in the classroom, and children spend time each day in planning and enacting sustained, collaborative sociodramatic peer play in prepared play centers. Specific techniques include having children develop play plans that articulate a social role and planned behavior, preparing specific play centers, and requiring sustained sociodramatic play daily. Tools includes other activities designed to enhance the development of child self-regulation skills: It restructures learning activities, replacing large-group activities and passive waiting time with small-group and peer-pairing activities that keep children more actively engaged in the learning process, and includes motor games and activities designed to practice self-regulation skills, such as pacing motor activity in time to fast or slow music, and games that require behavioral inhibition, such as Simon Says.

In an initial RCT, teachers and preschool children (ages 3–4) were assigned to classrooms that used either the Tools curriculum or a curriculum developed by the school district (Barnett et al., 2008). Tools was found to significantly improve the quality of teaching observed in the classrooms, including positive classroom structure and quality of the literacy environment and instruction, and teachers reported fewer behavior problems (Barnett et al., 2008). Assessment a year later also showed significant effects on children's EF skills (Diamond, Barnett, Thomas, & Munro, 2007); however, these latter assessments were made after teachers and children were allowed to change programs if desired, compromising the original randomization and introducing the potential for selection biases.

A more recent randomized trial (Wilson & Farran, 2012) compared Tools with usual practice preschools in six school districts and found no significant effects on child EF skills or other academic or behavioral outcomes measured. Similarly, Clements, Sarama, Unlu, and Layzer (2012) failed to replicate the positive effects of Tools. In the Clements et al. (2012) study, usual-practice preschools were compared with two intervention conditions: One included a preschool mathematics curriculum (Building Blocks), and the other paired Building Blocks with a modified version of Tools. Children in the Building Blocks condition outperformed those in the control group on two EF tasks (Head-Toes-Knees-Shoulders and Backward Digit Span), but children in the Building Blocks plus Tools condition did no better than the usual-practice control group on these tasks. Researchers have speculated that Tools is a complex intervention that may be difficult to deliver effectively without extensive professional development supports.

PROMOTING SOCIAL–EMOTIONAL LEARNING

A fourth approach to preventive intervention draws on research suggesting that emotion regulation, social problem-solving skills, and EF skill development are intertwined developmentally and that promoting emotion regulation and social problem-solving skills can enhance EF. Emotion regulation skills include emotional understanding (the ability to recognize and accurately label the emotional states of oneself and others), emotional coping (the ability to modulate affective arousal), and emotion display (the ability to control behavior in the face of affective arousal). Emotion regulation skills enable children to respond adaptively to their internal arousal, modulating their reactions to upsetting or exciting situations and controlling reactive impulses (Izard et al., 2001). Social problem-solving skills allow children to assess the problem, listen to and consider other perspectives, generate potential solutions, and negotiate a plan of action with the others involved (Zins & Elias, 2006). Good social problem-solving requires not only emotion regulation skills but also a willingness to act with feelings of caring and concern for the others involved and an understanding of accepted social norms and sanctions.

Emotion regulation and social problem-solving skills develop rapidly during the preschool and early elementary years and are supported by concurrently developing EF and language skills (Greenberg, 2006; Trentacosta & Izard, 2007). The neural areas that underlie EF have extensive interconnections with the ventral medial frontal and limbic brain structures associated with emotional reactivity and regulation, which allow EF and language skills (top-down regulation) to modulate the emotional and autonomic arousal systems (bottom-up regulation; Rueda, Posner, & Rothbart, 2005). Reflecting this interconnectedness, developmental studies show associations between preschoolers' developing emotional understanding and social problem-solving skills and their abilities to delay gratification, manage conflicts, and engage in goal-oriented and sustained learning efforts (Carlson & Wang, 2007; Denham & Burton, 2003; Trentacosta & Izard, 2007).

Teaching young children about their emotions as a strategy to build EF skills is based on a developmental model that places affective systems prior to the frontal cognitive systems in the sequence of development (see Greenberg, 2006). In infancy and early childhood, affective systems energize and motivate infants and young children to engage with others and with the environment, well before children can verbalize or reflect on their experiences (Greenberg, 2006). As children accumulate social experiences and as their cognitive and linguistic skills advance, their capacity to reflect on and appraise their emotional experiences and their ability to understand social cause and contingency also advance. Supported largely by implicit or incidental learning (e.g., learning through observation and experience), children develop schemas that link certain social experiences with feeling states, cognitive appraisals, and habitual response patterns (Izard, Stark, Trentacosta, & Schultz, 2008). When adaptive, these schemas foster the child's capacity to navigate and act on his or her social environment in goal-directed ways that balance self-protection with active exploration and interpersonal engagement. When maladaptive, these schemas privilege reactive, self-protective vigilance or protest and impede adaptive social engagement and flexible problem solving (Izard et al., 2008). Social–emotional learning programs are designed to facilitate the development of adaptive schemas (or overwrite habitual but maladaptive schemas) by making information about social–emotional exchanges explicit and more easily available to children, clarifying some of the mystery behind emotions and relationships and providing concrete suggestions and supports to help children develop more advanced emotion regulation and social problem-solving skills.

The PATHS (Promoting Alternative Thinking Strategies) Curriculum is a social–emotional learning program that focuses specifically on building the top-down higher order frontal cognitive control and language processes that will facilitate the modulation of lower level limbic impulses and emotional arousal (Greenberg, 2006). PATHS includes (a) an intensive focus on helping children to verbally identify and label feelings in order to manage them, including the use of emotion photographs, stories, and "feeling face" cards to help children identify and express their feelings; (b) lessons on caring and interpersonal concern, including the value of friendship and cooperation; (c) the use of explicit signals to cue and support intentional impulse control (e.g., a traffic "red light" for elementary children and "doing Turtle" for younger children, each guiding children when distressed to "tell yourself to stop, take a deep breath to calm down, say the problem and how you feel"); and (d) explicit guidelines for social problem solving and conflict resolution (identify the problem, generate solutions, consider consequences, and choose the best plan). In the version of the curriculum developed for young children, the Preschool PATHS Curriculum (Domitrovich, Greenberg, Cortes, & Kusché, 1999), teachers introduce and illustrate skill concepts with puppets, pictures, and story examples. Each lesson includes ideas for formal and informal extension activities that teaching staff can use throughout the day to generalize key concepts. Teachers are also encouraged to provide emotion coaching throughout the day, modeling feeling statements themselves when appropriate, helping children notice the feelings of peers, and prompting children to describe their own feelings. Teachers are also encouraged to watch for naturally occurring teachable moments, such as peer disagreements or conflicts. At these times, teachers are taught to help children stop and calm down (using "turtle") and then talk through the problem-solving steps of defining the problem and their feelings, listening to their friends' feelings, and generating ideas for how to solve the problem.

Two studies demonstrated positive effects of PATHS on EF skills. One examined intervention impact on 318 second- and third-grade children in classrooms randomized to receive the PATHS intervention or usual practice (Riggs, Greenberg, Kusché, & Pentz, 2006). Intervention teachers received a 3-day training workshop and weekly coaching in curriculum implementation. PATHS lessons were taught two or three times per week, and teachers also coached children to talk about their feelings, apply self-control, and follow the social problem-solving skill sequence to resolve conflicts. EF inhibitory control skills were assessed using the Stroop test and verbal fluency was examined. Compared with children in the usual-practice control group, children in PATHS classrooms showed significantly greater improvement in inhibitory control by the end of the year (Riggs et al., 2006). In addition, improvements in EF skills during the intervention year predicted lower rates of teacher-rated internalizing and externalizing behavior problems at the 1-year follow-up and mediated intervention effects on reduced behavior problems. In addition to documenting positive child outcomes, these findings provide empirical support for the conceptual theory of action that underlies the PATHS model.

In a second study, Preschool PATHS was implemented in the context of the comprehensive Head Start REDI (research-based, developmentally informed) program, which involved a set of enrichment activities led by classroom teachers: the Preschool PATHS curriculum, a dialogic reading program to enhance vocabulary and narrative understanding, sound games to foster phonemic awareness, and alphabet center activities to promote print awareness. In three Pennsylvania counties, 44 Head Start classrooms were randomly assigned to use the REDI program, and the others formed a usual-practice comparison group. Teachers were provided with 4 days of training and weekly classroom and individual visits by REDI coaches (for details, see Bierman, Domitrovich, et al., 2008). Observations conducted at the end of the year showed that REDI classrooms had more positive emotional climates than did usual-practice classrooms, with higher levels of emotion talk and greater support for child emotion regulation. REDI classrooms also scored more positively on classroom management (including positive limit setting and proactive management) and language use (including statements, questions, and rich, sensitive talk) and tended to have higher levels of instructional support (Domitrovich et al., 2009).

The Head Start REDI impact evaluation included 356 4-year-old children (86% of the eligible children in the participating classrooms). Hierarchical linear models that accounted for students nested in classrooms revealed positive effects for REDI on a number of the specific skills targeted by the intervention (e.g., vocabulary skills, phonemic awareness, print awareness, emotion knowledge, social problem-solving skills) as well as reduced aggression. REDI also showed an impact on children's EF, with children in REDI classrooms outperforming children in the usual-practice comparison classrooms on the Dimensional Change Card Sort ($p < .06$), which taps working memory, inhibitory control, and set-shifting skills (see Bierman, Nix, Greenberg, Blair, & Domitrovich, 2008 for details). No intervention effects emerged on other EF measures (Peg Tapping, Backward Word Span, Balance Beam), but a significant effect emerged on examiner ratings of self-regulation, with children from REDI classrooms being rated as more able to "pay attention," "sustain concentration," and "wait during and between tasks." Subgroup analyses revealed that REDI was particularly beneficial for children who started the year with low levels of behavioral inhibitory control. Improvements in EF skills partially mediated REDI intervention effects on emergent literacy and social–emotional competencies. In addition, significant intervention effects were evident a year later, as kindergarten teachers (who had no knowledge of the prekindergarten intervention) rated children who received REDI significantly higher on classroom learning engagement than did children who received usual-practice Head Start (Bierman et al., 2014).

OTHER PROMISING APPROACHES

Thus far, we have focused on intervention strategies shown by RCTs to promote EF skill development in young children. Two additional approaches are worth mentioning, although evidence of impact on the EF skills of young children is not yet available.

Physical Movement

Particularly among older adults, research has demonstrated that aerobic physical exercise provides cognitive benefits (Hillman, Erickson, & Kramer, 2008). Adolescents also appear to benefit, as research suggests that regular, aerobic physical activity may enhance verbal and math skills (see Sibley & Etnier, 2003, for a review). Much of this research is nonexperimental in nature, making causal interpretations difficult. For example, correlations between physical activity and academic performance may reflect the impact of activity on cognitive functioning, but these links might also represent the impact of third variables on both outcomes, such as family support or organizational skills, that support youth engagement in school and sports activities (see also Etnier & Chang, 2009). A number of studies show improved cognitive performance on EF tasks immediately following aerobic exercise when compared with performance prior to that exercise. However, far fewer studies have examined the longer term EF benefits of exercise intervention programs for children using randomized controlled trials (see Best, 2010, for a comprehensive review). We provide a brief discussion of findings from these randomized intervention studies that have shown promise for older children and adolescents but have not yet been evaluated with young children.

In one of the first experimental evaluations of the impact of aerobic exercise on children's cognitive functioning, Tuckman and Hinkle (1986) randomly assigned older elementary children (Grades 4–6) to a 12-week aerobic running class or to a usual-practice physical education class. Although EF skills were not evaluated directly, Tuckman and Hinkle reported significant intervention effects on a test that assessed flexible and divergent thinking, suggesting the potential of this intervention approach to improve EF. In a more recent study, Kamijo et al. (2011) randomly assigned 43 children (ages 7–9) to an after-school physical activity program ($n = 22$) or a wait-list control group ($n = 21$). The after-school program included 40 minutes of vigorous physical activity (e.g., visiting fitness stations and engaging in individual or small group activities and games), followed by a healthy snack and rest period and then 30 minutes of organizational games centered around a skill theme (e.g., dribbling). Effects on working memory were assessed separately for tasks at three levels of difficulty (remembering sets of single letters, three letters, or five letters). Significant benefits associated with the intervention emerged for working memory at the medium level of difficulty (three letters) but were less distinct at the lowest level of difficulty (one letter) and nonsignificant at the highest level of difficulty (five letters).

Davis et al. (2011) randomly assigned overweight elementary students (ages 7–11) to a no-intervention control group ($n = 60$) or to one of two after-school programs, involving either a high dose of exercise ($n = 56$, 40-minute sessions of running games, jump rope, soccer, etc.) or a low dose of exercise ($n = 55$, 20-minute sessions). After the 3-month intervention, children's performance was compared on the Cognitive Assessment System (CAS; Naglieri & Das, 1997), which measures integrative cognitive skills that use EF. Treatment benefits emerged on the Planning scale of the CAS, with the exercise groups performing significantly better than the control group did, and children in the high-dose condition performing significantly better than children in the low-dose condition did. However, no significant treatment effects emerged on the Attention, Simultaneous, or Successive scales of the CAS, which also use EF skills. No differences emerged between the exercise and no-treatment groups on the math or reading achievement tests, although children in the high-dose group outperformed those in the low-dose group on the math achievement measure (controlling for pretreatment scores). Although these findings are mixed, they provide some evidence for benefits of exercise to EF functioning in elementary-school-age children.

There are several hypotheses regarding the mechanisms by which aerobic physical activity promotes EF functioning. One focuses on the physiological changes induced by aerobic exercise, including increases in capillary blood supply to the cortex and alterations in neurotransmitter levels (particularly dopamine; Davis et al., 2011). This hypothesis is based on animal research that documents nonspecific neural activation associated with exercise that promotes robust and enduring neurogenesis in the learning and memory centers of the brain (see Best, 2010). A second hypothesis is that exercises that require complex and controlled movements activate and use EF, particularly when they must be done in a way that dynamically adjusts to changing conditions (Diamond & Lee, 2011). This hypothesis suggests that EF will be strengthened by exercises that incorporate complex movements but not by simpler activities that are more automatic, such as walking (Best, 2010). Finally, a third hypothesis is that the complex dynamics of rule-governed games might place demands on EF skills, thus strengthening them. For example, motivated by a goal of winning the game, children may need to constantly adjust their movements to coordinate their actions with their teammates, anticipate their opponents' moves, and make ongoing adjustments to their strategy and movements in response to other players' actions (Best, 2010).

Although the impact of physical activity on EF development has not yet been studied in young children, two studies suggest that it may be a promising approach. Lobo and Winsler (2006) randomly assigned 40 Head Start children to an 8-week experimental dance program or an attention control group. Although EF skills were not assessed in this study, the investigators found positive effects of the dance program on teacher and parent ratings of child social competence and reduced levels of internalizing and externalizing problems. It would be of value to know whether this kind of dance and movement intervention might also impact EF skills in young children.

In a second study, Tominey and McClelland (2011) randomly assigned 65 preschool children to active playgroups or an untreated control group. Playgroups included five to eight children and met twice weekly for 30-minute sessions for 8 weeks. They engaged in a curriculum of games selected to emphasize EF skills: inhibitory control (e.g., the Freeze Game) and attention set shifting (e.g., Red Light, Green Light). EF skills were assessed using a behavioral regulation task (Head-Toes-Knees-Shoulder [HTKS]) in which children are instructed to touch body parts that are the opposite of those being requested by the examiner (e.g., when the instructor calls "head," children are to touch their toes). Treatment had no overall effect on HTKS; however, additional analyses suggested positive treatment gains for children who had low scores at the pretreatment assessment. Treatment also enhanced letter–word identification skills, suggesting an impact on cognitive functioning.

With so little research examining the impact of physical movement on EF development among young children, it is not possible to determine the potential of this intervention approach. However, the preliminary findings suggest that further investigation of this intervention strategy may be worthwhile.

Parenting Interventions

Parenting interventions for infants and young children also warrant further study as a possible strategy for enhancing EF development. Certainly, there is evidence that the skills that support self-regulation begin to develop in infancy, and parents play a critically important role as socialization agents, directly affecting children's development of self-regulation (Fox & Calkins, 2003). There is evidence that working memory is affected by the quality of the home literacy environment, as well as by day-care or preschool attendance (Noble et al., 2007). Parents may influence language development (which is highly affected by family socioeconomic status), which in turn fosters EF skill development. In addition, sensitive, responsive adult–child interactions that provide scaffolding (i.e., sensitive support to facilitate successful goal-oriented activities) and help children label and understand their emotions and motivations may play a key role in fostering their developing capacities for self-regulation (Bernier et al., 2012; Hughes & Ensor, 2009); many home visiting programs that target child school readiness focus on promoting sensitive, responsive parenting, enriched language use and parent–child conversations, scaffolded play, and interactive reading (see Welsh, Bierman, & Mathis, 2014, for a review). However, the effects of these programs on child EF have not yet been explored.

There are several reasons to expect that these kinds of early parenting interventions might foster child EF skill development. These interventions may promote secure attachments, increasing feelings of security and reducing neuroendocrine and autonomic stress reactivity that impedes EF development (Bernier et al., 2012; Cicchetti, 2002). They may enrich support for child language development, which is intertwined developmentally with EF skill development (Noble et al., 2007). Finally, parenting interventions may improve external support for behavioral regulation, providing the limits and redirection that help children control their emotional reactivity and aggressive behavior, thereby creating a foundation for the internalization of self-regulation (Kopp, 1982).

FUTURE RESEARCH DIRECTIONS

As the studies reviewed in this chapter illustrate, a wide variety of intervention approaches show promise in terms of their ability to promote the EF skills of young children. To date, these different intervention approaches have emerged within different discipline and research traditions. Cross-talk among the investigative teams is limited. Looking forward, intervention development would benefit from more cross-disciplinary discussion, which might support integrative models and comparative designs. To help bridge the disciplinary divide, future research would benefit from (a) greater attention to the logic models underlying the various approaches and measurement models designed to examine mechanisms of change; (b) more consistency and rigor in the intervention trial methodology, meeting standards of evidence that are acceptable across the disciplinary fields and particularly meeting standards that are acceptable to the educational sciences, where eventual implementation is desired; and (c) an expanded focus on preschool and early elementary school outcomes, to better test the hypothesized links between the acceleration of EF skill development fostered by preventive intervention and later school success.

Articulating Logic Models and Measuring Mechanisms of Change

The capacity to make comparisons across intervention approaches and to identify strategies that might increase the impact of various approaches would be greatly enhanced by future studies that clearly articulate and measure the processes and change mechanisms that are thought to account for the intervention effects. Doing so will help to build knowledge of the unique and/or common mechanisms that are associated with improved EF in different approaches, thus informing basic research on EF development while also providing a basis to further refine and strengthen intervention components (Diamond & Lee, 2011). In addition, the approaches have different theoretical and empirical roots and may each be enriched by a consideration of the alternative models.

For example, several of the intervention approaches reviewed here were developed and evaluated first with adults and older adolescents before being adapted downward in age for use with young children. Working memory and attention control training programs, as well as programs focused on increasing aerobic physical exercise to promote EF, derived from successful intervention effects on older populations, may be enriched by considering research on the developmental processes associated with EF in early childhood. Particularly in the age range that is a focus of this chapter (ages 3–7), EF skills are emerging rapidly and their maturation is affected heavily by socialization experiences and intertwined skill development (language, emotion regulation), creating a context for intervention that is very different from adulthood or later childhood.

Conversely, other intervention approaches reviewed in this chapter were developed for a different purpose and have other central goals but show some evidence of impact on EF. For example, the Incredible Years Teacher Training Program has the primary goal of improving teacher–student interaction quality and classroom management to reduce child behavior problems and improve child social competence. Early childhood parenting programs that focus on improving sensitive, responsive parenting and enriching parent–child language have the primary goal of fostering child cognitive development and/or behavioral adjustment. By integrating models of EF more explicitly in these intervention designs and assessments, the impact on child EF might be strengthened. Better understanding the nature of their impact on EF might in turn inform improved intervention designs.

Finally, a third type of intervention reviewed here is one that targets the promotion of skills that are intertwined developmentally with EF. For example, academic tutoring programs (e.g., those used by Rabiner et al., 2010) focus on teaching academic content in specific domains. PATHS focuses on promoting emotion regulation, social problem-solving skills, and social competence, with a strong emphasis on promoting the language skills that support effective self-regulation and social functioning. Sociodramatic role-playing focuses on building narrative comprehension, perspective taking, and social interaction skills (Saltz et al., 1977). In each of these cases, domain-general EF skills may be strengthened because they are exercised in the context of domain-specific skill-building activities, resulting in dual gains in the content area of focus as well as EF skills. For example, Rabiner and colleagues (2010) found that computerized academic tutoring fostered attention skills as well as direct EF training but had the added advantage that it fostered academic learning as well (which the direct EF training did not). Comprehensive programs such as Tools of the Mind, which embed academic learning within a restructured classroom designed to enhance support for self-regulation, may represent a good way to strengthen EF during learning activities, but more specific and well-controlled research is needed to determine how best to structure academic or social–emotional learning activities in ways that maximize benefits for children's EF development.

As more comparative research is undertaken, the findings may well show that there is more than one way to effectively improve EF. It is also possible that the interventions that work best share some common features. As Diamond and Lee (2011) noted, many types of activities, perhaps even some not yet studied, can improve EFs if they possess certain features common to existing, effective interventions. These include opportunities for repeated practice on motivating tasks that require effortful EF, continually and gradually increasing levels of challenge, limited sit-and-listen time, and elicitation of joy, self-efficacy, and social bonding in children.

Measuring a Broad Range of Self-Regulation and School Adjustment Outcomes

The recent and intensive interest in EF among early childhood researchers and practitioners stems from a hypothesis that interventions that promote EF will have unique benefits for children by improving behavior, social–emotional functioning, and achievement. This hypothesis is based on developmental research that demonstrates predictive relationships between early EF and learning behaviors, functioning, and achievement (see Blair & Diamond, 2008). However, more experimental research is needed to test the causal linkages and determine whether (and to what extent) the promotion of EF with early intervention will have generalized behavioral or academic benefits for children. To better understand intervention impact, randomized trials need to include a broad range of outcome measures that allow for an assessment of generalized effects on nontargeted dimensions of self-regulation, as well as school-based academic and behavioral adjustment.

Behavioral adjustment, academic learning, and self-regulation are multiply determined, with EF skills being just one contributing factor. Among preschool children, for example, behavioral impulse control (as assessed by delay-of-gratification tasks or teacher ratings), emotion regulation skills, and language skills each affect school behavior and learning in ways that are distinct from the contribution of EF skills (Hughes & Graham, 2002). Whereas socialization (reflected by family socioeconomic status) has a significant impact on the development of EF and language skills, it is not associated with impulsivity (reward processing; capacity to delay gratification), reflecting different developmental determinants that interact to contribute to effective classroom engagement and learning behaviors (Noble et al., 2007). Similarly, although oppositional–aggressive behaviors have been linked with deficits in EF functioning in "hard to manage" preschool children (Hughes & Ensor, 2009), associations between EF deficits and behavioral problems are not always present (Bierman et al., 2009). Substantial research indicates that oppositional–aggressive behaviors are often instrumental, shaped and maintained by interpersonal contingencies and coercive family interactions (Webster-Stratton et al., 2001), and hence not necessarily an indication of EF or self-regulation deficits.

By measuring multiple dimensions of a child's self-regulation skills (e.g., EF, impulsivity, frustration tolerance) as well as the child's learning behavior and achievement in the classroom, intervention research may improve understanding of the specific effects of improved EF on children's school readiness as well as identify aspects of child self-regulation that require alternative or additional intervention approaches.

Improving Research Designs

Discipline-based differences in research methodology and design are evident in this area of research. For example, the direct EF training studies reviewed here analyzed only the subset of children who completed a minimum of training sessions (to ensure that those who are analyzed actually received the intervention), whereas school-based researchers typically run intent-to-treat analyses (to avoid selection biases associated with intervention dropout). Many of the smaller studies reviewed here conducted randomization at the level of the school, but analyzed at the level of the individual, without modeling the dependencies associated with the unit of randomization (school) or the unit of implementation (group). Certainly, smaller, less well-controlled pilot studies are appropriate to test the feasibility of a new intervention approach. However, to make inferences about the degree to which an intervention approach may improve outcomes for children in real-life education or community settings, more rigorous designs are required with intent-to-treat approaches, representative sampling, and analytic designs that account for the levels of randomization and implementation (Raudenbush & Bryk, 2002).

In addition, more careful study is needed to understand variations in intervention responding and the factors that might moderate the impact of an intervention approach. For example, exploratory analyses described in this review suggest that greater benefits in some interventions were observed among children with larger initial EF skill deficits (see Bierman, Nix, et al., 2008; Tominey & McClelland, 2011). Other forms of moderation may also emerge. More research is needed to explore potential interactions between type of program and characteristics of child participants, the broader school, and the neighborhood or family context. Research that can simultaneously examine programs based on different logic models in a variety of settings may help address the question "What works for whom, and under what conditions?"

Finally, almost nothing is known about dose effects and the amount of training or intervention experience that is needed to produce improvement in EF skills or associated self-regulated behaviors. In addition, little is known about the maintenance of gains over time and the possible need for booster intervention sessions to sustain effects. These are important topics for future research.

CONCLUSION

In recent years, developmental neuroscience research has generated new optimism regarding our capacity to intervene in ways that will reduce the early disparities associated with socioeconomic disadvantage and improve children's school success. In particular, EF research has expanded our understanding of early neural development and stimulated innovative approaches to prevention and early intervention. At the same time, caution is warranted in terms of the current evidence base supporting EF intervention in early childhood. A majority of the well-controlled studies of young children indicate promising but mixed effects on EF measures, and none have yet documented generalized and sustained effects on school behavior and achievement after school entry. In some cases, traditional intervention approaches targeting other primary goals (e.g., classroom management skills, academic tutoring) have outperformed innovative approaches directed specifically at promoting EF skills, in terms of their impact on children's school adjustment and learning. This may well be because stand-alone interventions that practice specific EF skills in a consistent and predictable manner do not prepare children well for the day-to-day classroom and peer interactions that are often unpredictable and emotionally laden. For this reason, interventions that can harness opportunities for children to practice self-regulation skills during naturalistic moments of challenge, guided by familiar adults, may have the greatest potential for generalized gains. The potential value of short-term interventions that target EFs deserves ongoing exploration, but it may be that promoting substantial and sustained gains in children's school readiness requires a broader focus, longer intervention time frames, and partnering with and supporting parents and teachers. In this context, attention to the neurocognitive developmental processes in intervention design and direct measurement of EF and related self-regulatory skills may contribute significantly to our understanding of developmental processes as well as to more powerful prevention and early intervention programs.

REFERENCES

Barkley, R. A. (2001). The executive functions and self-regulation: An evolutionary neuropsychological perspective. *Neuropsychology Review, 11*, 1–29. http://dx.doi.org/10.1023/A:1009085417776

Barnett, W. S., Jung, K., Yarosz, D., Thomas, J., Hornbeck, A., Stechuk, R., & Burns, S. (2008). Educational effects of the Tools of the Mind curriculum: A randomized trial. *Early Childhood Research Quarterly, 23*, 299–313. http://dx.doi.org/10.1016/j.ecresq.2008.03.001

Bergman Nutley, S., Söderqvist, S., Bryde, S., Thorell, L. B., Humphreys, K., & Klingberg, T. (2011). Gains in fluid intelligence after training non-verbal reasoning in 4-year-old children: A controlled, randomized study. *Developmental Science, 14*, 591–601. http://dx.doi.org/10.1111/j.1467-7687.2010.01022.x

Bernier, A., Carlson, S. M., Deschênes, M., & Matte-Gagné, C. (2012). Social factors in the development of early executive functioning: A closer look at the caregiving environment. *Developmental Science, 15*, 12–24. http://dx.doi.org/10.1111/j.1467-7687.2011.01093.x

Best, J. R. (2010). Effects of physical activity on children's executive function: Contributions of experimental research on aerobic exercise. *Developmental Review, 30*, 331–351. http://dx.doi.org/10.1016/j.dr.2010.08.001

Bierman, K. L., Domitrovich, C. E., Nix, R. L., Gest, S. D., Welsh, J. A., Greenberg, M. T., . . . Gill, S. (2008). Promoting academic and social–emotional school readiness: The Head Start REDI program. *Child Development, 79*, 1802–1817. http://dx.doi.org/10.1111/j.1467-8624.2008.01227.x

Bierman, K. L., Nix, R. L., Greenberg, M. T., Blair, C., & Domitrovich, C. E. (2008). Executive functions and school readiness intervention: Impact, moderation, and mediation in the Head Start REDI program. *Development and Psychopathology, 20*, 821–843. http://dx.doi.org/10.1017/S0954579408000394

Bierman, K. L., Nix, R. L., Heinrichs, B. S., Domitrovich, C. E., Gest, S. D., Welsh, J. A., & Gill, S. (2014). Effects of Head Start REDI on children's outcomes 1 year later in different kindergarten contexts. *Child Development, 85*, 140–159. http://dx.doi.org/10.1111/cdev.12117

Bierman, K. L., Torres, M. M., Domitrovich, C. E., Welsh, J. A., & Gest, S. D. (2009). Behavioral and cognitive readiness for school: Cross-domain associations for children attending Head Start. *Social Development, 18*, 305–323. http://dx.doi.org/10.1111/j.1467-9507.2008.00490.x

Blair, C. (2002). School readiness: Integrating cognition and emotion in a neurobiological conceptualization of children's functioning at school entry. *American Psychologist, 57*, 111–127. http://dx.doi.org/10.1037/0003-066X.57.2.111

Blair, C., & Diamond, A. (2008). Biological processes in prevention and intervention: The promotion of self-regulation as a means of preventing school failure. *Development and Psychopathology, 20*, 899–911. http://dx.doi.org/10.1017/S0954579408000436

Blair, C., & Razza, R. P. (2007). Relating effortful control, executive function, and false belief understanding to emerging math and literacy ability in kindergarten. *Child Development, 78*, 647–663. http://dx.doi.org/10.1111/j.1467-8624.2007.01019.x

Bodovski, K., & Youn, M. (2011). The long term effects of early acquired skills and behaviors on young children's achievement in literacy and mathematics. *Journal of Early Childhood Research, 9*, 4–19. http://dx.doi.org/10.1177/1476718X10366727

Bodrova, E., & Leong, D. J. (2007). *Tools of the Mind: The Vygotskian approach to early childhood education* (2nd ed.). Upper Saddle River, NJ: Prentice-Hall.

Carlson, S. M., & Wang, T. (2007). Inhibitory control and emotion regulation in preschool children. *Cognitive Development, 22*, 489–510. http://dx.doi.org/10.1016/j.cogdev.2007.08.002

Cicchetti, D. (2002). The impact of social experience on neurobiological systems: Illustration from a constructivist view of child maltreatment. *Cognitive Development, 17*, 1407–1428. http://dx.doi.org/10.1016/S0885-2014(02)00121-1

Clements, D. H., Sarama, J., Unlu, F., & Layzer, C. (2012, March). *The efficacy of an intervention synthesizing scaffolding designed to promote self-regulation with an early mathematics curriculum: Effects on executive function.* Paper presented at the meeting of the Society for Research in Educational Effectiveness, Washington, DC.

Davis, C. L., Tomporowski, P. D., McDowell, J. E., Austin, B. P., Miller, P. H., Yanasak, N. E., . . . Naglieri, J. A. (2011). Exercise improves executive function and alters brain activation in overweight children: A randomized, controlled trial. *Health Psychology, 30*, 91–98.

Denham, S. A., & Burton, R. (2003). *Social and emotional prevention and intervention programming for preschoolers.* New York, NY: Kluwer-Plenum. http://dx.doi.org/10.1007/978-1-4615-0055-1

Diamond, A., Barnett, W. S., Thomas, J., & Munro, S. (2007). Preschool program improves cognitive control. *Science, 318*, 1387–1388. http://dx.doi.org/10.1126/science.1151148

Diamond, A., & Lee, K. (2011). Interventions shown to aid executive function development in children 4 to 12 years old. *Science, 333*, 959–964. http://dx.doi.org/10.1126/science.1204529

Domitrovich, C. E., Gest, S. D., Gill, S., Bierman, K. L., Welsh, J. A., & Jones, D. (2009). Fostering high quality teaching with an enriched curriculum and professional development support: The Head Start REDI Program. *American Educational Research Journal, 46*, 567–597. http://dx.doi.org/10.3102/0002831208328089

Domitrovich, C. E., Greenberg, M. T., Cortes, R., & Kusché, C. (1999). *Manual for the Preschool PATHS Curriculum.* University Park: The Pennsylvania State University.

Dunn, L. M., & Dunn, D. M. (2007). *Peabody Picture Vocabulary Test, Fourth Edition.* Retrieved from http://www.pearsonclinical.com/language/products/100000501/peabody-picture-vocabulary-test-fourth-edition-ppvt-4.html

Elias, C. L., & Berk, L. (2002). Self-regulation in young children: Is there a role for socio-dramatic play? *Early Childhood Research Quarterly, 17,* 216–238. http://dx.doi.org/10.1016/S0885-2006(02)00146-1

Etnier, J. L., & Chang, Y. K. (2009). The effect of physical activity on executive function: A brief commentary on definitions, measurement issues, and the current state of the literature. *Journal of Sport & Exercise Psychology, 31,* 469–483.

Fox, N. A., & Calkins, S. D. (2003). The development of self-control of emotion: Intrinsic and extrinsic influences. *Motivation and Emotion, 27,* 7–26. http://dx.doi.org/10.1023/A:1023622324898

Greenberg, M. T. (2006). Promoting resilience in children and youth: Preventive interventions and their interface with neuroscience. *Annals of the New York Academy of Sciences, 1094,* 139–150. http://dx.doi.org/10.1196/annals.1376.013

Hanline, M. F., Milton, S., & Phelps, P. C. (2008). A longitudinal study exploring the relationship of representational levels of three aspects of preschool socio-dramatic play and early academic skills. *Journal of Research in Childhood Education, 23,* 19–28. http://dx.doi.org/10.1080/02568540809594643

Hillman, C. H., Erickson, K. I., & Kramer, A. F. (2008). Be smart, exercise your heart: Exercise effects on brain and cognition. *Nature Reviews Neuroscience, 9,* 58–65. http://dx.doi.org/10.1038/nrn2298

Holmes, J., Gathercole, S. E., & Dunning, D. L. (2009). Adaptive training leads to sustained enhancement of poor working memory in children. *Developmental Science, 12,* F9–F15. http://dx.doi.org/10.1111/j.1467-7687.2009.00848.x

Hughes, C., & Ensor, R. (2009). How do families help or hinder the development of executive function? *New Directions in Child and Adolescent Psychiatry: Special issue on social interaction and the development of executive function, 123,* 35–50.

Hughes, C., & Graham, A. (2002). Measuring executive functions in childhood: Problems and solutions? *Child and Adolescent Mental Health, 7,* 131–142. http://dx.doi.org/10.1111/1475-3588.00024

Izard, C., Fine, S., Schultz, D., Mostow, A., Ackerman, B., & Youngstrom, E. (2001). Emotion knowledge as a predictor of social behavior and academic competence in children at risk. *Psychological Science, 12,* 18–23. http://dx.doi.org/10.1111/1467-9280.00304

Izard, C., Stark, K., Trentacosta, C., & Schultz, D. (2008). Beyond emotion regulation: Emotion utilization and adaptive functioning. *Child Development Perspectives, 2,* 156–163. http://dx.doi.org/10.1111/j.1750-8606.2008.00058.x

Kamijo, K., Pontifex, M. B., O'Leary, K. C., Scudder, M. R., Wu, C. T., Castelli, D. M., & Hillman, C. H. (2011). The effects of an afterschool physical activity program on working memory in preadolescent children. *Developmental Science, 14,* 1046–1058. http://dx.doi.org/10.1111/j.1467-7687.2011.01054.x

Kaufman, A. S., & Kaufman, N. L. (2004). *Kaufman Brief Intelligence Test, Second Edition* [Measurement instrument]. Retrieved from http://www.pearsonclinical.com/psychology/products/100000390/kaufman-brief-intelligence-test-second-edition-kbit-2.html

Kerns, K. A., Eso, K., & Thomson, J. (1999). Investigation of a direct intervention for improving attention in young children with ADHD. *Developmental Neuropsychology, 16*, 273–295. http://dx.doi.org/10.1207/S15326942DN1602_9

Klingberg, T. (2001). Cogmed [Computer software]. Retrieved from http://www.cogmed.com

Klingberg, T., Fernell, E., Olesen, P. J., Johnson, M., Gustafsson, P., Dahlström, K., . . . Westerberg, H. (2005). Computerized training of working memory in children with ADHD—a randomized, controlled trial. *Journal of the American Academy of Child & Adolescent Psychiatry, 44*, 177–186. http://dx.doi.org/10.1097/00004583-200502000-00010

Klingberg, T., Forssberg, H., & Westerberg, H. (2002). Training of working memory in children with ADHD. *Journal of Clinical and Experimental Neuropsychology, 24*, 781–791. http://dx.doi.org/10.1076/jcen.24.6.781.8395

Kopp, C. B. (1982). Antecedents of self-regulation: A developmental perspective. *Developmental Psychology, 18*, 199–214.

Lengua, L. J., Honorado, E., & Bush, N. R. (2007). Contextual risk and parenting as predictors of effortful control and social competence in preschool children. *Journal of Applied Developmental Psychology, 28*, 40–55. http://dx.doi.org/10.1016/j.appdev.2006.10.001

Lobo, Y. B., & Winsler, A. (2006). The effects of a creative dance and movement program on the social competence of Head Start preschoolers. *Social Development, 15*, 501–519. http://dx.doi.org/10.1111/j.1467-9507.2006.00353.x

McClelland, M. M., Cameron, C. E., Connor, C. M., Farris, C. L., Jewkes, A. M., & Morrison, F. J. (2007). Links between behavioral regulation and preschoolers' literacy, vocabulary, and math skills. *Developmental Psychology, 43*, 947–959. http://dx.doi.org/10.1037/0012-1649.43.4.947

Morrison, A. B., & Chein, J. M. (2011). Does working memory training work? The promise and challenges of enhancing cognition by training working memory. *Psychonomic Bulletin & Review, 18*, 46–60. http://dx.doi.org/10.3758/s13423-010-0034-0

Naglieri, J. A., & Das, J. P. (1997). Cognitive Assessment System [Measurement instrument]. Itasca, IL: Riverside.

Noble, K. G., McCandliss, B. D., & Farah, M. J. (2007). Socioeconomic gradients predict individual differences in neurocognitive abilities. *Developmental Science, 10*, 464–480. http://dx.doi.org/10.1111/j.1467-7687.2007.00600.x

Owen, A. M., Hampshire, A., Grahn, J. A., Stenton, R., Dajani, S., Burns, A. S., . . . Ballard, C. G. (2010). Putting brain testing to the test. *Nature, 465*, 775–778.

Pears, K. C., Fisher, P. A., Bruce, J., Kim, H. K., & Yoerger, K. (2010). Early elementary school adjustment of maltreated children in foster care: The roles of inhibitory control and caregiver involvement. *Child Development, 81*, 1550–1564. http://dx.doi.org/10.1111/j.1467-8624.2010.01491.x

Posner, M. I., Sheese, B. E., Odludaş, Y., & Tang, Y. (2006). Analyzing and shaping human attentional networks. *Neural Networks, 19,* 1422–1429. http://dx.doi.org/10.1016/j.neunet.2006.08.004

Rabiner, D. L., Murray, D. W., Skinner, A. T., & Malone, P. S. (2010). A randomized trial of two promising computer-based interventions for students with attention difficulties. *Journal of Abnormal Child Psychology, 38,* 131–142. http://dx.doi.org/10.1007/s10802-009-9353-x

Raudenbush, S. W., & Bryk, A. S. (2002). *Hierarchical linear models* (2nd ed.). Thousand Oaks, CA: Sage.

Raver, C. C., Jones, S. M., Li-Grining, C. P., Metzger, M., Smallwood, K., & Sardin, L. (2008). Improving preschool classroom processes: Preliminary findings from a randomized trial implemented in Head Start settings. *Early Childhood Research Quarterly, 63,* 253–255.

Raver, C. C., Jones, S. M., Li-Grining, C., Zhai, F., Bub, K., & Pressler, E. (2011). CSRP's impact on low-income preschoolers' preacademic skills: Self-regulation as a mediating mechanism. *Child Development, 82,* 362–378. http://dx.doi.org/10.1111/j.1467-8624.2010.01561.x

Raver, C. C., Jones, S. M., Li-Grining, C., Zhai, F., Metzger, M. W., & Solomon, B. (2009). Targeting children's behavior problems in preschool classrooms: A cluster-randomized controlled trial. *Journal of Consulting and Clinical Psychology, 77,* 302–316. http://dx.doi.org/10.1037/a0015302

Riggs, N. R., Greenberg, M. T., Kusché, C. A., & Pentz, M. A. (2006). The mediational role of neurocognition in the behavioral outcomes of a social–emotional prevention program in elementary school students: Effects of the PATHS Curriculum. *Prevention Science, 7,* 91–102. http://dx.doi.org/10.1007/s11121-005-0022-1

Rosen, C. E. (1974). The effects of sociodramatic play on problem-solving behavior among culturally disadvantaged preschool children. *Child Development, 45,* 920–927. http://dx.doi.org/10.2307/1128077

Rueda, M. R., Posner, M. I., & Rothbart, M. K. (2005). The development of executive attention: Contributions to the emergence of self-regulation. *Developmental Neuropsychology, 28,* 573–594. http://dx.doi.org/10.1207/s15326942dn2802_2

Rueda, M. R., Rothbart, M. K., McCandliss, B. D., Saccomanno, L., & Posner, M. I. (2005). Training, maturation, and genetic influences on the development of executive attention. *Proceedings of the National Academy of Sciences of the United States of America, 102,* 14931–14936. http://dx.doi.org/10.1073/pnas.0506897102

Saltz, E., Dixon, D., & Johnson, J. (1977). Training disadvantaged preschoolers on various fantasy activities: Effects on cognitive functioning and impulse control. *Child Development, 48,* 367–380. http://dx.doi.org/10.2307/1128629

Shonkoff, J. P., & Phillips, D. A. (Eds.). (2000). *From neurons to neighborhoods: The science of early childhood development.* Washington, DC: National Academy Press.

Sibley, B. A., & Etnier, J. L. (2003). The relationship between physical activity and cognition in children: A meta-analysis. *Pediatric Exercise Science, 15,* 243–256.

Siegler, R. S., & Ramani, G. B. (2008). Playing linear numerical board games promotes low-income children's numerical development. *Developmental Science, 11,* 655–661. http://dx.doi.org/10.1111/j.1467-7687.2008.00714.x

Smilansky, S. (1968). *The effects of sociodramatic play on disadvantaged preschool children.* New York, NY: Wiley.

Thorell, L. B., Lindqvist, S., Bergman Nutley, S., Bohlin, G., & Klingberg, T. (2009). Training and transfer effects of executive functions in preschool children. *Developmental Science, 12,* 106–113. http://dx.doi.org/10.1111/j.1467-7687.2008.00745.x

Tominey, S. L., & McClelland, M. M. (2011). Red light, purple light: Findings from a randomized trial using circle time games to improve behavioral self-regulation in preschool. *Early Education and Development, 22,* 489–519. http://dx.doi.org/10.1080/10409289.2011.574258

Trentacosta, C. J., & Izard, C. E. (2007). Kindergarten children's emotion competence as a predictor of their academic competence in first grade. *Emotion, 7,* 77–88. http://dx.doi.org/10.1037/1528-3542.7.1.77

Tuckman, B. W., & Hinkle, J. S. (1986). An experimental study of the physical and psychological effects of aerobic exercise on schoolchildren. *Health Psychology, 5,* 197–207. http://dx.doi.org/10.1037/0278-6133.5.3.197

Vygotsky, L. S. (1967). Play and its role in the mental development of the child. *Soviet Psychology, 5,* 6–18.

Webster-Stratton, C., Reid, J., & Hammond, M. (2001). Social skills and problem-solving training for children with early-onset conduct problems: Who benefits? *The Journal of Child Psychology and Psychiatry, 42,* 943–952. http://dx.doi.org/10.1111/1469-7610.00790

Welsh, J. A., Bierman, K. L., & Mathis, E. (2014). Parenting programs that promote school readiness. In M. Boivin & K. Bierman (Eds.), *Promoting school readiness and early learning: The implications of developmental research for practice* (pp. 253–280). New York, NY: Guilford Press.

Welsh, J. A., Nix, R. L., Blair, C., Bierman, K. L., & Nelson, K. E. (2010). The development of cognitive skills and gains in academic school readiness for children from low income families. *Journal of Educational Psychology, 102,* 43–53. http://dx.doi.org/10.1037/a0016738

Wilson, S. J., & Farran, D. C. (2012, March). *Experimental Evaluation of the Tools of the Mind Preschool Curriculum.* Paper presented at the meeting of the Society for Research in Educational Effectiveness, Washington, DC.

Zins, J. E., & Elias, M. J. (2006). Social and emotional learning. In G. Bear & K. Minke (Eds.), *Children's needs III: Development, Prevention, and Intervention* (pp. 1–13). Bethesda, MD: National Association of School Psychologists.

14

CONCEPTUAL CLUTTER AND MEASUREMENT MAYHEM: PROPOSALS FOR CROSS-DISCIPLINARY INTEGRATION IN CONCEPTUALIZING AND MEASURING EXECUTIVE FUNCTION

FREDERICK J. MORRISON AND JENNIE K. GRAMMER

The previous chapters forcefully demonstrate that, across a broad spectrum of disciplines, spanning educational, developmental, cognitive, and neurophysiological perspectives, interest has mounted steadily in executive function (EF) and related constructs (cognitive control, self-regulation, effortful control, executive attention, work-related skills). A growing body of research has shown the importance of EF skills for children's success in school as well as for subsequent health, wealth, and reduced rates of criminality (e.g., Moffitt et al., 2011). However, despite advances in developing measures of EF and understanding the neurological underpinnings of EF skills, as well as efforts to intervene in the development of EF for children at risk, consensus on a number of questions fundamental to the study of EF has yet to be reached.

First, it is not clear whether constructs, as operationalized across disciplines, are all measuring the same underlying skill. Second, longitudinal measurement of the developmental course (both behavioral and neurological) of

http://dx.doi.org/10.1037/14797-015
Executive Function in Preschool-Age Children: Integrating Measurement, Neurodevelopment, and Translational Research, J. A. Griffin, P. McCardle, and L. S. Freund (Editors)

the underlying components of EF over the important school transition period is lacking at present. Finally, the malleability of EF (and its components, such as working memory, response inhibition, and attention control/flexibility), and particularly the impact of schooling on these abilities, has not been extensively charted.

Nevertheless, these concerns can also be viewed as research challenges and opportunities. In this chapter, we offer a series of proposals designed to yield a more comprehensive understanding of the nature and development of EF in children over the school transition period. Specifically, through a combination of (a) careful examination of the unitary versus componential nature of EF across the preschool to early elementary school period, (b) longitudinal research charting developmental trajectories of EF at multiple levels of analysis, and (c) experimental work to understand the malleability of early EF skills, we endeavor to derive a more unified theoretical and empirical perspective on the growth of EF.

MULTIPLE PERSPECTIVES ON EXECUTIVE FUNCTION

Development of the skills identified as EF (and related terms such as *self-regulation* and *effortful control*) has been receiving increasing attention from both basic and applied researchers (Anderson, 2002; Duckworth & Seligman, 2006; Luciano, 2003; Zelazo, Craik, & Booth, 2004). Developmentalists have focused on growth of EF from infancy to early adulthood (M. C. Welsh, 2001). Along with educational researchers, they have sought to understand the interplay between maturational and environmental factors that shape development of executive skills and the role of variability in children's self-control, which emerges even before children start school, on American children's academic achievement (Matthews, Ponitz, & Morrison, 2009). From a different perspective, neuroscientists have noted distinct differences between brain areas subserving basic cognitive functions (attention, memory) and those involved in integrating and coordinating attentional and memory skills, and have more recently explored differences in the neural bases of these skills in children as compared with adults (Luria, 1966; M. C. Welsh, Friedman, & Spieker, 2006). In addition, cognitive scientists have been analyzing the underlying components of EF (attention control/flexibility, working memory, response inhibition, planning) to ascertain their structure and function (Miyake, Friedman, Emerson, Witzki, Howerter, & Wager, 2000; Welsh, Huizinga, Granrud, Cooney, Adams, & van der Molen, 2002; Zelazo et al., 2004).

Although definitions and emphases differ, there is broad agreement that EF refers to cognitive skills, used for purposeful, future-oriented behavior, that underlie flexible adaptation to changing task demands, including regulation of attention, inhibition of inappropriate responses, coordination of information in working memory, and organization and planning of adaptive behavior (Blair, 2002; Botvinick, Braver, Barch, Carter, & Cohen, 2001; Eslinger, 1996; Klein, 2003; Shonkoff & Phillips, 2000; M. C. Welsh, 2002; Zelazo & Frye, 1998; Zelazo, Müller, Frye, & Marcovitch, 2003). Three key components, especially in younger children, include response inhibition, working memory, and attention control/flexibility.

There are significant questions about how the components of EF relate to one another. Though it is generally accepted that, in adults, components of EF are independent of each other although loosely correlated (Miyake et al., 2000), some have suggested that EF in childhood is best characterized as one general skill (e.g., Hughes, Ensor, Wilson, & Graham, 2009; Wiebe, Espy, & Charak, 2008; Wiebe et al., 2011). Evidence for a unitary EF construct in childhood is mixed, however, with additional data supporting three distinct EF components in children (Klenberg, Korkman, & Lahti-Nuuttila, 2001; Lehto, Juujärvi, Kooistra, & Pulkkinen, 2003; M. C. Welsh, Pennington, & Groisser, 1991). Although the composition of EF could change with development, with disassociations between EF components increasing as children get older (McAuley & White, 2011), it is also possible that the debate is confounded by differential sensitivity of measurement across age. Indeed, patterns of association change developmentally as children's EF skills become more sophisticated.

M. C. Welsh (2001) identified three major cycles of EF development that parallel data on cortical development (Thatcher, 1997)—18 months to 5 years, 5 to 10 years, and 10 to 14 years—with the cycle from late preschool through elementary school being perhaps the most dynamic. From a developmental and educational perspective, the second cycle is particularly intriguing, given that it straddles the period when children are starting formal schooling. Hence important questions arise concerning the role of experiences in educational settings (versus general development) in shaping growth of executive functioning across that important school transition period (Morrison, Bachman, & Connor, 2005).

CONCEPTUALIZING EXECUTIVE FUNCTIONS, SELF-REGULATION, AND EFFORTFUL CONTROL

Although often used interchangeably, the terms *executive function* and *self-regulation* do not always share the same definition. Each of these constructs originated historically from distinct disciplinary perspectives, which, in turn, have implications for the ways in which each has been measured. The term *self-regulation* stems from research by developmental and educational scientists, who emphasized utilization of child-friendly tasks (e.g., Head-Toes-Knees-Shoulders [HTKS]; Cameron Ponitz et al., 2008) with an emphasis on ecological validity, especially in a classroom context. In contrast, the term *executive function* has roots in cognitive psychology and neuroscience (Denckla, 2007). In these disciplines, the initial emphasis of research was on identifying, disentangling, and compartmentalizing the individual components of EF from a brain-based perspective using rigorous, fine-grained experimental assessments (e.g., Flanker and Go/No-Go tasks) and understanding deficits in these skills in individuals with cognitive disabilities.

Educational and Developmental Perspectives on the Development of Executive Function

Evidence for linkages between children's EF and achievement has accumulated steadily in recent years (Adams, Bourke, & Willis, 1999; Gathercole & Pickering, 2000; McClelland et al., 2007; J. A. Welsh, Nix, Blair, Bierman, & Nelson, 2010). For example, after controlling for general intelligence and attention control/flexibility, inhibition has also been identified as a unique predictor of math achievement and literacy in kindergarten (Blair & Razza, 2007; Espy, Bull, Kaiser, Martin, & Banet, 2008). In addition, children with better EF skills exhibit greater math abilities when compared with students with weaker EF skills (e.g., Bull & Scerif, 2001; Dobbs, Doctoroff, Fisher, & Arnold, 2006). Although these findings highlight the need to consider separate components of EF with respect to academic outcomes, few studies have included a battery of inhibition, working memory, and attention control/flexibility tasks and studied their unique contributions to various academic skills. In our own recent work we have explored relations between individual components of EF and children's mathematics and reading abilities (Lan, Legare, Ponitz, Li, & Morrison, 2011). In addition to finding evidence that working memory ability uniquely predicted most aspects of academic achievement, including academic tasks that required complex processing, our data also indicate that inhibition is a unique predictor of performance on math achievement tasks involving relatively simpler processes.

The term *self-regulation* has also been used by developmental psychologists to describe one element of temperament and refers to processes that control children's automatic responses to changes in their environment (Rothbart & Bates, 2006). In this framework, self-regulation is largely driven by effortful control, viewed as the capacity to regulate attention, behavior, and emotions. In conjunction with parent (and teacher) reports, child-level assessments of self-regulation and effortful control in this literature include those also used by neuroscientists to investigate EF. From this perspective, effortful control (and thus self-regulation) is supported by the development of the executive attention network. However, many of the measures used to assess children's effortful control are essentially identical to those used to assess aspects of children's EF skills. For example, a child-friendly version of a flanker task (Rueda, Fan, et al., 2004) has been described as measuring aspects of effortful control but is also seen by EF researchers as an assessment of attention control. Further, questionnaire items designed to reflect an effortful control factor in the Children's Behavior Questionnaire (e.g., "Is good at following directions") are the same as those measuring self-regulation on the Child Behavior Rating Scale (Bronson, Tivnan, & Seppanen, 1995). Recently, developmental psychologists have attempted to distinguish between EF and self-regulation. Raver and colleagues, for example, have used the term *self-regulation* to refer to a combination of children's EF and effortful control (Raver et al., 2011). Blair and Ursache (2011) suggested that EFs are not the same as self-regulation or self-control, conceptualizing the relations between the two to be bidirectional. From this perspective, self-regulation is relatively automatic, unconscious management of attention and emotional arousal in the service of goal-directed actions. EFs play a role in self-regulation in that they contribute to children's ability to regulate or manage arousal. In turn, EFs are also dependent on the regulation of emotions and behavior.

Although theoretical accounts of the relations between self-regulation and EF are informative, there are still many questions related to the operationalization and measurement of both. Indeed, despite the appearance of different constructs within the educational and developmental literature, the evidence that the constructs are measuring distinctly different skills is quite limited. The fuzzy distinction between EF and self-regulation (as well as effortful control)—in combination with existing debates about the measurement of both constructs—has contributed greatly to a proliferation of constructs, resulting in a kind of conceptual clutter whose similarities and differences are not readily apparent. Likewise, for discipline-specific reasons, numerous divergent measures of EF have proliferated, with little consensus on how they relate to each other, which has yielded a similar kind of measurement mayhem. From diverse perspectives, researchers have recently called for clarification in the way EF and self-regulation are defined, standardization of measurement in both constructs, and design of developmentally appropriate assessment tools in each domain that accurately measure children's skills (e.g., Schunk, 2008; Willoughby, Wirth, & Blair, 2011). Working toward these goals in a systematic way has important implications for uncluttering the conceptual landscape, deriving a more consistent measurement strategy, and ultimately developing a more unified approach to understanding EF and its development.

Educational and Cognitive Neuroscience Perspectives on the Development of Executive Function

In contrast to the confusion in the educational and developmental areas, cognitive and neurophysiological work with adults has developed a more uniform conceptualization and terminology of EF around the three components of attention control/flexibility, working memory, and response inhibition. In addition, advances in brain-imaging techniques and growing interest in brain development have greatly affected the rapid growth of the new field of educational neuroscience. As this field has grown, so have applications of neuroscientific methods (e.g., neuroimaging) to the study of school-related skills in reading (e.g., Schlaggar & McCandliss, 2007) and math (e.g., Ansari & Dhital, 2006), in addition to EF. Although this work has produced significant insights into the brain functions that underlie children's educationally relevant skills on laboratory tasks (Houdé, Rossi, Lubin, & Joliot, 2010) as well as the linkages between neurophysiological measures and academic achievement, fewer studies have focused on the impact of the school context on children's cognitive and academic growth. In our laboratory, we have launched a new investigation at the intersection of research on education, developmental psychology, and cognitive neuroscience to study the nature and sources of growth of executive functioning during the school transition. We have been gathering behavioral and event-related potential (ERP) data on prekindergarten, kindergarten, and first-grade children directly in the school setting using a portable electroencephalogram (EEG) system (Bio Semi).

In this work, we have been focusing on ERP components related to attention control/flexibility, response inhibition, and working memory, all of which develop during childhood. Most ERP studies have examined links between cognitive control processes and two ERP components that appear to reflect a network of structures (the anterior cingulate cortex and lateral prefrontal cortex) involved in detecting response conflict and attention control/flexibility. ERP researchers have focused on changes in related ERP potentials; specifically, the medial-frontal N2 and frontal P3 that follow them (Gehring, Gratton, Coles, & Donchin, 1992) during childhood appear to parallel changes in children's conflict-resolution and response-inhibition skills. In our recent work we have examined these processes using the Go/No-Go task (see, e.g., Botvinick et al., 2001). A general finding is that the amplitude and latency of the N2 and P3 potentials decrease with age, and that these ERP correlates become more adultlike as children become more skilled at tasks involving conflict resolution (Lewis, Lamm, Segalowitz, Stieben, & Zelazo, 2006; Rueda, Posner, Rothbart, & Davis-Stober, 2004; Rueda, Rothbart, McCandliss, Saccomanno, & Posner, 2005). Perhaps the most convincing evidence for a causal relationship between the ERP activity and EF, as well as for the impact of the environment in modifying EF, comes from a study in which a group of children underwent attention training, including training in conflict resolution. Children who underwent training showed better conflict resolution than did nontrained controls, and their N2 ERP component showed a pattern more similar to that in adults (Rueda et al., 2005). In addition to focusing on N2 and P3 potentials, we have also been focusing on the error-related negativity (ERN) that can be observed when individuals make an incorrect response on tasks that require the control of attention or inhibition of incorrect responses (Gehring, Lui, Orr, & Carp, 2011). Although the developmental data on the ERN are still growing (e.g., Davies, Segalowitz, & Gavin, 2004; Grammer, Carrasco, Gehring, & Morrison, 2014; Torpey, Hajcak, Kim, Kujawa, & Klein, 2012), the ERN presents another opportunity to explore the development of EF skills with EEGs.

Although there are cross-sectional data on the components of EF skills across childhood, we know of no reports of longitudinal data on changes in different ERP components. Developmental differences reported in cross-sectional investigations represent an important first step in documenting the average performance of children at specific ages, and this type of evidence has provided information about the age at which developmental changes in ERP components might be seen. However, with this type of data, it is not possible to examine the trajectories of individual children's development that correspond with gains in EF skills.

Longitudinal ERP data for each EF skill in children across this important period offers the opportunity to address a number of questions related to the development of these abilities at a neurological level that have yet to be resolved: (a) relations between behavioral and neurological indices of EF, (b) the stability of ERP components related to EF across childhood, and (c) associations between ERP components across EF tasks. For example, research has demonstrated that children (like adults) show an enhanced N2 component on trials in which they are required to inhibit a response in a Go/No-Go task (Lewis et al., 2006). In investigations using this task, although changes in behavioral measures are not always seen, age-related differences in ERP data for children have been identified (Cragg, Fox, Nation, Reid, & Anderson, 2009; Cragg & Nation, 2008). Examining behavioral and neurological data in combination using sophisticated longitudinal modeling techniques would provide insight into the changing relations between children's behavioral manifestations of EF skills and related ERP data. In addition, although little is known about the stability of ERP components across repeated assessments of tasks used frequently with young children, one report in which children were assessed using a flanker task to investigate the ERN over 2 weeks (Davies & Gavin, 2009) indicates that the test–retest correlations in children are relatively low, whereas similar assessments of adults across a few weeks and even 2 years reveal surprising consistency (Olvet & Hajcak, 2009; Segalowitz et al., 2010; Weinberg & Hajcak, 2011). Repeated assessments would allow for an examination of when and if greater stability in children's ERP activity occurs and the extent to which these changes are associated with maturation or experiences in school. Finally, despite high test–retest reliability of the ERN within task, relations across these tasks (Go/No-Go and flanker) in adults are much lower. We know of no similar reports from studies conducted with children. However, longitudinal ERP data across child-friendly versions of these same tasks could provide important evidence regarding the unitary versus componential structure of EF.

In our view, there are several reasons for incorporating a neurological perspective into the study of EF in children's academic development. Indeed, the possibility that schooling influences could produce effects on brain function prior to behavioral changes raises the possibility of detecting the influence of the environment prior to its behavioral emergence. In addition, incorporating neurological views and data will lead to a fuller understanding of the complex, multiple forces shaping children's growth. Findings from almost 3 decades of cognitive and neurological research have yielded a wealth of valuable data on the development of academic skills and EF. Building on this work, by noting the brain systems that subserve critical academically related cognitive abilities such as EF, we will move closer to specifying the neurological sources of individual differences among children who learn well and those who struggle to acquire EF skills.

MEASURING EF AND SELF-REGULATION

In the study of EF and self-regulation, researchers have relied on three main modes of data collection: laboratory-based measures, assessments in naturalistic settings such as the classroom, and teacher or parent reports. Each of these approaches offers both benefits and limitations to the study of EF and self-regulation that are particularly relevant to those interested in using these types of measures in school-based research. For example, many traditionally used laboratory-based assessments of EF with children have been adapted from tasks that cognitive psychologists and neuroscientists have used with adults. Reflecting the neural substrates believed to underlie the behavioral manifestations of subcomponents of EF, these computerized tasks capture finite differences in children's reaction time and accuracy rates in response to stimuli. Despite the rigorous control and precision afforded by these measures, it is not clear to what extent they reflect or predict behavior in the classroom (Bodnar, Prahme, Cutting, Denckla, & Mahone, 2007). This limitation has very real implications for the external validity and, in turn, the usefulness of findings resulting from neurophysiological assessments.

Alternatively, although classroom-based observational measures capture children in their natural environment, their sensitivity to the phenomenon of interest can be eroded by lack of experimental control introduced in the real world. In addition, because researchers can only passively observe what is happening in the classroom setting, it is often not possible to elicit specific behaviors of interest or differentially study each of the three aspects of EF. In our laboratory, we are working to refine and assess the use of three classroom-based measures of children's self-regulation (Lan et al., 2009)— one each for attention control/flexibility, working memory, and response inhibition. These tasks, which are conducted with small groups of children and administered by the children's teachers, have been successfully tested in prekindergarten and kindergarten classrooms. For example, in one of these tasks designed to assess children's response inhibition, children are instructed by their teachers to march in a circle. They are then told that they are supposed to freeze into a certain pose when music is played and to continue to march once the music stops. The speed and accuracy with which children can stop with the music serve as measures of children's ability to inhibit their response. Games such as this are frequently played by children in prekindergarten and elementary classrooms. As a result, not only are they easily administered with the assistance of teachers, but the students also really enjoy playing them.

In contrast to the time-intensive nature of direct assessments, teacher and parent report measures provide researchers with an efficient assessment from individuals with extensive experience with children. These techniques are also often viewed as more ecologically valid than are observations of children's behavior in the laboratory or classroom setting. Despite the obvious benefits, however, these reports are susceptible to bias (e.g., Derks, Hudziak, & Boomsma, 2009). In addition, evidence for consistency across teacher reports and performance-based measures is not always found in individual investigations (Bodnar et al., 2007).

Complicating the measurement of EF and self-regulation further are reports of weak linkages across different modes of measurement and inconsistent results across different measures (Bodnar et al., 2007; Lan & Morrison, 2008). It is possible that the assessment of EF and the assessment of self-regulation each tap unique aspects of these constructs that are greatly dependent on contextual factors. However, if these skills are highly related to children's academic development and success in school, yet their measurement is inconsistent, serious questions about the reliability of these linkages arise. Thus, it is important to examine the extent to which these measures—thought to assess similar constructs—share common variance.

WORKING TOWARD A UNIFIED CONCEPTUALIZATION OF EXECUTIVE FUNCTION

We believe that issues related to proliferation of constructs and measurement can also be seen as challenges and opportunities for future research. To this end, we offer three proposals.

Proposal 1: Exploring Associations Among Measures of Executive Function and Self-Regulation

It would be revealing to systematically examine relations among the measures of EF using both cross-sectional and longitudinal data. Results of factor analyses would permit researchers to address a number of important questions including the following.

Are Different Disciplines Measuring Different Constructs?

This fundamental question could be answered by directly examining the degree of association across measures derived from different disciplines (cognitive and neurophysiological, educational and developmental) within EF components (attention control/flexibility, working memory, response inhibition). To the extent that associations across disciplines, but within components, are strong and significant, these results would reveal that measures of EF, self-regulation, and effortful control are essentially tapping the same underlying skill. By implication, adoption of a more uniform nomenclature for these different measures would seem warranted.

Is Executive Function Unitary or Componential in This Age Range?

This question could be addressed by determining the best-fitting model for measures across EF components, within disciplinary perspectives at different ages as children transition into school. A one-factor solution at any grade would indicate that EF was best conceived as a unitary skill. From previous findings it is possible that, as children move from kindergarten to second grade, the factor structure will increasingly favor a componential model, with three factors likely emerging with greater experience in elementary school. It is also possible that the degree of unity across components will differ by disciplinary measure. Specifically, across disciplines the tasks measuring working memory seem relatively more uniform, including similar kinds of memory and processing demands. In contrast, the measures of response inhibition appear on the surface to be more disparate from one another, with the HTKS task making quite different behavioral demands than the Go/No-Go task does.

Does Context Influence Executive Function Performance?

Finally, it would be possible to examine the extent to which the context of testing influences children's performance and hence the associations obtained across disciplinary measures. Should the factors derived reflect unique testing environments (e.g., laboratory vs. classroom), these findings would clearly reveal that children's EF performance in a laboratory context was not strongly predictive of their classroom behavior. Conversely, results might show strong cross-context consistency, indicating that laboratory measures could be used as reliable indices of children's behavior in the classroom.

Proposal 2: Examining Developmental Changes in Executive Function and Self-Regulation Over Time

Although a number of recent investigations provide insight into the structure of EF in young children (i.e., unitary vs. componential), very little of this work has involved repeated assessments with children during the school transition. As a result, we know a great deal about the performance of children before and early in preschool (Carlson, 2005) but much less about their performance and development as they transition through prekindergarten and into elementary school. It is also important to examine whether and how these changing abilities relate to behavior in the classroom. Indeed, it could be the case that children who come into school with stronger EF skills (as assessed from using tasks derived from cognitive neuroscience) also exhibit stronger behavioral regulation on classroom-based measures. It is also possible, however, that the relations between these sets of skills are more limited than anticipated and that these different types of tasks tap into different abilities altogether. If so, the variance in children's achievement accounted for by measures of EF and self-regulation might not be shared significantly, or the patterns of these relations could change over time.

*How Does the Constellation of Executive Function
and Self-Regulation Skills Change Over Time?*

With longitudinal data on children's EF and regulatory skills measured at multiple levels, the ways in which these skills are related over time could be examined. As predicted for the cross-sectional data, it is likely that the separate components of response inhibition, attention control/flexibility, and working memory will become more clearly delineated as children get older. Contrasting longitudinal versus cross-sectional data, however, would reveal the extent to which they tell similar stories about the age-related changes in children's abilities. It is possible that developmental trajectories of these skills are masked in cross-sectional data. Because our knowledge of the development of EF skills is based largely on information gathered cross-sectionally, these findings offer only snapshots of the relations between children's skills at individual ages. As a result, there is still a great deal to be learned about the underlying developmental trajectories (both behavioral and neurological) of these skills.

In addition, changes in sets of skills as they relate to one another over time could be revealed in longitudinal analyses. For example, it is possible that (a) EF and classroom-based regulatory skills develop simultaneously, such that gains in one set of skills do not proceed in advance of the other; (b) elements of EF tapped by using laboratory tasks develop in advance of, and contribute to, future increases in classroom-based regulation; or (c) regulatory skills are developed in the classroom setting in advance of basic EF, and gains in these skills in the school context contribute to future EF abilities. Although subtle, the distinctions among these three models are meaningful when considering the development of these skills longitudinally. Moreover, this type of in-depth understanding has real-world implications for identifying the best way to intervene to improve children's EF and self-regulation, which is important for school success.

Proposal 3: Environmental Influences on the Growth of Executive Function: An Example From Schooling Research

Several lines of research point to the potential impact of schooling on the development of executive functioning. For example, given the growing evidence for cross-cultural differences in Chinese and American children's EF skills (Sabbagh, Xu, Carlson, Moses, & Lee, 2006; Wanless, McClelland, Acock, Chen, & Chen, 2011; Wanless, McClelland, Acock, Ponitz, et al., 2011), researchers (Lan et al., 2009) analyzed teacher discourse related to self-regulation in first-grade mathematics classrooms in China and the United States. A distinction was drawn between preparatory (given prior to start of task) and correctional instructions (given after the start of a task). Results were striking: 70% of instructions given by American teachers were correctional, whereas 70% of instructions given by Chinese teachers were preparatory. Recent efforts currently under way in our lab include coding of videotaped preschool and elementary school classrooms in China and the United States to document the extent to which teachers in both countries engage in instructional techniques that may be related to EF development. Although there are limitations to interpretations of these findings—including cultural variation in distributions of temperamental variables (Hsu, Soong, Stigler, Hong, & Liang, 1981) or in the prevalence of particular genes (Chang, Kidd, Livak, Pakstis, & Kidd, 1996) that might contribute to observed advantages in EF (Sabbagh et al., 2006)—it is equally likely that differences in the instructional environment of Chinese and American children may be tied to the observed cross-cultural differences in the development of EF.

Experimental Work

For the past several years, we have been using a natural experiment (designated "school cutoff") that permits assessment of the influence of a culturally valued learning experience (schooling) and circumvents some, if not all, of the serious biases found in other research. Each year, North American school boards proclaim that those children whose birth dates precede some specific date will be allowed to go to kindergarten or first grade while other children who just miss the cutoff date will be denied entry. Capitalizing on this arbitrary selection criterion, the methodology involves selecting groups of children whose birth dates cluster closely on either side of the cutoff date, thereby effectively equating the two groups of children on age. Background information gathered from parent questionnaires and direct assessments has routinely shown that the two groups are equated on critical control variables (e.g., IQ, socioeconomic status, preschool experience). With the groups matched on these dimensions, the children's progress may be compared using a pre–post design (with testing in the early fall and late spring of the school year). In other words, comparing the degree of change in the target skill from fall to spring in children who just made versus just missed the cutoff has allowed us to assess the impact of a relatively specific schooling experience on the growth of that skill.

In a series of studies over the past 15 years, the patterns of change across a broad range of domains and abilities appeared to be highly domain- and even sub-domain-specific (Bisanz, Morrison, & Dunn, 1995; Christian, Morrison, Frazier, & Massetti, 2000). For example, when considering the acquisition of mathematics skills, conservation of number has been found to improve as a function of age, whereas accuracy in mental arithmetic developed as a function of schooling experiences (Bisanz et al., 1995). Findings from recent quasi-experimental and experimental investigations have provided further evidence for the importance of schooling in the development of executive functioning. For example, Burrage and colleagues (2008) examined the influence of experience in preschool on growth of word decoding, working memory, and response inhibition. This quasi-experimental work using a school cutoff design suggests that schooling, and more specifically schooling in the years of prekindergarten and kindergarten, improves working memory for children who attend school compared with same-age peers who, because of arbitrary school cutoff dates, do not attend at the same time (Burrage et al., 2008).

Further evidence from a cluster-randomized school-based intervention (Raver et al., 2011) revealed that preschool-age children participating in the Chicago School Readiness Project exhibited significantly higher performance on EF tasks than did their peers in a control group. Moreover, results from this investigation indicate that there was a mediating role of children's EF on preacademic abilities, including letter naming and math skills. These findings complement those of Connor and colleagues (2010), who also found that an instructional intervention—which emphasized teacher planning and organization, classroom management, and opportunities for students to work independently—was most beneficial for children who started first grade with weaker EF skills.

Promoting Executive Function in the Classroom

What factors of the early classroom environment might be most important for the development of EF? Some hints can be drawn from the work of Raver and colleagues (2011), who concluded that children appeared to benefit from greater levels of structure in the classroom setting, including clearer routines, and less student–teacher conflict and coercion. They hypothesized that this increased structure may help children regulate their own behavior, which in turn would allow for more time focusing and maintaining their attention toward learning-related goals. Furthermore, evidence from classroom observations suggests that the teacher's use of specific instructional techniques that are related to aspects of children's cognitive development—including providing explicit goals, focusing children's attention, and requesting that they remember—are particularly important for children who exhibit lower regulation at the beginning of the school year (Coffman, Grammer, & Ornstein, 2009).

In our own work we have identified some elements of instruction that we feel are important to the development of EF skills. For example, there are sizable differences across first-grade classrooms in the ways in which teachers organize time spent in their classrooms—including the amount of time devoted to describing classroom procedures and preparing the class for assignments (Cameron, Connor, & Morrison, 2005). More time spent in these organizational aspects of instruction predicts fewer disruptive transitions and more time spent by children in independent, self-regulated activities. Current and ongoing work should explore these and other classroom practices in an effort to ascertain the mechanisms (instructional and noninstructional) that shape children's EF trajectories.

What Are the Influences of Schooling on the Growth of Executive Function?

Comparing the performance of older versus younger children within each grade, we would, partly on the basis of previous findings (Burrage et al., 2008), predict that significant schooling effects would be observed for working memory across kindergarten to second grade. In contrast, we expect smaller influences of schooling for measures of response inhibition. Predictions for attention control/

flexibility are less clear at this point, but given the role of attention in working memory, schooling effects might be anticipated here too. This pattern of findings would reveal that components of EF were differentially sensitive to schooling influences. Further, the results would favor a componential view of EF, given that different components react differently to the schooling experience. Finally, different components of EF might show different developmental trajectories, resulting from a combination of schooling and maturational influences.

It is clear that a more nuanced pattern of results could emerge. Neurological indices of schooling effects might predate evidence from behavioral measures (e.g., of response inhibition). These findings would reveal that schooling was influencing children's EF development but that it was detectable early on only neurologically. Such findings would highlight the value of neurological data for understanding how and when educational experiences impact children's development.

Moreover, schooling effects may show up earlier in laboratory-based measures than in classroom behaviors. Schooling may increase children's working memory or attention skills, as revealed using brain and behavioral measures on simpler, more tightly controlled tasks, but not until later on more complex, classroom assessments, where peer influences and other real-world factors intrude.

The proposal above represents one strategy for examining the malleability of EF in children. Other techniques include small-scale training studies as well as more ambitious school-based interventions.

CONCLUSION

The past 3 decades have witnessed an explosion of scientific work across several disciplines examining children's executive control processes. Notwithstanding the advances made within each field, the confusing array of constructs (conceptual clutter) and the dizzying variety of assessment tools (measurement mayhem) threaten to derail efforts to derive a more unified and hence fuller understanding of the nature and development of this critical skill. Our proposals represent one way to gain greater clarity and ultimately to integrate previously disparate perspectives into a more integrated approach.

REFERENCES

Adams, A., Bourke, L., & Willis, C. (1999). Working memory and spoken language comprehension in young children. *International Journal of Psychology*, *34*, 364–373. http://dx.doi.org/10.1080/002075999399701

Anderson, P. (2002). Assessment and development of executive function (EF) during childhood. *Child Neuropsychology*, *8*, 71–82. http://dx.doi.org/10.1076/chin.8.2.71.8724

Ansari, D., & Dhital, B. (2006). Age-related changes in the activation of the intraparietal sulcus during nonsymbolic magnitude processing: An event-related functional magnetic resonance imaging study. *Journal of Cognitive Neuroscience, 18,* 1820–1828.

Bisanz, J., Morrison, F. J., & Dunn, M. (1995). Effects of age and schooling on the acquisition of elementary quantitative skills. *Developmental Psychology, 31,* 221–236. http://dx.doi.org/10.1037/0012-1649.31.2.221

Blair, C. (2002). School readiness: Integrating cognition and emotion in a neurobiological conceptualization of children's functioning at school entry. *American Psychologist, 57,* 111–127. http://dx.doi.org/10.1037/0003-066X.57.2.111

Blair, C., & Razza, R. P. (2007). Relating effortful control, executive function, and false belief understanding to emerging math and literacy ability in kindergarten. *Child Development, 78,* 647–663. http://dx.doi.org/10.1111/j.1467-8624.2007.01019.x

Blair, C., & Ursache, A. (2011). A bidirectional model of executive functions and self-regulation. In K. D. Vohs & R. F. Baumeister (Eds.), *Handbook of self-regulation: Research, theory, and applications* (2nd ed., pp. 300–320). New York, NY: Guilford Press.

Bodnar, L. E., Prahme, M. C., Cutting, L. E., Denckla, M. B., & Mahone, E. M. (2007). Construct validity of parent ratings of inhibitory control. *Child Neuropsychology, 13,* 345–362. http://dx.doi.org/10.1080/09297040600899867

Botvinick, M. M., Braver, T. S., Barch, D. M., Carter, C. S., & Cohen, J. D. (2001). Conflict monitoring and cognitive control. *Psychological Review, 108,* 624–652. http://dx.doi.org/10.1037/0033-295X.108.3.624

Bronson, M. B., Tivnan, T., & Seppanen, P. S. (1995). Relations between teacher and classroom activity variables and the classroom behaviors of prekindergarten children in Chapter 1 funded programs. *Journal of Applied Developmental Psychology, 16,* 253–282. http://dx.doi.org/10.1016/0193-3973(95)90035-7

Bull, R., & Scerif, G. (2001). Executive functioning as a predictor of children's mathematics ability: Inhibition, switching, and working memory. *Developmental Neuropsychology, 19,* 273–293. http://dx.doi.org/10.1207/S15326942DN1903_3

Burrage, M. S., Ponitz, C. C., McCready, E. A., Shah, P., Sims, B. C., Jewkes, A. M., & Morrison, F. J. (2008). Age- and schooling-related effects on executive functions in young children: A natural experiment. *Child Neuropsychology, 14,* 510–524. http://dx.doi.org/10.1080/09297040701756917

Cameron, C. E., Connor, C. M., & Morrison, F. J. (2005). Effects of variation in teacher organization on classroom function. *Journal of School Psychology, 43,* 61–85. http://dx.doi.org/10.1016/j.jsp.2004.12.002

Cameron Ponitz, C., McClelland, M. M., Jewkes, A. M., Connor, C., Farris, C. L., & Morrison, F. J. (2008). Touch your toes! Developing a direct measure of behavioral regulation in early childhood. *Early Childhood Research Quarterly, 23,* 141–158. http://dx.doi.org/10.1016/j.ecresq.2007.01.004

Carlson, S. M. (2005). Developmentally sensitive measures of executive function in preschool children. *Developmental Neuropsychology, 28*, 595–616. http://dx.doi.org/10.1207/s15326942dn2802_3

Chang, F. M., Kidd, J. R., Livak, K. J., Pakstis, A. J., & Kidd, K. K. (1996). The worldwide distribution of allele frequencies at the human dopamine D4 receptor locus. *Human Genetics, 98*, 91–101. http://dx.doi.org/10.1007/s004390050166

Christian, K., Morrison, F. J., Frazier, J. A., & Massetti, G. (2000). Specificity in the nature and timing of cognitive growth in kindergarten and first grade. *Journal of Cognition and Development, 1*, 429–448. http://dx.doi.org/10.1207/S15327647JCD0104_04

Coffman, J. L., Grammer, J. K., & Ornstein, P. A. (2009, April). Understanding the interplay of the classroom context and children's self-regulation: Implications for the development of memory. In P. A. Ornstein & C. M. Roebers (Chairs), *Effects of schooling and instruction on developmental pathways in memory skills and executive functioning.* Paper presented at the biennial meeting of the Society for Research in Child Development, Denver, CO.

Connor, C. M., Ponitz, C. C., Phillips, B. M., Travis, Q. M., Glasney, S., & Morrison, F. J. (2010). First graders' literacy and self-regulation gains: The effect of individualizing student instruction. *Journal of School Psychology, 48*, 433–455. http://dx.doi.org/10.1016/j.jsp.2010.06.003

Cragg, L., Fox, A., Nation, K., Reid, C., & Anderson, M. (2009). Neural correlates of successful and partial inhibitions in children: An ERP study. *Developmental Psychobiology, 51*, 533–543. http://dx.doi.org/10.1002/dev.20391

Cragg, L., & Nation, K. (2008). Go or no-go? Developmental improvements in the efficiency of response inhibition in midchildhood. *Developmental Science, 11*, 819–827. http://dx.doi.org/10.1111/j.1467-7687.2008.00730.x

Davies, P. L., & Gavin, W. J. (2009). Reliability of ERN in children performing a visual flanker task. *Psychophysiology, 46*, S111.

Davies, P. L., Segalowitz, S. J., & Gavin, W. J. (2004). Development of response-monitoring ERPs in 7- to 25-year-olds. *Developmental Neuropsychology, 25*, 355–376. http://dx.doi.org/10.1207/s15326942dn2503_6

Denckla, M. (2007). Executive function: Binding together the definitions of attention-deficit/hyperactivity disorder and learning disabilities. In L. Meltzer (Ed.), *Executive function in education: From theory to practice* (pp. 5–18). New York, NY: Guilford Press.

Derks, E. M., Hudziak, J. J., & Boomsma, D. I. (2009). Genetics of ADHD, hyperactivity, and attention problems. In Y.-K. Kim (Ed.), *Handbook of behavior genetics* (pp. 361–378). New York, NY: Springer. http://dx.doi.org/10.1007/978-0-387-76727-7_25

Dobbs, J., Doctoroff, G. L., Fisher, P. H., & Arnold, D. H. (2006). The association between preschool children's socio-emotional functioning and their mathematical skills. *Journal of Applied Developmental Psychology, 27*, 97–108. http://dx.doi.org/10.1016/j.appdev.2005.12.008

Duckworth, A., & Seligman, M. P. (2006). Self-discipline gives girls the edge: Gender in self-discipline, grades, and achievement test scores. *Journal of Educational Psychology, 98,* 198–208. http://dx.doi.org/10.1037/0022-0663.98.1.198

Eslinger, P. J. (1996). Conceptualizing, describing, and measuring components of executive function: A summary. In G. R. Lyon & N. A. Krasnegor (Eds.), *Attention, memory, and executive function* (4th ed., pp. 367–395). Baltimore, MD: Paul H. Brookes.

Espy, K., Bull, R., Kaiser, H., Martin, J., & Banet, M. (2008). Methodological and conceptual issues in understanding the development of executive control in the preschool period. In V. Anderson, R. Jacobs, & P. J. Anderson (Eds.), *Executive functions and the frontal lobes: A lifespan perspective* (pp. 105–121). Philadelphia, PA: Taylor & Francis.

Gathercole, S. E., & Pickering, S. J. (2000). Working memory deficits in children with low achievements in the national curriculum at 7 years of age. *British Journal of Educational Psychology, 70,* 177–194. http://dx.doi.org/10.1348/000709900158047

Gehring, W. J., Gratton, G., Coles, M. G. H., & Donchin, E. (1992). Probability effects on stimulus evaluation and response processes. *Journal of Experimental Psychology: Human Perception and Performance, 18,* 198–216. http://dx.doi.org/10.1037/0096-1523.18.1.198

Gehring, W. J., Lui, Y., Orr, J. M., & Carp, J. (2011). The error-related negativity (ERN/Ne). In S. J. Luck & E. S. Kappenman (Eds.), *The Oxford handbook of event-related potential components* (pp. 231–291). New York, NY: Oxford. http://dx.doi.org/10.1093/oxfordhb/9780195374148.013.0120

Grammer, J. K., Carrasco, M., Gehring, W. J., & Morrison, F. J. (2014). Age-related changes in error processing in young children: A school-based investigation. *Developmental Cognitive Neuroscience, 9,* 93–105.

Houdé, O., Rossi, S., Lubin, A., & Joliot, M. (2010). Mapping numerical processing, reading, and executive functions in the developing brain: An fMRI meta-analysis of 52 studies including 842 children. *Developmental Science, 13,* 876–885. http://dx.doi.org/10.1111/j.1467-7687.2009.00938.x

Hsu, C., Soong, W., Stigler, J. W., Hong, C., & Liang, C. (1981). The temperamental characteristics of Chinese babies. *Child Development, 52,* 1337–1340. http://dx.doi.org/10.2307/1129528

Hughes, C., Ensor, R., Wilson, A., & Graham, A. (2009). Tracking executive function across the transition to school: A latent variable approach. *Developmental Neuropsychology, 35,* 20–36. http://dx.doi.org/10.1080/87565640903325691

Klein, C. (2003). Assessing the development of executive functions. *International Society for the Study of Behavioural Development Newsletter, 43,* 8–11.

Klenberg, L., Korkman, M., & Lahti-Nuuttila, P. (2001). Differential development of attention and executive functions in 3- to 12-year-old Finnish children. *Developmental Neuropsychology, 20,* 407–428. http://dx.doi.org/10.1207/S15326942DN2001_6

Lan, X., Legare, C. H., Ponitz, C. C., Li, S., & Morrison, F. J. (2011). Investigating the links between the subcomponents of executive function and academic achievement: A cross-cultural analysis of Chinese and American preschoolers. *Journal of Experimental Child Psychology, 108,* 677–692. http://dx.doi.org/10.1016/j.jecp.2010.11.001

Lan, X., & Morrison, F. (2008, July). *Inter-correlations among components of behavioral regulation and their relationships with academic outcomes in China.* Paper presented at the 20th Biennial Meeting of the International Society of Behavioral Development, Wurzburg, Germany.

Lan, X., Ponitz, C., Miller, K. F., Li, S., Cortina, K., Perry, M., & Fang, G. (2009). Keeping their attention: Classroom practices associated with behavioral engagement in first grade mathematics classes in China and the United States. *Early Childhood Research Quarterly, 24,* 198–211. http://dx.doi.org/10.1016/j.ecresq.2009.03.002

Lehto, J. E., Juujärvi, P., Kooistra, L., & Pulkkinen, L. (2003). Dimensions of executive functioning: Evidence from children. *British Journal of Developmental Psychology, 21,* 59–80. http://dx.doi.org/10.1348/026151003321164627

Lewis, M. D., Lamm, C., Segalowitz, S. J., Stieben, J., & Zelazo, P. D. (2006). Neurophysiological correlates of emotion regulation in children and adolescents. *Journal of Cognitive Neuroscience, 18,* 430–443.

Luciano, M. (2003). The neural and functional development of human prefrontal cortex. In M. de Hann & M. H. Johnson (Eds.), *The cognitive neuroscience of development* (pp. 157–180). New York, NY: Psychology Press.

Luria, A. R. (1966). *Higher cortical functions in man.* New York, NY: Basic Books.

Matthews, J. S., Ponitz, C., & Morrison, F. J. (2009). Early gender differences in self-regulation and academic achievement. *Journal of Educational Psychology, 101,* 689–704. http://dx.doi.org/10.1037/a0014240

McAuley, T., & White, D. A. (2011). A latent variables examination of processing speed, response inhibition, and working memory during typical development. *Journal of Experimental Child Psychology, 108,* 453–468. http://dx.doi.org/10.1016/j.jecp.2010.08.009

McClelland, M. M., Cameron, C. E., Connor, C. M., Farris, C. L., Jewkes, A. M., & Morrison, F. J. (2007). Links between behavioral regulation and preschoolers' literacy, vocabulary, and math skills. *Developmental Psychology, 43,* 947–959. http://dx.doi.org/10.1037/0012-1649.43.4.947

Miyake, A., Friedman, N. P., Emerson, M. J., Witzki, A. H., Howerter, A., & Wager, T. D. (2000). The unity and diversity of executive functions and their contributions to complex "frontal lobe" tasks: A latent variable analysis. *Cognitive Psychology, 41,* 49–100. http://dx.doi.org/10.1006/cogp.1999.0734

Moffitt, T. E., Arseneault, L., Belsky, D., Dickson, N., Hancox, R. J., Harrington, H., & Caspi, A. (2011). A gradient of childhood self-control predicts health, wealth, and public safety. *Proceedings of the National Academy of Sciences of the United States of America, 108,* 2693–2698. http://dx.doi.org/10.1073/pnas.1010076108

Morrison, F. J., Bachman, H. J., & Connor, C. M. (2005). *Improving literacy in America: Guidelines from research.* New Haven, CT: Yale University Press. http://dx.doi. org/10.12987/yale/9780300106459.001.0001

Olvet, D. M., & Hajcak, G. (2009). Reliability of error-related brain activity. *Brain Research, 1284,* 89–99. http://dx.doi.org/10.1016/j.brainres.2009.05.079

Raver, C. C., Jones, S. M., Li-Grining, C., Zhai, F., Bub, K., & Pressler, E. (2011). CSRP's impact on low-income preschoolers' preacademic skills: Self-regulation as a mediating mechanism. *Child Development, 82,* 362–378. http://dx.doi.org/ 10.1111/j.1467-8624.2010.01561.x

Rothbart, M. K., & Bates, J. E. (2006). Temperament. In N. Eisenberg, W. Damon, & R. M. Lerner (Eds.), *Handbook of child psychology: Vol. 3. Social, emotional, and personality development* (6th ed., pp. 99–166). Hoboken, NJ: Wiley.

Rueda, M. R., Fan, J., McCandliss, B. D., Halparin, J. D., Gruber, D. B., Lercari, L. P., & Posner, M. I. (2004). Development of attentional networks in childhood. *Neuropsychologia, 42,* 1029–1040. http://dx.doi.org/10.1016/j.neuropsychologia. 2003.12.012

Rueda, M. R., Posner, M. I., Rothbart, M. K., & Davis-Stober, C. P. (2004). Development of the time course for processing conflict. An ERP study with 4-year-olds and adults. *BMC Neuroscience, 5,* 39. http://dx.doi.org/10.1186/1471-2202-5-39

Rueda, M. R., Rothbart, M. K., McCandliss, B. D., Saccomanno, L., & Posner, M. I. (2005). Training, maturation, and genetic influences on the development of executive attention. *Proceedings of the National Academy of Sciences of the United States of America, 102,* 14931–14936. http://dx.doi.org/10.1073/pnas.0506897102

Sabbagh, M. A., Xu, F., Carlson, S. M., Moses, L. J., & Lee, K. (2006). The development of executive functioning and theory of mind. A comparison of Chinese and U.S. preschoolers. *Psychological Science, 17,* 74–81. http://dx.doi. org/10.1111/j.1467-9280.2005.01667.x

Schlaggar, B. L., & McCandliss, B. D. (2007). Development of neural systems for reading. *Annual Review of Neuroscience, 30,* 475–503. http://dx.doi.org/10.1146/ annurev.neuro.28.061604.135645

Schunk, D. H. (2008). Metacognition, self-regulation, and self-regulated learning: Research recommendations. *Educational Psychology Review, 20,* 463–467. http:// dx.doi.org/10.1007/s10648-008-9086-3

Segalowitz, S. J., Santesso, D. L., Murphy, T. I., Homan, D., Chantziantoniou, D. K., & Khan, S. (2010). Retest reliability of medial frontal negativities during performance monitoring. *Psychophysiology, 47,* 260–270. http://dx.doi.org/10.1111/ j.1469-8986.2009.00942.x

Shonkoff, J., & Phillips, D. (Eds.). (2000). *From neurons to neighborhoods: The science of early childhood development.* Washington, DC: National Academy Press.

Thatcher, R. W. (1997). Human frontal lobe development: A theory of cyclical cortical reorganization. In N. Krasnegor, G. R. Lyon, & P. S. Goldman-Rakic

(Eds.), *Development of the prefrontal cortex: Evolution, neurobiology, and behavior* (pp. 85–113). Baltimore, MD: Paul H. Brookes.

Torpey, D. C., Hajcak, G., Kim, J., Kujawa, A., & Klein, D. N. (2012). Electrocortical and behavioral measures of response monitoring in young children during a go/no-go task. *Developmental Psychobiology, 54,* 139–150. http://dx.doi.org/10.1002/dev.20590

Wanless, S. B., McClelland, M. M., Acock, A. C., Chen, F., & Chen, J. (2011). Behavioral regulation and early academic achievement in Taiwan. *Early Education and Development, 22,* 1–28. http://dx.doi.org/10.1080/10409280903493306

Wanless, S. B., McClelland, M. M., Acock, A. C., Ponitz, C. C., Son, S. H., Lan, X., . . . Li, S. (2011). Measuring behavioral regulation in four societies. *Psychological Assessment, 23,* 364–378. http://dx.doi.org/10.1037/a0021768

Weinberg, A., & Hajcak, G. (2011). Longer term test–retest reliability of error-related brain activity. *Psychophysiology, 48,* 1420–1425. http://dx.doi.org/10.1111/j.1469-8986.2011.01206.x

Welsh, J. A., Nix, R. L., Blair, C., Bierman, K. L., & Nelson, K. E. (2010). The development of cognitive skills and gains in academic school readiness for children from low-income families. *Journal of Educational Psychology, 102,* 43–53. http://dx.doi.org/10.1037/a0016738

Welsh, M. C. (2001). The prefrontal cortex and the development of executive functions. In A. Kalverboer & A. Gramsbergen (Eds.), *Handbook of brain and behaviour development* (pp. 767–789). Dordrecht, The Netherlands: Kluwer.

Welsh, M. C. (2002). Developmental and clinical variations in executive functions. In D. L. Molfese & V. J. Molfese (Eds.), *Developmental variations in learning: Applications to social, executive function, language, and reading skills* (pp. 139–185). Mahwah, NJ: Erlbaum.

Welsh, M. C., Friedman, S. L., & Spieker, S. J. (2006). Executive functions in developing children: Current conceptualizations and questions for the future. In K. McCartney & D. Phillips (Eds.), *The Blackwell handbook of early childhood development* (pp. 167–187). Malden, MA: Blackwell. http://dx.doi.org/10.1002/9780470757703.ch9

Welsh, M. C., Huizinga, M., Granrud, M., Cooney, J., Adams, C., & van der Molen, M. (2002, February). *A structural equation model of executive function in normal young adults.* Paper presented at the annual meeting of the International Neuropsychological Society, Toronto, Ontario, Canada.

Welsh, M. C., Pennington, B. F., & Groisser, D. B. (1991). A normative–developmental study of executive function: A window on prefrontal function in children. *Developmental Neuropsychology, 7,* 131–149. http://dx.doi.org/10.1080/87565649109540483

Wiebe, S. A., Espy, K. A., & Charak, D. (2008). Using confirmatory factor analysis to understand executive control in preschool children: I. Latent structure. *Developmental Psychology, 44,* 575–587. http://dx.doi.org/10.1037/0012-1649.44.2.575

Wiebe, S. A., Sheffield, T., Nelson, J. M., Clark, C. A., Chevalier, N., & Espy, K. A. (2011). The structure of executive function in 3-year-olds. *Journal of Experimental Child Psychology, 108*, 436–452. http://dx.doi.org/10.1016/j. jecp.2010.08.008

Willoughby, M. T., Wirth, R. J., & Blair, C. B. (2011). Contributions of modern measurement theory to measuring executive function in early childhood: An empirical demonstration. *Journal of Experimental Child Psychology, 108*, 414–435. http:// dx.doi.org/10.1016/j.jecp.2010.04.007

Zelazo, P. D., Craik, F. I., & Booth, L. (2004). Executive function across the life span. *Acta Psychologica, 115*, 167–183. http://dx.doi.org/10.1016/j.actpsy.2003.12.005

Zelazo, P., & Frye, D. (1998). Cognitive complexity and control: II. The development of executive function in childhood. *Current Directions in Psychological Science, 7*, 121–126. http://dx.doi.org/10.1111/1467-8721.ep10774761

Zelazo, P. D., Müller, U., Frye, D., & Marcovitch, S. (2003). The development of executive function in early childhood. *Monographs of the Society for Research in Child Development, 68*(3, Serial No. 274).

INDEX

ABOUT THE EDITORS

James A. Griffin, PhD, is the deputy chief of the Child Development and Behavior Branch (CDBB) at the Eunice Kennedy Shriver National Institute of Child Health and Human Development (NICHD), National Institutes of Health (NIH), and the director of the Early Learning and School Readiness Program. Prior to NICHD, Dr. Griffin served as a senior research analyst in the Institute of Education Sciences (IES) at the U.S. Department of Education; as the assistant director for the social, behavioral, and education (SBE) sciences in the White House Office of Science and Technology Policy (OSTP); and as a research analyst at the Administration on Children, Youth and Families (ACYF). Dr. Griffin's career has focused on research and evaluation efforts related to service systems and early intervention programs designed to enhance the development and school readiness of children from at-risk and disadvantaged backgrounds.

Peggy McCardle, PhD, MPH, is an affiliated research scientist at the Haskins Laboratories, New Haven, CT, and an independent consultant. She is involved in editing volumes related to literacy and learning, mentoring young scholars and researchers, and consulting in a variety of areas, including child language development and learning, bilingualism, education, and learning disabilities. In her role as former chief of the Child Development and Behavior Branch at the Eunice Kennedy Shriver National Institute of Child Health and Human Development she was actively involved in the workshop that was the impetus for this volume.

Lisa S. Freund, PhD, is the chief of the Child Development and Behavior Branch at the Eunice Kennedy Shriver National Institute of Child Health and Human Development (NICHD). She is a developmental neuropsychologist who is known for her neuroimaging studies with children from different clinical populations and was an NICHD-supported scientist for several years. She is currently responsible for a multi-faceted research and training program at NICHD to promote investigations, both basic and applied, to gain a deeper understanding of the developing brain and associated behaviors.